HISTORIC COASTAL NEW ENGLAND

"Covers a lot of ground thoroughly—with humor, a deft touch and irresistible detail. If you're planning a trip along the coast . . . this is a great guide . . ."

—*Courier Gazette*, Rockland, Maine

"A wonderful guidebook that serves the visitor . . . well."

—Dr. Daniel Snydacker, executive director,
Newport (R.I.) Historical Society
Museum and Library

"Packed with information . . . a useful volume for day trippers and long weekenders as well as vacationers."

—*Coast Star*, Kennebunk, Maine

HISTORIC COASTAL NEW ENGLAND

Guide to
People, Places, Architecture, and Attractions
from Greenwich to Kennebunkport

Second Edition

by

Barbara Clayton and Kathleen Whitley

A Voyager Book

The Globe Pequot Press

Old Saybrook, Connecticut

Architectural drawings on pages xii–xv by Jerrie Kishpaugh Hildebrand

All photographs not credited appear courtesy of authors.

Cover photo: Cape Neddick Light, Nubble Point, York, Maine

Library of Congress Cataloging-in-Publication Data
Clayton, Barbara.
    Historic coastal New England : guide to people, places, architecture, and
  attractions from Greenwich to Kennebunkport / by Barbara Clayton and Kathleen
  Whitley. — 2nd ed.
        p.   cm.
    "A voyager book."
    Includes index.
    ISBN 1-56440-650-4
      1. Atlantic Coast (New England)— Guidebooks. 2. Historic sites—New Eng-
  land— Atlantic Coast—Guidebooks. 3. Architecture—New England—Atlantic
  Coast—Guidebooks. 4. Atlantic Coast (New England)—History, Local. 5. Cities and
  towns—New England—Atlantic Coast—History. I. Whitley, Kathleen. II. Title.
  F12.A74C53 1995
  917.404'43—dc20   95-23870
                                                                       CIP

Manufactured in the United States of America
Second Edition / First Printing

CONTENTS

ACKNOWLEDGMENTS

Connecticut: *Greenwich:* Betsy Cullen, Barbara Freeman, Barbara Morgan, Mary Ann Smith, Susan Tritschler. *Stamford:* Russell Bastedo, Ron Marcus. *Norwalk:* Ralph Bloom, Lynn Hamilton, Robert Sbarge. *Westport:* Joan H. Dickinson, John Horkel. *Fairfield:* Lin Mulford, Chris Nevins, L. Corwin Sharp. *Bridgeport:* Mary Ann C. Freeman, Ben Ortiz, Lisa Tryon. *Stratford:* Bessie Burton, Hiram Tindall. *Milford:* Ruth and Richard B. Brockett, Karen Purcell. *New Haven:* Shirley Johnson, Lisa Broberg Quintana, Amy Trout. *Branford:* Betty M. Linsley. *Guilford:* Beverly Anderson, Penny Colby, Joel E. Helander, Mike McBride, Edith Nettleton, Juanita Strick. *Madison:* William T. Mills. *Clinton:* Robert Bischoff, Joan Davis. *Old Saybrook:* Harold Elrod, Jan Fenger, Donald and Dorothy Swan. *Old Lyme:* Elizabeth Hammond, Linda Legassie, Elizabeth Tashjian. *Niantic:* Joe Dippel, Sam Morrison, Frankie and John Reynolds. *Waterford:* Laura Fitch, Ted Tetreault. *New London:* Lisa Brownell, William E. Hare II, Valarie J. Kinkade, Penny Knowles, Lois Erickson McDonald, Lucille M. Showalter, Vivian Stanley. *Groton:* Elizabeth Butler, Carol W. Kimball. *Mystic:* Ellen Anthony, Norman F. Boas, Bernadette Bode, Elizabeth A. Gwillim, Peggy M. Pfeifer. *Stonington:* Louise D. Pittaway.

Rhode Island: *Westerly:* Tony Chiaradio, Gertrude and Isaac Smith. *Charlestown:* John Brown, Ann Crawford, Lawrence Oliviet, Cheryl Reves, Ella Sekatau. *South Kingstown:* Robert Ames, Phyllis Goodwin, William D. Metz, Ethel Rosenbalm, Saran Turnbaugh, Robert and Debra Sanborn VanCleef. *Narragansett:* Horace Cartter, Peter Gardiner, William D. Metz. *Block Island:* Sarah Geti, Ronald Gill. *North Kingstown:* N. A. Fuller, William J. Geary, Madeline Gifford, Lorrie MaGowan, Casey MacLaughlin, Mary Liz MacLaughlin, Althea McAleer. *East Greenwich:* Marion L. Fry, Marjorie Hale, Robert W. Merriam. *Warwick:* Hazel Kennedy, Mildred Longo, David Nash, Mary Jane Sorrentino. *Providence:* Barbara Applebaum, John T. Campanini, Jr., Violet Forbes, Albert T. Klyberg, Martha Mitchell, Tina Regan, Ted Sanderson, Elizabeth R. Tatian, Anthony Vecchio. *Barrington:* Marnie Hawkins. *Warren:* Walter Nebiker, Pat Redfern, Eileen Socha. *Bristol:* Janet Durst, David Ellis, Patricia A. Kenyon, Harriet Linn, Kevin O'Malley, Michael Pesare, Carol Sackett, Helen Tessler. *Portsmouth:* James Garman, Kevin O'Malley. *Middletown:* Benjamin C. Reed, Jr., Floride Taylor. *Newport:* Gladys Bolhouse, Bertram Lippincott III, Henry Joyce, Paul McConnell, Monique Panaggio, Benjamin C. Reed, Jr., Daniel Snydacker, Frank Winnert, Barbara Wright. *Jamestown:* Bob Brier, Ken Casewell, Mary Brooks Harding, Howard W. Harding, Patrick Hodgin, Mary R. Miner, Don and Heather Minto. *Tiverton:* John Berg, Carlton Brownell, Edna Snell. *Little Compton:* Carlton Brownell.

Massachusetts: *New Bedford:* Virginia Adams, Jean Bennet, Richard Kugler, Antone G. Souza, Jr., Tracy Texeira. *Fairhaven:* Debbie Charpentier, Carolyn Longworth. *Mattapoisett:* Priscilla Hathaway. *Marion:* H. Edmund Tripp. *Wareham:* Raymond Rider, Betty Wright. *Cape Cod:* Michael J. Frucci, Bill Norman, Elaine Perry. *Martha's Vineyard:* Angeljean Chiaramida, Randy Vega, Virginia Weckman. *Nantucket:* Deborah Miller, Elizabeth Oldham. *Plymouth:* Paula Fisher, Douglas Gray, Laurence R. Pizer, Peggy M. Timlin. *Kingston:* Doris M. Johnson. *Duxbury:* Alexandra B. Earle. *Marshfield:* Cynthia H. Krusell, William H. B. Thomas. *Scituate:* Kathleen Laidlaw. *Cohasset:* David H. Wadsworth. *Hull:* Daniel Johnson. *Hingham:* Winn Grotevant. *Weymouth:* Judith Patt. *Quincy:* H. Hobart Holly. *Boston:* Nancy Blodget, Petty Officer Brannan, Nancy Curtis, Michele Ellicks, Edie Shean-Hammond, Jonathan Hyde, Rich Tourangeau. *Lynn:* Jenny Beaujean, Ken Turino. *Nahant:* Mrs. Winthrop Sears. *Swampscott:* Dorothy Anderson. *Marblehead:* Victor Dyer, Dorothy Miles, Joan Von Sternberg. *Salem:* Mary Fabiszewski, Nancy Heywood, Marian Hubler, Mrs. John Pickering. *Beverly:* Joan Fairbanks, Kate Pinkham. *Gloucester, Annisquam, and West Gloucester:* Violet McCarthy, Judith McCulloch, Cayte Ward. *Rockport:* Stephen Rask. *Essex:* Diana Stockton. *Ipswich:* James Kyprianos. *Newbury:* Nancy Curtis. *Newburyport:* Ellie Bailey.

New Hampshire: *Hampton:* Harold Fernald. *Rye:* Louise Tallman. *New Castle and Portsmouth:* Nancy D. Goss, Kevin Shupe. *Isles of Shoals:* Frederick T. McGill, Jr., Laura Pokalsky.

Maine: *Kittery:* James Dolph, Joseph W. P. Frost. *York:* Richard Borges, Sarah Giffen. *Ogunquit and Wells:* Vicki Adams, Hope M. Shelley. *Kennebunk and Kennebunkport:* Joyce Butler, Susan C. S. Edwards.

We are especially grateful to our husbands, Lee Whitley and Ray Clayton, for their constant support, encouragement, and patience.

HOW TO USE THIS BOOK

We invite you to use this book as a guide to all the points of interest along New England's fantastic coast—to rediscover history and architecture, find sandy beaches and rocky cliffs, and acquaint yourself with people of today and yesterday.

Because hours and dates that sites are open vary from year to year, we have used the following general terms for your guidance:

Summer: open summer season

Extended season: open summer plus spring and/or fall

Open all year: open every month, four or more days per week

Limited hours: fewer than four days per week or fewer than three hours on days open

Fees vary so widely from one location to another that we simply say "Fee," "No fee," or "Donation."

The locator map introducing each state indicates the locations of towns and cities. The map accompanying each town or city shows the locations of individual points of interest.

The featured points of interest throughout this book are introduced by preliminary descriptions that appear in **boldface** type. These brief comments follow a basic format:

1.[1] General William Hart House,[2] *c. 1767*,[3] NRHP, HS.[4] 350 Main St.[5]
Open extended season, limited hours, and by appointment,[6] donation.[7]
Colonial gardens, exhibits, workshops.[8]

1. Number (noted on town map) of point of interest
2. Point of interest
3. Date of construction (if appropriate)
4. Abbreviation(s) for historical affiliation (*see* key below)
5. Address
6. When open (*see* "hours, dates" above)
7. Fee (*see* "fees" above)
8. Additional information

ABBREVIATIONS KEY

HS Historical Society
VI Visitor Information
NHS National Historic Site
NHL National Historic Landmark

NHM National Historic Monument
NRHP National Register of Historic Places
SPNEA Society for the Preservation of
  New England Antiquities

SETTING THE STAGE

Through this book we share with you the beauty of New England's ever-changing coastline and the excitement of discovering its historic and architectural landmarks. New England was the land of Pilgrims, Puritans, Royalists, and freethinkers. It was home to the leading whaling ports of the world, tinderbox of the American Revolution, and birthplace of United States presidents. As you tour the region's coastal towns, be aware of the trials, tribulations, hopes, and dreams of the many generations between the first adventurous settlers and today's busy citizens. Walk beaches; explore marshes and uplands. Browse through homes, museums, and historic buildings, for it is mainly through these physical reminders that you can picture and appreciate the ways of life that have preceded you.

The prelude to these New England lives and settlements began in England in the 1500s, when some members of the Church of England became dissatisfied with the ceremonialism of services and the authority of the clergy. Those wishing to "purify" the church became known as Puritans, and those wishing to separate and worship in their own way became known as Separatists. In 1608 a Separatist group led by William Brewster, tired of religious persecution, left England and settled in Leyden, Holland. Finding growing problems there, they sailed for the New World, where they believed they could live in peace with themselves and their God. These Separatists, now known as Pilgrims, founded Plymouth Colony in 1620.

Two years later, lands from the Kennebec River in Maine to the Merrimack River in northern Massachusetts, including Cape Ann, were granted to absentee landowners, Captain John Mason and Sir Ferdinando Gorges. They wanted to colonize land for England with Church of England Royalists (settlers loyal to the king) and adventurers and at the same time to create a successful commercial venture for themselves. Initial settlements were made in 1623 at Gloucester, Massachusetts, and Rye, New Hampshire.

Six years later in England approximately one thousand Puritans, led by John Winthrop, obtained and carried to the New World a charter for Massachusetts Bay Colony. They settled what is now Boston and developed a strong Puritan colony under Governor Winthrop. In 1635 independent thinker Roger Williams was tried in Boston by the Puritans and found guilty of new and dangerous opinions. Escaping across a frozen wilderness in midwinter, Reverend Williams and his followers founded Providence, Rhode Island, a colony based on religious freedom and respect for individual rights.

Paradoxically, by 1640, only a hundred miles away on the shores of Long

Island Sound, the New Haven Colony was established because its members were looking for a stricter Puritan lifestyle than was being practiced in Boston. During this same period Royalists were arriving in the Rye–Portsmouth, New Hampshire, and York, Maine, areas. The next ten years saw the growth of colonies, with Church of England Royalists and adventurers in northern New England and Puritans, Separatists, and religiously tolerant settlers in southern New England. Out of the Puritan settlements emerged the powerful Massachusetts Bay Colony, which in turn took over New Hampshire Colony in 1640, Maine Colony in 1649, New Haven Colony in 1663, and finally Plymouth Colony in 1691. Plymouth had paved the way for the other colonies and proved that settlers could survive, succeed, and prosper in the New World. Surviving on its own, Roger Williams's Providence Plantation opened its doors to those looking for religious tolerance.

During this period, coastal settlers, realizing the countryside was too difficult to tame for a profitable agricultural economy, turned to the sea. They reaped its bountiful resources of fish, whales, and seafood as well as using it as an avenue of trade with the world. Ships were built for domestic use and for profitable sale in England and France.

Along with religious turmoil and the everyday struggle for survival came a series of six wars (1675–1763) between Indians, supported by the French, and colonists, supported by England. For nearly four generations settlers' daily lives were constantly threatened by Indian ambush and sudden attack. When the threats finally ended, settlements grew and prospered, and colonists returned to their independent ways.

In order to replenish a depleted treasury and regain authority over the colonies, however, the English Parliament passed a series of acts in the mid-1700s. Seeds of separation sprouted quickly as colonists, in retaliation, defied the Acts of Assistance, Sugar Act, Stamp Act, and Townshend Acts and sponsored the Boston Tea Party and other such symbols of resistance. England closed the Port of Boston. The Continental Congress was formed, and once again colonists took up arms—at Concord, Lexington, Breed's Hill, Bennington, Fairfield, Norwalk, New Haven, New London, and Newport. It all culminated with the Treaty of Paris in 1783, resulting in a free and independent country.

Following the war resourceful Yankees set out for brighter horizons, establishing new and more lucrative trade routes with the East Indies, Russia, China, and India. New trade resulted in a more worldly wise society. Homes were furnished with the luxuries and exotic goods of the Far East, all of which enriched and enlivened the earlier Puritan way of life. Yet another conflict, the War of 1812, temporarily depressed the New England coastal economy; but it soon rebounded in a boom far surpassing anything previously known. The superior American fleet dominated the seven seas, amassing fortunes in whaling, trade, and passenger service. The American clipper ship with its billowing sails and sleek hull captured the spirit and pride of the maritime economy in the mid-1800s.

The advent of steam power in the same century profoundly affected coastal towns. The excitement of sail lost out to the efficiency of steam, and shipyards turning out sailing vessels grew strangely quiet. But as this industry declined, New England's resourceful craftsmen joined in the Industrial Revolution. First water-powered and later steam-powered factories sprung up along coastal rivers, turning home crafts into big business. In the late 1800s and early 1900s, New England became famous for its textile, shoe, clock, and furniture industries, to name only a few.

An economic bonus was the emergence of railroads, which took over coastal trade, broadened domestic markets, and ushered in a new and prosperous industry—tourism. Railroads provided quick and comfortable access to seashore areas, transforming what had been quiet farming, fishing, and shipbuilding towns into flourishing summer resorts. Today most coastal towns continue to attract large numbers of tourists, though the automobile and bus have replaced the railroad and coastal steamship as the preferred modes of travel.

The New England coast is equally inviting during the brilliant colors of autumn; or the lonely stark days of winter when snow meets the incoming tide; or when spring's first buds burst forth, beckoning you back to sandy beaches and rolling surf; or in summer when artists, tourists, and sunbathers gather to appreciate natural wonders. Come even when storms turn the ocean into a reckless giant assaulting beaches, harbors, and inlets with untamed fury. Come. Discover.

LIVING ARCHITECTURE

Studying New England's architecture reveals the fascinating lives of people. What people thought, what they valued, and how they survived is told by what they built. Earlier New Englanders adapted Old World ideas and applied "Yankee ingenuity." New England is fortunate in retaining many buildings from each architectural period. Using the following capsule descriptions as a bird watcher uses a field guide to birds you can distinguish these periods, find them represented throughout the tours, and better understand the people whose lives created them.

A FIELD GUIDE TO ARCHITECTURAL STYLES

Colonial (First Period) (c. 1620–1715). New England's first settlers, concerned with immediate survival, built shelters with designs probably influenced by a combination of remembered English huts, Indian wigwams, and available materials. Even while struggling with this strange climate, Indians, disease, and each other, these pioneers began the evolution of the Colonial period of American architecture. A family would often expand a primitive one-room home to two rooms by raising the roof. The plan was repeated on the chimney's other side to create the four-room center-chimney Colonial. A lean-to across the back might provide further rooms, forming a saltbox. Later owners sometimes modified this arrangement by raising the roof to add more rooms, losing the saltbox silhouette.

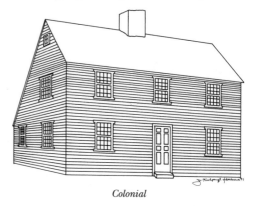

Colonial

Characteristics: Steeply pitched gable roof; massive central chimney; windows small, many-paned, randomly placed, close to eaves; entry not emphasized, door small, usually not centered; shingled or clapboarded walls nearly touch ground. Feeling: defensive, isolated, like sealed box.

Georgian Period (c. 1715–85). By about 1715, later in country areas, New England's prosperity set the stage for change in architecture. Improved communication brought books of building designs and new ideas, skilled immigrant craftsmen provided ability, and American industrial advancement provided tools to launch the Georgian period of classical architecture. Life was changing, with time now for more than mere practical survival. Areas were provided for purely social functions— spacious central halls, dining rooms, formal drawing rooms—and closets were added for expanded wardrobes.

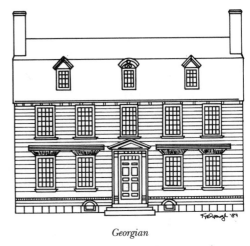
Georgian

Characteristics: Massive, symmetrical, intricate, harmonious; more windows with larger, fewer panes, balanced; door centered, arched or rectangular lights above; focus on decorative front entry, linteled windows, pedimented portico; quoined corners, some ashlar effect, water table and string course, horizontal focus; roof hip or gambrel, low pitch; ornamental eaves, more chimneys; fencing and balustraded captain's walk on roof; often two stories plus dormered third story, four rooms per floor; interior spacious, grand central hall and stairway; heavy elaborate molding and paneling, higher ceilings. Feeling: inviting, social, established, affluent.

Federal Period (c. 1785–1820). After the Revolution, Charles Bulfinch in Boston and Samuel McIntire in Salem, Massachusetts, ushered in the Federal style. Less massive than earlier Georgian, it was based on the work of the English Adam brothers. New England was reaping rewards from the sea—through whaling, shipbuilding, and world trade—and found the Federal style the most appropriate expression of this opulence.

Characteristics. Vertical focus, symmetrical, immense yet delicate, lighter than Georgian; usually 40 feet square; three stories tall; roof lowpitched, hip, balustraded, pierced by tall, slender chimneys; windows more numerous and larger, smaller on top floor, often Palladian window centered above portico; semielliptical

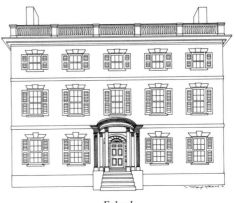
Federal

lights over door extending over side lights; elaborate fences, posts, finials; interior, ornate yet delicate woodwork, broad, sweeping stairs. Feeling: commanding, simple elegance, economic and social success, reflects confident new independence.

Greek Revival (c. 1820–50). As rewards from the sea produced the magnificent Georgian and Federal periods, so the receding economic tides caused by Jefferson's embargoes and the War of 1812 brought the Federal period to a close. With focus no longer on the sea, New England turned to broader national interests. Jefferson, blamed for New England's wounded economy, led American interest directly to the cultures and architecture of ancient Rome and Greece. In New England, Greek Revival gave architectural expression to a newly awakened regard for democracy.

Greek Revival

Characteristics. Greek temple features; stone, or wood cut and painted to resemble stone; usually on high granite foundation; low or flat roof, gable end or gable portico facing street; entrance not centered, transom and side lights around door rectangular; six-over-six windows, heavy lintels; Greek portico, small or extended across whole front; columns, pilasters at portico and corners; large, flat frieze tops wall, under eaves; ornamentation heavy. Feeling: powerful, grand display, intellectual freedom.

Victorian Era (c. 1830s–90s). The Industrial Revolution sparked intense changes in architecture. The theme was revivalism. Revivalism was the outgrowth of advances in communications and education, plus the technology of the Industrial Revolution. It was the expression of Victorian character—enthusiastic optimism and restless individuality. Fascinating and confusing, the nineteenth century's styles are selections

Gothic

and combinations from two thousand years of the world's finest architecture. Features were often varied and styles combined. The following Victorian styles are most frequently found along the New England coast.

Gothic characteristics (c. 1830s–70s). Often asymmetrical; pointed arch; steep roof, pointed gables, tall finials; tower or turret; pinnacles, battlements; gingerbread bargeboards; window tracery; veranda.

Italianate

Italianate characteristics (c. 1840s–90s). Rectangular; slightly pitched, gabled roof; projecting eaves with dominating brackets; tower or cupola; round-headed windows, often grouped; varied exterior colors; veranda, balcony; quoins.

French Second Empire characteristics (c. 1850s–90s). Combines colors, materials, heavy detail; always tall mansard roof, enveloping entire top floor, with curb at top; dormer windows; brackets featured.

French Second Empire

Queen Anne characteristics (c. 1870s–90s). Irregular plan and mass; variety of color, texture, windows; projections, gables, turrets; roofs high and multiple; chimneys emphasized, often incorporated into dormer window; veranda, balcony.

Queen Anne

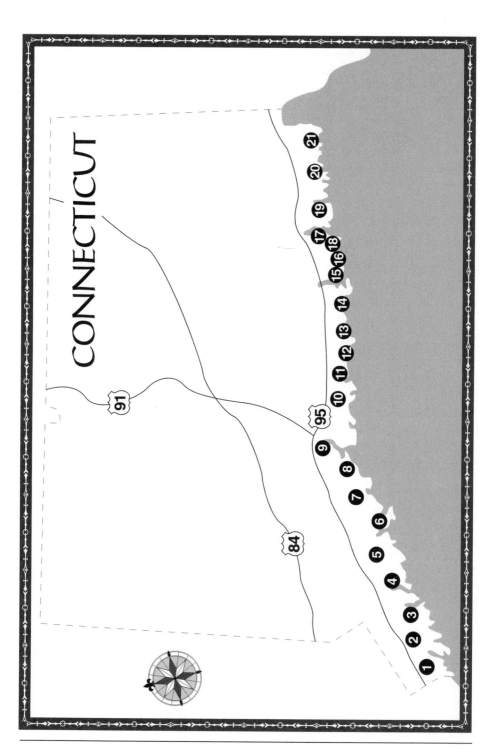

CONNECTICUT

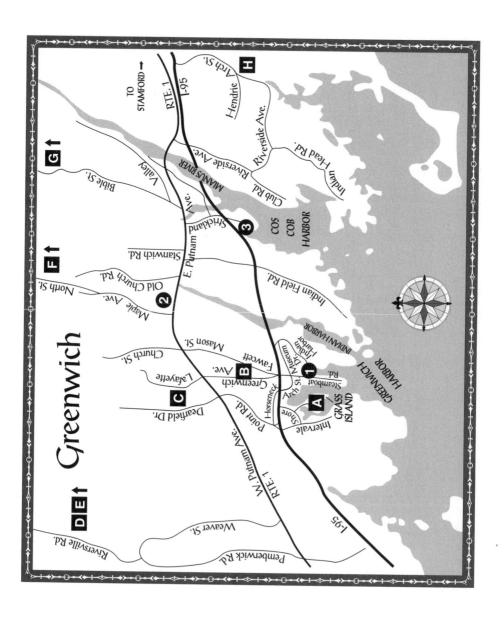

GREENWICH

This portal to New England's coast is a city of rolling countrysides, sandy beaches, charming shops, corporate headquarters, and beautiful homes illustrating a variety of architectural delights. Captain Daniel Patrick and Robert Feaks bought the land that became Greenwich from the Indians on July 18, 1640, for twenty five coats. The town was significant for its proximity to New Amsterdam (New York). Seeking protection from hostile Indians, Patrick signed a treaty with the Dutch on April 9, 1642. The settlement remained under Dutch authority until 1650.

During the Revolution, on February 26, 1779, British General Tryon and 1,500 men took possession of Greenwich, plundering and burning. Connecticut's General Israel Putnam escaped and rode to Stamford for help. That same evening at Mead's Tavern, when many British soldiers were full of hard cider, a militiaman shot close enough to General Tryon's head to make him order withdrawal. Putnam, returning with additional Continental troops and militia, harried the retreating British and captured several wagons of plunder.

Following the war Greenwich became a busy shipbuilding and shipping port. This ended in 1848 with the advent of the New Haven Railroad, which opened the area to summer visitors, commuters, and residential growth. The 1800s also saw active manufacturing along the Byram and Mianus rivers. Today Greenwich, a city of community service and cultural awareness, combines colonial and cosmopolitan lifestyles in a pleasing way. Famous residents have included Anya Seaton, Thomas J. Watson, Tom Seaver, Ivan Lendl, Dorothy Hammill, Glenn Close, John Twachtman.

1. BRUCE MUSEUM, *1912.* 1 Museum Dr., Bruce Park. Open all year, fee. Museum shop, lectures, special programs, workshops, spring Outdoor Crafts and fall Outdoor Arts festivals.

"Hawke's Nest" was the name for this massive granite home built in 1853 for Reverend Francis Lister Hawks, rector of New York City's St. Thomas Church. In 1858 Hawks sold his estate to wealthy textile merchant Robert Moffatt Bruce, who prospered during the Civil War manufacturing army blankets. An organizer of Greenwich Savings Bank and Greenwich Gas and Electric Lighting Company, Bruce was Greenwich's benefactor. His gifts included the 1905 Town Hall, Greenwich General Hospital, and park lands.

In the fall of 1993, the Bruce Museum reopened after a major expansion and renovation project. Featuring changing exhibitions in the arts, decorative arts, and natural sciences, the "new Bruce" also features a wing of permanent Environmental Galleries. These galleries include exhibits on the evolution of Long Island Sound (including a model of an archeological dig and a reconstruction of a Native American wigwam); a marine life "touch tank," with graphics and slide projections to add to the fun; and a life-size walk-through diorama presenting the region as it appeared prior to European contact and transporting visitors back to an era of pristine landscape.

2. PUTNAM COTTAGE, *c. 1690*. 243 East Putnam Ave. Open all year, limited hours or by appointment, fee. Putnam's Ride Monument, East Putnam Ave. and Old Church Rd. Headquarters, Putnam Hill Chapter of the DAR.

Israel Putnam was one of four original major generals elected by the Continental Congress in 1775. Veteran soldier and superb horseman, the sixty-one-year-old devoted Patriot made his famous Greenwich ride February 26, 1779. Alerted to the approach of outnumbering British soldiers near Knapp's Tavern, Putnam quickly dispersed his men to safer grounds, mounted his steed, and, with the enemy in hot pursuit, dashed down Put's Hill, a precarious descent where the enemy dared not follow. As shot tore through his hat, he looked back long enough to yell "Damn ye" and rode on to Stamford for reinforcements.

It is believed Putnam Cottage was built as a one- or two-room structure c. 1690; rooms were added as needed. Israel Knapp, grandson of an original Greenwich proprietor, obtained the property and, in 1754, a tavern license. During the Revolution, his tavern was a meeting place for Patriots. George Washington stopped here April 1776. Between 1780 and 1820 the stone wing was added, enlarging the tavern to its present

Putnam Cottage, Greenwich   (Bob Capazzo/Courtesy Putnam Hill Chapter, DAR)

size. An unusual pass through connects two huge fireplaces on the first floor. The building has been restored to evoke the Knapp Tavern era, with steeply pitched roof, rare scalloped shingles, and coarse rubble foundation. Inside, period furniture, including a Chippendale chair and tavern table of General Putnam and heirlooms from local families, speaks eloquently of Greenwich's heritage.

3. BUSH-HOLLEY HOUSE, *c. 1738*, NRHP, NHL, HS. 39 Strickland Rd., Cos Cob. Open all year, fee. Nineteenth-century barn, shed, wash house; adjacent 1794 house was Cos Cob's post office in early 1900s.

Referred to as "the house that never stopped living,"[1] the Bush–Holley House combines history and architecture and illustrates changes through three centuries. The early structure probably included a parlor, dining room, kitchen, and two bedrooms arranged around a central chimney. Here lived David Bush, granted mill rights on Strickland Brook in 1764. A farmer, miller, shipowner, and early entrepreneur, he became a wealthy and influential man. From the time Bush inherited his homesite, he made additions and improvements. He and his first wife had five children. After her death, he married Sarah Scudder Isaacs, who brought five children to Cos Cob. Together they had five more. Room was needed. By the time Bush finished building, he had added wings to the south and west of the original structure.

The property passed out of the Bush family in 1848. It was purchased by George Jackson Smith, who added a second-floor porch and Victorian windows in the parlor and dining room. In 1882 Edward P. Holley bought the house. In the early 1890s impressionist painter John Henry Twachtman asked Holley to open his home to Twachtman's art students. From that time until the 1920s, the house was a gathering place and inspiration for several generations of American impressionist artists, including J. Alden Weir, Frederick Childe Hassam, Theodore Robinson, Elmer MacRae, and Twachtman. Writers Lincoln Steffens, Willa Cather, Jean Webster, and Rose O'Neil were among the literary visitors. It was a lively and creative mecca, the first of numerous art colonies along the shore of Long Island Sound.

Edward Holley's daughter, Emma, married artist Elmer Livingston MacRae in 1900. They took over the boardinghouse from Emma's parents. In 1957, four years after Elmer MacRae died, widow Emma ended an unforgettable era in Greenwich art and literary life by selling the property to the Historical Society of the Town of Greenwich. The society restored the Bush–Holley House and opened it as a museum in 1959.[2]

BEACHES, PARKS, OTHER POINTS OF INTEREST

A. Roger Sherman Baldwin Park. Greenwich Harbor. Open all year. No fee. Summer concerts.

B. Greenwich Arts Council. 299 Greenwich Ave. Open for special events. Building originally 1905 Town Hall, gift of Robert M. and sister Sarah Bruce; classes, exhibits, lectures, music and dance studios.

C. **Greenwich Library.** Dearfield Dr. and West Putnam Ave. Films, tapes, oral history, coffee shop; lectures, Cole Auditorium, Hurlbutt Gallery with rotating displays.

D. **Audubon Center.** Corner Riversville Rd. and John St. Open all year. Fee. 280-acre preserve, 8 miles of trails, Mead Lake, visitor center, gift shop, exhibits, educational programs, field trips.

E. **Audubon Fairchild Garden.** North Porchuck Rd. off Riverville Rd. Open all year through Audubon Center. Fee. 127 acres, 8 miles of trails, more than 500 plant species—most native, some introduced by Benjamin Fairchild, creator of preserve. Given to National Audubon Society 1945; known for wildflowers.

F. **Town Parkland (Babcock Woods).** Wyckham Hill Ln. off North St. Open all year. No fee. Trails; hiking.

G. **Montgomery Pinetum.** Off Bible St., access from Montgomery or Pinetum lns. Open all year. No fee. Garden center, walks; picnicking.

H. **Binney Park.** Hendrie Arch St., Old Greenwich. Open all year. No fee. Paths, picturesque setting; picnicking.

STAMFORD

S tamford is a city of architectural contrasts. It prides itself on diversity—cultural, ethnic, social, economic, religious. Architectural diversity is evident in the houses of worship, from the modern First Presbyterian Church to the classic meetinghouses on Old Long Ridge Road to magnificent Gothic St. Mary's on Atlantic Street. Corporate headquarters in modern office buildings gleam amid historic buildings downtown.

It all began in 1640 when Captain Nathaniel Turner, agent for New Haven Colony, bought land from Ponus, an Indian sachem. The next year twenty-eight pioneers from Wethersfield settled Stamford. In 1692 witchcraft terror swept down from Massachusetts. Accused Elizabeth Clawson faced trials that drew the attention of governor, legislature, and prominent ministers. She survived being "bownd hand & foot & put into the water"[3] and later was declared not guilty. Soon Connecticut's General Court advised against witchcraft trials. Stamford was a supply and training center during the Revolution and a significant contributor to the Industrial Revolution. Today Stamford serves as a showcase of harmony between business success and historic preservation.

1. DOWNTOWN ATLANTIC STREET WALK. Atlantic St. south from Broad St. Whitney Museum of American Art, Fairfield County, lobby of Champion International Corporation. Atlantic at Tresser Blvd. Open all year, tours by appointment, no fee. Parking in Champion underground garage, entrance Tresser Blvd.

You can best appreciate the old and new by walking Atlantic Street: the classical **Ferguson Public Library**, the **Stamford Center of the Arts**, **Palace Theatre**, NRHP, and the Beaux arts classical **Old Town Hall**, NRHP.

In contrast, Champion's ultramodern polished glass and steel skyscraper houses the **Whitney Museum of American Art, Fairfield County.** The side entrance provides a sudden oasis of quiet amid beautiful plantings. Champion Greenhouse has an ongoing exhibition program and special shows. The Whitney Museum has five changing exhibitions of contemporary art as well as American masters, with detailed catalogues. The modern grand hall also hosts gallery talks and a variety of educational and performing arts programs.

2. HOYT–BARNUM HOUSE, *1699*, NRHP, HS. 713 Bedford St. Open all year, limited hours, fee.

Stamford's oldest documented structure is a simple Connecticut Colonial that remains

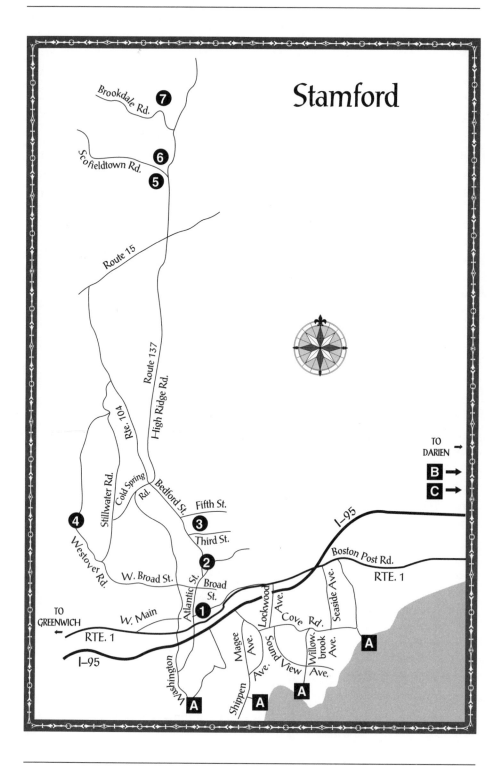

on its original site, now surrounded by the modern city. Joshua and Mary Hait (Hoyt) owned this land, which came to their son, Samuel, after Joshua's death in 1690. By 1699 Samuel Hoyt was an established blacksmith, an important person at a time when iron was usually imported and so scarce that pieces were either repaired or recast. Here Hoyt began his home for his first bride, Susanna Slason. The detailed inventory of Samuel's estate included pewter, more than one bed, and much land—indications of his wealth and community significance. The house probably began with one room, with riven, not sawn, wall boards and whitewash consisting of lime to kill bugs. The massive central chimney could date to this first period. The smaller fireplaces are probably modifications. Other rooms were added to accommodate the family, which grew to fourteen children born of two wives. Three centuries of families have lived in this beautifully maintained house with its period furnishings.

3. FIRST PRESBYTERIAN CHURCH, *1958.* 1101 Bedford St.

When you walk into the sanctuary, you are not prepared for the overwhelming effect of light and color, the beautiful, bold, "Joseph's coat of many colors" characteristics of the stained glass windows. The effect is strong, reassuring—inviting you, by its very magnificence, to worship. The grounds are gloriously planned and maintained, providing a view of serene clusters of colors and peaceful rolling lawns against the building's striking slate exterior. The church is silhouetted against the sky-reaching height of the carillon tower. Gardens frame the view and enhance the feeling of ageless beauty and reverence. The fish-shaped church was designed by Wallace K. Harrison, director of planning for the United Nations buildings and an architect of Rockefeller Center, Lincoln Center, and the World Trade Towers. The stained glass windows were created by Gabriel Loire. More than one hundred stones embedded in surrounding walks represent spiritual giants of Judeo/Christian tradition.

4. FORT STAMFORD, *1781 site,* NRHP. 900 Westover Rd. Open all year, no fee. Formal perennial gardens. Parking restricted to residents in summer.

Charged "to erect some small fortifications to prevent a surprise from enemy's horse . . . and to make choice of a strong woody ground where to hutt his troops,"[4] Stamford's Brigadier General David Waterbury built and fortified Fort Stamford. Designed by Colonel Rufus Putnam, it was intended for both offense and defense. From here attacks were launched against foraging raids made by British troops from nearby New York and Long Island. The fort was ordered built less than six weeks after a pastor and his people were attacked. When Reverend Moses Mather, pastor of Middlesex (Darien) Congregational Church, defended the Revolution from the pulpit, his home had been plundered. When he proposed making examples of Tories, Tories seized him from the pulpit, appropriated valuables from the congregation, and marched Mather and about fifty other men to prison in New York. Five months later Mather was exchanged, one of the fortunate ones to survive.

An outline of the fort, seen on markers at the site, suggests a rectangle measuring about 135 feet by 165 feet, with redoubts at all four corners. Barracks, with chimneys for warmth and cooking, connected the defenses. No buildings remain, but redoubts can be found with stone and earth walls high enough for protection, low enough to fire over.

5. STAMFORD HISTORICAL SOCIETY MUSEUM. 1508 High Ridge Rd. Open all year, fee. Research library, publications, lectures, events.

To collect, preserve, and interpret Stamford's historical materials from the 1600s to the present—these are the goals of the Stamford Historical Society, founded in 1901. Their museum and research facility is headquartered in this former school building (built 1914). Changing exhibits feature textiles, tools, decorative arts. The twentieth century is recorded in textiles and apparel collections and papers from former mayors of Stamford. A permanent exhibit displays Stamford's industrial beginnings, from the time water power and railroads drew Linus Yale and Henry R. Towne to move their lock company here in 1868. By 1916 the company grew from 30 workers to more than 5,000 and gained the city recognition as home of Yale lock. Another early industry is Pitney-Bowes, still headquartered in Stamford. Their model M postage meter was first used commercially on November 16, 1920.

6. STAMFORD MUSEUM AND NATURE CENTER. 30 Scofieldtown Rd. Open all year, fee. Museum, art galleries, planetarium, observatory, early New England working farm, trails, country store; hiking, picnicking; art shows, concerts, programs.

Watch artists at work and children feeding geese as you walk the grounds of a grand Tudor mansion set amid many pieces of fine sculpture and landscaped pools. Wander across the estate to the early New England farm with its 1750 barn and live animals. Walk woodland wildlife trails through 118 acres, and picnic beside the lake or a pond or stream. One path leads to the Bartlett Arboretum.

Galleries of North American Indian exhibits, natural history, and art, plus changing exhibits featuring kites, birds, minerals, or miniatures are found in the manor house. The mansion was built for millionaire department store founder Henri Bendel in 1931–32, inspired by Maidenhead, England, manors—Shoppenhange, c. 1288, and Ockwell, c. 1467. A patron of the arts, Bendel graced his mansion with his art collections and sixteenth-century furnishings. The museum's auditorium is the old Bendel music room, without organ or furnishings, which were sold to make the house seem less haunted to a later owner's children.

7. BARTLETT ARBORETUM, University of Connecticut, 151 Brookdale Rd.
Open all year, no fee. Arboretum, gardens, greenhouse, horticultural reference library, exhibits, publications; courses, guided walks, lectures, workshops.

The arboretum, with its many labeled plants, is a fine place to enjoy solitude and to learn. Over half of the sixty-three acres are natural woodlands, marsh, meadow, and lake—accessible by trails. Until the state purchased the site in 1965, this was the home of Bartlett Tree Company, which is still headquartered in Stamford. In 1913 Dr. Francis A. Bartlett moved here with his family and began tree surgery and grafting among the existing fruit orchards and native oak, maple, and hickory trees.

There are about twenty acres in cultivated gardens and plant collections, including exotic trees, herbarium collection, perennial border, dwarf conifers, rhododendrons, and small ornamental trees. Pollarded trees (with tops cut back to the trunk) were used by Dr. Bartlett to evaluate pesticides. Others planted by him over sixty years ago include the chestnut, pecan, hickory, hazel, and walnut trees that still surround his research laboratory, now the Education Building. The Bartletts' home is now the Administration Building.

BEACHES, PARKS, OTHER POINTS OF INTEREST

A. Stamford beaches and parks. Parking limited to residents in summer.

B. Darien: Bates–Scofield Homestead, c. 1736. 45 Old Kings Hwy. North. Open summer, limited hours. Donation. Classic Connecticut saltbox, moved here 1964; massive central stone chimney, attractive plantings, memorial herb garden, local history exhibits, research library.

C. Darien: Stephen Tyng Mather House, 1778, NHL. 19 Stephen Mather Rd. Summer home of founder of National Park Service.

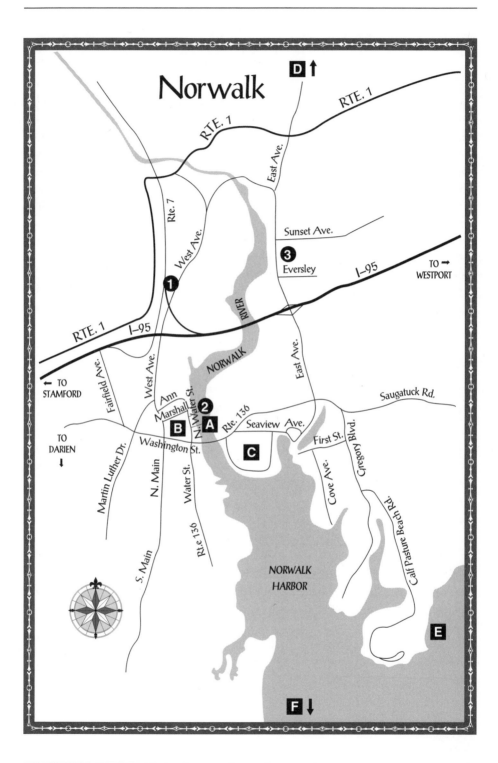

NORWALK

Norwalk, a city of historic, ethnic, cultural, and economic pride, was founded in 1640 by Daniel Patrick and Roger Ludlow. As Ludlow's claim was settled first, he is considered the "father of Norwalk." With a promise of thirty settling families, the Connecticut Colony declared Norwalk a town September 11, 1651. Norwalk quickly developed as a farming community. In Revolutionary times the *Gamecock,* under Norwalk's Captain Lemuel Brooks, became Connecticut's first commissioned privateer. These intrepid privateers harassed the British Navy, causing them to retaliate. On July 11, 1779, Major General William Tryon and 2,600 Hessian and British soldiers attacked the city. Colonial generals Samuel Parsons and Oliver Wolcott positioned 1,000 men on heights beyond the common. Severely outnumbered, they withdrew as British burned the town, leaving only six houses untouched along their battle route.

The determined Norwalkers rebuilt, adding coastal trade and shipbuilding to their farming world. The 1800s saw the hatting (most prominent), garment, home builders' hardware, and locks industries bolster the economy. The tidal flow of the Norwalk River plus ideal salt density and water temperatures of Long Island Sound provided the right conditions for oystering, an industry pursued since Indian days. Oystering peaked in the period 1885–1910, going from harvesting public beds to sophisticated aquatic oyster farming; small Norwalk oysters were considered delicacies in England and Europe. Oystering came back in the 1950s, and today Norwalk has the largest oyster business in Connecticut. Norwalk has come through economic highs in the late 1800s and lows in the 1900s to today's resurgence. The once-deteriorating waterfront is being restored and rebuilt, combining ambiences of the past with modern building techniques. Norwalk's oyster and art festivals and boat shows keep alive history and traditions while displaying the varied talents of the city's people.

1. LOCKWOOD–MATHEWS MANSION, *1864,* NRHP, NHL. 295 West Ave. Open extended season, fee. Guided tours, special functions, exhibits, gift shop; lectures, student internships, trips.

Step inside this fifty-room mansion to appreciate nineteenth-century elegance and wealth. Built for Ann Louisa and LeGrand Lockwood and designed by Detlef Lienau, it began a new era of opulence. The mansion copied sixteenth-century chateaus of France and added Renaissance, Second Empire, and contemporary Victorian elements to create its "chateauesque" style. (Twenty years later Newport, Rhode Island, mansions followed the Lockwoods' prototype into a Golden Age.) Master craftsmen from Europe used rare woods in exquisite inlaid and carved woodwork. They created parquetry floors, frescoed and paneled walls, ceiling motifs, gold work, marble, and

Lockwood-Mathews Mansion Museum, Norwalk   (Lockwood-Mathews Mansion Museum, Inc.)

etched glass. Woodworkers received 50 cents and stonecutters $1 per day. The hand-cut granite house boasts a 42-foot skylighted octagonal rotunda, conical roofed towers, quoins, dormers, steeply pitched gables, turrets, and iron balustrades. Its beauty surrounds you as you move from room to room, absorbing the constant flow of museum quality craftsmanship. The house centers in the rotunda, where the Lockwoods entertained and displayed their superb art collection.

Other rooms include a dining room, library, billiard and music rooms, drawing room, conservatory, card room, Moorish room, four rooms where music boxes are now displayed, and bedrooms for family and servants. Advanced for its time, the mansion had steam heat and burglar alarms as well as bowling alleys and a theater. The thirty-acre estate includes gate house, carriage house, ice house, gardener's cottage, chicken coops, lodge, and stables.

LeGrand Lockwood, treasurer of the New York Stock Exchange, made money on Wall Street in steamships, railroads, and banking. Desiring a summer home, the Lockwoods returned with their six children to their native Norwalk to build this mansion, which they called "Elm Park." Construction took four years and cost nearly $2 million. During a gold manipulation on Black Friday (September 24) in 1869, the year they moved in, Lockwood lost most of his capital. He was forced to mortgage Elm Park to

Lake Shore and Michigan Railroad and Commodore Cornelius Vanderbilt. Sadly, he died before he could recoup his losses. His wife, unable to make payments, was evicted when Commodore Vanderbilt foreclosed in 1874.

Two years later Elm Park was purchased for $90,000 by New York importer Charles Mathews and his wife, Rebecca. Their family lived here for three generations, enjoying the mansion in the lavish manner for which it was created. The last of the children, Florence Mathews, lived here until her death in 1938. In 1941 Norwalk bought the property for $170,000 for a city park. During and following World War II, the grounds were used for Victory Gardens and the building for city offices, public meetings, and free concerts. In 1961 the Common Interest Group saved the building, threatened by demolition, and a museum corporation started the estate's restoration back to glory and new uses.

2. THE MARITIME CENTER. 10 North Water St. Open all year, fee. Aquarium, maritime history museum, IMAX movie theater, educational programs, hands-on exhibits, study cruises; snack bar, gift shop.

Long Island Sound is the background for this unique aquarium with more than 125 species. Special exhibits, galleries, marine displays, a seal pool, a marine science wet lab, and murals unfold the world of Long Island Sound marine life before your eyes. You come nose to nose with sharks as they swim by, with only the thickness of the glass separating you. You learn about the region's maritime history and see amazing nature films on a movie screen six stories high.

3. CITY HALL COMPLEX. 125 East Ave. Open all year, no fee. City offices, Norwalk Museum and Reference Library; concerts.

The old Norwalk High School, built 1936–38, has been adapted and converted into the new City Hall. The colonial-style beauty of the cherished high school auditorium was preserved in what is now the Concert Hall. Original Palladian windows, chandeliers, paneling, and dentiled moldings have been restored in this acoustically fine hall where Duke Ellington, U.S. military bands, chamber orchestras, community choruses, and other performing artists have played to full houses.

The City Hall section is now a modern flow of offices. The pièces de résistance are mural paintings of Fairfield County life in the 1930s that are displayed throughout the complex. Fifty paintings in Norwalk were originally done by six artists commissioned by President Franklin D. Roosevelt's WPA, 1935–41. Many are restored and hang here in the City Hall, post office, library, and Maritime Center. In the atrium of City Hall is Harry Townsend's *Purchase of Norwalk*. Other paintings on the first floor include panels from Mark Twain's books, including *Connecticut Yankee in King Arthur's Court* by Justine Gruelle. Second-floor paintings are familiar local scenes by Alexander J. Rummler plus a self-portrait. Third floor displays paintings of Norwalk's major industry—oystering.

Canvases are done with such reality that figures seem to speak to you, inviting you into the painting. Though Depression-era art, the paintings give a feeling of lightness, contentment, and deep-rooted American values.

BEACHES, PARKS, OTHER POINTS OF INTEREST

A. **Sheffield Island Lighthouse,** NRHP. Open summer. Thirty-minute scenic and informative ferry ride (fee) from Hope Dock by Maritime Center, North Water and Washington sts.; 3-acre island park, 1868–1902 stone ten-room lighthouse, original lightkeeper's 1826 stone cottage; simple light tower predated present light. Bird watching, picnicking; guided tours.

B. **Historic South Norwalk,** NRHP, NHL, NHD. Washington, Water, Marshal, South and North Main sts. Open all year as shops, restaurants, businesses. Nineteenth-century economic center that declined, now a revitalized and tastefully restored waterfront neighborhood.

C. **Veteran's Memorial Park.** Seaview Ave. Open all year. Boat launch, fee.

D. **Cranbury Park.** Follow East Ave. north, becoming Newtown Ave., to Grumman Ave., left on Grumman to park. Open all year. No fee. 130 acres, picnicking, mansion for parties.

E. **Calf Pasture Beach.** Calf Pasture Beach Road. Open all year. Seasonal parking fee.

F. **Norwalk Islands.** Limited access by boat through National Audubon Society; five islands are part of Audubon bird sanctuary.

WESTPORT

John Green was one of the five original "Bankside" farmers who settled (c. 1648) in what later became known as Greens Farms, west of what is now Sherwood Island State Park. Later, others settled along the Saugatuck River, forming Saugatuck Village, named Westport in 1835. In this active shipping port, pedlar ships, reminiscent of Mississippi River boats, frequented local waters, adding their own special character. Soon coastal beauty and Colonial ambience lured artists, writers, and actors. A fascinating town to visit, Westport is affluent today with cultural and artistic flair and loyalty to New England traditions.

1. **WHEELER HOUSE, *1795*, NHRP, HS. 25 Avery Pl. Open all year, limited hours or by appointment, no fee. Educational programs, exhibits, museum shop, research center, library.**

This gracious, Victorian Italianate, probably first built as a salt box, was a wedding gift from Captain Ebenezer Coley to son Micahel in 1795. A later owner, Farmin Patchin, who received the property in 1846, built the two-story, octagonal, cobblestone barn in the rear of the property. It is being restored to serve as a museum for Westport's history.

In 1865, owners Morris and Mary Bradley enlarged and converted the home to its present Victorian style. In time the house passed to daughter Julia, who married Charles Wheeler, and later to their son, Dr. Lewis Wheeler. Dr. Wheeler, who once served as surgeon aboard President Woodrow Wilson's yacht, was a prominent doctor in Westport, living here until his death in 1958. The property was sold to the Westport Historical Society in 1981.

The house, particularly the parlor and kitchen, has been restored to represent the era of Morris and Mary Bradley, a time of renewed prosperity and growth following the Civil War. Notice the seven-piece black walnut parlor suite, marble-topped tables, and fancy lady's desk of the Victorian era.

BEACHES, PARKS, OTHER POINTS OF INTEREST

Beach sticker fee for nonresidents at all city beaches in summer.

A. **Nature Center for Environmental Activities.** 10 Woodside Ln. Open all year. Fee. Sixty-two acres with trails, natural history museum, lifelike dioramas, aquarium, hands-on tidal pool, exhibits and Bentz scope in Discovery Room; greenhouse, live animals, reference library; nature sanctuary dedicated to study, preservation, rehabilitation, and enjoyment of native plants and animals in peaceful, inviting environment; gift shop, picnicking, hiking. Nature-oriented nursery school; wildlife hotline, animal rehabilitation program—more than

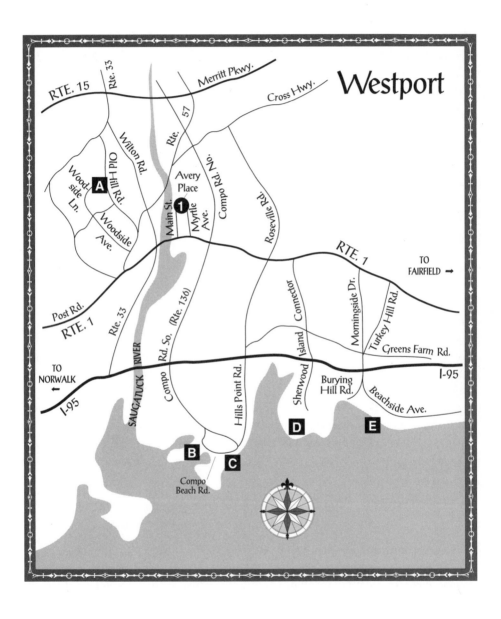

1,000 helped annually; natural history field courses, field trips, special events, educational programs on and off campus.

B. **Compo Beach.** Compo Beach Rd. Open all year. Twenty-nine acres, concessions, bath house, playground, yacht basin, lifeguards; picnicking, swimming.

C. **Old Mill Beach.** Hills Point Rd. Open all year. Small beach mainly for local residents; swimming.

D. **Sherwood Island State Park.** I-95, exit 18. Open all year. Parking fee in summer. Named for settler Daniel Sherwood of England's Sherwood Forest; 2-mile beach, 234 acres, concessions, rest rooms, pavilion, lifeguards; picnicking, swimming, fishing.

E. **Burying Hill Beach.** Beachside Ave. Open all year. Small rocky beach adjacent to Sherwood Park; lifeguards; swimming.

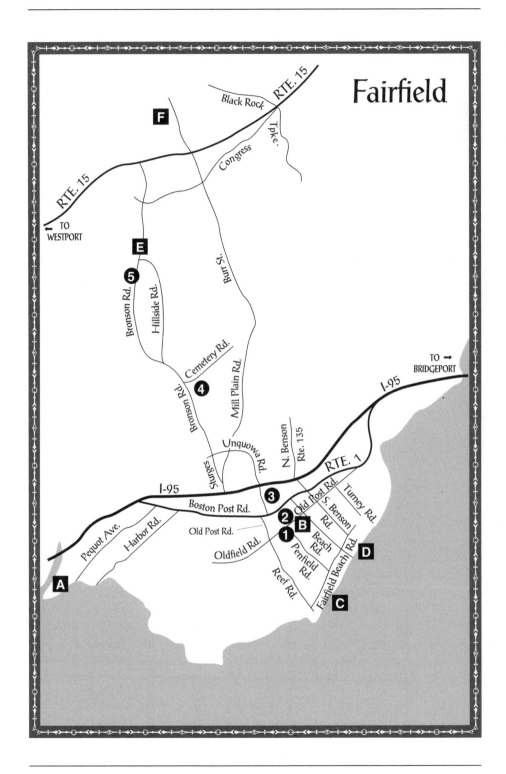
Fairfield

FAIRFIELD

Fairfield has the flavor of a small colonial town with city advantages. Roger Ludlow, former deputy governor of Massachusetts, founded the town in 1639 with a small group of men and many cattle. Before that, the land was farmed by the Unquowas clan of the Paugussett tribe, which summered at the seashore to fish and plant corn. Ludlow planned lots along the Old Post Road, which was at that time an Indian trail between villages. It later became the communication path of the colonies. Fairfield farms yielded well during their first century, enough to ship wheat, flax, timber, and livestock to Boston, New York, and the West Indies in trade for nails, textiles, furnishings, and molasses to make rum. During the Revolution, Fairfield's "whaleboat fleet" harassed British ships, capturing or burning many. Twenty-three-year-old Samuel Smedley captained the 230-ton *Defense* and her crew of 130 men, seizing more than eight British ships. Ruthless British Brigadier General Tryon and his Hessians retaliated. They kidnapped Colonel Gold Selleck Silliman, who was in charge of the Patriots' coastal defenses. They attacked Fairfield, occupied the town, and burned more than two hundred homes and all public buildings.

Fairfield has three historic districts listed on the National Register: Fairfield, Greenfield Hill, and Southport. **Fairfield** (B on map) includes historic town-owned buildings—the Old Town Hall, Sun Tavern, Victorian Cottage and barn, Burr Homestead—plus the DAR-owned Old Academy. All are open for functions or by appointment. Along Old Post Road from Post Road to Turney Road parade historic homes ranging in architecture from Colonial to Georgian, Federal, Greek Revival, and Victorian. A fine walking tour guide pamphlet is available at the Fairfield Historical Society (2).

Greenfield Hill (E) is a charming village of historic homes, many pre-Revolutionary, surrounding the simple white-clapboarded Congregational Church. Bell tower and steeple rise above the village green, where a magnificent copper beech tree presides. The annual Dogwood Festival has drawn visitors for more than fifty years. In the late 1700s Pastor Timothy Dwight opened an academy in Greenfield Hill for young men and women. He later became president of Yale College.

A small village called Mill River in the 1700s, **Southport** (A) grew to become a center of commerce and elegant homes. Shipping the Southport onion kept the harbor profitable throughout the 1800s. Walk through the quaint, harbor-centered village to see historic homes of Colonial, Federal, Greek Revival, Gothic, and Victorian architecture.

1. BURR HOMESTEAD, *c. 1793.* **Old Post Rd. at Penfield Rd. Open by appointment.**

The Burr Homestead was built to replace a house burned by the British in spite of General Tryon's promise to save it. The original home was built about 1700 by Peter Burr, chief justice of the Connecticut Colony. It descended to grandson Thaddeus Burr, deputy of Fairfield, sheriff, commissioner, member of the Committee of Correspondence and the Council of Safety, and a justice. Here Burr gave haven to John Hancock, Dorothy Quincy, and Sam Adams during the occupation of Boston. Dorothy Quincy and John Hancock were married here August 28, 1775. It is said that other visitors included George Washington, Benjamin Franklin, the Marquis de Lafayette, James Otis, and John Adams. Aaron Burr, a dashing cousin of Thaddeus, is said to have tried to woo Dorothy Quincy away from John Hancock when Hancock and Adams went on to Philadelphia. John Singleton Copley painted portraits of Thaddeus and his wife Eunice Dennie Burr.

The present mansion was probably built by Fairfield carpenter-architect Daniel Dimon in late Georgian–early Federal style. Its owner remodeled it into Greek Revival in the 1830s by removing dormers, lifting the roof, and adding full-height columns.

2. FAIRFIELD HISTORICAL SOCIETY MUSEUM. **636 Old Post Rd. Open all year, fee. Research library, museum shop, publications, home-restoration resource center; oral history and other programs, schools outreach.**

Four centuries of Fairfield life are exhibited in this fine museum. Changing exhibits highlighting Fairfield and area history are featured. The society's costume collection, the largest in southern New England, contains more than 10,000 items, including 200-plus hats. Exhibits include paintings, prints, home and farm tools, toys and dolls, household objects and furnishings, and decorative pieces. The research library centers on genealogy, decorative arts, and local history, and includes manuscripts, maps, architectural drawings, microfilm, photos.

3. CONNECTICUT AUDUBON SOCIETY BIRDCRAFT MUSEUM AND SANCTUARY. **314 Unquowa Rd. Open all year, limited hours, fee. Museum, trails.**

"Life for the birds whose household words are songs in many keys" is the motto in stone at the pillared entrance. The first private songbird refuge in the country, this six-acre sanctuary was given by Annie Burr Jennings and directed by Mabel Osgood Wright from 1914 to 1934. Enter the grounds and you are immediately in a world apart; you hear birds over the rush of traffic, which soon fades. Touch exhibits at this natural history museum are geared for children—dinosaur footprints, dioramas of wildlife, live bees. Changing exhibits include 2,000 mounted birds and mammals. The sanctuary is also a bird banding station.

4. OGDEN HOUSE, *c. 1750*, HS. **1520 Bronson Rd. Open extended season, limited hours, and by appointment; fee. Eighteenth-century gardens, wildflower trail.**

Remarkable in its unchanged simplicity, the Ogden House remains in a peaceful residential setting where an even earlier house had been. This typical New England saltbox was built for David and Jane (Sturges) Ogden at the time of their marriage. It served the Ogden family for 125 years and is furnished in accordance with the 1774 inventory of David Ogden. The earliest Ogdens were farmers, successful but, as their inventory indicates, not wealthy. They had furniture but no clocks, paintings, or prints. They had some silver, much land, but also debts. Paint layer analysis indicates the interior was repainted about every fifty-five years. The huge fireplace in the kitchen is 5 feet high and 10 feet wide. Georgian features appear in paneled walls—some chamfered-cut with raised center panels—enclosed beams, and window woodwork. Yale architectural studies suggest Dutch influence as well as New England Colonial.

5. BRONSON WINDMILL, *1893–94*, NRHP. **3015 Bronson Rd. Exterior view only, no fee.**

In 1891 financier Frederic Bronson built a large mansion that was designed by Richard Morris Hunt. It was constructed on the site of the home of Timothy Dwight. Dwight was pastor at Greenfield Hill and president of Yale College in 1795. The windmill was the main water source for Bronson's large dairy farm. The weathered, patterned shingles and ogee-shaped roof are original. A large wooden tank within the 80-foot octagonal tower, an underground cistern, and much original machinery remain.

BEACHES, PARKS, OTHER POINTS OF INTEREST

C. **Penfield Beach and Rickards Beach.** Fairfield Beach Rd. Open all year. Parking fee in summer. Bathhouses, pavilion, 800-ft. beach. **Penfield Reef Light.** Marks mile-long Penfield Bar, dangerous landmark in Sound; one of most stylish lighthouses, built 1874, Second Empire design, red-topped light tower projects from one side of white-capped granite house; legend tells of drowned light keeper whose ghost returns to save victims on Christmas Eve.

D. **Jennings Beach.** Beach Rd. and South Benson Rd. Open all year. Parking fee.

F. **Connecticut Audubon Society Fairfield Nature Center.** 2325 Burr St. Open all year. Museum no fee. Trail fee. Museum store, 168 acres, 6 miles of trails, greenhouse, nature walk for handicapped; habitat of marsh, ponds, woods, fields; exhibits of snapping turtles, pond life, plus changing exhibits; natural history reference library; programs, classes, some with live animals.

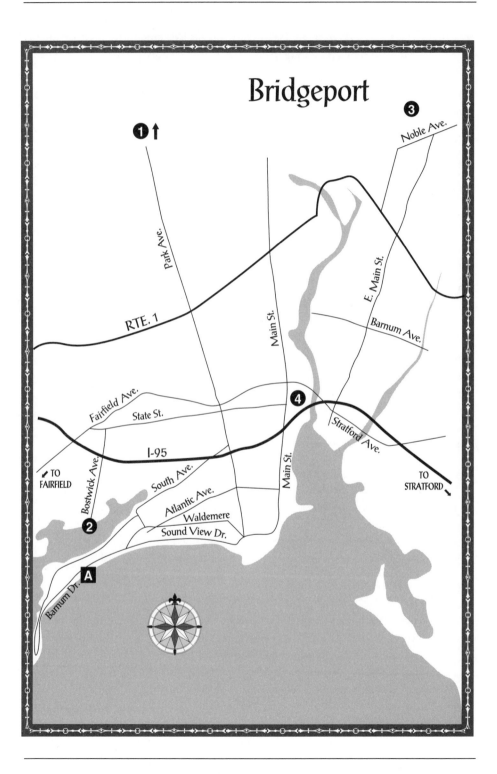

Bridgeport

BRIDGEPORT

Bridgeport is an industrial city with gracious residential areas and an historic past. It was part of Stratford until incorporated separately in 1821. It became a city in 1836 and is now the state's largest. Bridgeport's first important economy was whaling. The advent of railroads brought industry to make the city a major manufacturing and financial center. Here the first gramophones became Columbian Phonograph Company; Elias Howe invented the first sewing machine; and P. T. Barnum began the "Greatest Show on Earth."

1. THE DISCOVERY MUSEUM. 4450 Park Ave. Open all year, fee. Fine arts galleries, hands-on science and art exhibits, planetarium shows daily, Challenger Space Center with mini-missions on weekends, gift shop, programs.

The focus of this exciting museum is on interactive art and science. Changing art exhibitions are featured on the main level. In the lower-level science galleries you can push a button, watch a gear mesh, and move a complicated mechanism to produce power. The upper level is an experiment-filled lab where you become a scientist. Walk inside an electric wall outlet or listen to a life-size model of Michael Faraday talk about electricity. Transformers, motors, generators, batteries, strobes—all displays draw you to participate: move the ball, direct the rod, swing the pendulum, pedal the energy producer. Art and science join in the light exhibit, where video cameras and computers record your motions and paint your image in moving, blending color. Fascinating hands-on creative workshops for adults and children are another feature of this museum—"Connecticut's adventure in art and science."

The museum is situated on the edge of **90 Acres Park,** city parkland with nature trails. Within the park is the **Capt. John Brooks House,** a restored house museum with some original furnishings. Built in 1788 and moved to this site, it is the oldest house in Bridgeport and was lived in by only one family.

2. CAPTAIN'S COVE SEAPORT. One Bostwick Ave. Open all year, no fee. Marina, restaurant, wharves, shops, boats.

It's a modern marina with a flair—a people's place. You can picnic at tables on wharves suspended over water, explore tiny, individually housed shops, dine or self-serve, take a cruise, or stroll the wharf. In the restaurant a 35-foot model of the *Titanic* is suspended above one part of the room. The central bar is topped by the bridge of the *Mary Ellen Carter,* and a nearly life-size model of Sikorsky's S44 Flying Boat of World War II hovers over the other third of the room. If she's in port, you can tour the HMS *Rose,* replica of a Revolutionary War–era 24-gun frigate that engaged in skirmishes in the English

Channel in the Seven Years War, helped capture Havana and Martinique in 1761, and was intentionally sunk off Savannah, Georgia, in 1779 to block the approach of a French invasion fleet. Now the largest operational wood sailing ship in the world, the *Rose* replica was built in Lunenberg, Nova Scotia, with some of the original wood.

3. BEARDSLEY ZOO AND PARK. Noble Ave. Open all year, fee. Lake, ball fields, gift shop, concessions, picnicking, tennis.

When wealthy cattleman James Beardsley donated more than 100 acres and Frederick Olmsted designed Beardsley Park, they were thinking of a simple rural park. But this was Bridgeport, home of P. T. Barnum. Barnum, who had exercised his animals along the streets of Bridgeport, found the park a fine place for these strolls. The idea of a zoo took shape in 1920. Citizens contributed animals to the menagerie, including some Barnum "retirees."

The zoo's thirty-six-acre outdoor habitat is now home to more than three hundred specimens of eighty or more species of animals. The emphasis is on North and South American animals, though Siberian tigers remain. Rare red wolves have been born here and reintroduced to the wild in the Species Survival Plan. Exotic animals range from anteaters to zebras. The indoor South American tropical rain forest exhibit with waterfall and stream is barrier free: Animals and birds are free, and people walk behind glass walls in darker areas that discourage birds from entering. Here you'll see crocodiles, turtles, spider monkeys, boas, margay cats, sloths, agouti, and marmosets. The Children's Zoo has a New England farm setting.

4. THE BARNUM MUSEUM, *1891*, NRHP. 820 Main St. Open all year, fee. Museum shop.

The museum parades the legacy of the world's greatest showman and Bridgeport's former benefactor and mayor, Phineas Taylor Barnum. The museum building is wildly appropriate—a mix of Romanesque with touches of Byzantine and Gothic. On the first floor you are greeted by an animated statue of P. T. Barnum. You meet Barnum the man and learn he was sixty when he began his circus. That was April 10, 1871, when they performed to a crowd of 10,000 in Brooklyn. By 1889 the show was the greatest wonder of the world, according to its creator. On this floor there is a re-creation of the library in Barnum's first Bridgeport mansion, "Iranistan," and a contemporary gallery mounting traveling art shows. On the second floor the focus is Barnum's Bridgeport of the 1800s. A gallery features Barnum's four Bridgeport mansions and depicts the distinctive architecture, character, and fate of each. To show Bridgeport as a city rich in opportunity, a huge revolving exhibit of costumes, sewing machines, buttons, corsets, typewriters, helicopters, ammunition, cigars, and razors illustrates items manufactured here.

On the third floor meet Barnum the showman. You hear circus music and background sounds before you can see the magnificent circus in miniature, "The Greatest

The Barnum Museum, Bridgeport   (The Barnum Museum, Bridgeport, Conn.)

Show on Earth." A 1,000-square-foot moving scale model of the three-ring circus, it was hand carved by William Brinley over a period of sixty years. Here are circus performers with all the circus trappings, from big top to small living tents. In all the model contains more than 500,000 pieces.

BEACHES, PARKS, OTHER POINTS OF INTEREST

A. Seaside Park. Atlantic or South Ave. to Barnum Dr. Open all year. Fee. 4.5-mile beach, lifeguards, bathhouses, concessions; picnicking. 200 acres given by P. T. Barnum, his statue here. **Black Rock Harbor Light or Fayerweather Island Light** at eastern end of park built 1823; Bridgeport citizens restored it and the area.

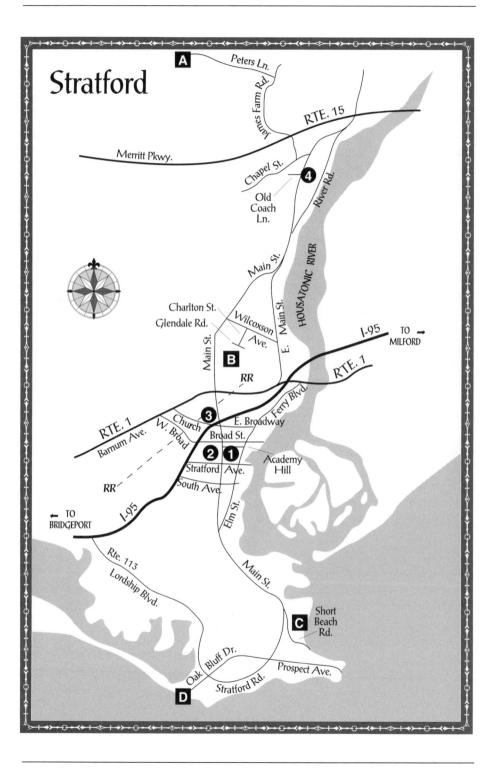

Stratford

STRATFORD

S tratford is picturesquely located on Long Island Sound at the mouth of the Houstonic River. A community with a strong colonial heritage, it was founded in 1639, when the congregation of Reverend Adam Blakeman settled on the river at "Cupheag" ("small harbor" in the Pangusett Indian language), now called Mack's Harbor. In the seventeenth and eighteenth centuries Stratford was an active shipbuilding port.

1. JUDSON HOUSE, *c. 1750*, NRHP, NHL, HS. 967 Academy Hill. Open extended season, limited hours, fee. Permanent and changing exhibits.

The Captain David Judson house may have influenced Connecticut architecture, for it is believed the curved pediment of its doorway became a model for doorways throughout the state. The original door with bull's-eye glass and the wide overhangs of the gable are rare features. The huge central chimney serving six fireplaces and post-and-beam second floor illustrate a transition from saltbox to Georgian architecture.

Step inside this carefully restored home of an eighteenth-century community leader and his family. Furnishings are based on David Judson's 1761 inventory and son Abner's 1775 inventory. The parlor features a 1760 piano, which belonged to William Samuel Johnson, framer and signer of the Constitution, and—like his father—president of Columbia College (now Univeristy). The piano was displayed at Mount Vernon for more than fifty years. A set tea table draws your imagination to niceties of yesteryear. The dining-room table with antique Canton china invites you to dine in a nineteenth-century period. The decorative paneling, c. 1800 mantel, and built-in corner cupboard with original glass and hardware speak of greater elegance. The house boasts two kitchens with massive fireplaces. During Abner Judson's time five slaves lived and did the cooking in the cellar. Such quarters provide a rare insight into New England slavery. Throughout the home, period furnishings and displays of farm and home implements illustrate life in the 1700s.

Behind Judson House is the **Catherine Bunnell Mitchell Museum** with exhibits illustrating Stratford history from 1639 to the mid-1800s. There are collections from the French and Indian, Revolutionary, and Civil wars, items from Stratford's China trade, local Indian artifacts, early documents, paintings, a rare profile and bill of sale for slave Flora, and changing exhibits done by the Stratford Historical Society.

2. MAIN STREET WALK. Academy Hill to Church St. Open all year, no fee.

Main Street from the Judson House north is a fascinating variety of Colonial and Victorian architecture in a traditional New England setting. On the right is **Christ Episcopal**

Captain David Judson House, Stratford   (Stratford Historical Society/Ruth P. Tabor)

Church, organized in 1707—the oldest parish in the oldest diocese in the Anglican church outside of England. First rector Samuel Johnson, Yale graduate and former Congregational minister, instructed future Anglican clergy in the church rectory. During the French and Indian Wars British troops used the earlier church building's weathercock for target practice. That same rooster perches proudly atop the present church. Next door is the **Old Episcopal Burying Ground,** where Reverend Samuel and his son William Samuel Johnson are buried. At 2103 Main is the **1799 Johnson House,** where Samuel Johnson's grandson Samuel William lived. This Georgian with Federal architectural elements was lived in by a Johnson until 1913. The **Stratford Library** at 2203 Main combines an original 1896 Romanesque section with the newer 1924 Captain John Sterling Memorial Building. At 2283 is the 1886 **Sterling House,** built by John W. Sterling, Jr., and designed by Yale building architect Bruce Price. Now a community center, the Romanesque thirty-room mansion boasts a gargoyle over the side entrance. Sterling left over $25 million to Yale University, making possible the graduate school, four buildings, and eighteen Sterling professorships. At 2301 Main is the **First Congregational Church,** gathered in 1640. This fifth building gracefully combines original 1859 Victorian Gothic style with 1950s neo-Colonial trim on the front door and steeple.

3. NATIONAL HELICOPTER MUSEUM. Off Main St. at railroad station. Open extended season, limited hours, no fee.

Home of Sikorsky Aircraft, Stratford is honored as the birthplace of America's helicopter industry. This museum is the only one solely dedicated to this industry. Here through photos (many rare) and text you can relive the history of the helicopter from its early concepts through Igor Sikorsky's original model VS-300 to the present. Photo exhibits, including the work of inventors from all over the world, bring alive the excitement and accomplishment of the helicopter.

The museum is housed in the c. 1848 Eastbound Railroad Station of New York and New Haven Railroad. This building was the subject of a painting by Edward Lamson Henry, *The 9:45 Accommodation, Stratford, Connecticut,* which is on display at the Metropolitan Museum of Art.

4. BOOTHE MEMORIAL PARK AND MUSEUM, *1663*, NRHP. Main St., opposite Old Coach Ln. Open extended season, no fee. Thirty-two acres, twenty buildings, rose garden, exhibits, playground, picnicking, cross-country skiing, sledding.

"I made it all myself" is the excited cry of schoolchildren visiting Boothe Park. They learn through hands-on experiences. Some start with wheat, threshing it, grinding the grain into flour, then using the flour to make pancakes, which never tasted better. Others do woodworking, weaving, and rug making. This unusual park/museum fosters knowledge and appreciation of early Americana through collections, exhibits, education, and varying architectural innovations. The Boothe family home was built about 1820 on an earlier Boothe 1663 foundation. In 1913, brothers Stephen and David Boothe, wanting to save and share America's past, began collecting and displaying artifacts and creating buildings, with a different architectural emphasis. They topped a hay barn with a clock tower from a Massachusetts church acquired in exchange for a Eureka carpet sweeper. They built a forty-four-sided blacksmith shop and an ice house that tells the story of the early ice industry. Further additions were Merritt Parkway toll booths, a basilica for outdoor church services, and a redwood technocratic cathedral symbolic of Depression days. A miniature windmill, decorated according to events, became a focal point.

Displays include farm implements, tools, home furnishings, antique buggies and carriages, baskets, and much more. For special occasions, such as an Easter Service for 4,000 or benefits for local groups, the Boothes opened their grounds. They shared collections and park atmosphere and provided gifts, food, and entertainment free of charge. The tradition continues today, for the Boothes left their estate to Stratford, which dedicated it as a park in 1955. Here unusual buildings and peaceful surroundings evoke a pleasant sense of nostalgia intermingled with historic pride.

BEACHES, PARKS, OTHER POINTS OF INTEREST

A. Roosevelt Forest. Peters Ln. Open all year. No fee. 250 acres, nature museum, playground, wildlife area; hiking, biking, picnicking, fishing, ice skating, sledding.

B. Longbrook Park and Brewster's Pond. Glendale Rd., off Main St. by way of Wilcoxsin Ave. and Charlton St. Open all year. No fee. Ball fields, concessions, wading pool, playground; biking, picnicking, ice skating, sledding.

C. Short Beach Park. Short Beach Rd. off Stratford Rd. Open summer. Beach sticker. Playgrounds, ball fields, tennis, concessions, lifeguards; hiking, sailing, swimming, biking, picnicking, fishing.

D. Long Beach. Oak Bluff Dr. Open summer. Nonresident beach stickers and boat-launching permits sold at Recreation Office. Lifeguards; fishing, hiking, sailing, swimming.

MILFORD

The English country–style stone Memorial Bridge is the grand entrance to Milford, where Route 162 spans the Wepawaug River. Built in 1889, the intriguing bridge symbolizes Milford's early years. A 40-foot granite tower stands guard over fifty-five memorial stones lining the bridge. Among them are memorials for "Free Planters," first pastor Peter Prudden, and "Seven Pillars" of the original church. The settlement, founded 1639, was originally part of the conservative New Haven Colony. After Milford joined the liberal Connecticut Colony in 1665, conservative Puritan Robert Treat and followers, objecting to suffrage for people other than Puritans, moved south and founded Newark, New Jersey. (They later returned to Milford.) Through the years fishing, oystering, and clamming, along with farming and an experimental seed industry, strongly influenced Milford's lifestyle. In recent years summer visitors have added their wealth and way of life to this growing seacoast town.

1. MILFORD HISTORICAL SOCIETY WHARF LANE MUSEUM COMPLEX, HS. 34 High St. Open extended season, limited hours, donation.

The three homes of the Wharf Lane Complex are surviving witnesses to life in eighteenth-century Milford. The c. 1700 **Eells–Stow House,** the oldest, is a "mystery house." Its architecture is different from the usual early-1700s house plan. It has a cove overhang, middle passageway, and small diamond windows of the Elizabethan era; two chimneys normally attributed to a later period; and a dog-legged stairway with unique handrail showing supporting balustrade from first to second floor. The kitchen probably evolved from an open lean-to. The rear ell was added in 1880, making it a two-family house. While the frame and layout are original, much of this intriguing building has been restored or reconstructed. Many Milford-made chairs are displayed in the house.

Samuel Eells, Jr., inherited the property from his father, Major Samuel Eells, who came to Milford in 1663 with his bride. A copy of Major Eells's wedding portrait hangs in the parlor. (The original is in the National Gallery of Art in Washington, D.C.) After 1754 the home was sold to Stephen Stow, a successful coastal schooner captain who was also a good man. On New Year's Eve 1777 a British prison ship put ashore 200 smallpox-stricken colonial soldiers. Unselfish settlers took them in; Captain Stow cared for many of the sick until the town hall was converted to a hospital the following day. Sadly, Stow was a victim of the dread disease. He and others are buried in a common grave at the Old Burying Ground on Prospect Street. Other notable graves are Connecticut Governors Robert Treat, Jonathan Law, and Charles Hobby Pond.

The **Stockade House** is named for Nathan and Abigail Clark's 1659 house, the

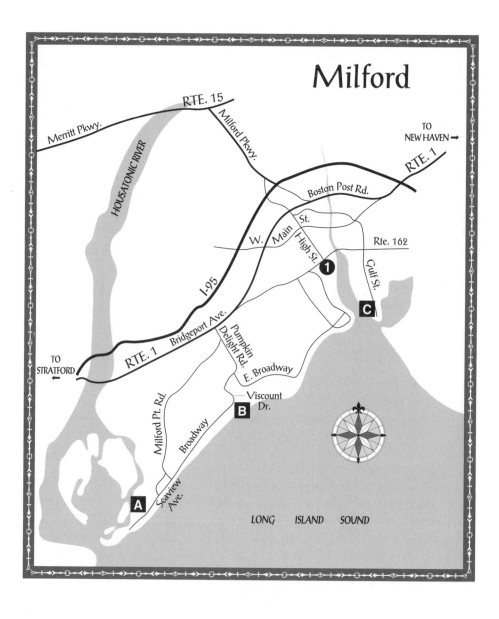

Milford

RTE. 15

Merritt Pkwy.

HOUSATONIC RIVER

Milford Pkwy.

TO
NEW HAVEN →

RTE. 1

Boston Post Rd.

W. Main St.

High St.

Rte. 162

I-95

1

Gulf St.

C

Bridgeport Ave.

Pumpkin Delight Rd.

E. Broadway

RTE. 1

TO
STRATFORD
←

Milford Pt. Rd.

Viscount Dr.

B

Broadway

A

Seaview Ave.

LONG   ISLAND   SOUND

first built outside the Stockade. In 1780 Michael Peck constructed the present building using beams and framework from the 1659 structure. The building was moved here in the 1980s. The rare built-in bookcase, much of the raised paneling, some beams, the framework, and the chimney stones are original. Notice the unusual shallow corner fireplace in the borning room, early 1900s portrait of Dr. Richard L. Eells, and early 1800s portrait of John Alden's descendant, Willie Flint. In 1920 this building was Milford Hospital.

The c. 1785 **Bryan–Downs House,** built by Captain Jehiel Bryan, was taken down and stored for several years before being erected here. Today it houses the permanent Claude C. Coffin Indian collection, including more than 4,000 prehistoric Indian artifacts. It has changing exhibits relating to Milford and a general store selling items of local interest.

BEACHES, PARKS, OTHER POINTS OF INTEREST

A. National Wildlife Refuge. Milford Point Rd. and Seaview Ave.; take right fork, not private road. Open all year. No fee. Has 12-acre beach, 890 acres of mud flats, two small offshore barrier beaches, nesting areas for terns, views of Long Island Sound.

B. Walnut Beach. Viscount Dr. Open summer. Parking fee. Rest rooms, lifeguards; swimming.

C. Gulf Beach. Gulf St. Open summer. Parking fee. Concessions, fishing pier, lifeguards, volleyball; swimming.

Oyster Houses, *by Alexander J. Rummler*   (Norwalk City Hall WPA Paintings Collection)

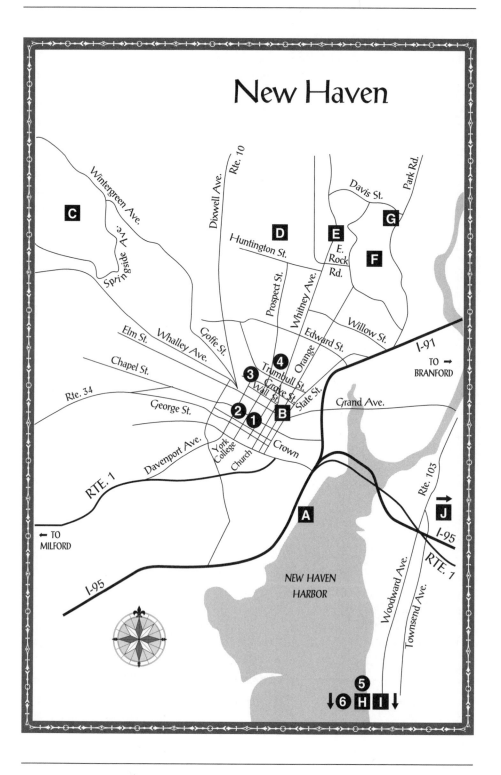

New Haven

NEW HAVEN

N ew Haven grew from a quiet green to a modern city with a fascinating composite of architectural styles, corporate headquarters, and cultural centers. All are within the shadows of the ivy halls of Yale University, third oldest in the nation.

In 1637 Theophilus Eaton and John Davenport led conservative Puritans from London, England, to establish a settlement here on Long Island Sound. They bought land from the Indian sachem Momauquin, founding New Haven November 24, 1638. Combining with other settlements, in 1643 they formed the New Haven Colony that would include today's Connecticut towns of Stamford, Milford, New Haven, East Haven, Fair Haven, Branford, Guilford, and Madison. Puritan congregations governed by their members were established in each settlement and discouraged all other churches. In civil matters the colony adopted John Cotton's code of law, one of the first written in the New World. All went well until 1660, when the Connecticut Colony obtained a charter claiming the New Haven Colony. After three bitter years, New Haven Colony gave in and joined the Connecticut Colony. Had things gone differently, one of the original states might have been called New Haven. From 1701 to 1875 New Haven was a twin capital with Hartford.

The day after blood was shed at Lexington, New Haven's Benedict Arnold took a stand for liberty, forcing selectmen to open the powder house for the Connecticut Governor's Foot Guard. Before the war ended New Haven was attacked by the British, and Benedict Arnold became a traitor. After the war New Haven became a maritime community specializing in coastal and West Indies trade and later a manufacturing and railroad center. Famous eighteenth- and nineteenth-century residents included Noah Webster, Eli Whitney, James Hillhouse, Samuel F. B. Morse, and Charles Goodyear.

1. NEW HAVEN GREEN HISTORIC DISTRICT, *1812–16*, NRHP, NHL. Bounded by Chapel, College, Church, and Elm sts.

The sixteen-acre Green, center of New Haven life for more than three hundred years, was the center of nine "squares" in the original 1638 village plan. The early Green was marketplace, drill field, and pasture with courthouse, county house, and grammar school. By 1814 the buildings, except the courthouse, were gone, replaced by today's three historic churches standing in supportive unity on the south side of this green oasis. West are Gothic Revival stone buildings of Yale University; north the Colonial or Beaux-arts Ives Memorial Library and Greco-Roman New Haven County Courthouse; east a Colonial Revival building, a high Victorian Gothic City Hall, and a classic Greek post office amid dramatic modern structures.

Trinity Church, 1815, one of the oldest Gothic Revival churches in the nation, was designed by Ithiel Town. Its Episcopal congregation dates to 1752. In the magnificent interior, exquisite Tiffany windows, fourteenth-century-style painted glass windows, and arched motifs sweep eyes and thoughts heavenward. The focus is the chancel area with its carved marble altar; delicate tile, brass and marble pulpit; brass eagle lectern; and sculptured figures of the reredos.

Center Church, United Church of Christ, is the oldest congregation on the Green. The imposing Federal brick building, with elegantly detailed steeple set above a classical entrance, has unusual wreathed ox-skull ornamentation, symbolic of Saint Luke and the priesthood. This fourth meetinghouse was designed by Asher Benjamin and adapted and constructed by Ithiel Town in 1814. Inside, simple grandeur is reflected in a domed ceiling with unusual plaster relief supporting a Waterford chandelier. As of old, New Haven founder and first minister John Davenport stands behind the pulpit in the arched Tiffany window. The church, literally built on the foundation of its early members, stands above New Haven Colony's burial ground, dating to the church's 1638 gathering. Descend steps to an unusual indoor cemetery under the sanctuary floor. Here are buried John Davenport's wife; the first wife of Benedict Arnold; Jared Ingersoll; and, behind the church, regicide John Dixwell.

The Federal-style **United Church on-the-Green** was built in 1814 by David Hoadley, designed by Ebenezer Johnson. Its Federal elegance is stated in balanced dentilled and gabled brick front facade showing delicate egg-and-dart moldings in arched doorways. The white bell tower is topped by a windowed cupola with feather weather vane. Inside, the sanctuary has been restored in keeping with its early Federal appearance and has original chandelier and shallow-dome ceiling. In the 1740s a group of "New Lights," people seeking changes in the established church, separated from Center Church to form United Church. Here in 1855 Henry Ward Beecher preached against slavery.

2. YALE UNIVERSITY. York, Chapel, Elm, and College sts. Open all year.

In 1716 "Collegiate College" moved to New Haven from Old Saybrook, and two years later the college was renamed in honor of its first major private benefactor, Elihu Yale. This institution of higher learning has been inspired by many distinguished minds, each leaving an influence on the great complex of knowledge and tradition and architecture that is Yale.

The architecture of Yale is a mix of styles—Georgian, Gothic, Victorian, Georgian Revival, and varieties of modern. On the old campus quad is the oldest building, **Connecticut Hall** (College Street near Chapel Street, NHL, built 1752). Similar to Harvard's Massachusetts Hall, it was the dormitory of Eli Whitney, Nathan Hale (class of 1773), Noah Webster, and William Howard Taft. **Harkness Tower** (1917–21, High Street), centerpiece of **Memorial Quadrangle,** was designed to provide a feeling of English tradition. It was the first creation of James Gamble Rogers, architect of the general Gothic plan of the university. The tower is the icon of Yale, 216 feet tall, ending in a spray of stone, with Yale's values and traditions depicted in sculptures on its facades. The **School of Art and Architecture** building (York at Chapel) was designed by Paul Rudolph. Of hammered concrete aggregate within and out, it demonstrates unique use of space, variety, and shock. The **David S. Ingalls Hockey Rink** (Sachem Street), designed by Eero Saarinen, is concrete with an aluminum roof suspended by cables from a central arch, like a huge tent. The design suggests the sweeping rushes of hockey or the shape of a whale. The **Payne Whitney Gymnasium** (Tower Parkway) was the world's largest until the builders of the Moscow Olympian facility came here with tape measures.

• **Yale University Art Gallery,** 1111 Chapel St. Open all year, no fee. Sculpture garden, museum shop, publications, lectures.

America's first university art gallery was founded in 1832 with John Trumbull's gift of one hundred paintings. Art from every major period is augmented by special changing exhibits in five gallery floors. Here are treasures of ancient Americas, Egypt, Near East, Greece, and Rome—for example, the Mithraeum from Dura-Europos, sanctuary of the Persian sun god. Nineteenth- and twentieth-century European art is well represented—Peter Paul Rubens, Frans Hals with his twinkling-eyed portraits, Van Gogh, Millet. American experience in the decorative arts and furnishings includes Georgia O'Keeffe's *The Blue Wave, Maine.*

• **Yale Center for British Art.** 1080 Chapel St. Open all year, no fee. Reference library, research, museum shop, publications, lectures.

This fine museum and research institute opened in 1977, exhibiting British paintings, prints, rare books, sculpture, and drawings from Paul Mellon's collection. Classical art is featured—Sir Joshua Reynolds, George Stubbs (two whole rooms), Thomas Gainsborough, J. M. W. Turner (a wonderful roomful), John Constable. More modern artists are also represented; works include a sensitive sculpture of Albert Einstein and collage of images of Elvis Presley. Four floors of treasures provide a chronological survey of British art. Important in contemporary architecture, the building was the last designed by architect Louis I. Kahn, who died in 1974.

• **The Beinecke Rare Book and Manuscript Library.** Wall and High sts. Open all year, no fee.

Walk upstairs past rare books seen behind glass in stacks in the center of the building. Comfortable couches allow time to study light patterns emerging through 1¼-inch-thick translucent marble walls, which allow natural light but not enough to damage collections. From the exterior this modern building stands in rare harmony with its more classical neighbors. The Vermont marble, granite, bronze, and glass structure was designed by Gordon Bunshaft. Permanent exhibitions include the Gutenberg Bible (one of five in this country, twenty-one in the world) and Audubon's *Birds of America.*

• **The Yale University Collection of Musical Instruments.** 15 Hillhouse Ave. Open fall though spring, limited hours, no fee. Lectures, concerts.

More than 800 European and American instruments from the sixteenth to the twentieth century are in this fine collection. Permanent exhibits include an array of strings, one a Stradivarius. Ancient horns have serpents' bodies. The second-floor exhibit room features keyboard instruments from the collection of Morris Steinert, whose gift began the museum in 1900. The museum is devoted to the history of music through documentation and exposition of its instruments. Hillhouse Avenue is a neighborhood of elegant homes of the mid-1800s.

• **Peabody Museum of Natural History,** 170 Whitney Ave. Open all year, fee. Museum "dino store," lectures, events, workshops.

Dinosaurs dominate. The skeleton of 65-foot *Brontosaurus excelsus,* the thunder lizard, towers over a huge room full of dinosaurs, turtles, birds. On the wall is the 110-foot-long Pulitzer Prize–winning mural, *The Age of Reptiles,* by Rudolph F. Zallinger. New England's largest museum of natural history also features mineralogy, meteorites, invertebrates, mammals, and ancient cultures. A huge Olmec stone head from Mexico, the remarkable collection of mammalian-evolution fossils from nineteenth-century Yale paleontologist O. C. Marsh, and the realistic Birds of Connecticut exhibit are particularly interesting.

3. GROVE STREET CEMETERY, *1797.*

Enter this historic burial ground through a massive Egyptian Revival gateway, reminiscent of Pyramids. Inside are a Victorian chapel and beautifully landscaped roadways. In this tranquil cemetery, one of the first to lay out family plots, are buried Samuel Morse, Noah Webster, Eli Whitney, Roger Sherman, Charles Goodyear, Theophilus Eaton, James Pierpoint, and Ithiel Town.

4. NEW HAVEN COLONY HISTORICAL SOCIETY MUSEUM.
114 Whitney Ave. Open all year, fee. Research library, gift shop, educational program, films, lectures, hands-on classes.

The new City Hall had just opened. A petition, requesting the formation of an association for collecting and preserving documents and relics relating to the New Haven Colony, was presented October 6, 1862. Inspirer Horace Day further helped the cause by holding incorporation meetings at William A. Reynolds's home, built on the foundation of the manse of New Haven founder John Davenport. Success was assured. The New Haven Colony Historical Society was founded November 14, 1862. Today it is headquartered in this dignified Colonial Revival brick building with marble-pillared entrance. It houses a superb research library of 30,000 printed items, genealogies, and 250 collections of handwritten manuscripts. Off the Ionic-columned central rotunda are permanent exhibit rooms displaying New Haven tablewares, A Visual History of New Haven, paintings, Eli Whitney's cotton gin, and special period furnished rooms.

Outstanding changing exhibits have included "Free Men: The Amistad Revolt and American Anti-Slavery Movement" and "Seizing the Light: Masterworks of the Photograph Archive."

5. BLACK ROCK FORT AND FORT NATHAN HALE, NRHP. Woodward Ave. Open summer, no fee. Views, picnicking across road.

Forts have commanded this site since 1657. On July 5, 1779, nineteen men in the 1775 Black Rock Fort defended New Haven against British attack until their ammunition ran out. Spiking their guns, they withdrew. Today the log fortification provides peaceful harbor views. In 1807 the area was renamed Fort Hale in honor of Revolutionary War hero Nathan Hale. Enlarged and rebuilt slightly inland in 1863, the current fort, with earth-covered concrete bunkers and surrounding moat, suggests Civil War readiness. Yet wildflowers growing atop gun placements, a unique drawbridge, and Memorial Flag Court speak of peace rather than war.

6. PARDEE–MORRIS HOUSE, *c. 1780*, NRHP. 325 Lighthouse Rd. off Woodward Ave. Open summer, limited hours, fee.

From 1671 to 1918, through war, British attacks, imprisonment, prosperity, financial setbacks, and building restoration, eight generations of Morrises and their descendants lived at this same site. Militia Captain Amos Morris—freeman, selectman, church deacon—owned the 170-acre farm when on July 5, 1779, the British attacked, burning the home and later imprisoning Morris and his son, Amos junior, who escaped. Amos senior was released after promising not to do anything against the British. It appears the house was rebuilt on the same foundation. The lintel over the kitchen door bears the inscription "Capt. A. M. 1767" from an addition made by Amos in that year, possibly indicating that part of the edifice survived the burning. By the time Amos III inherited the farm, financial problems were looming on the horizon; parcels of land were sold and mortgages taken. In the 1880s Amos III's son Julius opened a boardinghouse. His son, Edwin, the last Morris to live here, sold lots on Morris Point. In 1915, Morris descendant, William S. Pardee, bought the home and began restoration. Upon his death in 1918, the house was left to the New Haven Colony Historical Society.

The Georgian wood farmhouse with gabled ends of granite, possibly showing Dutch influence, is restored to the time of the first and second Amoses. Major doorways with bull's-eye glass welcome you to the central hall, off of which are front parlors, a rear kitchen, and office or additional parlor. A two-story frame addition on the north end has an unusual ballroom on the second floor. In the first-floor parlors are "hearts and crown" and "York" chairs, 1610 Bible box, and family portraits. The room gives a sense of the comfortable lifestyle of a prominent and successful farmer of the 1700s. Furnishings are authentic to the period.

BEACHES, PARKS, OTHER POINTS OF INTEREST

A. Long Wharf, I-95 exit 46. Early pork-packing plants, now modern commercial buildings; Long Wharf Theater, fee; M/V *Liberty Bell* cruises, summer, fee.

B. Connecticut Children's Museum, 291 Orange St. Open all year. Fee. Hands-on parent-child interacting activities, infants to preschool.

C. West Rock Ridge State Park. Wintergreen Ave. and Springside Ave. Open all year. No fee. **"Judges Cave,"** hiding place for Edward Whalley and William Goffe when sought by Charles II for part in execution of Charles I of England; 428 feet high; hiking, picnicking.

D. Connecticut Agricultural Experiment Station, 1875, NHL. 123 Huntington St. Open all year for testing, agricultural questions, and problems. First state-supported agricultural experiment station.

E. Eli Whitney Museum, NRHP. Whitney Ave. at Armory St., Hamden. Open all year. Fee. Exhibits relate to Eli Whitney's industrial and creative genius; overview of industrial use of site from 1798 to 1979. Offers exceptional educational hands-on programs for all ages; 1816 Barn offers community cultural events.

F. East Rock Park. East Rock Rd. Open all year. No fee. During 1779 British attack many took refuge here; 359 feet high by ½ mile wide, 647 acres. Bird sanctuary, nature trails, ball fields, war memorial, panoramic views; picnicking, hiking.

G. Pardee Rose Gardens. 180 Park Rd. Open all year. No fee. Greenhouses; garden memorial to Nancy Marie English Pardee by son William Scranton Pardee.

H. East Shore Park. Woodward Ave. Open all year. No fee. Playgrounds, tennis, harbor views.

I. Lighthouse Point Park. 2 Lighthouse Rd. off Woodward Ave. Open summer. Parking fee. Antique Coney Island–style 1916 carousel, NRHP, fee; 90-foot 1840 lighthouse (not open) used 1845–77; site where British landed July 5, 1779, to be repulsed two days later; 82 acres, bathhouse, concessions, trails, views, boat rentals, natural history displays, pavilion; fishing, picnicking, swimming.

J. Shore Line Trolley Museum, NHS. I-95 exit 51 east, signs to 17 River St., East Haven. Open extended season. Fee. 100 trolley cars 1860–1982; founded by Branford Electric Railway, NRHP, oldest operating suburban trolley line; 3-mile narrated trip, trolley rides to car barns, restoration shop/museum, gift shop; picnicking.

BRANFORD

B ranford has preserved the beauty and tradition of its Town Green, where
three churches, the Town Hall, and the old Academy stand. The land was
purchased from the Indians by the New Haven Colony in 1638 and settled
in 1644. A simple white spire towers above the New England Gothic Episcopal
church. The Town Hall, a stately Greek Revival with massive column-supported
portico, contrasts with First Congregational Church next to it. The Congregational
church, whose congregation was gathered in 1644, has a tall steeple and clock
tower atop its brick building. At the lower end of the Green is the Baptist church, a
Greek Revival in white clapboard with black shutters and square belfry. The
Academy of 1820 is white-clapboarded, with quaint cupola atop the tower and
small-paned twelve-over-twelve windows. From the Green Route 146 leads to the
shore, to Stony Creek, and on to Guilford. It is designated a Scenic Road and is a
peaceful drive past beautiful residential and ocean scenes.

1. HARRISON HOUSE, *1724*, NRHP, HS. 124 Main St. Open summer, limited hours, no fee. Herb garden.

This beautiful old saltbox has housed only two families in its long history. It was built
two rooms over two rooms by Nathaniel Harrison, whose descendants remained until
1800. Then the Linsley family lived here until 1938, when architectural historian J.
Frederick Kelly bought the house and reclaimed it to its time. Hand-hewn oak corner
posts, huge chamfered summer beams, exposed joists, corner cupboard, and large fireplace are features. Period furnishings include seventeenth-century chests from Branford and a bedspread made by a Linsley ancestor. The Branford Historical Society has
a growing collection of manuscripts, photographs, and other materials relating to
Branford history, buildings, and families.

2. JAMES BLACKSTONE MEMORIAL LIBRARY, *1896*. 758 Main St. Open all year, no fee.

Timothy Beach Blackstone built this magnificent Greek Revival structure to honor his
father, James Blackstone, born in Branford in 1793. Designed by architect Solon S.
Beman of Chicago, the white Tennessee marble building cost about $300,000 and took
three years to build. The Ionic columns of the portico, marble doorways, and egg-and-
dart moldings are copies of the Erechtheum on the Acropolis in Athens. The impressive interior is done in pink and gray marble, with mosaic floors and a 50-foot dome.
Oliver D. Grover did the eight large mural paintings within the dome on the subject of
the evolution of bookmaking. Open doorways, supported by Ionic columns with gold

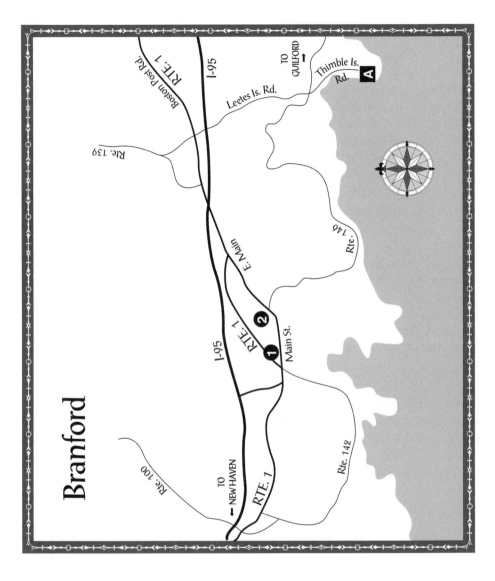

leaf entablatures, lead to separate stacks. The reading room has the feeling of a comfortable private club and serves as concert and lecture hall.

OTHER POINTS OF INTEREST

A. Stony Creek. Thimble Island Rd., town dock. Thimble Islands seem close enough to touch; tours to islands; busy town wharf of working and pleasure boats, Puppet House Theater with plays, concerts.

GUILFORD

Guilford is a town of beautiful historic houses, many within easy walking distance of the centuries-old Town Green. The tree-shaded Green is surrounded by four churches, the 1894 Town Hall, the library, quaint shops, and historic houses. Walk down Broad and Fair streets for a tour in architecture—Colonial, Federal, Greek Revival, Octagon, French Second Empire, Italianate. Guilford's historic town center and many houses are listed on the NRHP.

In 1639 Puritan leader Reverend Henry Whitfield arrived with about forty men, some with families. Aboard one of the three ships men signed the "Guilford Covenant," similar to the Mayflower Compact. They bought land from Squaw Sachem Shaumpishuh of the Menuncatuck Indians. She made her mark, a bow and arrow, on the deed. Sister of the New Haven area chief, she had also made her mark on that deed. Guilford was home to Sam Hill (as in "run like Sam Hill"), who ran for many offices. Quarries here supplied stone for the Statue of Liberty base.

Sachem's Head, an area of Guilford, was named for a captured Pequot who was executed by Uncas of the Mohegans in 1637. His severed head was wedged in the fork of a tree.

1. HENRY WHITFIELD HOUSE, *1639*, NRHP, State Historical Museum, Old Whitfield St. Open all year, fee. Museum shop.

You know it is not the usual house museum when you first see the English late-medieval-style stone house that was home to Reverend Henry Whitfield, spiritual leader of Guilford's founders. Oldest remaining stone house in New England, it was one of four stone houses built for the power structure people of this early settlement. Legend says Indians helped transport fieldstone, which was mortared with yellow clay mixed with burned, crushed shells, obtained from piles of shells left by Indian shellfishers. The north chimney and one half of the great hall were probably completed before the 1639 winter. Walls slant outward toward the bottom—they are over 30 inches thick in the basement and 18 inches at the third floor—in this home built as a fort.

The building was restored following documented evidence and reclaimed accurately for the period. J. Frederick Kelly, in a 1930s WPA project, found treasures from other Connecticut houses being torn down. Each material was documented, stored, and used to reclaim other historic structures such as this. The more than 2-foot-wide wall boards Kelly installed in the great hall came from this supply.

In the 33-foot-long great hall, treasures include the Governor William Leete wainscot chair, made of American oak about 1650 for a founder of Guilford and governor of New Haven and Connecticut colonies. Displayed here is the only known eighteenth-

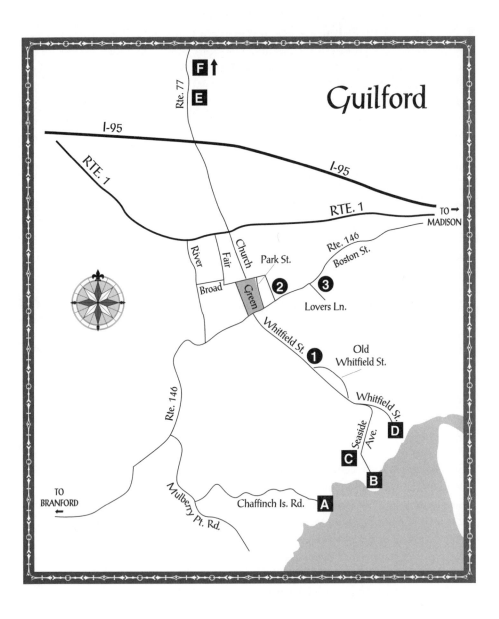

1639 Henry Whitfield House, Guilford   (Courtesy Henry Whitfield State Historical Museum)

century American communion board in existence, dating to 1713, from the Guilford church. It was in this house that the town's first Catholic mass also was held, sponsored by a mid-1800s tenant. The room shows the decorative reality of the seventeenth century, when the fireplace was the basic lighting device. In the attic the structure itself is exhibited—the bare bones of its architecture. Here also is the oldest town clock left in New England, built by Ebenezer Parmelee and placed in the Guilford church steeple in 1726.

2. HYLAND HOUSE, *c. 1660.* 84 Boston St. Open extended season, fee.

The house itself is a museum uniquely preserved for study. The lean-to, added about 1720, probably by grandson Ebenezer Parmelee, completed the saltbox style and covered much of the rear exterior. On that preserved exterior you can see tapered clapboards—hand hewn—and 1⁄16-inch–thick glass, all probably original and dating to the 1600s. From the second floor you have a clear view into the attic, around the immense chimney to the original extreme pitch of the roof. Roman numerals indicate how the early builders matched pieces. Slanted walls in the east parlor present a mystery. No one can explain why they intentionally slant to the extent that you wonder how the china stays in the cupboard. The shelves are level, only the walls and cupboard slant. The house displays period furnishings—most notable are a Bible box on its own standard, the 1810 needlepoint rug created by just one lady, and the raised embroidery called "stump work" dated 1669.

3. THOMAS GRISWOLD HOUSE MUSEUM, *1774*, NRHP. 171 Boston St. Open extended season, fee. Library, working blacksmith shop, farmers' museum, Colonial gardens; lectures.

You feel the quiet presence of living history in this classic Connecticut saltbox, where one family lived for nearly two centuries. Family life in the late 1700s to mid-1800s is interpreted. The house, described in J. Frederick Kelly's book *Early Domestic Architecture of Connecticut,* features an unusual round-back Guilford cupboard, rear double batten door, and original latchkey front door. Griswold treasures include a 1760 Queen Anne cherry lowboy, gilt-framed mirror, and c. 1700 corner cabinet. You'll see a chair from a founding family, a costume collection, an array of early hearing aids, and a silent piano, used for practice by traveling concert pianists in the early 1800s.

BEACHES, PARKS, OTHER POINTS OF INTEREST

A. **Chaffinch Island Park.** Chaffinch Island Rd. Open all year. No fee. Tiny island, no beach; picnicking.

B. **Jacobs Beach.** Guilford Point, Seaside Ave. Open all year. Parking fee in summer. Lifeguards, rest rooms; swimming.

C. **Chittenden Park.** Across from Jacobs Beach. Open all year. No fee. Ball fields.

D. **Town Boat Landing.** Whitfield St. Open all year. No fee. Marina; fishing poles like masts along rocky shores, beach, marsh grass; Coast Guard Auxiliary, dock master, two restaurants. See **Falkner Island Light,** NRHP. Built 1802, 3 miles outside harbor; island name first appeared in deed from Uncas, Mohegan chief; named for falcons no longer there, island now home to protected Arctic, common, and roseate terns.

E. **Guilford Handcrafts Center.** 411 Church St. Open all year. No fee. Fine arts and handcrafts educational facility, gallery with changing exhibits, shop.

F. **Lake Quonnipaug.** Rte. 77 about 8 miles north of I-95. Open all year. Parking fee in summer. Beach, boat launch, rest rooms; swimming.

MADISON

M adison, a quiet coastal town with a deep sense of history and community, relates closely to the sea. Originally part of Guilford, this became a separate town and was named for President James Madison in 1826. The historic Green, watched over by the First Congregational Church, is surrounded by Old Lee Academy and historic homes dating from 1740. Native-born Daniel Hand, a southern merchant in partnership with George W. Williams before the Civil War, became both wealthy and generous. He financed the Daniel Hand High School and gave $1.5 million for the education of black people in the South. At that time Hand was the largest donor in the United States to a benevolent society.

1. ALLIS–BUSHNELL HOUSE AND MUSEUM, *c. 1785*, HS. 853 Boston Post Rd. Open summer, limited hours, no fee. Herb garden.

From the street this house appears an unpretentious post-and-beam garrison Colonial, but inside it is a beautifully restored two-family home with mirror-image front rooms on the first floor and a double kitchen. Originally the Allises built a one-story two-family home. In 1815 the Bushnells opened the first floor for single-family living and built a second floor. A Victorian wing was added in 1860. Each section of the home has been restored to its construction era. The parlors retain original paneling, wainscoting, enclosed beams, and unusual corner fireplaces and cupboards. Early Windsor chairs, period furniture, and the original Madison Green deed on the wall set the colonial-era tone. The elongated kitchen with two fireplaces illustrates life in the nineteenth century, showing Connecticut-made redware, stoneware batter pail and jug cooler, iron Betty lamp, perforated tin lantern, and bench table. The 1860 wing has Victorian furniture along with an unusual hearing aid, a stereopticon, and an 1826 W. Geib piano, which belonged to Julia Ward Howe's mother. Second-floor rooms display nineteenth- and twentieth-century toys and Madison costumes, and one room is a small library. At the top of the stairs are medical memorabilia from Dr. Milo Rindge, who had offices here in the early 1900s. Earlier medical techniques are illustrated with such unfamiliar devices as craniotomy forceps, intestinal tucker, mouth gag, and gallbladder trocar.

A painting in the front hall brings to life Cornelius Scranton Bushnell, born here July 18, 1828. Bushnell was an organizer of the Union Pacific Railroad and a wealthy shipbuilder. He sought greater shipbuilding horizons as main financier of the steam powered iron *Monitor,* which fought the *Merrimac* during the Civil War battle of the "ironclads." A model of the *Monitor* is in the rear museum. Other Madison artifacts there include Indian relics, early utensils and tools, ship half models, and a diorama of

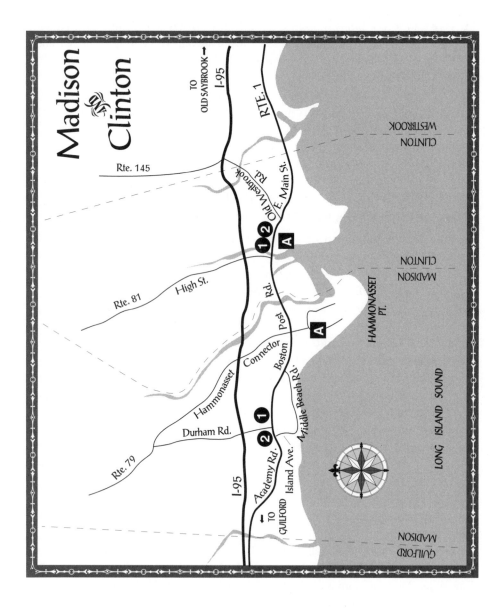

Madison's Jitney Players, who began American summer theater here in 1923. Since 1922 the Madison Historical Society has owned the house and museum.

2. DEACON JOHN GRAVE HOUSE, *1685*. **581 Boston Post Rd. Open summer, no fee. Educational programs, crafts, lectures.**

This classic seventeenth-century garrison Colonial is being restored under the watchful eye of expert Abbott Cummings and will be furnished using the 1685 inventory of John Grave, Jr. The beaded clapboard house, with twelve-over-twelve windows, exposed timbers, and unusual tree laths, is an educational and architectural tool as well as an historic house. Inner structural areas will be visible through hinged wall openings. The original east section was a one-over-one house. During those early years Graves served as justices of the peace, schoolteachers, church deacons, and militia captains.

In the early 1700s the central chimney and west side were added. Small steps cut in the central chimney led to a hiding place for arms during the French and Indian Wars. The rear section was added during the Revolution. For over a century this home, owned only by Graves and their descendants, was an "ordinary" (an inn). It was purchased in 1983 by the Deacon John Grave Foundation.

BEACHES, PARKS, OTHER POINTS OF INTEREST

A. **Hammonasset State Beach.** Rte. 1 and Hammonasset Connector. Open all year. Summer parking fee. Connecticut's largest waterfront park; 2-mile beach, bathhouse, pavilion, concessions; picnicking, swimming, camping, fishing. **Meigs Point Nature Center** offers nature walks in forest and along salt marsh and beach; nature programs, wildlife exhibits.

CLINTON

(see locator map, page 50.)

C linton residents, true to their New England heritage, have been farmers, fishermen, and shipbuilders since the early settlers in 1663. First known as Homonoscitt, in 1667 the area became the plantation of Kenilworth, later called Killingworth. By 1838 the southern school district separated to become Clinton. During the early 1700s the community was home to Collegiate College, forerunner of Yale University.

1. STANTON HOUSE, *c. 1789.* 63 East Main St. (Rte. 1). Open summer, no fee. General store, exhibits.

This was sacred educational ground. Near the well stood the earlier home of Reverend Abraham Pierson. In October 1701 the General Court of Connecticut granted a charter for a "collegiate school" to ten trustees, one of whom was Pierson. The school was located in Saybrook and was ultimately to become Yale University. Pierson, elected first president and rector, taught students. As local minister he could not leave his duties to teach in Saybrook, so held classes in his home here in Clinton until his death in 1707.

Adam Stanton built this double-chimney house using, it is believed, beams from Pierson's home. The front parlors have unique common walls with the central hall: Wooden panels hinged at the ceiling can be swung up and hooked, creating one large front room. The front parlor has French wallpaper and a revolving tea table. As you walk through the house notice the paneling and convenient cupboards around many fireplaces. In the sitting room see blue Staffordshire china and Chippendale chairs; in the dining room turtleback Hitchcock chairs, mahogany sideboard, and a drop-leaf table; in the kitchen a serviceable 8-foot fireplace and 1600s court cupboard. Upstairs is the bedroom where Marquis de Lafayette spent a night in 1824. Behind it is the Buckingham Room used by Connecticut's Civil War governor, William Buckingham, uncle by marriage to Lewis E. Stanton, donor of the house.

Records show the store active 1804–64. It carried ice skates, hardware, yard goods, tea, spices, patent medicines, molasses, glassware, hairpins, leather goods—a little of everything. Adam Stanton's office was adjacent. Behind that was Sally Stanton's spinning room. The attic holds local artifacts.

2. CAPTAIN ELISHA WHITE HOUSE, *c. 1750,* HS. 103 East Main St. Open all year, limited hours, no fee.

This stately Georgian home with curved brick pediments over front door and first floor windows was built by Captain Elisha White and is believed to be the earliest brick house on the Connecticut shoreline between New Haven and New London. Locally referred to as "the Old Brick," the Captain Elisha White House is a very early example of a center-hall Georgian Colonial, featuring chimneys at either side of the house. Each room has its own catty-cornered fireplace—a marked design change from the center-chimney architecture then prevalent outside of urban areas in Colonial America.

The house has passed through a number of Clinton families, including three sea captains: White, Griswold, and Redfield. In 1814 it became a two-family home; the owners literally split the house and property down the center. In 1986, the last owner, Sally Hull MacMillan, left "the Old Brick" in her will to the Clinton Historical Society. With deep-set windows and window seats, wide-board floors and beautiful rolling grounds featuring Colonial-style herb gardens, "the Old Brick" is a fitting home for the historical society's nineteenth-century portrait and landscape collection, period furniture, and the society's library. The gardens may be viewed at any time; there is a saying in Clinton that the gate to "the Old Brick" is always open.

BEACHES, PARKS, OTHER POINTS OF INTEREST

A. **Clinton Historical Society Room.** Andrews Memorial Town Hall, East Main St. Open all year, limited hours. No fee. Displays of china, glassware, silver, clothing, dolls, tinware, home utensils, Native American and Clinton artifacts.

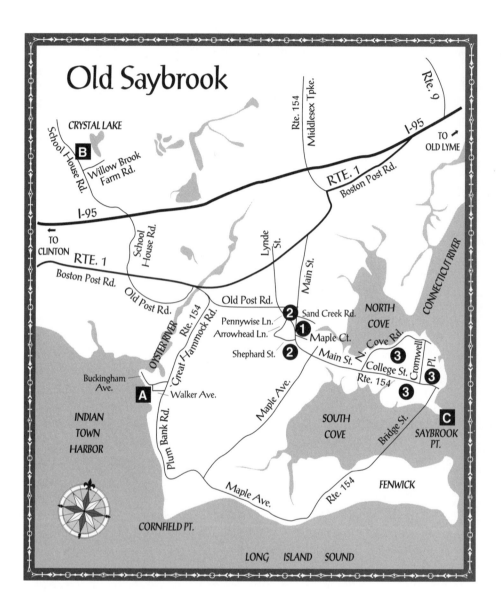

OLD SAYBROOK

Indians called it *Pashbeshauke,* "place at the river's mouth." The Dutch called it *Zeebrugge,* "sea bridge." Today this place where the 407-mile Connecticut River meets Long Island Sound is the picturesque boating, fishing, and resort community of Old Saybrook. In 1635 agents of patentees Lords Saye, Sele, Brooke, and others, founded the colony now known as Old Saybrook. As the colony grew, parishes became the separate towns of Essex, Chester, Deep River, Lyme, Old Lyme, Westbrook, and Old Saybrook.

In 1701 Collegiate College, forerunner of Yale University, was formed by ten Puritan ministers and located in Saybrook. Initially classes were held in Clinton, with commencements in Saybrook at the home of Reverend Thomas Buckingham. From 1707 to 1716 classes were in Saybrook. During that time the college's library, one of the finest in New England, was housed at Buckingham's home. When the college moved to New Haven in 1717, Saybrook refused to give up the library, questioning the legal right to move the college. But in spite of attempts to undermine bridges and delay carts, more than 1,200 books (260 mysteriously disappeared) were taken to New Haven.

True to Saybrook's nautical lifestyle, the *Turtle,* first submarine made for battle, was built here by David Bushnell in 1776. A one-man sub run by hand power, it had limited use in the Revolution.

1. GENERAL WILLIAM HART HOUSE, *c. 1767,* NRHP, HS. 350 Main St.
Open extended season, limited hours, and by appointment; fee. Colonial gardens, exhibits, workshops.

Colonial major general, wealthy coastal and West Indies trader, successful merchant, a founder of the Republican Party in Connecticut, and six-time gubernatorial candidate William Hart built this elegant home for his bride, Esther Buckingham, great granddaughter of Reverend Thomas Buckingham. General William Hart was son of Reverend William Hart, minister of the First Congregational Church next door, and grandson of John Hart, who earned Collegiate College's first bachelor of arts degree. During the Revolution William was an active major, and, with his brothers, armed ships as effective privateers, bringing in large spoils that added to the Hart wealth.

Today the home is an interpretative house/museum with front rooms restored to different times in William Hart's life. The Federal period parlor is set as if the general had just left home to transact business at the docks. The parlor on the right shows an earlier colonial time, when the general was a strong supporter of Jefferson and the Republican party and was involved in Western Reserve lands, where he owned thou-

General William Hart House, Old Saybrook   (Old Saybrook Historical Society/Roger Epply, artist)

sands of acres. The central hall, featured in J. Frederick Kelly's book *Early Domestic Architecture of Connecticut*, displays an unusual curvature in the banister, possibly of Irish influence. The large dining room, with Greek Revival elements, relates to the house's use as a girls' boarding school in the mid-1800s. The library emphasizes the Victorian period. Its fireplace has unusual Sadler and Green transfer-print tiles, illustrating Aesop's Fables, made in Liverpool, England, 1765–99. The rear kitchen section with large working fireplace was probably built earlier, moved here, and attached at a later date. The shed behind was probably used as a schoolroom. Upstairs are bedrooms with period furnishings, family portraits, and Saybrook genealogies. A rear room is a library. Another displays Saybrook, Hart, and Governor John Winthrop, Jr., memorabilia.

Outside, molded cornices, wide corner boards, Doric-columned portico with quoined front doorway, and clapboards increasing in width as they flow upward add grace to this early Georgian home, which speaks of the success of the Harts.

2. MAIN STREET WALKING TOUR. Walk Main St. from Old Post Rd. to Maple Ave. for a flavor of Old Saybrook. Houses private.

The **Humphrey Pratt Tavern,** NRHP, 287 Main Street, was for years a stage stop on the New Haven to Boston run and later Saybrook's first post office. At **338 Main,** unusual for New England, is a c. 1873 Gothic copied from a home in England. Legend reports Lafayette made a purchase at the **Store for the Humphrey Pratt Tavern,** now **James Pharmacy,** when it was located at the corner of Old Post Road and Main. The store, moved here in 1874, was later owned by Anna Louise James, Connecticut's first black woman pharmacist. Across the Green, NRHP, is the 1840 Greek Revival **First Church of Christ,** fourth building of the Congregational church founded 1646. Reverend William Hart served as minister for forty-eight years. **395 Main** was the c. 1773 home of

General Hart's brother Samuel. At **500 Main** is the house Dr. Samuel Eliot built in 1737 for bride-to-be Mary Blague. He died before they were married. Two years later Mary married Reverend William Hart to become matriarch of the Saybrook Harts.

3. SAYBROOK POINT. Off College St. left on North Cove Rd. Meandering drive along cove, moored boats point into the wind.

Amid beautiful homes overlooking the water are the 1750 **William Tully House** at 135 and **Black Horse Inn** at 175 North Cove Road, both NRHP. Continue on Cromwell Place back to College Street. To the right is **Cypress Cemetery,** with graves of General William Hart and Lady Alice Fenwick, wife of Governor George Fenwick. Next to the cemetery is a site marker for **Collegiate College.** Away from town on College Street is the site of **Saybrook Fort,** 1636, first fortification in Connecticut. Its first commander, Lion Gardiner, originally designed the fort as a palisaded earthen embankment surrounded by a moat with a cannon in each corner. Gardiner's son was the first white child recorded as born in Connecticut. A statue of Lion Gardiner stands near the fort he engineered. The fort was removed in 1871 to make way for tracks and turntable for the **Connecticut Valley Railroad,** which ran until 1922. Ferries ran between Saybrook Point and Fenwick, carrying passengers and later railroad cars until 1911.

From Saybrook Point **Lynde Point Lighthouse** is visible across South Cove in Fenwick Borough, a prestigious summer area where Katharine Hepburn has a summer home. Built in 1838, the lighthouse is known as "Inner Light." It was manned until 1973 but is now automated, its fixed white light shining 13 miles out to sea. In 1886 **Saybrook Breakwater Light,** known as "Outer Light," was erected on the west jetty to protect ships entering the Connecticut River.

BEACHES, PARKS, OTHER POINTS OF INTEREST

A. **Harvey's Beach.** Off Great Hammock Rd. Open all year. Fee. Swimming.

B. **Crystal Lake Town Park.** Schoolhouse Rd. Open all year. No fee. Crystal Lake, 180 acres, trails, playground, rest rooms, amphitheater; skating, picnicking.

C. **River Cruises.** Saybrook Point, Rte. 154. Open summer. Fee.

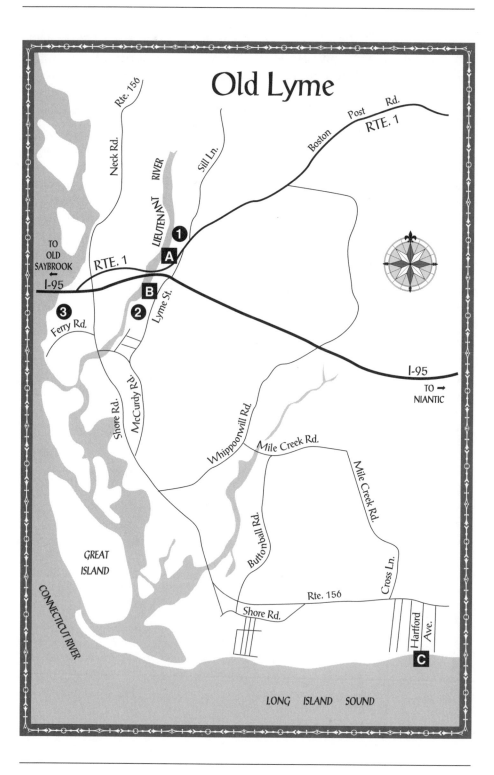

OLD LYME

Old Lyme's stately homes, traditional white-steepled First Congregational Church, inviting back roads along orderly stone walls, tranquil woods, tidewater marshlands, and rugged rocky coast are all potential landscapes vying for an artist's brush. In the early twentieth century Lyme attracted artists from all over the country, becoming a center for American Impressionism. Lyme separated from Saybrook in 1665. Its main industry in the eighteenth and nineteenth centuries was shipbuilding, resulting in more than sixty sea captains' homes. It has also been home to two Connecticut governors, Matthew Griswold and his son Roger Griswold. Today, as of old, artists, vacationers, fishermen, and devoted residents enjoy the peaceful, scenic atmosphere.

1. FLORENCE GRISWOLD MUSEUM, *1817*, NHL, HS. 96 Lyme St.
Open all year, fee. Exhibits of New England decorative arts, American Barbizon and American Impressionist art, local architecture and history, herb and perennial gardens, Chadwick studio, bookshop; lectures, workshops.

In this regal home is a gracious blending of American history, art, and architecture. In 1899 Barbizon-style artist Henry Ward Ranger found in Old Lyme a perfect harmony of light, color, and countryside—similar to the atmosphere around Paris, art capital of the world in the 1800s. As a result, from 1900 to the 1930s Ranger and other artists summered in Old Lyme, many staying at Florence Griswold's boardinghouse. After acclaimed American impressionist Childe Hassam arrived in 1903, the Barbizon style gave way to Impressionism, and the Griswold home and Old Lyme became one of the most famous centers of American Impressionism. In this historic home you share a milestone in the cultural acceptance and artistic development of a new American art style. Visiting rooms where artists lived and worked, walking the Griswold property, experiencing the Chadwick studio, and seeing town and country scenes the artists painted is like coming face to face with the artists and seeing the world through their eyes.

This late Georgian mansion with Federal elements and rear wing from an earlier house was built for William Noyes by Samuel Belcher, designer of First Congregational Church. Sea captain Robert Griswold purchased the home in 1841. Following his death his wife and daughters opened a finishing school. Daughter Florence inherited the home in 1899. She solved her financial problems by taking in summer boarders, American landscape painters. Thus Florence, daughter of a sea captain and patron of the arts, represented and united the two worlds of Old Lyme.

Today the mansion has been restored and is furnished in styles reflecting the many years the house has been occupied. The Federal front hall dates to construction in 1817. The Empire parlor reflects the era of Captain Griswold and his family, when

Dining Room, Florence Griswold Museum, Old Lyme   (Courtesy Florence Griswold Museum, hdqrs. Lyme Historical Society)

sailing ships were in their heyday. The parlor door panels give you a first glimpse of the legacy left by resident artists. Florence's bedroom, with her parents' bed and her washbasin, stand, and lamp, speaks of her reign as art patron and landlady. The dining room is the artists' priceless gift. Here many of the artists painted panels showing their talents and varying styles over an eighteen-year period. Only the best artists were invited to paint panels, a much sought-after honor. Over the mantel Henry Rankin Poore's caricature of the artists, *The Fox Chase*, forever reminds you of the artists' comradery and personalities. Other rooms are galleries with changing exhibits from the museum's collections of fine and decorative arts, including more than 600 paintings, prints, and watercolors. There are works by Childe Hassam, Allen Talcott, William Chadwick, Willard Metcalf, Henry C. White, and Louis P. Dessar.

2. LYME STREET WALK. Rte. 95 south to McCurdy St. Houses private, church open all year for services and through church office.

Walk Lyme Street to sense the peace and beauty of this seaside town's main street, where local history and varying architecture combine to tell the story of Old Lyme. **Lyme Academy of Fine Arts,** 79 Lyme, is housed in the 1817 John Sill House, which combines architectural symmetry with creative arts. Samuel Belcher, designer of the Florence Griswold Museum and the First Congregational Church, also designed this late Georgian. It features a Palladian window with louvered fanlight and rare curving cantilevered stairway. Across the street, third house south of Route 95, is the Gothic **Bartlett House,** NRHP. Called a "cottage residence" by designer Alexander Jackson Davis, this 1814 house with Gothic gingerbread is an unusual style for the area. At 76 Lyme is the former home of Impressionist artist **Charles Ebert.** An interesting Italianate with Greek Revival features, it shows fluted Doric porch columns, dentils, and egg-and-dart molding. Step inside the **Town Hall** to see paintings by Lyme artists throughout the building. On Lyme Street opposite the First Congregational Church is the c. 1700 **McCurdy House,** a fine example of a building that expanded over the years to a 90-foot, eight-gable home to meet the growing needs of its owners, all McCurdy descendants. When wealthy merchant John McCurdy lived here, George Washington was a guest (April 10, 1776). Lafayette stayed here July 27, 1778, while his troops camped in a local orchard. He returned in 1824.

Often portrayed in paintings, **First Congregational Church** stands proudly at Lyme and Ferry streets. The original building, designed by Samuel Belcher, burned July 3, 1907. Using the old foundation and pictures, the congregation completed the present replica—fireproof with an inner core of steel and concrete and a slate roof— in 1910. Rising above the Ionic-columned portico is a magnificent Christopher Wren–style steeple with clock and belfry supporting a cloud-piercing spire topped by a gold leaf finial. Inside, in shades of white and cream, a 32-foot dome with gold leaf border, chancel panels with gold leaf Greek fret, and chancel dome with gold leaf Greek honeysuckle combine to give a feeling of openness, light, and majesty.

3. NUT MUSEUM. 303 Ferry Rd. Open extended season, limited hours, and by appointment; fee plus a nut.

"Nuts are works of art for the soul as well as the body. Nuts teach gentleness and respect. They are hard on the outside, soft and sweet on the inside,"[5] says the creator/curator Elizabeth Tashjian of this unusual house/museum. Inside this Gothic mansion, nuts are king. Every table, wall, and shelf displays nuts in a variety of forms, from the actual fruit or seed to nut-shaped ceramics, nut masks, nut music, nut sculpture, nut jewelry and scrimshaw, and murals and paintings of nuts, nutcrackers, and nut plants. The nuts are displayed elegantly on tapestries and fine fabrics and are considered works of art, from the tiniest to a 35-pound coco-de-mer nut from a Pacific island.

BEACHES, PARKS, OTHER POINTS OF INTEREST

A. Lyme Art Association Gallery. 90 Lyme St. Open extended season. Donation. Changing member artists exhibits.

B. Lyme Academy of Fine Arts, NRHP. 84 Lyme St. Open all year by appointment. No fee. Art exhibits by school and local artists, nationally recognized art faculty; classes, festivals, and fairs.

C. Sound View Beach. Shore Rd. Hartford Ave. access. Open. No fee. Lifeguards, swimming. Limited street parking, parking lot fee.

NIANTIC

Niantic is an uncrowded coastal town of historic homes, relaxed living, and inviting beaches. A village within East Lyme and originally settled as part of Saybrook, Niantic drew more people with the advent of the railroad in 1851. Boardinghouses, hotels, then summer homes developed. Two resorts began as religious colonies—the Connecticut Spiritualists Campmeeting Association and the Baptist Seaside Resort Association.

1. THOMAS LEE HOUSE, *1660*; Little Boston School, 1734, HS. 230 West Main St. (Rte. 156). Open summer, fee. English herb garden

Archaeologist and architect Norman Morrison Isham studied and restored the Lee house in 1914. This conservative expert concluded he had seldom seen a house more interesting. This oldest wood frame house in Connecticut may have begun in 1641 as a one-room shelter for Phoebe Lee and her children. Phoebe's husband, Thomas, had probably secured the land before their arrival either as a grant or through his friend and neighbor Matthew Griswold. Sadly, Thomas Lee died aboard ship. Son Thomas Lee added the west wing about 1690. Shortly after 1712 a lean-to was built on the old front, and the staircase was moved to the new front. In the mid-1700s the western walls were plastered, fireplace walls paneled, beams cased, and wider windows installed. The structure of the house is a treasure for architectural studies, with reports from the Research Department of Colonial Williamsburg Foundation, Yale, and Isham to aid the student.

The Lee family has been documented by Reverend Joseph Lee of the third generation. The account includes the story of "Bride Brook Park." Betty, daughter of the second Thomas Lee, married in 1646, despite her father's objections, in an unusual ceremony. Governor Winthrop's son conducted the services with a river (now called Bride Brook) separating the couple from the minister. A chest with thirteenth-century hinges and the initials of the bride and groom is displayed within the house. Other Lee descendants were pastors, farmers, judges, doctors, a governor, the operator of the first submarine in the Revolution, and U.S. President Grover Cleveland. Only Lee descendants have lived here, except during a brief period of deterioration when the house was used as a chicken coop before being rescued by the East Lyme Historical Society in 1914. President William Howard Taft was present at the dedication celebration.

Upstairs you can see an original casement window in place (one of two in the state), and shadow-molded wide boards. Rare furnishings from the 1600s are mostly English, with some from Connecticut and Pennsylvania.

The **Little Boston School** was the first district school between New York and Boston. Governor Joseph Talcott ordered Lee to set aside land for the school in 1734.

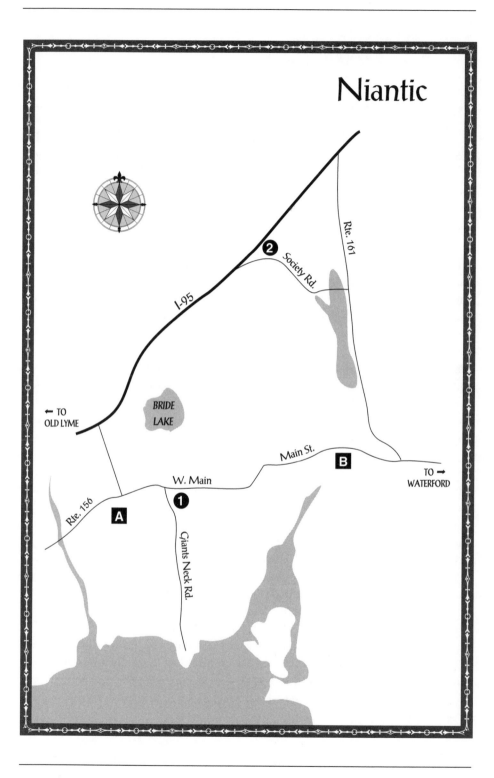

Navigation, astronomy, Latin, and Greek were taught. Jonathan Comstock, son of the first headmaster, wrote the first book on physics in English in this country. The last class was held in 1922.

2. SMITH-HARRIS HOUSE, *c. 1845*. **33 Society Rd. Open summer, no fee.**

A fine example of country Greek Revival, the house was built by Thomas Avery. The first floor is a house museum of Americana—costumes, quilts, furnishings, china, utensils—from the mid-1800s. The farmyard looks as if the family just left for a short visit, leaving an old hay rake and other scattered tools. There are a corn crib, a restored barn, and a tool shed. Town buildings are on land once part of the farm.

BEACHES, PARKS, OTHER POINTS OF INTEREST

A. **Rocky Neck State Park.** Rte. 156, exit 72 from I-95. Open all year. Fee in summer. Park with 561 acres, .75-mile white sand beach, ball fields, bathhouse, boardwalk, pavilion; swimming, camping, hiking, fishing, picnicking.

B. **Millstone Energy Center.** 278 Main St. Open all year. No fee. Hands-on activities, video displays, marine aquaria, Geiger counter, computer games, stereographic hologram, tours, publications.

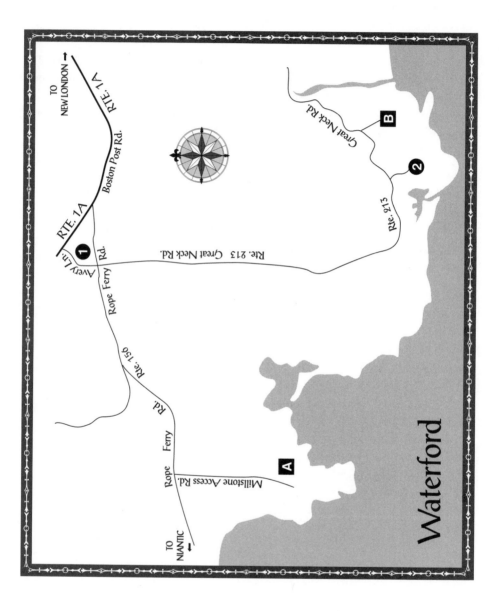

Waterford

WATERFORD

Waterford is a town of pleasant homes, parks, and Millstone Nuclear Power. Settled in 1645, it was mainly a fishing, trading, and farming community. It was part of New London until October 8, 1801, when it was incorporated as a separate town.

1. HISTORIC JORDAN GREEN. Rope Ferry Rd. (Rte. 156) and Avery Ln.
Open summer, no fee. Herb garden, corn crib, smokehouse, education center, blacksmith shop, community and school programs, apple orchards.

Some of the town's historic buildings are gathered here in a village setting. The **Jordan Park House,** the original Waterford Library building, is now a community center and the office of the Waterford Historical Society, Inc. The **Beebe Phillips Farmhouse** (c. 1839) interprets farmhouse living in the nineteenth century in displays of well-equipped country kitchen and other appropriate furnishings. The **Jordan School House** (1740) is Waterford's oldest existing public building and is restored to its 1740s time. Desks line walls and benches face windows. Education exhibits and woods used in the restoration are marked with their sources; for example, the fireplace lintels are from the home of Captain Jonathan Caulkins, who served under Norwich-born Benedict Arnold at the Battle of Saratoga in 1777. The **Stacy Barn Museum** education complex is set up for farm animals and for the display of carriages, tools, and a cider press—all used in hands-on programs. On the way to the working blacksmith shop, where the forge is ready to fire and tools are arrayed, you pass a three-hole outhouse, a remnant of life in times past.

2. HARKNESS MEMORIAL STATE PARK. Great Neck Rd. (Rte. 213).
Open all year, fee. Mansion museum, grounds, formal gardens, stable complex; summer music festival; picnicking, fishing.

Acres of lawns sweep from the mansion to the sea, and formal gardens recapture the grandeur of another age. The elegance is quiet, not ostentatious. Edward and Mary Harkness were wealthy yet conservative. They had five summer homes, but they were also philanthropists. Edward Harkness donated more than $200 million from his father's earnings from Standard Oil. The Harknesses had a working self-sufficient farm and sent vegetables and flowers to local hospitals. Mary Harkness had many projects, usually anonymous, and finally gave this estate to be used for public health. She helped children with disabilities, a cause that developed into Camp Harkness. Now about 100 acres of the 234-acre estate form a recreational site for Connecticut's handicapped. Cottages house more than 200 people and day campers are welcomed. Campers learn living and vocational skills as well as enjoy themselves.

The Italianate villa mansion, named Eolia, has forty-two rooms and panoramic views of the Sound. Construction of the concrete and limestone block mansion began in 1902. Climbing actinidia vines cover much of the plain facade. Storm damage necessitated extensive restorations, completed in 1992. Restorers traced old auction sales lists to find furnishings that had been sold at the Harknesses' deaths. The gardens were restored to Mrs. Harkness's plans—Oriental, Italian, and cutting gardens and greenhouses. The stable and garage complex is also restored. Here tile and wood floors, stone and paneled walls house an indoor squash court, two bowling alleys, huge billiard room, and a garage complete with a turntable to move the family's limousines.

BEACHES, PARKS, OTHER POINTS OF INTEREST

A. **Millstone Nature Trail.** Millstone access road off Rte. 156. Open all year. No fee. Millstone was granted to John Winthrop; in 1737 millstones quarried here; some larger stones used in many forts. Quarry activity peaked 1910; now Millstone Nuclear Power Station; nature trails with guide booklets and signs.

B. **Eugene O'Neill Theater Center.** Great Neck Rd. (Rte. 213). Open for performances, limited season. Fee. National Playwrights Conference, American Soviet Theater Initiative, National Music Theater Conference, classes, workshops.

NEW LONDON

N ew London—builder of ships since 1660—was the second largest whaling port in the world in the mid-1800s. The city offers a wealth of museums and preserved history amid modern industry, pleasant homes, and schools of higher education. In 1646 John Winthrop, Jr., son of the Massachusetts Colony governor, led more than forty Puritan families to settle Pequot Plantation: the area that included what is now Waterford and Groton as well as New London. The colonial seaport was one of the best, a natural harbor on the Thames River, a drowned valley, deep and wide near the coast. Coastal and West Indies trade—sugar, molasses, rum—prospered.

With the Revolution, privateers and warships outfitted here. On September 6, 1781, Benedict Arnold led British troops to retaliate. More than twenty-five British ships and 800 troops attacked Fort Trumbull from the land, as traitor Arnold knew it was designed to defend only from the sea. The fort fell. British burned buildings, ships, supplies, and, when the wind shifted, most of New London. During the War of 1812, a two-year blockade by the British ended in a Peace Ball at the courthouse. Both Americans and British attended, having become accustomed to each other's presence in New London.

New London preserves her long history with museums, the Bank Street Waterfront Historic District, and many buildings listed on the National Register of Historic Places.

1. MONTE CRISTO COTTAGE, NHL. 325 Pequot Ave. Open extended season, fee.

Eugene O'Neill, the only American playwright to receive the Nobel Prize and four Pulitzer Prizes, spent his boyhood summers here. The cottage was named for his actor father's most famous role. As a young man, Eugene promised that his then-famous father would be known as Eugene O'Neill's father. His father, who was supporting two adult sons at the time, probably laughed. Eugene O'Neill used his detailed memories of this New London house as a setting for *Ah, Wilderness,* his only comedy, and *Long Day's Journey into Night.* He also wrote *Mourning Becomes Electra* and *Desire under the Elms.* A photo of Eugene at age seven—on ledges overlooking the water, intently drawing the scene—was the source for an endearing statue. It is now valued by a New London that looked askance at O'Neill's nonconforming presence during his lifetime. A smaller copy of the statue is featured here in this home of O'Neill memorabilia. You can see a multimedia presentation about O'Neill, sit in his study, read one of his plays set here, and picture the action. The O'Neill Theater Center (see Waterford) operates the museum, and their guide introduces you to the house, family, characters, and ghosts.

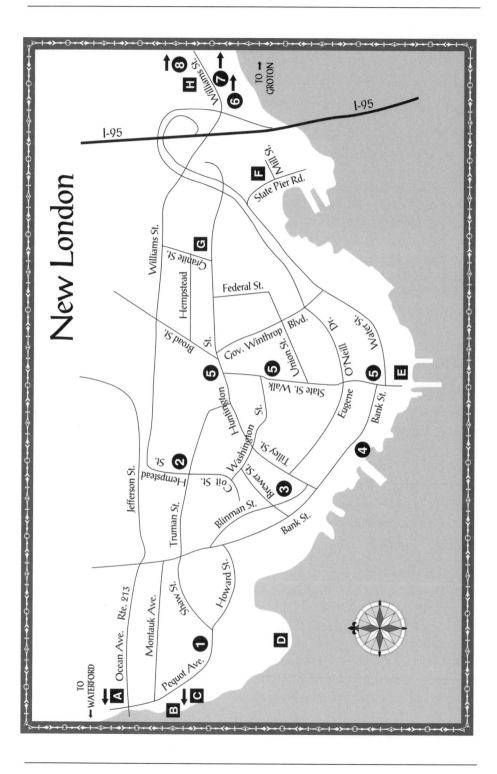

New London

2. HEMPSTED HOUSES, NRHP. 11 Hempstead St. Antiquarian and Land-mark Society. Open extended season, fee. Programs.

The Hempsted houses interpret life of average middle-class New London families—a slice of 300 years of real life. The **Joshua Hempsted House** (c. 1678), oldest in New London, was begun by Joshua, son of Robert Hempsted, a founder of the city. Joshua's grandson, another Joshua, expanded the house and kept a detailed diary (now published) from 1711 until his death in 1758. This wonderful record of the house, the Hempsteds, and life at that time provides the basis of the interpretation.

The house was continuously lived in by Hempsteds until 1937. It is preserved and re-created from architectural studies and is furnished according to the diary, with 30 percent of the pieces from the Hempsted family. The hall was the general all-purpose room where the family ate, slept, and entertained. The musket on the summer beam may have belonged to the first Joshua, and the plank chair and the bed are from the family. Seaweed, which you can see in a cut-out section, insulates walls. Gunpowder for the town militia was stored in the tall attic. Many in town rushed to help remove it when the chimney caught fire in January 1746. The right side of the house was added in 1728 by the diarist's son Nathaniel, Sr. It shows the difference of fifty years—brick fireplaces, taller ceilings, larger windows. It was never finished. Nathaniel died, his wife returned to her family, and their newborn baby was left with the wet nurse, his other children with his parents.

Outside, the hand-split oak clapboards are exact replicas of the early Colonial exterior, with its steep slopes and many gables. Well and sweep are in the original places, near the memorial to Stephen Hempsted, one of the few wounded to survive at Fort Griswold (see Groton); he joined the western movement and became governor of Missouri.

The **Nathaniel Hempsted House** (1759), built nearly a century later, displays changes in architecture and the continuity of the family's maritime heritage. Before the Revolution, Nathaniel was a rope maker. His granite house, built on granite ledge, was then right on the water. It could have been part of the rope walk, with rigging strung through the door and stored in the attic. Walls are 2 feet thick, covered with plaster. The kitchen oven projects in beehive shape on the outside. Five brothers who lived here, nephews of Nathaniel, were sea captains. Most died at sea before their fortunes were made.

The Hempsted houses interpret life of family and community through authentic period furnishings, architectural detail, and a knowledgeable guide.

3. SHAW MANSION, *c. 1756*, NRHP, HS. 11 Blinman St. Open extended season, fee. Library open all year, formal gardens, gazebo.

The rough gray granite of the stolid exterior doesn't hint at the breadth of decorative arts displayed within. The mansion was built for successful merchant and shipowner

Captain Nathaniel Shaw and family. Stone was quarried from granite ledges of the grounds for this conservative Georgian mansion. The full-width front porch and wing with balustraded deck roof were added about 1840–50, when the family made many interior changes, including lowering the floors of the first floor to make higher ceilings. Shaw ships sailed for Providence, Newport, Boston, New York, Philadelphia, and later the West Indies. During the Revolution, son Nathaniel, Jr., a leading Patriot, was named naval war agent for the state. His home served as Connecticut's naval office. This helped make New London a center for privateers and warships and drew British attack. Visitors included Governor Trumbull, Nathan Hale, Lafayette, and George Washington, who dined and slept here.

The house museum interprets the social history of the family, New London, and decorative arts. Descendants lived here until the house was acquired by the New London County Historical Society in 1907. Furnishings include pieces from the family, six family portraits by Ralph Earl, a large textile collection, and the mirror and dining-room table used by George Washington. A special room features changing exhibitions from the society's collection. The Victorian parlor is accurately furnished from an 1870 family photograph. The most unusual features are the major fireplace walls, which are all stone. No one knows how the solid stone on these interior walls was applied or created. The research library contains more than 5,000 volumes and manuscripts plus a solid nineteenth-century collection of New London newspapers and letters from figures such as George Washington, John Hancock, and Benedict Arnold.

4. U.S. CUSTOM HOUSE, *1833*, NRHP. 150 Bank St. Open all year, limited hours, fee.

Rock solid of rough-cut and polished granite, this building is the oldest operating customhouse in America. It was designed by the first Federal architect, Robert Mills, whose many Federal buildings include the Washington Monument. This, the nation's first Federal-style customhouse, was almost lost when the U.S. government put it up for sale in 1983. The New London Maritime Society was formed to save and restore the historic structure. Custom offices remain on the second floor, and a significant maritime museum opened in 1990.

As you step through the front door, feel the soft patina of the wood from Georgia live oak timbers taken from the USS *Constitution,* "Old Ironsides." In the twentieth-century Ships Room see a scale model of the *Turtle,* first war submarine. In the Captain Comstock and America's Cup Room see flags, photographs, and memorabilia from the 1870 *Magic* and 1871 *Columbia* sailed by New London's Captain Comstock and crew. In the halls are paintings of nineteenth-century mayors influential in New London's maritime history. The Main Gallery, overlooking the river, is where men registered and cleared ships and signed on for voyages. Now the gallery features a working Fresnel lens from the New London Ledge Lighthouse, lighthouse records and certificates, a special section on Arctic voyages, ship models, and navigational instruments.

Climb the cantilevered flying stairway, feel the well-worn stone steps where generations of seamen have walked. The second-floor gallery displays marine paintings and is used for receptions and lectures. Above the galleries is an observatory, where a customs officer could watch shipping to be sure all paid proper customs. Sometimes an officer would perch on a high chair atop the roof while another officer stood ready on the dock. If a ship tried to avoid customs, a signal was given from the roof, and the offender was quickly apprehended.

The lower level, with entrance from the Maritime Heritage Park on the Thames River side, has arched and vaulted ceilings. Here are exhibits relating to navigation and New London's supremacy as a whaling center. In this beautifully preserved customhouse you feel the excitement of the sea and realize how it affected New London.

5. WHALE OIL ROW AND STATE STREET WALK. Walk from corner of Federal and Huntington sts. east to State St. and downhill to City Pier.

At Federal and Huntington streets is **St. James Episcopal Church,** organized 1725 and seat of Samuel Seabury, America's first Episcopalian Bishop 1785–96. This majestic Gothic Revival erected in 1850 sets the tone for neighboring **Whale Oil Row,** NRHP, four Ionic-pillared Greek Revival homes. These mansions, built in 1830, speak of the wealth and success of early whaling sea captains and merchants; three were sold to whaling merchants and one to the Union Bank president. At Huntington and Broad streets is the 1784 **State Court House,** NRHP, a prefab drawn here by oxcart from Lebanon and believed designed by Isaac Fitch. It has always been a courthouse for sessions of the Superior Court of Connecticut. In addition it served as meetinghouse, social hall, and hospital. The late Georgian has keystone lintels, quoined front doorway, and square fluted pilasters flanking a Palladian window.

Across the street, the imposing Richardsonian Romanesque **Public Library,** NRHP, is the gateway to the varying architectural and historical moods of State Street. The original library building was a gift from Henry Philemon Haven, one of New London's most prosperous whaling merchants. Notice the massive construction, boldly segmented arches, and contrasting colors and textures of stone.

Walk State Street, one of the main commercial roadways since Revolutionary days, past eighteenth-, nineteenth-, and twentieth-century buildings. Look above street level to appreciate restored facades. The building at **300–302 State Street,** opposite Meridian Street, has intriguing Doric pilasters with Wedgwood-like bas relief designs of swans and sea life depicting New London's early dependence on the sea. At **290 State Street** is the exclusive Thames Club for men, founded in 1869. At Washington Street is the 1856 **First Baptist Church.** Across State Street there is interesting detail over the entrance to the 1896 **Mohican Hotel,** noted for its interior brass and marble ornamentation and roof garden. Many hotels were here from the mid-1800s into the 1900s.

At Union Street the **First Congregational Church,** gathered 1642, combines its early heritage with the present fortresslike 1850 Gothic Revival building. Notice the deep-set windows, the massive stone Gothic design duplicated in the softer wood of the doors, and the sky-reaching steeple above a clock tower. The church's first minister, Richard Blinman (Blynman), came from Gloucester, Massachusetts, where he was their first minister. Controversy arose when Gurdon Saltonstall, minister 1688–1708, strongly opposed John Rogers's Rogerenes. They were a group who refused to pay taxes to support the Congregational church, official church of the colony. Saltonstall won the argument in 1708 when he became governor, persecuting the Rogerenes.

Across Union is **City Hall,** originally built in 1854–56 and extensively remodeled in 1912 to the present Renaissance Revival style. At the Parade, early militia ground at the foot of State Street, is the 1896 **Soldiers and Sailors Monument** built on the site of New London's first fort (1691–1777). Nearby is old Union Schoolhouse, known as **Nathan Hale School,** where Hale taught from March 1774 to July 1775 before joining the colonial army. Serving in Lieutenant Colonial Thomas Knowlton's Rangers, Hale volunteered to go behind British lines to obtain needed information for General Washington. On his way back he was caught and executed September 22, 1776. His final words echo down through the years, "I only regret that I have but one life to lose for my country."[6]

At the foot of State Street is a Romanesque gateway, the 1888 **Union Station,** NRHP, designed by Henry Hobson Richardson. It was built on the river near **City Pier,** where in earlier days wagons, trolleys, ships, and trains met to transfer cargo and passengers. Today cars, trucks, buses, ferries, and trolleys have added to that brotherhood of transportation, creating a modern transportation hub.

6. UNITED STATES COAST GUARD ACADEMY. Mohegan Ave. off Williams St. Open all year, no fee. Visitor center and gift shop, museum, *Eagle,* dress parades spring and fall.

The Coast Guard invites you to visit its beautiful 125-acre site on the Thames River. If the tall ship *Eagle* is in port, you can board the commissioned square rigger on weekend tours. The visitor center presents the U.S. Coast Guard Academy through a film of academy life and displays of Coast Guard equipment—helm or ship's wheel, ship's binnacle, magnetic compass, gyro compass, engine order telegraph. The huge eagle suspended outside the center is a copy of the *Eagle*'s figurehead. The original eagle was removed in the 1950s and is in the academy's museum.

Drive through the pleasant campus. Along the way, you'll probably see cadets marching in formation. At the waterfront are myriad modern small boats in neat array, contrasting with the proud barque *Eagle.* She was built in 1936 in Hamburg, Germany, as a training ship for German naval cadets. She sailed from Bremerhaven, and was renamed the *Eagle* after being taken as a war prize in 1946. You've reached the museum when you see the navigation light on one corner and an old Coast Guard cutter on the other. The museum displays the history and presence of the Coast Guard through paintings, instruments, maps, models, and small boats.

The academy began in 1876 as the Revenue Cutter School aboard the schooner *Dobbin*. The barque *Chase*, based in New Bedford, housed the school from 1878 until 1900, when it was based in Arundel Cove, Maryland. In 1910 Fort Trumbull became the land base until the academy moved to this site in 1932.

7. LYMAN ALLYN ART MUSEUM. 625 Williams St. Open all year, donation. Research library, shop, programs. Deshon Allyn House, *1829*, NRHP.

The elegant interior is the perfect setting for this fine community museum of comprehensive art. It was founded by Harriet Allyn in memory of her father, Lyman Allyn. The stately structure was designed by Charles Platt. Delicately detailed arched entries lead to ten galleries of changing and permanent exhibits. The research library contains more than 7,000 volumes of art history centering on decorative arts. Resources also include an outstanding collection of drawings plus an extensive costume study collection.

Galleries of early New England furnishings and decorative arts are instructive as well as beautiful. Each style is described, and there are examples to study. You walk across huge Oriental rugs to a Federal period dining room containing Hepplewhite and Sheraton furniture set with an unusual 1825 pattern of Staffordshire china by Hall. On the second floor are fine arts from the Orient, Near East, Greece, Rome, and Africa—paintings, sculpture, masks, carvings, and ceramics, such as the glazed fourteenth-century Chinese terra-cotta *Head of Lohan*. On the lower floor a fantastic fifteen-room oversize dollhouse is fully occupied by dolls and furnishings of the 1850s. Victorian dollhouses and furnishings in three scales, plus dolls and toys—like a three-horse-drawn fire truck with fireman—entice the eye.

The **Deshon Allyn House** on the grounds is open through the museum. The stately random-granite Federal has hipped roof, round-arched windows, dressed stone quoins, a Palladian window, and a recessed entrance flanked by Ionic columns and side lights. Built by prosperous whaling master Captain Daniel Deshon and lived in by whaler Captain Lyman Allyn, the house contains elegant Empire furnishings.

8. THAMES SCIENCE CENTER. Gallows Ln. off Williams St. Open all year, fee. Shop, nature trails, educational programs for children and teachers, guided trips, summer camp.

The focus and strength of the center are programs that make studying science exciting and educational for children. Included are "Honeybee Boogie," "Robot Acts Assembly," "Life at the Seashore," and many other applied environmental science programs. Teachers come from all over the country to study here through national science grants. The museum's major permanent exhibition is "Time and the River," a series of hands-on stations revealing the geology of the Thames River basin and how people respond to the opportunities the land presents. A fiber-optic map shows the 1,474-square-mile watershed area the Thames River draws from. Push buttons to watch the river flow; to follow the sun, moon, and tides; and to watch tides rise from Greenwich to New London. Here are a diorama of the Pattagonsett salt marsh, a touch-and-feel tank, a live hive of honeybees, a station to hear songs of local birds.

BEACHES, PARKS, OTHER POINTS OF INTEREST

A. **Ocean Beach Park.** Rte. 213 just over line from Waterford, foot of Ocean Ave. Open summer. Fee. Amusement park, .75-mile-long beach, pool, playground, water slides, miniature golf, boardwalk, boats, rides, arcade, concessions, dining, gift shop; picnicking, swimming.

B. **New London Harbor Light.** Pequot Ave. Private. Rebuilt 1801, automated 1912, on rocky outcrop near mouth of Thames River. First tower, finished 1760, was of stone, 24 feet diameter, 64 feet tall, with wood lantern. Was fourth light in colony, shipping taxed to support light and keeper. During Revolutionary War guided privateers to shelter in New London; October 1, 1791 President Washington signed contract with Nathaniel Richards of New London to supply oil to the light. In War of 1812, light extinguished for military reasons. Current light 89 feet tall, octagonal, pyramidal, coursed freestone, smooth-hammered, one of the finest masonry lights.

C. **New London Ledge Light and harbor view from Pequot Ave. near New London Harbor Light,** 1909, NRHP. Mouth of harbor, about a mile off shore. Looks like a mansion floated out to sea; full-size French Second Empire house, eleven rooms on two floors, red brick, white trim, dormers in mansard roof; lantern in center on top, electrified by cable to Avery Point. Ghost legend: Light keeper's wife ran away with a Block Island ferry captain, keeper jumped from light to his death; later unexplained opened doors, footsteps, lights on and off attributed to keeper's ghost.

D. **Fort Trumbull.** U.S. Naval Underwater Systems Center. Pequot Ave. just past Howard St.; view from B and C. Not open to public. Remains of walls of fort, intact 1790 powder house, officers' quarters, brig; site of Revolutionary attack; present fort built 1840s, served during Civil War.

E. **Thames River Estuary Maritime Heritage Park.** Plans call for future park linking City Pier, Custom House, Bank Street Historic District, Fort Griswold, Coast Guard Academy, *Nautilus,* Shaw Mansion; will revolve around Thames River.

F. **Ye Olde Town Mill.** 8 Mill St., off State Pier Rd. Open all year, limited hours. No fee. Original mill built 1650 for John Winthrop, Jr., governor of Connecticut, industrial entrepreneur; rebuilt 1712; 1800 gristmill, overshot water wheel, spill-way, grindstone, chiseled support beams, stonework still in place.

G. Ye Antientest Burial Grounds, 1653. Huntington St. Legend says Benedict Arnold watched New London burn from here.

H. Connecticut College Arboretum. Williams St., across from main entrance to Connecticut College. Open all year. No fee. 425 acres, trails; self-guided tour with brochure; variety of ecosystems; open ledge with glacial erratic deposits; ravine, tidal marsh; 300 woody plants on 20 acres, including laurel, holly, viburnum, azalea, conifers, red maple; wildflowers; 200 acres natural areas, wildlife; hiking, picnicking.

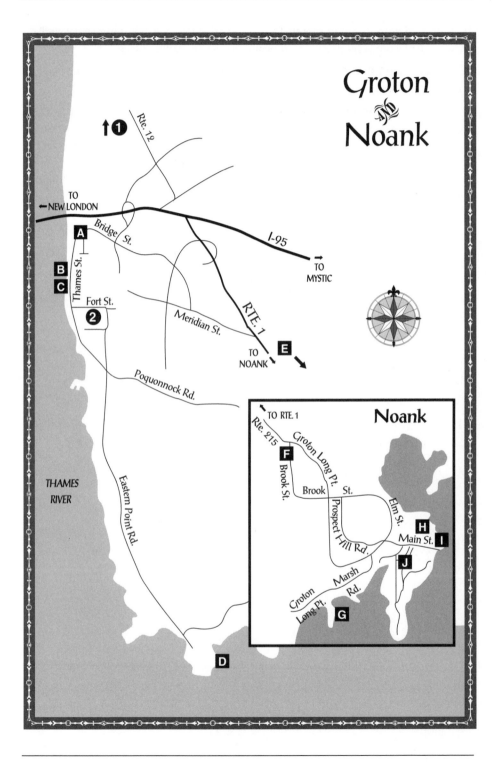

GROTON AND NOANK

G roton, the submarine capital of the world, began as part of Pequot Plantation (New London), founded under the leadership of John Winthrop, Jr.,
in 1646. In 1705 the newly incorporated town was named Groton, in
honor of the Winthrop estate in England. Early livelihood came from farming and
the sea—shipbuilding and maritime trade along the coast and with the West
Indies. Patriot privateers drew the wrath of the British and prompted their savage
attack on New London and Fort Griswold. This was the only major Revolutionary
battle in Connecticut and the last in New England. After the Revolution, Groton
people built ships, milled at every stream, traded, and searched for seals and
whales throughout the world. In 1868, residents and the state presented land for a
navy yard, officially commissioned during World War I as a submarine base. Now
500 acres, it is the country's largest. Submarines are not only based here and
exhibited in museums, they are built in Groton by the Electric Boat Division of
General Dynamics. The firm delivered seventy-four submarines during World War
II, as well as the nations's first nuclear sub, the USS *Nautilus,* now on display.

Noank, in contrast, retains the village atmosphere of an older, more peaceful
fishing and shipbuilding era. Victorian and Greek Revival homes line quiet roads
with many places to stop to picnic and appreciate water views.

1. USS NAUTILUS MEMORIAL SUBMARINE FORCE LIBRARY
AND MUSEUM, NHL. Crystal Lake Rd. off Rte. 12. Open all year, no fee.
Museum, library, gift shop, submarine tour, film.

There is no doubt in your mind that you've arrived at the right place. Myriad small
subs surround the front of the museum, and the black conning tower of the *Nautilus*
rises from the riverside. Midget subs include a Japanese Mato A from the 1930s, an Italian Maiale and German Seehund HU 75 from World War II, and Simon Lake's *Explorer*
from 1936, the last boat created by the pioneer designer/builder of research submarines. Inside, the focus is the history of submarines. The self-guided tour starts with
a model of Captain Nemo's ship *Nautilus* from Jules Verne's *Twenty Thousand Leagues
under the Sea.* Trace the development of subs as you walk the long wall of models in historical order. Displays reenact history, from Bushnell's 1775 *Turtle* to the Navy's first
sub, USS *Holland SS1,* launched in 1897, to the current Trident sub. Enter a World
War II Fleet Boat Control Room or the Attack Center; look through a periscope, adjust
it, and find the *Nautilus* at the pier. Upstairs see the *Nautilus* room, a huge fleet boat
model, and the library. The museum staff announces a sub coming upriver and all rush
to the pier for a closer view, a real-life demonstration amid the history of submarines.

Board the *Nautilus,* "first and best," a National Landmark after twenty-five years and nearly 500,000 miles. This first nuclear-powered sub steamed 62,562 miles, over half while submerged, on her first uranium fuel core. That distance would require more than two million gallons of diesel fuel. On August 3, 1958, *Nautilus's* commander announced, "For the world, our country, and the navy—the North Pole." They had reached it after ninety-six hours and 1,830 submerged miles under ice. Climb down to the torpedo room and follow passageways to the galley, officers' quarters, enlisted mess and quarters, control room, and attack center—a fascinating walk through life on a sub. Bunks piled on bunks, sinks squeezed into corners, every inch utilized for the 111 crew members. The museum is created and maintained with military precision and perfection. Yet you feel no hurry as you study the exhibits and soak in the history of submarines at this popular museum for all ages.

2. FORT GRISWOLD STATE PARK, NRHP. 57 Fort St. Open extended season, no fee. Sixteen-acre site with museum, historic house, gardens.

Two 1830 issue cannons flank the entrance to this Revolutionary War fort, symbolic of the terrible battle that was waged here. On September 6, 1781, the British arrived in force, aiming to remove the threat of privateers and divert Washington's attention from his move south toward Cornwallis and Yorktown. Led by traitor Benedict Arnold, the forces split at the Thames, half the force attacking and burning New London. The other half, about 800 men, landed in Groton, where local Patriots had the advantages of a completed fort, with magazines full, and woods and swamps to slow British invasion. The defenders, about 165 militia, valiantly responded to two charges by the enemy until they were overpowered. The commander of Fort Griswold, Colonel Ledyard, was forced to surrender. He was immediately killed with his own sword. Massacre followed. At least eighty-eight of the garrison died, and most of the rest were badly wounded. A cart carrying American wounded plunged down the hill, out of control, and hit a tree. The few survivors were taken to the Avery house. British Major Montgomery was buried in the fort's parade ground, the rest of the British in unmarked graves. The fort retains the original star-shape form, remarkably intact. You can still walk through the sally port, a tunnel through the earthen wall, which leads to a covered ditch. From the top of the wall you look down on the 1840 fortifications, hot shot furnace, magazine, stone walls. You can appreciate the height advantage of the fort's placement and the panoramic view of Thames and Sound.

Monument House Museum, a small solid structure of stone blocks and water-rounded beach stones, contains exhibits of life in Groton—Indian, trade, Civil War, and whaling collections. A detailed diorama of Fort Griswold captures the action on the day of the attack. The **Monument** is a 134-foot-tall pyramid of stone blocks, taller than any surrounding trees. Names of men who fell at the fort are engraved at the entrance. A spiral stone stairway leads to the top and an expansive view of cities, river, and Sound.

Ebenezer Avery House was built about 1750 by a naval ensign, Ebenezer Avery, who was later wounded in the massacre. Here the wounded who survived the wagon crash were sheltered, Avery among them. He survived, lived a long life as a tailor, and had four wives, all named Elizabeth. Now well-tended perennial and herb beds line the walk and invite you to enter. Period furnishings interpret Avery family life, Groton, and the Revolutionary War. It is maintained by Avery Memorial Association.

BEACHES, PARKS, OTHER POINTS OF INTEREST

A. National Submarine Memorial. Circle at Bridge, Fairview, and Thames sts. Open all year. No fee. Memorial to fifty-two subs downed in World War II; huge conning tower surrounded by flags and memorials, finished granite wall with accurate carved silhouette of each sub with name, date damaged, fate of crew.

B. *Hel-Cat II*. 181 Thames St. Open extended season. Fee. Steel fishing boat.

C. *River Queen II*. 193 Thames St. Open extended season. Fee. Cruise Thames River, see USS *Nautilus,* Trident subs under construction, submarine base, U.S. Coast Guard Academy.

D. Project Oceanology. End Eastern Point Rd., through University of Connecticut campus to water. Open all year. Fee, reservations; private nonprofit. Summer 2½-hour oceanographic cruise aboard 55-foot *Enviro-lab* research vessel; drag net, examine catch with instructors, take water samples, do tests. School year extensive marine education program. On former Plant family estate with Gothic mansion facing wide expanse of lawns, sea, lighthouse; Morton Plant's father built railroad to Florida; son continued railroading, was philanthropist, paid for town hall.

E. Bluff Point Coastal Reserve State Park. Rte. 1, then south on North Rd. to end Depot Rd. Open all year. No fee. Site of Governor Winthrop home; 806 acres, 100-acre tidal salt marsh, rocky bluffs, sandy beaches, forest; hiking, fishing, swimming (thirty-minute walk to beach), picnicking.

F. Haley Farm State Park. Brook St., Noank. Open all year. No fee. On 198 acres are old shoreline farm, fields, woods, orchards, ponds, stone walls, paths, 8 miles bike trail.

G. Esker Point Beach. Marsh Rd., Noank. Open all year. Parking fee in summer. Lifeguards, concessions, rest room, picnic tables and grills under shade trees; swimming.

H. Noank. Village of well-kept Greek Revival (example: classic Moses Latham House, 1845, at 59 Main), Italianate, and Gothic homes, many on Main St.; winding narrow roads; views of harbor, inlets, boat yards, and marinas from Riverview Ave., Pearl St., and Marsh Rd.

I. Town Beach and Dock. Main St., Noank. Open all year. No fee. Tiny beach next to Univeristy of Connecticut MSI Marine Research Lab, Sea Research Foundation for Mystic Aquarium that aids rescued animals; limited parking.

J. Noank Historical Society Museum. Sylvan Rd. By appointment. Exhibits of photos, art, shipbuilding, fishing, Indian relics.

MYSTIC

Mystic in earlier years was a vibrant shipbuilding center and seaport. Today in this town of Colonial and Victorian buildings, you see tidy white houses of the early maritime community along with gracious homes of sea captains and wealthy merchants. During the Revolution, Mystic patriots sailed the seas and harassed the British, who called Mystic "an accursed little hornets' nest."[7] During the Gold Rush era, shipbuilders competed to build the fastest ship to San Francisco. Mystic won with the *Andrew Jackson,* built in 1860, which made the trip in eighty-nine days and four hours, nine hours ahead of the famous *Flying Cloud.*

Walk Gravel, Clift, Pearl, High, and Eldridge streets to see historic homes, many with dates and names to help you savor the mystique of the days of billowing sails in nineteenth-century Mystic.

1. **MYSTIC SEAPORT MUSEUM. Rte. 27. Open all year, fee. Village, old ships, marina, planetarium, children's museum, library, gift shop, food; boat rentals, classes and races; special daily events, films, visiting exhibits, college courses.**

A huge ship's anchor, tall masts silhouetted against the sky, and boats reflected in the Mystic River greet you as you enter this recreated nineteenth-century seaport. The seventeen-acre New England village boasts sixty or more structures authentic to the time when clipper ships were lords of the sea. It is all here, whether you are an "old salt" coming to reminisce and participate, an historian to study maritime history, or a visitor to enjoy attractions. Mystic Seaport Museum stands on the site of two shipyards, the 1837 Geo. Greenman & Co. and the 1851 Charles Mallory & Sons. Many a record-breaking vessel slid down the ways in the 1800s. One, the *David Crockett,* made twenty-five runs around Cape Horn to San Francisco, a record never equaled.

In 1929 the Marine Historical Association formed to begin this unique museum, bringing to it historic New England buildings and erecting reproductions of others on the site. Here it would have been natural to see the mighty *Charles W. Morgan,* 1841, NHL, docked at its wharf. The *Morgan,* built in New Bedford, is the last of the wooden whaling fleet of whaling's golden age. In eighty years at sea the *Morgan* made thirty-seven voyages, with trips lasting up to four years, and brought in a total of 54,483 barrels of oil and 152,934 pounds of whalebone. Board the ship, which sailed under twenty-one different captains, and thrill to the imagined shout of "Thar she blo-o-ows." Below decks see the captain's cabin, forecastle, steerage, and blubber room.

Nearby is the 1882 square-rigged Danish training ship originally christened *Georg*

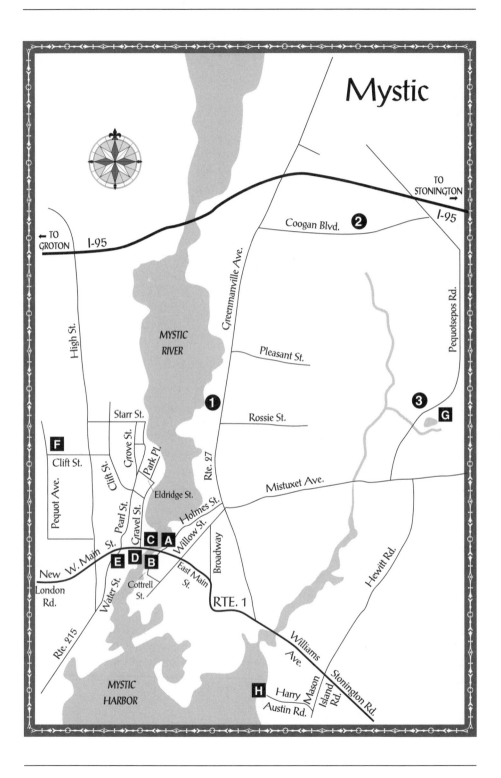

Stage, which trained generations of Danish seamen. Australian Alan Villiers, captain and writer, bought her in 1934, renaming her *Joseph Conrad* for his favorite marine writer. She continues her legacy of training here, where students live aboard and learn fundamentals of sailing, seamanship, weather, and maritime history. Visit the 1921 two-masted, gaff-rigged fishing schooner *L. A. Dunton*. Each of her ten 14-foot dories held two men and tubs with 1,800 feet of fishing line and 300 hooks, one every 6 feet, for cod fishing. The restored 1908 steamboat *Sabino* makes daily trips (fee) on the river. Once an island ferry in Casco Bay, Maine, she is believed to be the last operating coal-fired passenger steamer in the United States. At the shipyard watch boats being restored by skilled craftsmen using nineteenth-century tools and techniques combined with modern-day technology. The museum has a collection of more than 400 restored vessels.

To be part of early seafaring life, step inside the ship's chandlery, where all the necessities for a ship's voyage can be found. Visit the village exhibits and talk with craftsmen using age-old methods with the skill and respect of true artists. Watch whaleboat demonstrations, sailors aloft furling sails, costumed staff drawing your imagination back a century and more. The **Stillman Building** exhibits ship models, paintings, and scrimshaw. The **Mallory Building** brings Mallory shipbuilding to life, and the **Wendell Building** displays figureheads. The **R. J. Schaeffer Art Gallery** has changing marine art exhibits. There is something here for everyone.

2. MYSTIC MARINELIFE AQUARIUM, 55 Coogan Blvd. Open all year, fee. Gift shop and bookstore, picnic area, University of Connecticut college credit courses, field trips, classes for all ages, school programs.

Separated by less than an inch of glass, stand eye to eye with beluga whales and Atlantic bottlenose dolphins. Watch their graceful bodies whirling and diving underwater in the indoor three-pool complex. Whales and dolphins exhibit natural behaviors during daily demonstrations in the 1,200-seat Marine Theater.

The two-and-a-half-acre outdoor Seal Island complex features four different species of seal and sea lion. Their barking forms a noisy backdrop for these pinnipeds, which range from 8-pound pups to 2,400-pound adults. Unusual elephant sea lions molt annually, losing skin and fur. An expanded collection of large, graceful Steller's sea lions can be seen in the Alaskan Coast exhibit. This threatened species is part of the aquarium's continuing efforts to bring attention to species declining in number. In the nearby Penguin Pavilion, the customarily formally attired penguins also molt annually, losing their feathers. African black-footed penguins can also be seen. Visitors watch these flightless birds frolic above and below the water. Mystic Aquarium is a founding member of the Northeast Region Stranding Network, which rescues stranded marine animals along the North Atlantic coast. The Aquarium is credited with the rehabilitation and release of two Atlantic whitesided dolphins and numerous seals.

3. DENISON HOMESTEAD, *1717*. Pequotsepos Rd. Open extended season and by appointment, fee.

Ann Borodell Denison Gates had a dream that became reality. Growing up in this home, where her ancestors had lived since 1717, she wanted to see it preserved. Annie Gates started with a tea, a tent, and 700 guests, who became charter members of the Denison Society on August 16, 1930. Now her home is toured annually by thousands. Each year the Denison clan gathers from every part of the globe for Denison Day at the old homestead. The original 700 has become 1,100 and growing.

Before the house was built, Captain George Denison erected a stockade here in the mid-1600s. Captain Denison was commander of Connecticut troops in King Philip's War and instrumental in the capture of Canochet, which helped end Indian hostilities. Captain Denison's grandson George built the present home for his bride,

The Charles W. Morgan, Mystic Seaport, Mystic   (Mystic Seaport Museum/Mary Anne Stets)

Lucy Gallop. Today the home shows family life from 1717 to the death of Annie Gates in 1941. Restored in 1946, the house has only Denison family furnishings. To speak to eleven generations, each room has been restored to a different period. The dark wood of the kitchen illustrates the Colonial style with trimmer arch, walk-in fireplace, 1740 flintlock, iron pots, and pewter and wooden utensils. The lighter Federal parlor speaks of the next century with wallpaper, enclosed beams, ceiling moldings, and raised paneling. A melodeon, bird-of-paradise Chippendale mirror, silver coffee urn, and coin silver teaspoons relate to a more comfortable way of life. Upstairs the Revolutionary War bedroom has gunstock corners, rough-cut wooden ceiling molding, and a tester embroidered by Captain George Denison's second wife, Lady Ann Borodell, when a teenager in Ireland. The pre–Civil War bedroom shows an ornate Franklin iron stove, 1800s Denison trunk, painted ceiling moldings, and paneled and plaster walls. Downstairs in the twentieth-century room are memorabilia from Annie Gates. Her presence is felt as you move room to room and era to era reliving the days of Denisons.

BEACHES, PARKS, OTHER POINTS OF INTEREST

A. Whaler's Wharf. Holmes St. Open summer. Fee. Cruises.

B. Cottrell Wharf. Cottrell St. Open summer. Fee for Mystic River cruises.

C. Mystic Bascule Bridge. Rte. 1, center of town. Boats line up, red lights flash, traffic stops, bells ring, a foghorn sounds, massive weights drop, and the span rises quietly, allowing fishing boats, sailboats, steamboats, windjammers, and world-class yachts to pass through.

D. Steamboat Wharf. Southwest side of drawbridge. Open summer. Fee for cruises aboard replicas of nineteenth-century gaff-rigged schooners.

E. Mystic Art Association Gallery. Water St. Open summer. No fee. Member exhibits.

F. John Mason Monument. Pequot Ave. and Clift St. Monument commemorates victory over Pequot Indians.

G. Denison Pequotsepos Nature Center. Pequotsepos Rd. Open all year. Fee. Wildlife sanctuary on 125 acres, natural history museum, native wildlife exhibits, live owls, guided and self-guided trails, wildflower meadow, ponds, wetlands, marsh, uplands, nature trips, braille trails, gift shop, environmental programs.

H. Williams Beach. Harry Austin Rd. Open extended season. Fee. Playground, ball fields, lifeguards; boating, picnicking, swimming.

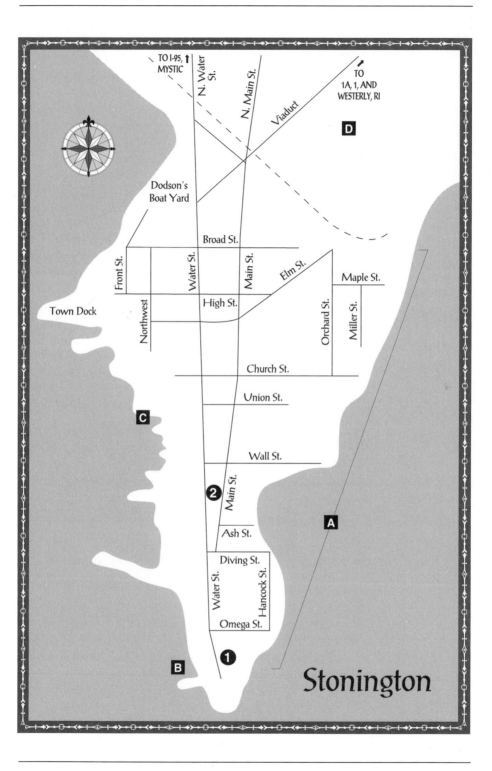

TO I-95,
MYSTIC

N. Water St.

N. Main St.

Viaduct

TO
1A, 1, AND
WESTERLY, RI

D

Dodson's
Boat Yard

Broad St.

Front St.

Water St.

Main St.

Elm St.

Maple St.

Northwest

High St.

Orchard St.

Miller St.

Town Dock

Church St.

C

Union St.

Wall St.

2

Main St.

A

Ash St.

Diving St.

Water St.

Hancock St.

Omega St.

1

B

Stonington

STONINGTON

Since 1649, when Stonington was settled, the economic base of this most easterly harbor in Long Island Sound has been the sea—fishing, whaling, sealing, trading. In the winter of 1820–21, when he was twenty-one years old, Captain Nat Palmer of Stonington discovered Antarctica while on a sealing trip on the 47-foot sloop *Hero*. He had sailed with four other Stonington-manned boats in search of seals. He met a Russian squadron of ships under Admiral Bellingshausen. The Russian commander bestowed on Palmer the honor of being first to claim the sighting of the long peninsula reaching north from below South America, now called Palmerland. In 1844, as an innovative designer and builder of clipper ships, Captain Palmer broke the speed record to Hong Kong with the *Houqua*.

In 1837 the railroad was completed from Boston south to Stonington, which flourished as the stopping place for travelers who came by steamboat from New York to meet trains from Boston. Stonington still has an active fishing fleet and retains its authentic eighteenth- and nineteenth-century New England coastal village atmosphere. Well-maintained historic homes line quiet, narrow streets with panoramic marine views.

1. OLD LIGHTHOUSE MUSEUM, *1840*, HS. 7 Water St. Open extended season, and by appointment, fee. Parking at Point (no fee).

Here's your chance to get inside a lighthouse, climb the circular stone stairs to the top, and enjoy a panoramic view of harbors and Sound. The 35-foot-tall octagonal stone lighthouse was rebuilt to replace the 1823 original when erosion forced a move to higher ground. The keeper's dwelling is combined with the light in fortresslike construction. Museum collections include Stonington salt-glaze pottery, whaling gear, farm tools, China trade treasures, ship models, dollhouses, and furnishings, as well as a fourth-order Fresnel lens and photographs of Long Island Sound lighthouses. Early portraits represent founding families, many of whose descendants are still in town and help preserve the character of the village. Cannonballs from the Battle of Stonington in the War of 1812 are displayed, one still imbedded in the hearthstone in which it lodged. Changing exhibits include one on penmanship and tools created with the aid of American Velvet Company, producers of velvet in Stonington since 1895 and now one of the few remaining producers in the country.

2. CANNON SQUARE. Just south of Wall St.

These cannons were main actors in a deadly drama in 1814. On August 9 four British warships commanded by Sir Thomas Hardy, protégé of Lord Nelson, threatened Stonington village. The *Ramillies* (74 guns), the *Pactolus* (38 guns), the *Dispatch* (22 guns), and the bombship *Terror* gave the villagers one hour to leave. "We shall defend the place to the last extremity; should it be destroyed, we shall perish in its ruins"[8] was the reply. At sunset the bomb ship *Terror* warped (hauled itself by means of its anchor) closer to the village, followed by barges carrying Congreve rockets and launches with short cannons. Stonington's two eighteen- and one six-pound cannon were the villagers' only defense. First mounted in earthworks, then moved to the Point, the cannons were fired until ammunition ran out, then the defenders spiked the cannons. When more ammunition was located, the defenders dragged the cannons by oxen to a blacksmith's shop to remove the spikes. They fired again and holed the *Dispatch*. A day of truce and negotiations suddenly ended when the *Terror* renewed her attack, and *Pactolus* and *Ramillies* warped closer to the village. Stonington's cannons were hauled to where a landing was expected. It didn't happen. The British force left Stonington. No life was lost, though forty buildings were damaged. An expert has said wars are about the way people react to threats.

Across from the cannons, in the 1851 Ocean Bank building, hangs the sixteen-star, sixteen-bar flag made in 1796 by the ladies of the Congregational Church and flown during the Battle of Stonington.

BEACHES, PARKS, OTHER POINTS OF INTEREST

A. **Stonington Village Walk.** Water, Main, and Broad sts. Park at Point. Narrow streets lined with historic buildings from the eighteenth and nineteenth centuries; architecture Colonial, Georgian, Federal, Greek Revival, Italianate, French Second Empire, Queen Anne; from simple vernacular of talented artisans' and fishermen's homes to more elaborate creations; a Robert Mills Custom House of 1827 on Main Street, Stonington Library, United Church; fishing fleet based at Town Dock off High Street, where steamships brought passengers for rail to Boston.

B. **duBois Beach.** Water St. Open all year. Fee in summer. Park at Point.

C. **Harbor Recreation Pier.** Open all year. No fee. Walk-through on Union Street, small covered wharf, benches, harbor views.

D. **Barn Island State Wildlife Management Area.** Rte. 1 to Palmer Neck Rd. Open all year. No fee. Boat launch, paths.

RHODE ISLAND

(AT = Abbreviated Tour)

RHODE
ISLAND

95

WESTERLY

T he romantic tradition of Westerly reports the first settlers to be John and Mary Lawton Babcock, who eloped by boat from Newport in 1648. Farming, shipbuilding, and trade formed the economic base. Early in the nineteenth century, the Pawcatuck River was utilized with the establishment of cloth mills, first woolen, then cotton. A huge cotton mill and twelve double houses, built in 1849 for White Rock Company and bought in 1874 for Fruit of the Loom, can still be seen. In the mid-1800s, stonemason Orlando Smith saw large granite outcrops, took an option on about 300 acres, and began a high-quality granite industry that flourished. After the Civil War every town and village commissioned granite monuments to honor their soldiers. Eventually granite became too expensive to quarry so far below the surface, and the industry died in 1955.

The town has the distinction of being a twin town with Pawcatuck, Connecticut. The two communities honor their mutual historic ties as well as crossing state lines to share the same main post office and railroad station.

1. BABCOCK–SMITH HOUSE, *c. 1732*, NRHP, HS, Orlando Smith Trust.
124 Granite St. Open summer, fee. Museum shop, Colonial gardens.

This pre-Revolutionary house has been home to two interesting families. It was built for Dr. Joshua and Hannah Stanton Babcock and was lived in by their descendants until 1817. Grandson of a first settler, Dr. Babcock was a surgeon, chief justice of the colony's Supreme Court, member of the General Assembly when independence was declared, major general of the militia, member of the colony's War Council, and a founder of Brown University. He was the first Rhode Islander to graduate from Yale. Before 1772, his friend Ben Franklin, who visited him here, appointed him postmaster. He had a post office and general store, probably in the attached ell. In 1848 Orlando Smith bought the house and the land, which then became the source of the successful granite industry. Smiths lived here until 1972. The house is furnished from the two families' collections.

The early Georgian house retains original beaded clapboards and beautiful swan's-neck broken-pedimented front entry. Heavy Georgian moldings cap tall, narrow windows. The ell was redone in the mid-1800s, acquiring Greek Revival elements, and the entrance porch was an 1885 addition. The copper beech tree is centuries old, and the boxwood hedge and brownstone walk could be as old as the house. The house underwent Victorian changes, but in 1928 restoration expert Norman Isham reclaimed it.

Inside, you follow Babcock and Smith families through portraits and possessions. The parlor features original raised paneling on fireplace wall and on a scallop-shell

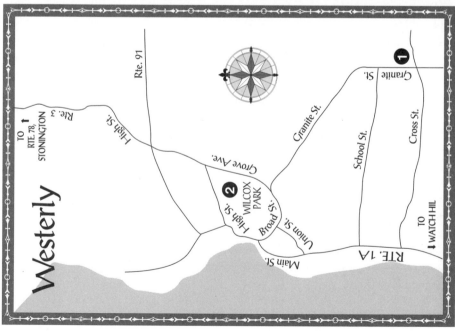

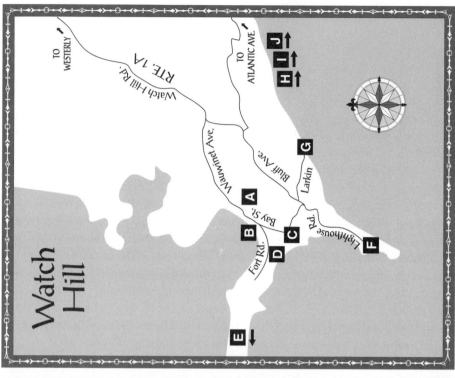

Babcock-Smith House, Westerly   (Orlando R. Smith Trust)

corner cupboard with butterfly shelves. Both are highlighted by pilasters with triple capitals. The front-hall staircase has a shipwright-created stair balustrade with three alternating designs of balusters, curving molded handrail, and corkscrew turned newel post. In the dining room are portraits of the families' first sons, Colonel Harry Babcock and Orlando R. Smith. Harry was a flamboyant genius in the French and Indian and Revolutionary wars, said to have kissed the queen on the cheek when presented, and later asked to leave the military. Furnishings from two centuries are eclectic, both primitive and sophisticated—Queen Anne daybed, Connecticut highboy, Hepplewhite sideboard, several tall-case clocks, and China trade treasures like the two Chinese ivory-inlaid tables of Charlotte and David Babcock. A painting of Captain David Babcock's ship *Young America,* on which the family lived for several years, hangs in the parlor. The house is administered by the Westerly Historical Society and the Orlando Smith Trust.

2. WESTERLY CENTER WALK. Open all year, no fee. High and Broad sts. and Grove Ave. around Wilcox Park Historic District.

Westerly's prosperity in the nineteenth century is expressed in public buildings and private homes—the Old Town Hall, 1872; the Town Hall and Court House, 1912; and the Richardsonian Romanesque **Westerly Public Library,** which contains a public art gallery. Behind the library is **Wilcox Park,** eighteen acres with flowers, shrubs, statues, fountains, duck pond, and area for the visually impaired. The suddenly quiet oasis with paths through shaded beauty was designed by Frederick Law Olmsted. The park and neighborhood are lined with Greek Revival and Gothic-style houses to appreciate. Away from the center, **Westerly Hospital** displays Florence Nightingale's nurse's cap and a volume of her writing in the lobby, given by her Westerly relatives.

BEACHES, PARKS, OTHER POINTS OF INTEREST

A. Watch Hill. South on Rte. 1A, parking on Bay St. Village of winding streets, hills with Victorian houses, water views.

B. Ninigret Statue. Bay St. Sculptured by Enid Yandell in 1914, Niantic Indian chief faces mouth of Pawcatuck River and little Narragansett Bay; memorial benches.

C. Flying Horse Carousel. c. 1867. End of Bay St. Open all year. Operated summer, fee. Built by Charles W. F. Dare Co.; perfect tiny horses, each hand-carved from one piece of wood with real tails and manes, leather saddles, and agate eyes, are suspended from center frame and swing out when carousel operates (to help riders grasp brass ring).

D. Watch Hill Beach and Bathhouses. End of Bay St. Open all year. Summer fee. Popular open beach, lifeguards, bathhouses.

E. Napatree Point Beach and Conservation area. Open all year. No fee. Walk from Bay St. through parking lots, past yacht club, along harbor to signed path; trails through dunes, sand; wildlife, views, ruins of Spanish American War fort at end of point.

F. Watch Hill Point Lighthouse, 1856, NRHP. Lighthouse Rd. Private. Walk along winding road of large estates to view light; site of early watchtower and beacon. Present light built to replace 1807 wood light, used oil until 1930; granite 3-story square light plus white-painted stuccoed oil house, brick signal house, brick keeper's house; well preserved example of nineteenth-century lighthouse complex. Site of wrecks; in 1812 Oliver Hazard Perry, commanding a coastal patrol vessel, ran on rocks in fog. View Napatree Point and beyond to Fisher's Island Sound and lighthouse.

G. East Beach. Walk in right of way at Larkin and Bluff. Open all year. No fee. Sandy beach from Watch Hill Light to Ocean House Hotel.

H. Atlantic Beach. Atlantic Ave. Open all year. Parking fee. Popular 3-mile-long beach; no facilities on beach, concessions line road.

I. Misquamicut State Beach. Atlantic Ave. Open all year. Fee in summer. Popular beach, center of 7-mile strip; lifeguards, rest rooms, showers.

J. Atlantic Beach Park. Atlantic Ave. Open summer. Fee. Roller skating, water slides, amusements, mini golf, batting cages.

CHARLESTOWN

T housands of years ago Indians lived here. They came to the coast to hunt, fish, and plant in summer, then moved inland for protection against the fierce winter. In Charlestown an Indian heritage still exists—land, culture, ceremonies, historic sites, the presence of the Narragansett Indian Tribe.

Charlestown separated from Westerly in 1738 and was named for King Charles II of England, grantor of the Rhode Island charter of 1663. The Pawcatuck River provided power for many textile mills in the early nineteenth century. Industrial mill villages formed, with the town center near Cross' Mills, site of two gristmills. Route 1 provides access (be aware of left lane reverses) to large public parks, open beaches, a tourist information center, and many fine art galleries.

1. CHARLESTOWN HISTORICAL SOCIETY SCHOOLHOUSE, 1838, NRHP. Rte. 1A, grounds of Cross' Mills Public Library. Open summer, limited hours, no fee.

Walk into a schoolhouse of old. Desks of varying ages and sizes face the old potbelly stove and blackboard. An 1874 Franklin fifth reader rests on a desk. A wall cutout reveals the old construction of this completely restored one-room school.

2. HISTORIC VILLAGE OF THE NARRAGANSETT INDIANS, NRHP. Access by permission of Tribal Council at junction of routes 2 and 112 ("a" on map).

Here the Longhouse People gathered. Clans and families built wigwams and a longhouse, the cultural center of the seminomadic tribe. Hand-hewn granite blocks formed the recently burned **Narragansett Indian Church** (b), which replaced the c. 1750 wooden church. Samuel Niles, first Indian minister, was buried here in 1785, and the graveyard behind the church bears many Indian family names. Original hard wooden benches with straight backs face altar and wooden cross. Flowers are in every window. Picture this once-active Indian tribal village as you drive along the smooth dirt road and arrive at the meetinghouse. In the open clearing in front of the church, tribes and clans from all over the nation still gather the second Saturday and Sunday in August as they have for more than three centuries. Descendants of blood chiefs Canonicus and his nephew Miantonomi are still part of the Narragansett tribal government.

The Royal Indian Burial Ground (c), NRHP, open all year, no fee, is off Narrow Lane (first dirt road on the left past the old landfill). A path leads up through the twenty-acre undeveloped state park to graves believed to be of colony-appointed Sachem Ninigret and his family. In the peaceful open grassy area, a protective iron railing encloses the rough stone markers from the 1700s.

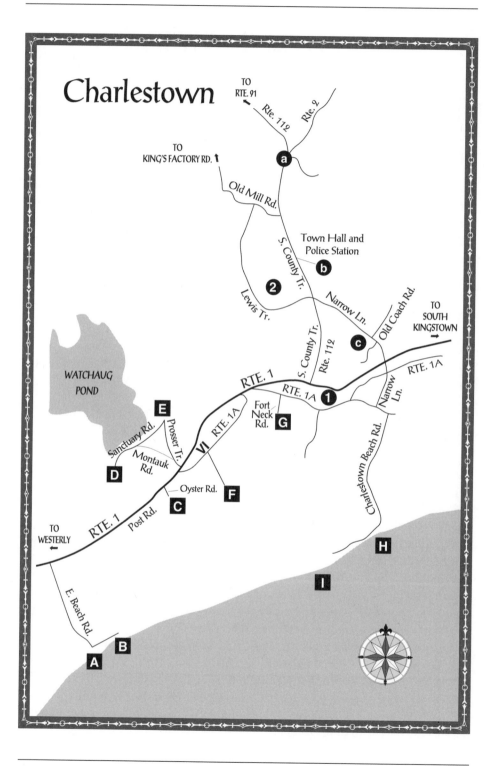

BEACHES, PARKS, OTHER POINTS OF INTEREST

A. Sam Ferretti Blue Shutters Town Beach. East Beach Rd. Open all year. Fee. Lifeguards, bathhouse, concessions; sandy beach, surf, open to Block Island Sound.

B. East Beach (state). East Beach Rd. Open all year. Fee. 3 miles of uncrowded ocean barrier beach with heavy surf; covered at high tide, sharp drop-off in one area; lifeguards; picnicking. Ninigret salt pond on other side of barrier beach: windsurfing, shellfishing.

C. Ninigret National Wildlife Refuge. Oyster Rd. Open all year. No fee. Borders Ninigret Park; nature trails.

D. Kimball Wildlife Refuge. Montauk to Sanctuary Rd. Open all year. No fee. 29 acres, trails to Watchaug Pond, small nature center; Rhode Island Audubon.

E. Burlingame State Park. Off Prosser Trail. Open all year. No fee. 2,100 acres; beach on Watchaug Pond, boat launch, covered picnic areas; camping entrance off Rte. 1.

F. Ninigret Park. Entrance Rte. 1A. Open all year. No fee. 172 acres; 3-acre spring-fed pond, sandy beach, rest rooms, playground, picnic grills, tables, ball fields, tennis, celestial observatory (fee), health exercise track, criterium 10-speed bike–racing course. Frosty Drew Memorial Nature Center, open all year, limited hours or by appointment; donations; displays, programs, trails.

G. Fort Ninigret, NRHP. Fort Neck Rd. Open all year. No fee. Beautiful, peaceful site on cove of sheltered salt pond; iron railings protect and outline remains of early 1600s Dutch trading post; rubble earthworks rise slightly above shallow moat; large rough fieldstone in center. Niantic Indians here after Dutch, now memorial to Niantics and Narragansetts; possibly 1637 site of Captain John Mason's meeting with Niantics and alliance to destroy the Pequots.

H. Charlestown Beach. Charlestown Beach Rd. Open all year. Fee. Lifeguards, bathhouse; volleyball on beach.

I. Charlestown Breachway. Charlestown Beach Rd. Open all year. Fee. Lifeguards, boat ramp, rest rooms; small, open beach; surfing, fishing.

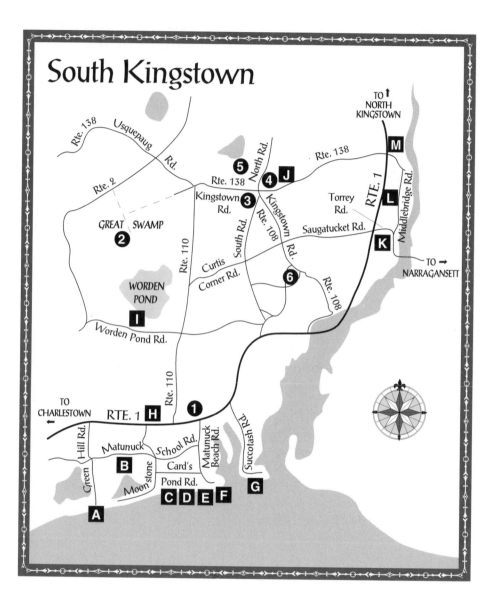

South Kingstown

SOUTH KINGSTOWN
(WAKEFIELD, MATUNUCK, KINGSTON)

South Kingstown is a composite of natural beauty, from Great Swamp and Worden Pond through rolling verdant countryside to white sandy beaches on Block Island Sound. It was originally part of Kings Towne, which divided in 1723 into North and South Kingstown. The latter was basically the Pettaquamscutt Purchase, land bought from Narragansett Indians in 1658. The first settlement was on Tower Hill. A courthouse was built there in 1733. By the mid-1700s, however, Little Rest (Kingston) 5 miles to the west had become a cultural and business center for neighboring plantations, and in 1752 the courthouse moved to Little Rest, making it the county seat. In the historic year of 1776 a third courthouse (today's Kingston Library) was built. Here sessions of the state assembly met until 1791 as one of five rotating capitals of Rhode Island.

Wakefield Village, at the head of Point Judith Pond, is South Kingstown's main port. Matunuck, another of South Kingstown's coastal communities, was the birthplace of Commodore Oliver Hazard Perry. Though outnumbered, Perry's fleet defeated the British in the Battle of Lake Erie, September 10, 1813. His succinct report echoes down through the years, "We have met the enemy and they are ours."[9] The sea has been a major influence on the lifestyle of South Kingstown for centuries.

1. EDWARD EVERETT HALE HOUSE, *1880s.* Off Rte. 1, opposite Matunuck Beach Rd. Private.

Here summered the author of the classic *The Man without a Country*. Edward Everett Hale's dedication to his country may have been strengthened by the short life of his granduncle Nathan Hale (see New London 5). In addition to writing, Edward Hale was a Unitarian minister, editor, and humanitarian. A leader in the Lend-a-Hand charity movement, he followed their motto: "Look up and not down, look forward and not back, look out and not in, lend a hand."[10] His home on the hill is recognized by the H in the shutters. Below the house is the **Robert Beverly Hale Memorial Library,** named for Edward's beloved son, who died of typhoid fever at age twenty-three. The library was given in his memory by friends and family in 1896.

2. GREAT SWAMP. Entrances off Rte. 2 and at intersection of rtes. 138 and 110; latter leads to wildlife preserve. Open all year, no fee. Five miles of trails, wildlife, birding; hunting, fishing, canoeing, hiking.

On this site New England forces struck a severe blow in King Philip's War. After Philip became chief of the Wampanoag Indians, relations between red and white men deteriorated rapidly, ending in war. December 19, 1675, colonial troops from Plymouth, Massachusetts, and Connecticut under General Josiah Winslow marched from Smith's Castle to surround an island in the Great Swamp fortified by Narragansett and Wampanoag Indians. Midwinter conditions made it possible to maneuver on frozen swampland. Setting fire to the camp, 1,000 colonials killed more than 500 Indians. Of the colonists, 80 lost their lives and 150 were wounded. Philip, not present at the battle, fought with even greater intensity until his capture and death in August 1676. A tall, naturally sculptured stone monolith reaches skyward as a silent symbol of the lives that were lost here. Surrounding stone memorials stand for the different colonies that took part in the attack.

3. OLD WASHINGTON COUNTY JAIL, *1792*, Pettaquamscutt HS. 2636 Kingstown Rd., Kingston. Open extended season, limited hours, fee. Genealogical and historical library.

The inviting jailer's house belies the cold reality of granite cell blocks added in 1858 and used until 1956. On the first floor are cold, dank men's cells; each held two men in windowless barred constraint. Men showing good behavior might be allowed to have visiting time in the corridor for a quick game of checkers. In contrast, women's cells above were larger, with solid doors for privacy and a cherished window. Today they are display rooms; one-room schoolhouse, musical instruments room, Indian room with hand-carved case telling story of Hiawatha, toy room, loom room, and Kingston artifacts room.

The two-and-a-half-story granite jailer's home is furnished to show life in South Kingstown for the last 300 years. Each room features a local personage and period. The Potter Room, once the sheriff's office, relates to Judge Potter and family. Upstairs the Eldred Room is named for an early graduate of University of Rhode Island. The Mumford Room includes parts of the old Mumford house, a Narragansett planter's home. The Civil War Room evokes that era through local documents, uniforms, and memorabilia. Outside, a Colonial garden creates a peaceful backdrop.

4. KINGSTON HISTORIC DISTRICT WALKING TOUR, NRHP. Kingstown and South rds. Houses private.

Kingston Village was called Little Rest until 1825. The name may have come from its being a place to rest after travelers came up the long hills—or from the fact that during court and general assembly sessions "little rest" could be had by residents. The many eighteenth- and nineteenth-century taverns and inns suggest the second possibility. To enjoy Kingston's charm, walk Kingstown Road, noting house names and dates from the church to South Road. **Kingston Congregational Church,** 1820, was first organized at Tower Hill in 1732. The 1832 **Church House,** erected on the foundation of Kingston's 1752 courthouse, has been a school, fraternity, residence, and parsonage.

The building at **2590 Kingstown** was a stagecoach stop and inn named, in turn, Barker House, Kingston Inn, and Babcock Hotel. Its taproom had an unusual hinged partition to keep liquor off-limits on Sundays.

On the near corner of South Road is the 1738 **Elisha Reynolds home:** store, boardinghouse, home of the first local newspaper (*Rhode Island Advocate*), blacksmith shop, boot factory, and summer home for opera star Madame Pauline Lucca, now Tavern Hall Club and apartments. Across South Road is the **John Moore House.** The east side was built in 1710, making it the oldest house in the village. At one time sheep lived in the attic during the winter.

Cross Kingstown Road, walk west by the 1774 **Joe Runnels Tavern.** At 2587 Kingstown is **South County Art Association,** housed in the home of early member Bernon Elijah Helme (see 5). Helme's home was originally two houses, joined for Landholders Bank in 1818. The older section was a 1754 saddler's shop. At the corner is **Kingston Library** (NRHP), originally built as Colonial-style Kings (Washington) County Courthouse in 1776. It served as a state house until 1791 and as county courthouse until 1891. In 1876, it was remodeled to French Second Empire with mansard roof and front tower added. The original belfry was moved to the top of the new tower. The building became a library in 1895. Adjacent is the stone 1857 **County Records building** housing records.

5. UNIVERSITY OF RHODE ISLAND, *1892.* Kingstown Rd. Open all year for functions; historic Watson House open by appointment, donation. Public programs, classes, tours, performing arts.

The roots of this nationally known university go back to the federal Hatch Act of 1887, which induced the state to establish an agricultural experiment station and school. In 1888 Kingston postmaster and general store owner Bernon Elijah Helme promoted the purchasing of the 140-acre **Oliver Watson Farm** as a campus for the new agricultural school, which became the University of Rhode Island in 1951. Over the years the restored c. 1796 **Watson House** served as farm manager's home, tearoom, faculty home, fraternity house, dormitory, nursery school, and kindergarten. Still part of the university, it retains its original structure and contains period furnishings and changing exhibits. It also provides a fine working laboratory for students in history, art, architecture, archaeology, textiles, and Colonial furnishings. Its 8-foot central chimney serves six fireplaces. Special items include a loom belonging to Quaker Billy Rose, a 1700s wagon bench, a Watson family four-poster bed, rope spring beds, and a corn-husk mattress.

6. VILLAGE OF PEACE DALE. Rte. 108. Museum of Primitive Art and Culture. 1058 Kingstown Rd. Open all year, limited hours, donation.

The Village of Peace Dale was named by village founder Rowland Hazard for his wife,

Mary Peace Hazard. Rowland Hazard built this highly successful nineteenth-century textile mill complex 1847–83. He also built Peace Dale Congregational Church, designed by the architects of New York's St. John the Divine Cathedral. The Hazards continued to share their fortunes with the town by donating the Village Green as a park, organizing the first fire company in the state, and building Narragansett Pier railroad depot and Hazard School as well as the 1908 Neighborhood Guild building for industrial arts and recreational programs. The mills, originally powered by water from Saugatucket River, speak eloquently of a nineteenth-century town/family industry. A shawl for Abraham Lincoln was made at these mills, which now operate under new owners.

Hazard's 1856 Peace Dale Office Building at Kingstown Road and Columbia Street was company store, post office, and boardinghouse. The top floor housed employee recreation, making it the birthplace in 1856 of the U.S. Industrial Recreation Movement. Today the building houses various businesses and the **Museum of Primitive Art and Culture,** which displays archaeological and ethnological collections of tools, weapons, household utensils, beadwork, fishing and hunting gear, Indian pipes, and other artifacts used by Indian tribes from Alaska to Australia, from Stone and Bronze ages to the present.

Across the road is the **Hazard Memorial Library,** built 1891 in Richardsonian Romanesque style, given by Rowland Hazard's sons in his memory. On the grounds is the interpretive bronze sculpture *The Weaver* by world-renowned artist Daniel Chester French, 1920. French is known for his seated *Abraham Lincoln* in the Lincoln Memorial, Washington, D.C., and for his *Minuteman* in Concord, Massachusetts. The sculpture here, commemorating weavers from prehistoric times to modern-day industrial workers, was given by Hazard's daughter, Caroline, one-time president of Wellesley College.

BEACHES, PARKS, OTHER POINTS OF INTEREST

A. **Green Hill Beach.** Green Hill Rd. Open all year. No walk-on fee, parking fee. Sandy beach; swimming.

B. **Trustom Pond National Wildlife Refuge.** Matunuck School Rd. Open all year. No fee. Trails, wildlife; fishing.

C. **Theater-by-the-Sea,** NRHP. Card's Pond Rd. Open summer. Fee for performances. Continuous since 1933; restaurant.

D. **Roy Carpenter's Beach.** Card's Pond Rd. Open summer. Fee. Lifeguards, store; swimming.

E. **South Kingstown Town Beach at Matunuck.** Matunuck Beach Rd. Open all year. No walk-on fee, parking fee. Rest rooms, pavilion, lifeguards; swimming, picnicking.

F. Mary Carpenter's Beach. Matunuck Beach Rd. Open all year. Fee. Bathhouse, swimming.

G. East Matunuck State Beach. Succotash Rd. Open all year. Fee. Lifeguards, concessions, bathhouse; picnicking, swimming, fishing.

H. Perryville Trout Hatchery. Old Post Rd., Perryville. Open all year. No fee. Fish used to stock state waters; tours, opportunities to feed fish.

I. Worden Pond. Worden Pond Rd. Open all year. No fee. Rhode Island's largest natural freshwater lake; boat launch; fishing.

J. Fayerweather House, c. 1820. Rte. 138, Kingston. Open summer. No fee. Built by blacksmith George Fayerweather. Of Afro-Indian ancestry, Fayerweather married Indian princess, lived here with their twelve children; descendants lived here for eighty years, carrying on father's trade; daughter Sarah Harris was first black to attend Prudence Crandall, all-white girls' school in Canterbury, Connecticut, and thus a principal in Connecticut's famous Black Law case. Craft demonstrations, classes, workshops.

K. Torrey Graveyard. Rte. 1 and Torrey Rd. All that is left of Tower Hill settlement, once a tiny hamlet in Rhode Island's frontier; now a busy thoroughfare. Land originally given by Sewalls to build meetinghouse in 1707; graves date from 1700s–1900s, such as Helmes, Oatleys, Torreys, and, in 1944, Bernon Elijah Helme.

L. Pettaquamscutt Rock or Treaty Rock. Middlebridge Rd. opposite John St. Open all year. No fee. Probable site of Roger Williams and William Coddington's purchase of Aquidneck Island from Narragansett Indians 1637–38; also Pettaquamscutt land purchase from Narragansett Sachems Kachanaquant and Quequaquenuet by settlers Wilbor, Hull, Porter, Wilson, and Mumford 1657–58. Trail leads uphill to rock, approximately 10-minute walk.

M. Hannah Robinson Tower and Rock. Rtes. 1 and 138. Open all year. No fee. Wooden tower overlooks countryside and Narragansett Bay. Tradition tells of Hannah Robinson, beautiful daughter of wealthy Quaker plantation owner, who eloped with French dancing teacher against family's wishes; deserted by husband, she became fatally ill; while being brought home by forgiving father, asked to stop here where she played as a child to see the familiar view before she died.

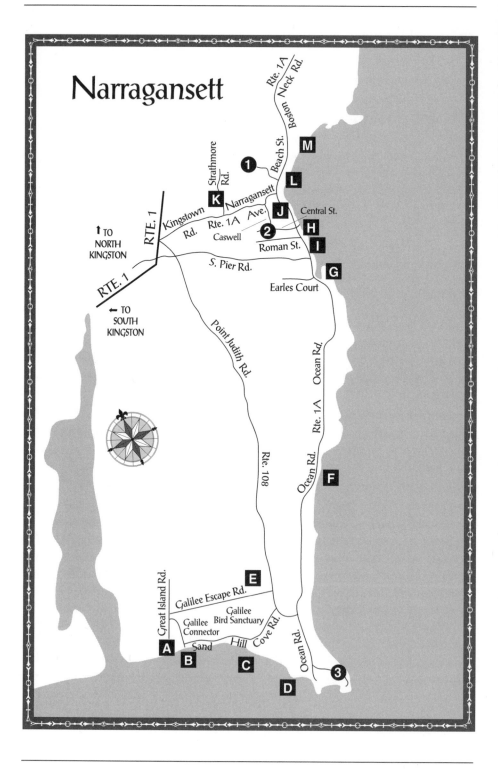

Narragansett

NARRAGANSETT

An elegant resort center flourished here from the 1870s until about 1920. Drawn to beautiful beaches and lush woods, the sophisticated elite arrived in the prosperous years of industrial and commercial expansion following the Civil War. Rhode Island Civil War governor and U.S. Senator William Sprague and his celebrated wife, Kate Chase, built "Canonchet Mansion" and were followed by others who created large estates and about a dozen grand hotels. Narragansett Casino covered almost a square block. In 1900 fire destroyed all but the Towers of the Casino, and by 1920 most hotels and summer estates had succumbed to fire or removal. The wishing well, South Pier at Ocean Road, is a reminder of Green Inn, last of the grand hotels, burned in the 1980s.

But this was not the first occupation of Narragansett by the wealthy. In the eighteenth century the "Narragansett Planters," with extensive land holdings, developed a rich pastoral economy that supplied exports to the West Indies and other markets. The American Revolution and a declining economy later wiped them out, leaving few traces from this earlier important period. Now the popular resort community is a successful combination of turn-of-the-century elegance, modern homes, rental housing, and many beautiful sandy beaches with easy access.

1. SOUTH COUNTY MUSEUM AND CANONCHET FARM. Off Rte. 1A across from Narragansett Town Beach Pavilion. Open extended season, fee. Gift shop, working print shop, lectures, historic skills workshops.

You drive through parts of 174-acre Canonchet Farm, once the manor of fun-loving Governor then Senator William Sprague and his wife, Kate Chase Sprague, who later died in poverty. Ruins—a tall stone foundation with heavy granite lintels and stone arches—were once the carriage house, all that remains from the legendary estate. The museum appears to be part of a village from the past. It is like a large country store or barn, with alcoves of special exhibitions where you're invited to touch, pick up, learn how it works. The arrangement of items, tools, instruments, maps, diagrams, and labels creates an excellent self-guided tour. Historically accurate exhibits include Country Kitchen, General Store, Cobbler's Shop, Narragansett Cheese, Maritime and Fishing, Child's Bedroom, Toys of Yesteryear, Textiles, Gentleman's Study, Growing a Crop, and Vehicles, including fire engines, milk wagon, mail wagon, and a horse-drawn hearse. The focus of the museum is to keep alive two centuries of historic heritage, handcrafted technology, and everyday life of a Rhode Island village.

2. ST. PETER'S-BY-THE-SEA, *c. 1870.* Central and Caswell sts. Open all year for services, mornings, and by appointment; no fee.

Granite blocks and buttresses, bell tower with anchors as symbolic door hinges, and seventeen treasured stained glass windows, some with molded and fluted textures, distinguish this elegant Episcopal church. The congregation grew from a group gathered by Joseph Dulles, whose great-grandson became secretary of state. The first church was built in 1869 but destroyed by a storm less than a year later. Only the cross remained standing. The next day the church trustees resolved to build this stone church. One of the Tiffany stained glass windows is a memorial to summer resident Varina Jefferson Davis, daughter of Confederacy President Jefferson Davis. Florence Brevoort Kane, noted sculptress and member of the congregation, created a bronze statue of Christ and two bas-relief memorials. The 1879 pipe organ still operates by bellows in this beautiful sanctuary.

3. POINT JUDITH LIGHTHOUSE, *1816,* NHS. 1460 Ocean Rd. (Rte. 1A). Grounds open all year, no fee.

The windswept point seems a world apart, nearly surrounded by waters of Block Island Sound and the open Atlantic. Sails and powerboats dot the horizon. The Block Island ferry heads toward the breakwater marking the entrance to Point Judith Pond and safe harbor at the working fishing village of Galilee. Many ships have been wrecked off Point Judith—giving it the name "Cape Hatteras of New England"—including *Normandy* in 1864, *American Eagle* in 1870, and *Swallow* in 1900. During the Revolution, a tower beacon stood here. In 1810 the first light was established by William Ellery, a signer of the Declaration of Independence. For years tower watchmen logged every boat, to the smallest sail. During World War II rescuers aided a boat torpedoed 4 miles off the point. Today the 51-foot brown-capped lighthouse continues to guide mariners.

BEACHES, PARKS, OTHER POINTS OF INTEREST

A. **Village of Galilee.** Great Island Rd. Open all year. No fee. One of few remaining active fishing villages; commercial fishing boats line wharves; plenty of fresh fish for sale; ferry to Block Island, sightseeing boats, charters.

B. **Galilee Beach (or Salty Brine State Beach).** Galilee Connector and Sand Hill Cove Rd. Open all year. Fee. Lifeguards, rest rooms; named in honor of broadcaster and Good Samaritan Salty Brine. Nearby **Galilee Bird Sanctuary,** bounded by Galilee Connector and Galilee Escape Road.

C. **Captain Roger W. Wheeler Beach (or Sand Hill Cove Beach).** Sand Hill Cove Rd. Open all year. Fee. Lifeguards, bathhouses, concessions; picnicking, swimming.

D. **East Breakwater.** End Ocean Rd. Open all year. No fee. Fishing.

E. Fishermen's Memorial State Park. Point Judith Rd. and Galilee Escape Rd. Open all year. Fee. Camping.

F. Scarborough State Beach. Ocean Rd. Open all year. Fee. Lifeguards, bathhouses, concessions, gift shop, gazebos, observation deck, large open sandy beach; picnicking.

G. State Pier. Ocean Rd. near Earles Ct., on South Pier Rd. (sign says Pier 5). Open all year. No fee. Boat launch; fishing.

H. The Towers. 1883, NRHP. Ocean Rd. between Central and Roman sts. **Chamber of Commerce Information Center.** Open all year. No fee. Remaining part of Narragansett Pier Casino, designed by McKim, Mead and White; Westerly granite blocks topped by conical roofs; parallel pair of stone arches with curved towers at ends, linked by long gallery room above; spans Ocean Road. Louis Sherry, New York caterer, was steward superintendent at height of Casino's fashionable popularity; after mortgagee sale he ran Casino until September 12, 1900 fire.

I. The Coast Guard House, built as North Pier Life Saving Station, 1888, NRHP. 40 Ocean Rd. Open all year as restaurant. Romanesque rock-faced granite, unusual arched windows, designed by McKim, Mead and White.

J. Canonchet Memorial. Green between Towers and Narragansett Beach. Open all year. No fee. Statue honors Tribal Chief Canonchet of the Narragansetts; 6,000-pound limestone sculpture by Robert K. Carsten, 1977; concert gazebo, flagpole.

K. Narragansett Indian Monument. Kingstown Rd. and Strathmore Rd. Open all year. No fee. Carved from one Douglas fir by Peter Toth, 23-foot-tall head is one of forty-one in country honoring Indians; deep expression and experience mark Indian's face.

L. Narragansett Town Beach. Beach St. across from entrance to #1. Open all year. Fee. Lifeguards, bathhouses, concessions; popular large open sandy beach with room for all; swimming.

M. Canonchet Club Beach. Town beach, also called Narragansett Pier Beach Club or North Pavilion. Beach St. north of L. Open all year. Fee. Lifeguards, concessions, pavilion; swimming.

BLOCK ISLAND

(Ferries run to the island year-round or seasonally, depending upon point of departure. See Old Harbor, below, for more information.)

Stepping ashore on Block Island, you shed the outside world. Peaceful surroundings ease tensions and open your mind to the excitement and vitality of island breezes, endless ocean views, warm sands, inviting waters (including 365 freshwater ponds), and intriguing marshlands and moors. Wander this unspoiled island. Victorian hotels built in the late 1800s still greet summer visitors. In spite of updating and new additions, they transport you back into that earlier period of gracious living.

First discovered by Giovanni da Verrazano in 1524, the island was explored by Dutch navigator Adrian Block, who charted it as Adriaen's Eylandt, in 1614. Soon colonists from Massachusetts settled on the secluded isle, becoming farmers, fishermen, and shipbuilders. In 1672 the island became a chartered town called New Shoreham, now better known as Block Island. During the Revolution the Battle of Block Island took place nearby when a British frigate defeated five Continental ships a little after midnight on April 6, 1776. Block Island was the perfect hideaway for privateers, smugglers, and deserters at different times in its history. The first harbor was at the foot of Dodge Street. By 1878, with the help of a breakwater built by the federal government, the area known as Old Harbor became the center of activity. Summer of 1875 saw the steamer *Canonicus* bring 10,000 passengers to Block Island to enjoy the healthy climate and scenic beauty, opening a new era of tourism and island economy. Today the island preserves its lifestyle, welcoming visitors to its unspoiled Victorian charm.

1. OLD HARBOR. Dodge and Water sts.

Ferries all year from Point Judith, R.I., and in summer from Providence, New London, and Newport; home to island's fishing fleet, breakwater built 1870–76, commercial center since 1700s, town of New Shoreham; shops, hotels, restaurants, bike and moped rentals; fishing.

2. BLOCK ISLAND HISTORICAL SOCIETY MUSEUM. Former Woonsocket House, Old Town Rd., Ocean Ave., and Corn Neck Rd. Open summer. Fee.

Ongoing and changing exhibits.

3. CLAYHEAD NATURE TRAIL, MAZE. Off Corn Neck Rd. Open all year. No fee.

Trails lead to northeastern shore through pine forests and bayberries, along scenic high bluffs of Clay Head to Settler's Rock (see 4) at Sandy Point; spectacular views.

4. SETTLER'S ROCK. Corn Neck Rd., Cow Cove. Open all year. No fee.

Marks landing place of first white settlers in 1661, purchased island for 400 pounds sterling; courageously landed on island with no natural harbor and inhabited by Narragansett Indians.

5. NORTH LIGHT, *1867*. Sandy Point, NRHP, Corn Neck Rd. Open summer. Fee.

Oldest island light, fourth on site; built to last of 18-inch Connecticut granite with Italianate-style masonry windows; light shone 13 miles at sea; abandoned 1970, replaced by automatic light 1972; acquired by town of New Shoreham 1984, restored, light rekindled 1989; interpretative maritime center; set in twenty-eight-acre wildlife and bird preserve; admittance to gull rookery in bordering dunes forbidden.

6. NEW HARBOR OR GREAT SALT POND. West Side Rd. Open all year. No fee.

Large protected harbor, created by the opening of a breach way in late 1890s; offers 1,400 acres of safe anchorage for boats of every size, docking for Montauk Ferry, marina, tourist facilities, boat rentals, quahog digging.

7. BLOCK ISLAND CEMETERY. West Side Rd.

Burial ground dating to seventeenth- and eighteenth-century settlers who turned this isolated island into a home.

8. GREENWAY. Old Mill Rd. Open all year. No fee.

Walking trails to historic places, unusual ecological habitats, ponds, fields, Enchanted Forest, Turnip Farm, Rodman's Hollow (see 9); island and ocean views, guided tours available.

9. RODMAN'S HOLLOW. Cooneymus Rd. Open all year. No fee.

Wildlife refuges; natural ravine from Glacier Age, paths meander near sea level, surprising ocean views; adjoins Black Rock acreage and R.I. Audubon Society's Lewis–Dickens Farm.

10. MOHEGAN BLUFFS. Mohegan Trail. Open all year. No fee.

Cliffs 200 feet high offer magnificent views of ocean and Southeast Light; dirt path and stairs lead to water's edge.

11. SOUTHEAST LIGHT, *1874*. Southeast Light Rd. Grounds open all year. Lighthouse restoration 1995. Exhibits open in summer. Fee when lighthouse open. Breathtaking views.

Sixty feet high, 201 feet above ocean, highest location for lighthouse in New England; gingerbread trim, 1875 French Fresnel lens seen 20 miles at sea until 1990, when temporary light replaced it; erosion precipitated moving lighthouse 245 feet to safety. Light relit August 27, 1994, fixed with first-order Fresnel lens.

BEACHES, PARKS, OTHER POINTS OF INTEREST

No fees for beaches, parking; surf fishing all around island.
Please do not climb on dunes; they are carefully preserved.

A. **Ballard's Beach.** Spring St., south of ferry dock, by Ballard's Restaurant. Sandy beaches; swimming.

B. **Esta Park.** Water St. Overlooks harbor; benches, views.

C. **Fred J. Benson Town Beach.** Corn Neck Rd. Sandy beach, lifeguards, bathhouse (fee); swimming.

D. **Crescent Beach Area.** Corn Neck Rd. Sandy, moderate surf; swimming.

E. **Charlestown Beach.** West Shore at Dead Man's Cove. Swimming.

F. **Black Rock Beach.** Black Rock Rd. Rhode Island's southernmost beach overlooking Atlantic; sand and stones, rough undertow, remote.

G. **Mohegan Bluffs Beach.** South shore beneath cliffs; rough surf; sand and boulders, steep stairs to beach, views, swimming.

NORTH KINGSTOWN
(SAUNDERSTOWN, WICKFORD)

T wo silver arrowheads face one another over red leopards on a field of silver. This is North Kingstown's coat of arms, derived from Richard Smith, first permanent settler and builder of Rhode Island's first plantation. In the early 1600s Indian Sachem Canonicus's village at Cocumscussoc bordered on what would become North Kingstown's largest village, Wickford. Here Canonicus's friend Roger Williams established a trading post near the Pequot Indian Trail, much of which is now Old Post Road. At the same time Richard Smith settled nearby. In 1651 Williams sold his trading post to Smith. Smith created this plantation—a prototype for large rural plantations, rivaling southern plantations and beginning a unique economic, agricultural, and social system that flourished until the Revolution.

Enterprising Lodowick Updike, Smith's grandson, surveyed, laid out, and sold lots in "Updike's Newtown" about 1709. The community was later named Wickford for Wickford, England, birthplace of Connecticut Governor John Winthrop's wife, Elizabeth. An active coastal trade kept docks bustling and ship-yards racing to turn out much-needed vessels in the first half of the 1800s. Then, as in other coastal towns, the age of steam slowed trade, quieted docks, and brought the Wickford economy to a low ebb. In the late 1800s docks came alive again, this time with summer visitors, tourists, and artists. Today, thanks to preservation and local pride, Wickford is a treasury of eighteenth- and nineteenth-century homes, many built by Updike descendants.

1. GILBERT STUART BIRTHPLACE AND SNUFF MILL, *1750*,
NRHP, NHL. 815 Gilbert Stuart Rd., Saunderstown. Open extended season, fee.

America's famous eighteenth-century portrait painter, Gilbert Stuart, was born here in 1755. From his room young Gilbert could hear the rhythmic sounds of the undershot waterwheel providing power for the family snuff mill. From this rural setting he went on to paint the wealthy and famous of two continents. While studying in England, Gilbert painted *The Skater*, which skyrocketed his career as a portraitist in England and Ireland. Returning to America in 1792, he painted portraits of such notables as John Adams, John Quincy Adams, Thomas Jefferson, James Madison, George Washington, Revolutionary war heroes, and wealthy statesmen. He is best known for his unfinished oval portrait of George Washington, as seen on the first U.S. postage stamp and on the one-dollar bill. Copies of Stuart's paintings adorn the walls of his birthplace.

Stuart's father, a Scottish immigrant, built this gambrel-roof, two-and-a-half–story building with living quarters above and New England's first snuff mill below. It is the

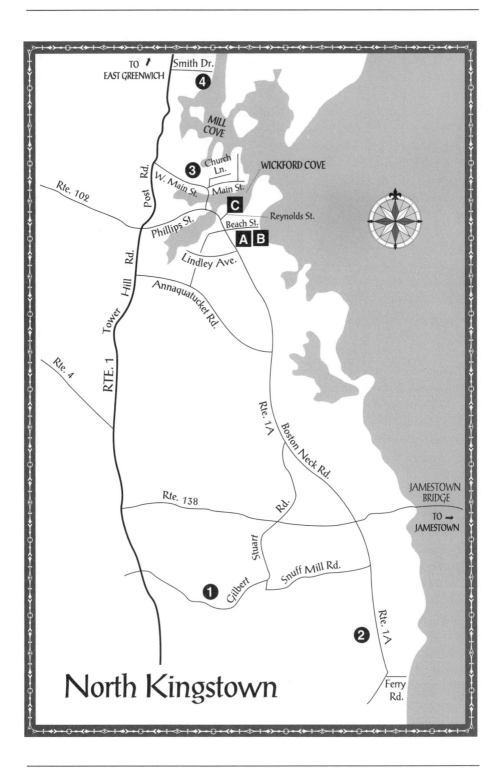

TO
EAST GREENWICH

Smith Dr.

4

MILL
COVE

WICKFORD COVE

Rte. 102

Post Rd.

W. Main St.

3

Church
Ln.

Main St.

Reynolds St.

C

Phillips St.

Beach St.

A **B**

Lindley Ave.

Tower Hill Rd.

RTE. 1

Rte. 4

Annaquatucket Rd.

Rte. 1A

Boston Neck Rd.

JAMESTOWN
BRIDGE

TO →
JAMESTOWN

Rte. 138

Stuart Rd.

1

Gilbert

Snuff Mill Rd.

2

Rte. 1A

Ferry
Rd.

North Kingstown

site of the first and last true water-powered snuff mill in America. The restored building combines furnishings of a working man's eighteenth-century home with memorabilia and machinery from the home/factory. The adjoining gristmill once ground corn for New England's favorite Johnny Cakes. The picturesque Mettatuxet River provides power as it has for nearly two and a half centuries.

2. SILAS CASEY FARM, *c. 1750*, NRHP, SPNEA. 2325 Boston Neck Rd. Open extended season, limited hours, fee. Tours of house, barnyard, and gardens.

This plantation, still a working farm, allows a glimpse into the world of eighteenth-century farming and its evolution to the present. Atop a picturesque hill, set off by century-old stone walls, the house overlooks Narragansett Bay and Jamestown Island. Daniel Coggeshall built the home, originally with five rooms around the central chimney. From the time his daughter and son-in-law Silas Casey inherited the farm until they donated it to SPNEA, this house was lived in by Casey descendants. Caseys were prosperous shipowners, gentlemen farmers, and statesmen who related closely to Newport both economically and culturally. Family furnishings can be found throughout the three rooms open to the public. Thomas Lincoln Casey was an engineer involved in building the Washington Monument and Library of Congress. His survey equipment is on display. The dining room features china from the 1700s and portraits of Casey generations. Paintings, documents, and furniture throughout speak of changing lifestyles of Casey descendants over 200 years. A bullet hole in the parlor door testifies to an encounter between sailors from British ships blockading Narragansett Bay and local Patriots during the Revolutionary War.

3. WICKFORD HISTORIC DISTRICT, NRHP. Tower Hill and Post rds. north to Mill Cove, south to Lindley Ave. Homes private.

Walk the area to enjoy an interesting variety of eighteenth- and nineteenth-century Colonial, Georgian, and Federal homes as well as Victorian summer homes, many named and dated. On Main Street alone there are fifteen houses built in the 1700s. **Cyrus Northrop's 1803 House** at 90 Main is typical of early 1800s, showing an interesting pedimented fanlight over the front door. **St. Paul's Episcopal Church,** 1847, NRHP, oversees the historic street at 76 Main. The Romanesque Revival–style frame church features a three-story clock tower with open arched belfry and sky-reaching spire. The round arch motif is carried out in doorways, windows, and corbel trim. Inside are elegant stained glass windows.

A memorial flagstone walk "The Greeneway," leads from Main Street to **Old Narragansett Church,** 1707, NRHP, 60 Church Lane, open summer, no fee. This historic frame church building, moved here in 1800, is one of the oldest standing Anglican church buildings in North America. The exterior features rounded arched windows

Old Narragansett Church, North Kingstown   (Old Narragansett Church Committee)

and a broken segmented-arched pediment over the front door. Inside, box pews, wine-glass pulpit, reading desk, seventeenth-century altar, and slave galleries are in keeping with the Colonial setting. Surprisingly, altar and pulpit are on different sides of the church. Traditionally the altar in Anglican churches is on the east end. The church was built in the Puritan style, thus placing the pulpit opposite the main entrance. Climb the steps to see the antique self-contained organ built by renowned English organ builder Bernard Smith about 1660—the oldest church organ in use in the country. Tradition says it was built for Charles II of England. Smith used secondhand pipes dating to the 1590s. Rebuilt in 1680, the organ has been restored to that date. The first Sunday in August the church's precious gift of Queen Anne Communion silver is used. Lack of heat and electricity restrict services to summer months. Portraitist Gilbert Stuart was baptized here April 11, 1756.

4. SMITH'S CASTLE, *1678*, NRHP. Rte. 1. Open extended season, limited hours, ongoing restoration, no fee. Docents, lectures, films, gardens.

Last of the great Rhode Island plantation houses to survive, this is the only one still standing from which Roger Williams preached. Smith's Castle is a golden thread connecting the earliest days of Rhode Island with the present. Here you learn of plantation life and how its unique society affected the development of Rhode Island. In 1651, when Roger Williams went to England as a special envoy, friend Richard Smith bought his trading post. Smith's home became part trading post, part home, part stockade, and part inn known as Smith's Castle. Here using slave and native American labor, Smith raised breeding stock, dairy cows, sheep, and swine. His wife Joan's Cheshire cheese became so popular it started an industry of its own. Richard Smith, like Roger Williams, believed in religious freedom and opened his home to visiting preachers, giving them opportunity to express themselves.

During King Philip's War Indian prisoners were brought to the Castle, and colonial forces assembled here to organize the Great Swamp encounter. Indians retaliated by burning the Castle, then owned by Richard, Jr., in 1676. Two years later, using the old foundation and charred timbers, Richard rebuilt, continuing the prosperous plantation. When Richard, Jr., died childless in 1692, Smith's Castle passed to nephew Captain Lodowick Updike. During four generations of Updikes, the plantation flourished both socially and economically until Wilkins Updike's bank foreclosed and sold to Benjamin Congdon in 1812 to pay a debt of honor.

The house you visit today has been altered and added to. Different rooms speak of different centuries. On the left the 1600s room shows life during the time of Richard Smith, Jr., with wide floor boards, a charred corner post from the original house, open beams, and period furnishings. In the Updike Room, portraits of Updikes oversee the dining room with its painted paneling and Queen Anne and Hepplewhite furniture. About 1740 Daniel Updike made extensive changes, installing elegant wood paneling, enclosing corner posts and beams, and building a new staircase. He incorporated the rear lean-to kitchen into the house, using part of the original Richard Smith fireplace and mantel. The room over the lean-to was the scene of many parties, meetings, and celebrations, for this was a center for the local aristocracy.

BEACHES, PARKS, OTHER POINTS OF INTEREST

A. Beachwood House. End Beech St. Wickford. Senior center, gift shop. Part of Updike farm 1600s–1800s; Dyer family home 1872–1921; summer home R.I. Governor Elisha Dyer 1897–1900; inn 1921–68.

B. Wickford Art Association Gallery. Beech St., next to Beechwood House. Open all year, limited hours. Donation.

C. Town Hall, 1888, NRHP. Reynolds St. and Boston Neck Rd. (Rte. 1A). Open all year. No fee. Richardsonian Romanesque.

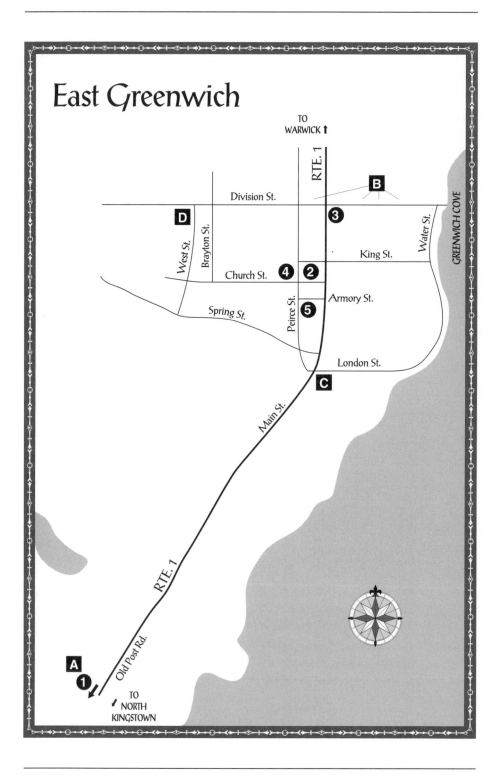

East Greenwich

EAST GREENWICH

Situated on four hills, East Greenwich looks out over Greenwich Bay. The settlement was incorporated in 1677 and named for Greenwich, England. Early land grants were given to grantees in appreciation of services in King Philip's War. During the Revolutionary War determined settlers defended their homeland, building Fort Daniel and organizing the Kentish Guards under James M. Varnum and Nathanael Greene. Following the war fishing thrived, and sea captains and merchants were involved in trade with many foreign ports. Warehouses lined the shore north of King Street, active docks kept coopers, riggers, and carpenters busy. Small factories and mills added to the life of the busy seaport. By 1750 East Greenwich was the county seat and for a time one of the five rotating capitals of Rhode Island. In 1790, here was one of the first calico block-printing shops in the United States. Embargoes of the early 1800s brought change. Cotton mills developed along Hunts River, and a bleachery was established at the south end of town on the Mascachaug River, creating the town's textile industry. Today East Greenwich looks to the sea as a popular yachting center.

1. NEW ENGLAND MUSEUM OF WIRELESS AND STEAM, *1964*,
NRHP. Rte. 1, west on Frenchtown Rd., left on Tillinghast Rd., shortly on left.
Open summer, limited hours and by appointment, fee. Reference library.

This unusual museum was established to preserve and illustrate the engineering history of steam engines and wireless communication. It is an ideal place for radio or steam engine enthusiasts. Inside the Steam Building are stationary steam engines of all sizes, powers, and shapes. Many are running, showing the excitement and efficiency of steam. Ten engines were made in Rhode Island, one by George Corliss of Providence, at one time the largest manufacturer of stationary steam engines. There is an engine made by the boat-building Herreshoffs and a Sears Roebuck 1899 engine listed for $250 in their catalog. Engines are powered by boilers ranging from modern oil-fired models to earlier donkey-type boilers.

The Wireless Building has an outstanding collection of wireless receivers and transmitters, both commercial and domestic. Their technical progression can be followed from crystal sets through vacuum tubes, from about 1900 to 1950. Here you see Marconi's equipment from the turn of the century, crystal receivers, pre-1920 spark transmitters, and radios by early manufacturers: Atwater Kent, Crosley, Federal, Grebe, and Magnavox. There are the first eight models of RCA, a consortium created in 1919 by Owen D. Young of General Electric along with AT&T, Westinghouse, and others. Here is an 1884 Paul Nipkow type of mechanical scanning disc and a 1934 scanning wheel TV set—forerunners of modern television. There are displays relating to Karl F. Braun, Amos Emerson Dolbear, Thomas A. Edison, Edwin Armstrong, Reginald A. Fessenden, and Guglielmo Marconi. The Massie System of Wireless Telegraph Station building once located at Point Judith, Narragansett, is on the grounds. Its second floor is just as it was when an active wireless station in 1907.

Each fall the museum sponsors "Yankee Steam-Up," when private collectors show and explain their engineering classics.

2. KENT COUNTY COURTHOUSE, *1803*, NRHP. 127 Main St. Open all year, tours by appointment, no fee.

The courthouse is Georgian in style, with balustraded roof framing a square clock tower topped by a cupola. It is on the site of an earlier 1750 building where Rhode Island's General Assembly enacted a charter to form Rhode Island College (Brown University) March 2, 1764. On June 12, 1775 they voted to charter and arm two sloops to protect trade. Abraham Whipple was appointed commander, creating the first colonial navy. The present building was erected in 1803. Remodeled in 1909, the interior houses a beautifully designed courtroom with delicate crenellated molding around the elevated judge's bench and rope molding ornamenting wainscoting and witness stand. The semivaulted ceiling and broken pediment with finial over the doorway add to the grandeur of the room.

3. VARNUM MEMORIAL ARMORY AND MILITARY MUSEUM, *1914*. Main and Division sts. Open all year by appointment, no fee.

The medieval-looking fortress was built in memory of General James M. Varnum by the Varnum Continentals to perpetuate customs and traditions of the Revolutionary War and to encourage patriotism. It houses a working armory on the main floor with a military museum on the lower level. Here are uniforms, weapons, and armaments from Revolutionary days through the Vietnam action days to the present.

4. GENERAL JAMES MITCHELL VARNUM HOUSE MUSEUM, *1773*, NRHP. 57 Peirce St. Open summer and by appointment, fee.

A scenic location and an elegant home created the perfect setting for General Varnum and his wife, Martha Child of Warren, Rhode Island. James Varnum was in the first graduating class of Rhode Island College (Brown University) in 1769. He was admitted to the bar in 1771 and settled here in East Greenwich. Drawn to the military in 1774, he became the first commander of the Kentish Guards and by 1777 a distinguished Continental brigadier general. He fought with honor at the battles of Boston, Long Island, White Plains, Rhode Island, and Valley Forge. Varnum's eight-room home was a meeting place during the war, where he met with Generals Lafayette, Rochambeau, Greene,

Sullivan, and Washington. After the war Varnum became a member of the Society of the Cincinnati and the Continental Congress. He pleaded the historic legal case, Trevett v. Weeden, the first time a legislative act was declared unconstitutional. At age forty, when a director of the Ohio Company of the Northwest Territory and a federal judge, Varnum moved west and helped to found Marietta, Ohio. There he died in 1789.

Today the dentiled late Georgian mansion invites you into its carefully restored interior. The dining room is the most elegant room. Notice the dentiled molding and broken pediment over the fireplace, which was copied by architect Stanford White. Large Chinese temple vases were gifts from the Sultan of Muscat to a local ship captain for shipping Arabian horses to Queen Victoria. Across the hall is the drawing room, with 1797 mahogany pianoforte and Chinese sewing table. The red-paneled library is furnished as Varnum's office. There is an unusual c. 1750 English reading chair and the walnut wing chair of Governor William Greene, Sr. The Colonial kitchen displays a huge fireplace and period furnishings set against the warm patina of old paneling.

On the second floor is the master bedroom with biblical Delft fireplace tiles and a Sheraton writing desk with ivory eagle escutcheons, symbolic of the Society of the Cincinnati. In a bedroom used by Lafayette hangs a rare picture of Napoleon given by Lafayette to General Varnum. The meeting room displays a Lafayette bowl and General Varnum memorabilia. Outside, lovely grounds provide a setting reminiscent of the gardens of Monet.

5. ARMORY OF THE KENTISH GUARDS, *1842*, NRHP. Armory and Peirce sts. Open all year by appointment, no fee.

This Greek Revival building with hobnail doors and shutters holds memorabilia of the famous Kentish Guards, active during the Revolutionary War. This proud voluntary militia was formed in 1774 by fifty-six citizens, with James M. Varnum first commander and General Nathanael Greene, Washington's second in command, a charter member. Fifth oldest chartered military company in the country, it is unusual in that it was incorporated as an independent company subject only to the Rhode Island governor. The guards served with honor in the Revolution (building Fort Daniel, which overlooked the harbor) and in the War of 1812, the 1842 Dorr War, and the Civil War. Members have served in every war through Vietnam.

BEACHES, PARKS, OTHER POINTS OF INTEREST

A. **Frenchtown Park.** Frenchtown Rd. off Rte. 1, access opposite elementary school. Open all year. No fee. Park of 140 acres, trails, pond, remains of 1812 stone mill known as Tillinghast's factory; picnicking, fishing.

B. **Historic District,** NRHP. Division, Peirce, and London sts. and Greenwich Cove, Main St. Once Pequot Indian trail.

C. Colonel Micah Whitmarsh House, 1767, NRHP. 294 Main St. Open as offices. First brick house in town; Whitmarsh, colonel of Kentish Guards, served at Valley Forge and Battle of Rhode Island.

D. Windmill Cottage. 1818, NRHP. 144 Division St. Private. Bought in 1866 by Henry Wadsworth Longfellow as gift for his friend Professor George Washington Greene, grandson of General Nathanael Greene; the c. 1790 octagonal windmill was moved in 1870 and placed on the west side of the cottage to serve as a study for Professor Greene.

WARWICK

Warwick was founded by one of New England's most colorful colonists, Samuel Gorton. He left England for religious and civic freedom, arriving in Boston in 1636. Within two years he was banished from Plymouth for daring to oppose magistrates who censured his maidservant for smiling in church. Then he was asked to leave Portsmouth for quarreling with authorities. Next, he was refused freemanship in Roger Williams's Providence, the epitome of tolerance. He left Providence after participating in a bloody street riot and arrived in Pawtuxet, Rhode Island, where inhabitants panicked and applied to Massachusetts for protection. Gorton and a small group of followers settled in January 1645 on land they had purchased two years before—an area that was to become Warwick. Meanwhile, Pawtuxet settlers induced Indians to revoke Gorton's purchase of land and enlisted Massachusetts Bay Colony to oppose his settlement. The summer of 1645, three commissioners and forty men came from Boston to arrest Gorton and six others. They confiscated livestock and forced remaining Gortonites to leave. Gorton was judged guilty of blasphemy, which was punishable by death, but months later he was released from prison and banished. Gorton went to England to get protection from Massachusetts and returned with Robert Earl of Warwick's guaranty in 1648. Relative peace reigned after his return until King Philip's War in 1675, when settlers left and their homes were destroyed.

Development of mills—fulling, grist, saw—evolved into textile mills, beginning with Job Greene's cotton mill in 1794, four years after Samuel Salter's first mill in Pawtucket. Warwick is still a city of villages, which emerged from the many mill villages. Thirty-nine miles of coastline provide space for many boats and marinas as well as successful inland industries.

1. PAWTUXET VILLAGE HISTORIC DISTRICT. Post Rd. Buildings private.

Though demolished during King Philip's War, Pawtuxet rose again and was a busy seaport by the Revolution, with thirty registered boats busy in the triangular trade. The historic center is now a seaside village of seventeenth- to twentieth-century homes in their waterfront summer resort setting. **Christopher Rhodes House** (c. 1800, NRHP, 25 Post Road, private, "a" on map) is a fine example. It was home to Christopher Rhodes, successful cotton manufacturer, organizer of Weybosset Bank, militia brigadier general, and member of Rhode Island General Assembly. The delicately carved pedimented center entrance with fanlight is the focus of this early Federal.

Gaspee Point (NRHP, off Narragansett, residents only in summer, no fee, "b" on

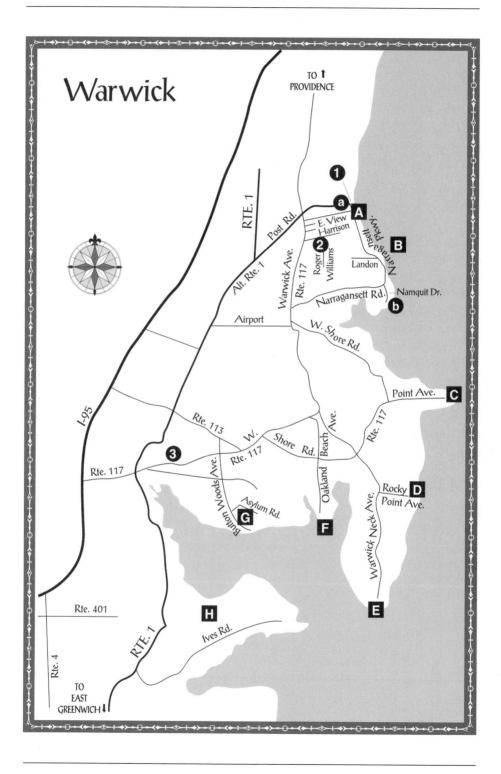

Warwick

map) is a sandy point of land on Narragansett Bay. Off shore, on June 9, 1772, one of the first overt acts of the Revolution occurred. The British ship *Gaspee,* enforcer of hated trade laws, ran aground here early in the morning. At Sabin Tavern in Providence, John Brown met with a group to plot her destruction. After midnight Captain Abraham Whipple led fifty men in eight longboats to this point. They surprised the crew, put them ashore, and set fire to the schooner. Patriots cheered the news, and all King George III's investigations and promised rewards drew no information or arrests. Now the event is celebrated every year for several days in late May or early June.

2. JOHN WATERMAN ARNOLD HOUSE, NRHP, HS. 11 Roger Williams Ave. Open limited hours and by appointment, no fee.

The Arnolds of this land go back to the town's very founding, when William and wife Christian Arnold moved here from Providence about 1638 to settle their 10,000 acres of land along the Pawtuxet River. Their son Benedict became the colony's first governor, also great-grandfather to traitor Benedict Arnold. Another son, Simon, was father to Israel, who farmed this section in the next century. Here Arnolds lived until early 1900s.

The farmhouse is late eighteenth century, typical of rural homes of the time, a basic Colonial with added ell. The interior has paneling in the dining room, wide plank floors, simple mantels, and period furnishings. The Count Rumford fireplace, a smaller fireplace built into a larger one, using the space between to retain heat, is one of two in Rhode Island. Precious objects remain from the family's long heritage—a plate that belonged to Peregrine White, Samuel Gorton's soup tureen, an early-1700s William and Mary chest of drawers from the Arnold family.

3. WARWICK MUSEUM, Kentish Artillery Armory, *1912*, NRHP. 3259 Post Rd. (Rte. 117). Open all year, no fee. Lectures, slides, tours, classes.

The focus is on visual arts and Rhode Island's cultural heritage. Known and emerging artists' works are displayed in changing exhibitions which also include objects from other collections. The museum's home is the Kentish Artillery Armory, red brick with projecting corner towers and parapets with battlements. The Kentish Light Infantry was organized in 1797 and continued here as the Kentish Artillery until the 1970s. Located in the heart of Apponaug Village, the armory is near the 1835 **Warwick City Hall** (NRHP), a red brick of varying courses with imposing clock tower. Both were designed by William Walker and Son.

BEACHES, PARKS, OTHER POINTS OF INTEREST

A. **Pawtuxet Park.** East View St. off Narragansett Pkwy. Open all year. No fee. Small beach, scenic green on water, boat launch, benches, water views; picnicking. **Narragansett Parkway** offers water views along coastal section of road.

B. Salter's Grove. Narragansett Pkwy. at Landon Rd. Open all year. No fee. Boat launch, small playground, view south to Gaspee Point and beach; fishing, hunting.

C. Conimicut Point Park. Point Ave. off Rte. 117. Open all year. Fee. Concessions, expansive beach, views, peaceful setting.

D. Rocky Point Amusement Park, c. 1915. Rocky Point Ave. Open summer. Fee. Large amusement park, carousel, shore dinners, beach.

E. Warwick Neck Lighthouse. End of Warwick Neck Ave. Exterior view only. No fee.

F. Oakland Beach Park. Oakland Beach Ave. Open all year. Fee. concessions, large beach on Greenwich Bay.

G. Warwick City Park. Asylum Rd. Open all year. Fee. Lifeguards, rest rooms, swings, boat dock. concessions, bike path, nature trails; 170 acres of woods, sand dunes, beach; picnicking, swimming.

H. Goddard State Park. Ives Rd. Open all year. Fee in summer. Huge, beautifully maintained park of 489 acres on Greenwich Bay. Cited as "the finest example of private forestry in America," woodlands grew from tree-planting project begun with Henry Russell's planting acorns in 1874; continued by Colonel Goddard, whose family gave this land to the state in his memory. Golf course, saltwater beach, bridal path and rings, fields, performing arts center in restored carousel building, naturalist program; bathhouse, concessions, boat ramp, picnic tables, fireplaces, shelter, gazebo, lifeguards; golf, swimming, hiking, cross-country skiing, ice skating.

PROVIDENCE

The name "Cornerstone State" is aptly applied to Rhode Island. Here in the 1600s were articulated ideals that would become cornerstones of this country—true democracy, separation of church and state, freedom of religion and conscience, and the right to elect political leaders, with heads of families having equal votes regardless of size of land ownership or religious beliefs. Radical principles, yes, but here were planted the seeds of our democracy.

Two names stand out in Providence history, Williams and Brown. The first gave it life and a vision, the second growth and prosperity. Roger Williams, born in London about 1603, studied law and theology at Cambridge. Disagreeing with Church of England teachings, he and his wife, Mary, sailed for the New World, settling in Boston. He was distressed by Puritans who did not grant to others the religious freedom for which they themselves had left England, and he was outspoken about British land grants versus Indian sovereignty. Thus, he was encouraged to leave Boston. He tried Salem and Plymouth but was still unable to live in harmony with both local leaders and his conscience. Williams was brought to trial in Boston in 1635. Found guilty for holding new and dangerous opinions, he was banished to England. Escaping across a frozen wilderness in midwinter, he and a few followers settled near the Moshassuck River and founded Providence Plantation, "gift of God," in 1636.

Seven years later Williams went to England to secure a charter for Providence and Newport on Aquidneck Island, then called Rhode Island; thus came the legal name of "Rhode Island and Providence Plantations." Williams died in 1683, leaving a legacy of free thinking, equal opportunity, and individual integrity. He was a true champion of democracy.

The Brown family has been prominent in Providence since Chad Brown was minister of the Baptist Church in the 1600s. Succeeding generations were Baptist ministers until merchant Nicholas and brothers John, Joseph, and Moses created the family firm of Nicholas Brown and Company. The activities of this company ran the gamut from manufacture of spermaceti candles to Far Eastern trade—all profitable ventures.

In addition to possessing business acuity, the Browns shared their talents and money with Providence. Joseph designed some of the city's most beautiful homes, including the famous John Brown House. John, one of the wealthiest merchants and manufacturers in Providence, initiated trade between China and Providence. He named three of his ships for George Washington, built Washington Bridge, and was great-grandfather of Nathanael and John Brown Herreshoff (see Bristol 6). Moses, a Quaker, gave land, and his son gave the money to establish the Moses

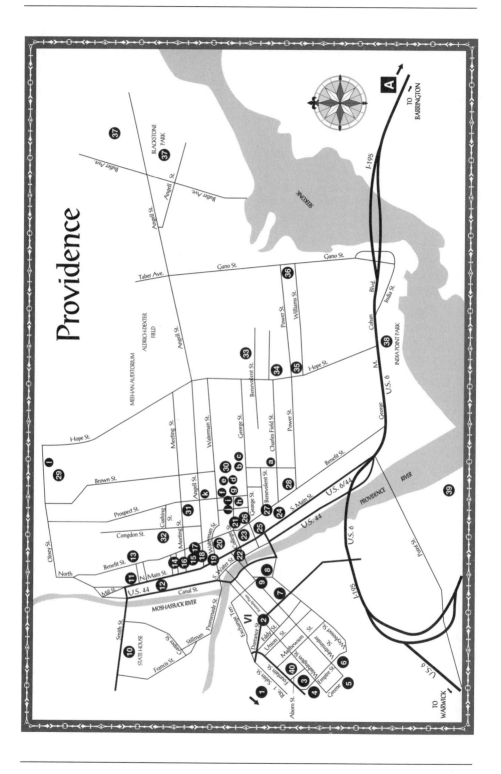

Providence

Brown Friend's School. Nicholas, Jr., gave so much support to Rhode Island College that it was renamed Brown University in his honor.

Over the years Providence went from farming to a maritime community. Merchants went from trading with Europe and the West Indies in the "triangle trade," through privateering, to trade with the East Indies and China. They brought wealth and rare and beautiful goods from the Far East. During the Revolution Providence was well protected by forts and by its location on Narragansett Bay. Following the war Providence prospered on the open seas until the War of 1812, after which the city turned inland to factories and mills. Textile, tool, silver, and jewelry manufacturing brought many immigrant workers, who added their traditions to the heritage of Providence. Today this is a city of historic architecture, ethnic variety, economic expansion, social awareness, and great pride in its heritage.

1. ROGER WILLIAMS PARK, *1880–1905,* NRHP. Off Rte. 1, entrance Elmwood Ave. or Park Ave. Open all year. No fee.

One of most beautiful municipal parks in country, 430 acres with 140 acres of ponds and lakes, began with gift of 102-acre family farm willed to city by **Betsy Williams,** great-great-great-granddaughter of Roger Williams; her **1773 home,** NRHP, with period furnishings, open summer; original park section designed 1878 by Horace S. W. Cleveland of Chicago. **Dalrymple Boat House,** 1895; Queen Anne building houses park office, warming area for ice skating, boat rentals. Colonial Revival **Casino,** 1897, houses special events. **Benedict Temple to Music,** 1924, is Greek temple theater for performing arts at base of natural amphitheater near Cunliff Lake; as many as 15,000 attended performances at turn of century. **Charles H. Smith Greenhouse and Hartman Gardens** have plants on display and for sale. **Bandstand** picturesquely situated in lake behind casino offers summer concerts. **Carousel Village,** fee, family entertainment area, has refreshments, carousel, train ride. **Pony Rides,** summer, fee. **Park Museum of Natural History and Planetarium,** fee, in elegant replica French chateau, dramatically lit at night; beautiful and meaningful ceiling and wall murals greet you in the impressive central hall; exhibits center on natural history, natural resources, and North American and Pacific cultures; five-year rotation of exhibits such as seasons of Narragansett Bay Worlds, from smallest plant and animal species to overview of the bay; gift shop, lectures, special events, films. **Cormack Planetarium** seats sixty in domed theater; changing programs of the heavens explored through electronics; astrology week. **Zoo,** fee; on thirty-six acres, stresses conservation, education, and enjoyment for everyone; Elephant Pavilion, Tropical America indoor free-flight aviary reproducing a neotropical rain forest, endangered species exhibits and breeding, black-footed penguins, International Farm, Sea-Lion Pool, African Plains Exhibit; four acres of natural wetlands with trails, 1893 Menagerie Center, gift shop and cafe. Extensive collection of bronze statues throughout park.

2. KENNEDY PLAZA, CITY HALL PARK, AND CITY HALL,
1874–78, NRHP, NHL, NHS. Dorrance St. Open all year. No fee.

City Hall, impressive Second Empire style similar to Louvre in France, designed by Samuel F. J. Thayer; interior boasts elegant marble staircase, brass and fine woodwork; visit **Council Chamber,** beautiful interior, and **Aldermen's Chamber,** dramatic gold stars against blue sky ceiling. **Kennedy Plaza and City Hall Park,** 1892, includes **General Ambrose Burnside Equestrian Statue,** 1887; **Carrie Brown Bajnotti Memorial Fountain,** 1901, cast by Gorham Silver Company; **Soldiers and Sailors Monument,** 1871; **Major Henry H. Young Memorial,** 1911. **Union Station,** Exchange Terrace, 1898: Beaux arts–style buildings created dramatic railway entrance, once used by 300 trains a day. **Greater Providence Convention and Visitors Bureau,** 30 Exchange Terrace, tourist information.

3. LEDERER THEATER, *1917*, NRHP. 197–203 Washington St. Open as theater.

Home of Trinity Square Repertory Company; built as movie palace, Majestic Theater, with fancy beaux-arts design: white terra-cotta and brick–sheathed facade with green and gold accents, paneled and balustraded parapet; inside, second-level gallery provides view of stained glass rotunda.

4. PROVIDENCE PUBLIC LIBRARY, *1900*, NRHP. 225 Washington St. Open all year. No fee.

American Renaissance style; massive thirteen-bay facade; collections of Irish and Italian culture, slavery, ship models, whaling, printing, architecture, Civil War.

5. CATHEDRAL OF SAINTS PETER AND PAUL, *c. 1889*. Greene and Westminster sts.

Gothic Revival style by Patrick C. Keeley; dramatic massive structure in sandstone ashlar, cruciform design with elegant rose windows, square crenellated towers; Cassavant organ, 6,330 pipes from 6 inches to 32 feet; on site of first Roman Catholic church in Providence.

6. BENEFICENT CONGREGATIONAL "ROUNDTOP" CHURCH, *1809*, NRHP, 300 Weybosset St.

Original design brought from Dublin, Ireland, by Reverend James "Paddy" Wilson; built by Barnard Eddy and John Newman; remodeled 1836 in Greek Revival style by James C. Bucklin, who added four-column Doric portico with frieze to original brick-faced stone building, gilded and enlarged dome, added classical cupola fashioned after monument to Lysicrates, Athens; gallery has two-level Ionic columns; church's presence in 1809 encouraged residential growth in this part of city.

7. ARCADE BUILDING, *1828*, NRHP, NHL. 65 Weybosset and 130 Westminster sts. Open all year as shops.

Greek Revival, massive Ionic-columned porticos made of stone and glass; Weybosset facade designed by Russell Warren, Westminster facade by James C. Bucklin. First indoor shopping mall in country; skylighted three levels of open shops connected by cast iron–railed balconies with picturesque lamp posts, gable roof.

8. UNITED STATES CUSTOM HOUSE, *1855–57*, NRHP. 24 Weybosset St. External view only.

Second customhouse in Providence, replaced 1790 one on Water St.; reminiscent of city's early maritime prominence. Italian Renaissance Revival, rusticated stone, cupola atop metal dome, central entrance and windows enclosed within five molded arches; designed by Ammi B. Young, first supervising architect of U.S. Treasury; was also post office and district court; named for Congressman John E. Fogarty; notice interesting contrasts of varied architecture in the area.

9. TURKS HEAD BUILDING, *1913*. Westminster and Weybosset sts. External view only.

Building shaped to fit street intersection; "Turk's head" relief on facade, symbol of nineteenth-century store that had ship's figurehead in Turk's head form.

10. RHODE ISLAND STATE HOUSE, *1895*, NRHP. 82–90 Smith St. Open all year. No fee. Tours.

Designed by Charles P. McKim of McKim, Mead and White; late Renaissance Revival with beaux-arts classicism, modeled after U.S. Capitol; one of five self-supporting domes in world, first in country, second in size only to St. Peter's Basilica, Rome; 235 feet above ground, dome stands on colonnaded drum surrounded by four smaller cupolas; side wings bring length to 333 feet. Faced with white Georgian marble, north side has arcaded porte cochere and south side arcade is topped by two-story loggia; atop dome overlooking the city stands 11-foot gold leaf bronze statue created by George T. Brewster and cast by Gorham representing **Independent Man,** symbolizing Rhode Island's determination to allow freedom of thought, conscience, and religion (smallest state, but greatest freedom).

Inside, columned House of Representatives decorated with magnificent needlepoint tapestries of Greek and Roman scenes; in green and gold Senate Chamber thirteen original states' seals border curved ceiling, eagles support clock over columned podium; Royal Charter of 1663 and Gaspee Commission exhibited at Senate entrance; elaborate Governor's Reception room boasts portrait of George Washington by Rhode Island–born Gilbert Stuart, a moon sample, 4,205-troy-ounce Gorham silver service presented in 1905 to USS *Rhode Island* by people of Rhode Island; magnificent State

Rhode Island State House, Providence   (Alex Tavares)

Library, carved wood and gold leaf ceiling bordered by sixteen printers' marks; 149 feet above the rotunda floor is 50-foot mural designed by James A. King, painted by Giorgio DeFelice, depicts historic Rhode Island events; hallways display paintings of governors and political leaders; famous Civil War Gettysburg cannon at entranceway.

11. CATHEDRAL CHURCH OF ST. JOHN, *1811*, NRHP, NHL, NHS.
271 North Main St. Open all year, no fee.

Design by John Holden Greene illustrates change in church architecture, adding Gothic Revival elements to Georgian style; replaced 1722 King's Chapel used since founding of Episcopal church in Providence; name changed to St. John after Revolution; became cathedral 1929; 62-foot dome ceiling holds Waterford chandelier with golden umbrella reflector; seventeenth-century altar believed from Durham Cathedral, England; seventeenth-century William and Mary chair; sanctuary entered through elegant oak screen, carvings from Bluecoat School, London; library; gravestones date from 1700s.

12. ROGER WILLIAMS NATIONAL MEMORIAL, *1965*, NRHP. North
Main St. Open all year, no fee.

Visitor center, 4½-acre national park commemorates Williams and site where he first settled; land given in memory of Isaac Hahn, first Jewish citizen elected to office in

Providence; Hahn Memorial marks site of spring used by Williams, designated in 1721 for public use in perpetuity. Visitor center exhibits relate to Williams's life, plantation, and belief that all should have freedom of conscience; Williams statue, waysides, slide show.

13. BENEFIT STREET, *1750s.* **College Hill. Houses private.**

Originally Back Street, dirt way running behind houses to family graveyards, orchards, and gardens; later straightened and improved, thus "benefiting" citizens by relieving congestion on parallel Towne Street (South and North Main streets). Benefit Street now lined with more than 100 preserved, restored, and dated historic buildings, known as "Mile of History"; varying architectural styles parallel city's growth and history from mid-1700s to late 1800s, one of best groupings of Colonial homes in country. South Benefit Street relates to early prosperous seaport era. **John Reynolds House,** 1783–92, 88 Benefit, was home of poetess Sarah Helen Whitman, courted by Edgar Allan Poe for four years; she broke engagement one month before he died, was immortalized in Poe's poem, "To Helen"; also birthplace of Jabez Gorham, founder of Gorham Silver Company, whose home was at 56 Benefit Street. **Sullivan Dorr House,** 1809, 109 Benefit, ornate grand Federal mansion designed by John Holden Greene, is fine example of wealthy merchant's home in early 1800s; Sullivan made fortune as consul in China; son Thomas Wilson Dorr led 1842 Dorr Rebellion seeking suffrage for nonlandowners.

14. OLD STATE HOUSE/SIXTH DISTRICT COURTHOUSE, *1762,* **NRHP, NHL. 150 Benefit St. Open all year, no fee.**

Seat of colonial government and social life; State House until 1900. Washington and Lafayette entertained here; Rhode Island's General Assembly renounced allegiance to King George III here May 4, 1776—two months before formal Declaration; 1783 Assembly repealed restricted voting rights of Roman Catholics; 1784 Assembly passed act starting emancipation of slaves. Brick Georgian-style building once overlooked salt marsh cove filled in about 1890s; on North Main Street side two-story tower entrance topped with clock added 1851; interior updated 1906 to Sixth District Court; former council chamber only room to retain original appearance; today houses Rhode Island Historical Preservation Commission and Heritage Commission.

15. SHAKESPEARE'S HEAD, *1772,* NRHP. **21 Meeting St. Open all year as Preservation Society headquarters.**

Built by John Carter, printer who apprenticed under Benjamin Franklin; Carter ran bookshop here "at the sign of Shakespeare's head"; post office when Carter appointed postmaster by Franklin; in 1762 William Goddard and mother, Sarah, began *The Provi-*

dence Gazette and Country Journal, town's first newspaper, which Sarah ran; center of activity during Revolution. Taped cassette and guided neighborhood tours.

16. BRICK SCHOOL HOUSE, *1769,* NRHP. 24 Meeting St. Open through Providence Preservation Society; Georgian style.

First brick school in Providence. One of first free schools in country; stored ammunition during Revolution; housed Brown University classes before college was built and during Revolution; early school for black children, open-air school, later school for handicapped children.

17. PROVIDENCE MARINE CORPS ARTILLERY/STATE ARSENAL, *1839,* NRHP. 176 Benefit St. Open all year, limited hours.

Designed by Russell Warren; Gothic Revival, crenellated battlement towers, metal window shutters, arched entrance with hobnailed door; housed troops and ammunition during Dorr Rebellion; early state arsenal; Civil War paintings.

18. PROVIDENCE ART CLUB, *1789.* 10 Thomas St. Open all year by appointment.

Built by Seril Dodge, sold to Avis Brown, widow of Nicholas Brown; in 1906 original delicately detailed Federal parlor mantel removed, used in several different homes, found by Brown descendant, returned here in 1990 to its rightful place. Attached building at 11 Thomas Street, 1791, art gallery open for exhibits, no fee; also built by Seril Dodge; he and brother, Nehemiah, were silversmiths beginning vital Providence industry; Jabez Gorham apprenticed under Dodge; became art club in 1880, second oldest in country.

19. FIRST BAPTIST MEETING HOUSE, *1775.* NRHP, NHL. 75 North Main St.

Oldest Baptist Society in America, oldest of any denomination in state, founded 1638 by Roger Williams. Third building on site; designed in Georgian tradition by Joseph Brown; five-tier 185-foot steeple designed after James Gibbs's St. Martin's-in-the-Fields Church, London, from Gibbs's book of architecture; arched window design throughout, Palladian window over entrance, rusticated wooden quoins; inside, 1792 Waterford crystal chandelier, three-sided gallery supported by Ionic columns; Brown University commencements held here.

20. MUSEUM OF ART, Rhode Island School of Design, *1926.* 224 Benefit St. Open all year, fee.

Outstanding small museum, exhibits classical art, Oriental prints and textiles; huge tenth-century Japanese Buddha; nineteenth- and twentieth-century American, British, and French art; medieval to modern art, costume collection; lectures, concerts, films. **Pendleton House,** 1904–06, copy of museum benefactor Charles Leonard Pendleton's home, contains American furniture from 1700s and silver, china, paintings, and decorative art from Pendleton's lifelong collection.

21. PROVIDENCE ATHENAEUM, *1836.* 251 Benefit St. Open all year. No fee.

Center of early literary and intellectual life of city; society founded 1831, merged with Providence Library Company dating to 1753, thus one of oldest libraries in country; houses rare and valuable books; Edgar Allan Poe and sweetheart Sarah Whitman often met in library stacks. Granite Greek Revival building, Doric columns, original wrought iron fence; design influenced by four different architects.

22. MARKET HOUSE, *1775,* NRHP. South Main St. Rhode Island School of Design classrooms.

Area originally crossroads for Wampanoag and Pequot Indian trails; brick building designed by Joseph Brown and Stephen Hopkins was on edge of Providence River (now filled in) facing drawbridge; sheltered city's first marketplace, two stories with first-floor open arched arcade, now windowed in; shops and warehouses were on riverbank, laden wagons brought wares; center of civic and commercial life and resistance meetings during Revolution, plaque tells of tea burning in Market Square March 2, 1775; housed French troops during Revolution. Local government until City Hall built 1878; in 1797 St. John's Lodge of Masons added third floor, first masonic hall in Rhode Island; east end projection designed by James C. Bucklin added 1833. Plaque tells of 1815 storm with 11-foot-plus tides; 1938 storm saw 13-foot-plus tides and 95-mph winds.

23. PROVIDENCE COUNTY COURT HOUSE, *1930–33.* 250 Benefit St. Open all year. No fee.

Superior and supreme court of Rhode Island; on site of James Brown's c. 1722 waterfront shop and distillery; Georgian Revival style, imposing nine-story complex of granite and limestone, central 250-foot clock tower.

24. JOSEPH BROWN HOUSE, *1774.* 50 South Main St. Private.

Home of prominent Providence architect, designer of brother John Brown's house and Baptist Church. Considered signature house of Providence; unusual roofline, balustrade, and ogee gable showing curved dentiled pediment. Original entrance was on second-floor level, stairs descended to lawn running to river's edge; legend says French soldier rode his horse up the steps to the entrance, but horse would not descend and was led through house and out garden door; Providence Bank founded by John and Moses Brown occupied building 1791–1916; earlier, site of Field Garrison House where Roger Williams watched Providence burn in 1676 during King Philip's War.

25. STEPHEN HOPKINS HOUSE, *1707*, NRHP, NHL. 15 Hopkins St.
Open extended season, limited hours. No fee.

Home of Stephen Hopkins from 1742 to 1785, nine-term colonial governor, signer of Declaration of Independence, Continental Congress delegate, Rhode Island superior court chief justice, founder of Providence Library Company and *Providence Gazette and County Journal;* instrumental in bringing Brown University to Providence and its first chancellor. Bought original building, now rear ell, in 1743, added two-story front section; originally built on corner of Hopkins and South Main, moved here 1927. A Quaker, Hopkins preferred simple unadorned surroundings; home has Colonial and Georgian elements; interior restored to Hopkins era has shell cupboard, unusual mantels; Colonial garden; Washington slept here. Headquarters of Colonial Dames of America in Rhode Island.

26. ATHENAEUM ROW/BROWN AND IVES BLOCK, *c. 1845*.
257–267 Benefit St.

Early Greek Revival row houses designed by Russell Warren, featuring Doric porticoes.

27. FIRST UNITARIAN CHURCH, *1816*, NRHP. Benefit and Benevolent
sts. Open all year, tour through sexton.

Architect John Holden Green's masterpiece; elegant Federal with Gothic elements modeled after Boston's New South Church, designed by Charles Bulfinch. Four-tier clock tower, lofty steeple; urn finials decorate exterior; second church building on site; has largest and heaviest bell cast by Paul Revere.

28. JOHN BROWN HOUSE, *1786–88*, NRHP, NHL, HS. 52 Power St.
Open extended season and by appointment. Fee.

John Brown one of most influential personages in Providence in 1700s; slave trader, privateer owner, patriot, philanthropist; owner of iron foundries, spermaceti candleworks, rum distilleries; began China trade from Providence; known for his resistance and leadership in burning British customs schooner *Gaspee* in 1772 (marker South Main and Planet streets); conducted business from grand Georgian-style home high above the city, starting trend to live away from business area.

One of most elegant houses in country, it reflects Brown's prestige and power in post-Revolutionary era; last house designed by brother, Joseph Brown, with construction overseen by John's son James; three-story sandstone and brick, projecting central block with pediment against balustraded roof, recessed Palladian window above columned portico; majestic interior, fourteen rooms, copies of French wallpapers, exquisitely carved woodwork; elaborate moldings, fireplaces, and doorways; period furnishings include Brown family pieces; two gracious rooms off central hall for entertaining. Brown hosted George Washington and Thomas Jefferson August 19, 1790; John Quincy Adams felt it most magnificent home he had seen; John Brown's daughter Salley Brown Herreshoff was last Brown to live here.

29. COLLEGE HILL HISTORIC DISTRICT, *c. 1730–1880*, NRHP, NHL.
Olney St., Cohan Blvd., Hope St., and Providence River.

High, prominent location, area originally settled by Roger Williams; 300 intact eighteenth- and early nineteenth-century buildings, one of largest collection in country; mainly residential; Brown University and Rhode Island School of Design.

30. BROWN UNIVERSITY, *1764*. College, Prospect, Waterman, and Brown sts. Founded as Rhode Island College, seventh oldest in country; came to Providence 1770, named in 1804 for Nicholas Brown, Jr. Tours through Corliss–Brackett House, 45 Prospect St.

Annmary Brown Memorial ("a" on map), 1903–07. 17 Brown St. Open all year by appointment, no fee. Neo-Renaissance style; General Rush C. Hawkins and Annmary Brown Hawkins buried in crypt; center for Renaissance studies, European and American paintings.

John Carter Brown Library (b), 1904. George and Brown sts. Open all year, no fee. John Carter Brown was son of Nicholas Brown and grandson of John Carter (see **15**). Rare books, superb Americana collection, map collection 1477–mid-1800s; Indiana limestone, beaux-arts style, classical gem.

Dr. Samuel Gridley Howe Memorial Flagpole (c). Near George St. gate. Mast from C. Oliver Iselin's yacht; base gift of American Hellenic Educational Progressive Association. Howe was chief surgeon in Greek War of Independence 1820–29, founder of Perkins Institute for the Blind, husband of Julia Ward Howe, who wrote "Battle Hymn of the Republic."

University Hall (d), 1770, NRHP, NHL. Prospect St. at College St. Administrative offices; oldest building at Brown, designed to resemble Princeton's Old Nassau Hall; during Revolution military barracks and hospital; four-story Georgian-style brick, bell cupola.

Manning Hall (e), 1834. Prospect St. Open all year. Greek Revival with Doric columns, designed by Russell Warren; replica of Diana-Propylaea Temple at Eleusis; named for James Manning, first president and at one time only faculty member; gift of Nicholas Brown, Jr.; chapel and library until 1878, when Robinson Hall became library; today chapel on second floor.

Carrie Tower (f), 1904. Corner Prospect and Waterman sts. Erected in memory of Carrie Brown Bajnotti; 95-foot clock tower of ornate stone and brickwork.

Van Wickle Gates (g), 1901. Given by Augustus Van Wickle (see Bristol 7), ornate iron gates to College Green open twice a year, in fall for first day of classes and spring for commencement.

John D. Rockefeller Jr., Library (h), 1964. 10 Prospect St. Open all year. Fee. Main university library, houses more than two million volumes. Special government documents section open all year, no fee.

John Hay Library (i), 1908–10. 20 Prospect St. Open all year. No fee. Built by Andrew Carnegie for friend John Milton Hay, assistant private secretary to Lincoln, secretary of state under presidents McKinley and Theodore Roosevelt. American Renaissance style; houses university's special collections: Webster Knight Stamp Collection containing uncanceled blocks of U.S. postage stamps from first issued in 1847; Charles Woodberry McLellan Lincoln Collection; Harris Collection of American Poetry and Plays; Anne S. K. Brown Military Collections.

List Art Building (j), 1971. 64 College St. Open school year. No fee. Brown University art departments; designed by Philip Johnson; triangular jags of roofline with skylights add dramatic modernity to college hill skyline; **David Winton Bell Gallery,** major historical and contemporary art.

Corliss–Brackett House (k), 1875–82, NRHP. 45 Prospect St. Open all year as administrative offices; college tours. Nineteenth-century large high Victorian Italianate villa, brick and sandstone with four-story corner tower; elegantly carved woodwork of South American walnut and mahogany. Designed by inventor George Corliss as his home; here he brought Bermuda to Rhode Island to help ailing wife; he designed an early thermostatically controlled heating and cooling system that kept air temperature constant within one degree; also devised hydraulic elevator; invented Corliss Steam Engine. House later owned by screen playwright Charles Brackett, who wrote *Sunset Boulevard.*

Ladd Observatory (l), 1891. 210 Doyle Ave. off Hope St. Open summer, limited hours. No fee. Telescope, lectures.

31. WOODS–GERRY MANSION, *1860,* NRHP. 62 Prospect St. Open all year as Rhode Island School of Design administrative offices and art gallery. No fee.

RISD one of most prestigious art schools in country, founded 1877; building grand Italianate of brick and sandstone courses, bay, arcaded porte cochere, French windows to terrace; largest house of its period on highest point in city; designed by Richard Upjohn of New York for Dr. Marshall Woods; later home of U.S. Senator Peter Gerry; site of Revolutionary War alarm beacon atop an 85-foot mast to warn militia of British. Gardens have contemporary sculptures.

32. PROSPECT TERRACE. Congdon St.

Park with extensive views of city's varied and fascinating skyline; Roger Williams Memorial Monument, in which he is entombed, erected 1939.

33. NELSON WILMARTH ALDRICH HOUSE, *1822*, HS. 110 Benevolent St. Open all year as museum. Fee.

Changing exhibits; Federal house designed by John Holden Greene; later home of Nelson W. Aldrich, Rhode Island's U.S. senator under McKinley, T. R. Roosevelt, William Taft; Aldrich-Vreeland Banking Act and Aldrich Plan formed basis for Federal Reserve System; daughter Abby married John D. Rockefeller; son Winthrop Aldrich, U.S. ambassador and uncle of Vice President Nelson Rockefeller, also lived here. Headquarters of Rhode Island Historical Society.

34. GOVERNOR HENRY LIPPITT HOUSE, *c. 1863*, NRHP, NHL. 199 Hope St. Open extended season and by appointment. Fee.

Lippitt was Rhode Island governor 1875–76; Renaissance Revival, denticulated medallion cornice, projecting central entrance with pediment and Corinthian-columned semielliptical porch, entablature with foliate frieze; second-level pedimented tripartite window; porte cochere; beautiful wood and marble work, wall and ceiling stenciling, ornate chandeliers.

35. LIBRARY OF THE RHODE ISLAND HISTORICAL SOCIETY, *1822*. 121 Hope St. Open all year. No fee.

One of oldest in country: Rhode Island–related histories, documents, genealogies, books, newspapers, microfilm; largest collection of pre-1800 Rhode Island imprints; manuscripts 1642 to present; personal papers of Roger Williams and Moses Brown; photos, paintings, collections relating to Rhode Island business, women's labor history; twentieth-century collections.

36. ROGER WILLIAMS LANDING PLACE MONUMENT, NRHP, Gano St. between Power and Williams sts.

Williams first stepped ashore here in 1636; passive park.

37. BLACKSTONE PARK. Angell St. Open all year. No fee.

Narragansett Boat Club, oldest rowing club, founded c. 1851; river grove.

38. INDIA POINT PARK. India St. Open all year. No fee.

Here John Brown had piers in eighteenth century from which he traded with China and East Indies; at low tide hull of wrecked ship is visible. Today city park; information center, nautical museum, harbor views, playground.

39. FOX POINT HURRICANE BARRIER, *1961*. Near mouth of Providence River. Barrier protects 280 acres of low-lying Providence; closed when storms threaten. Tours during waterfront festival.

40. RHODE ISLAND BLACK HERITAGE SOCIETY. 46 Aborn St. (opposite Lederer Theater, #3). Open all year. No fee.

Museum relating to black history, culture, and art; library, changing exhibits.

OTHER POINTS OF INTEREST

A. **Crescent Park Carousel,** 1895, NRHP, NHS, NHL. I-195 exit 44, Route 103 to end of Bullocks' Point Ave., East Providence. Open extended season. Fee; Sixty-six different moving figures carved by Charles I. D. Looff, hand-carved moving figures on an A. Ruth and Sohn neo-Baroque band organ; 1985 State Symbol of Folk Art.

BARRINGTON

B arrington has a long, patchwork-quilted past. Wampanoag Indians were here when Plymouth Colony established a trading post on the west side of Barrington River in 1632. Three decades later, Reverend John Myles and others left Rehoboth because of their Baptist faith. They established the first white settlement here in what would become Barrington, named for Lord Barrington, an advocate of religious tolerance. By 1685 Plymouth allowed "rights of conscience," legally permitting the already established Baptist church, which local Congregationalists also supported. In 1692 Massachusetts Bay Colony took over Plymouth Colony, and once again only Congregational churches were publicly supported. The Baptist church endured, however, obeying the letter though not the spirit of the law.

The town had a unique political organization, with settlers divided into three socioeconomic classes. An incident in 1681, when five persons and their heirs were named permanently to the highest class, precipitated the abolition of this undemocratic plan. At different times Barrington was part of towns in both Massachusetts and Rhode Island; twice it became a separate town, and it gained final independence in 1770.

Shipbuilding, fishing, and agriculture made up the early economic base. In 1898 railroad connections brought people to build country homes and estates on quiet winding roads along scenic coastline and coves and among rolling fields, lakes, and forests. Brickmaking, agriculture, and shellfishing industries were strong in the early 1900s. Boatyards and marinas are important today for repair, storage, and mooring of pleasure craft and commercial fishing boats.

1. HAINES MEMORIAL PARK. Washington Rd. and Narragansett Ave. Open all year, fee for picnic tables and fields. Boat dock.

This pleasant state park along the Providence River has plenty of parking to let you enjoy boating, fishing, picnicking, and access to **East Bay Bicycle Path,** the well-developed 14.5-mile path that extends from Providence to Bristol.

2. BELTON COURT, *1905–06,* NRHP. Middle Hwy. at Primrose Hill. Open all year as Zion Bible Institute, drive through, no fee.

Originally a private home built by Frederick S. Peck, this imposing mansion later became the campus of Barrington College and is now part of Zion Bible Institute. The granite rubble mansion has a gable roof, wraparound porch, and rear porte cochere.

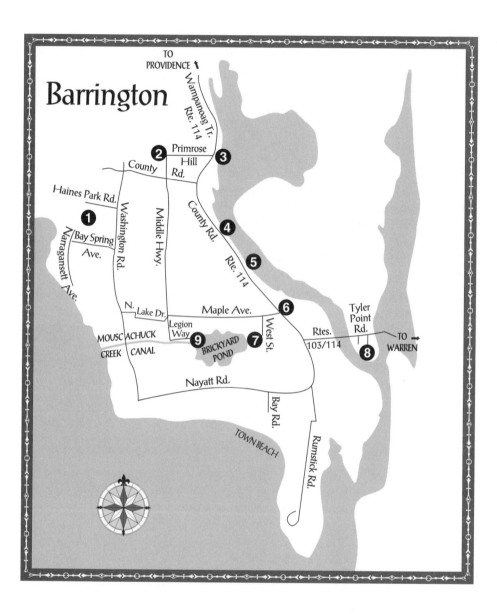

In 1918 the crenellated corner tower and ballroom were added to complete the eclectic romantic architecture of Belton Court.

3. OSAMEQUIN NATURE TRAILS AND BIRD SANCTUARY,
Wampanoag Tr. (Rte. 114). Open all year, no fee.

Within these forty-two acres of tidal wetlands and uplands, marked nature trails wander through varied coastal plant and animal habitats. You can look across Hundred Acre Cove, the estuary of Barrington River, and appreciate Rhode Island's cleanest and most extensive inland estuarine system.

4. WALKERS FARM. County Rd (Rte. 114). Open all year, no fee. Parking, pier, boat launch, family farm plots to rent, fishing.

Boating, fishing, and peaceful relaxing are available on thirty acres of open land in this scenic setting on Hundred Acre Cove.

5. BARRINGTON CONGREGATIONAL CHURCH, *1806.* **461 County Rd.**

A pleasant setting on Barrington River is the background for this historic church. The Congregationalists' first meetinghouse, in which they met with the Baptists, was burned in King Philip's War. In 1710 they built their own church. It is believed timbers of the building were carried upriver over ice to this site. A beautiful stained glass window is centered over the simply framed front door, with steeple and belfry above.

6. BARRINGTON CIVIC CENTER, NRHP; Town Hall, *1888;* Library, *1917.* 283 County Rd. Open all year, no fee.

The English Tudor Town Hall of stone and half-timbers, complete with steep gable roof and corner turrets in Romanesque style, commands the hill. It was designed by Stone, Carpenter, and Willson. The stones of the first story are memorial stones contributed by farmers and others of the community. The Library was founded in 1806 as Barrington Library Society and originally didn't allow fiction. It was reorganized as Barrington Public Library in 1880. The **Barrington Preservation Society Museum** is open limited hours and by appointment. The **Peck Center Playground,** behind the parking lot, a remarkable modern playground for children under twelve, is full of mazes, slides, swings, with handicapped access.

7. VETERANS MEMORIAL PARK. West St. Open all year, permit for grills, no fee. Fields, rest rooms, picnic tables, East Bay Bicycle Path access. Parking within park.

There is plenty of room within the 245-acre town park to fish, walk paths through woods and fields, or picnic under trees on the bank of Brickyard Pond.

8. TYLER POINT CEMETERY. **Tyler Point Rd.**

Ancient stones stand on sheltered point between the Barrington and Warren rivers. The first marked grave dates to 1702. This small cemetery for the earlier Baptist church is said to contain the unmarked grave of Reverend John Myles. On some stones you can find unusual motifs, one a portrait.

9. MOUSCACHUCK CANAL. **Legion Way. Open all year, no fee.**

A path through woods follows the canal to Brickyard Pond. The canal was a horse canal for the former brickyards. It was used to transport high-quality finished bricks to Narragansett Bay, where they were loaded onto ships and carried all over the world. The last brickyard closed in 1948.

Barrington Town Hall, Barrington (Barrington Preservation Society)

WARREN

Warren's[11] deep river channel helped shape its history, beginning with Wampanoag Indians who lived on the river in their village of Sowams. In 1621 Pilgrims Edward Winslow and Stephen Hopkins visited Chief Massasoit at his headquarters here. They brought gifts for the chief—a laced red coat and a copper chain. Two years later Winslow saved the chief's life when he restored him to health. Their friendship grew. After Massasoit died in 1661, however, the harmony he and Plymouth had established was tested. There were misunderstandings when Indians hunted on and used land they had "sold" to Plymouth. The chief's eldest son, Wamsutta, was arrested as a suspect in a planned revolt and died on the way home. His brother Metacom, known as Philip, vowed to exterminate all whites. King Philip's War lasted fourteen months, ending with Philip's death in 1676.

In the early 1800s, molasses, sugar, and coffee were traded with the southern colonies and West Indies, especially Cuba. In 1820 Warren's first whaler, the *Rosalie*, left harbor, and in 1865 the last Warren whaler was destroyed by a Confederate ship in the Civil War. Meanwhile the first cotton mill began in 1847, and by the 1860s textiles dominated. Oystering was a major commercial success; the industry began in the 1880s with small oyster-shucking houses and developed with the addition of oyster seedbeds and eventually large packing houses. The 1938 hurricane effectively ended that industry, leaving one oyster house, today remodeled as the Wharf Tavern. Now oysters are brought to Warren for processing.

Some clipper ships were built here. Several went into the tea trade with China and the 1849–50 Gold Rush in California. Luther Blout, builder of more than 280 vessels, now builds excursion boats and ferries for use throughout the world. Warren shipbuilders built homes with particular skill, and many of their houses survive today. Trim gambrel cottages with tiny dormers; Colonials with central chimneys; Georgians, Federals, and Greek Revivals of more prosperous times; Victorians—all provide architectural variety and interest.

1. WARREN'S WATERFRONT HISTORIC DISTRICT. Water and Main sts. Open all year, no fee.

You can walk through 350 years of history, through the growth of a New England seaport and whaling center to the textile era and beyond. Many buildings have been restored; others are being revived. All listed here are private except where noted. **James Barton House** ("a" on map), c. 1848, 37 Liberty Street, is an early Victorian with Greek Revival elements at doorway and corners. James Barton and three brothers were Warren sea captains. James founded the *Warren Gazette* and in 1867, a man ahead of his

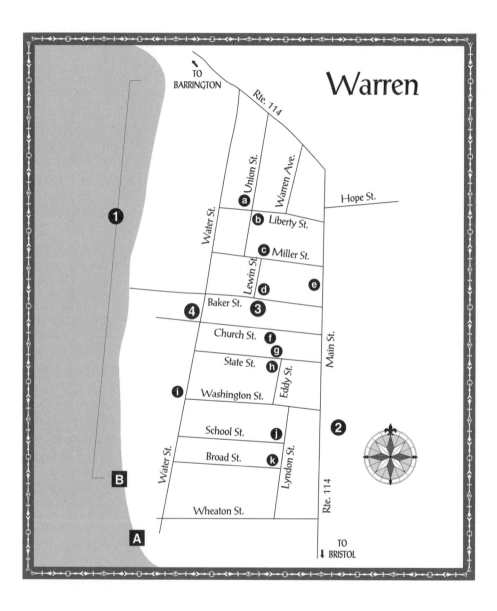

time, hired women as compositors. **John R. Wheaton House** (b), 1833, 90 Union Street, is Greek Revival with three tiers of parapets. The top two feature closed panels alternating with openwork Chippendale-style panels. The house, built for successful merchant and councilman Wheaton, was possibly designed by Russell Warren.

Miller–Abbot House (c), 1789, 1802 addition, 33 Miller Street, was built for Nathan Miller, Revolutionary War hero. In 1847 the Abbot family bought it. Commodore Joel Abbot was Admiral Matthew C. Perry's second in command when they opened the door to Western trade with Japan in 1853. **Masonic Temple** (d), 1796, Baker and Lewin streets, is open by appointment. This Federal has elaborate woodwork typical of Warren—hand-carved quoins and a modillion band repeated in pediments over doors framed by Ionic capitals atop fluted pilasters. The second floor was constructed with timbers from British ships sunk in Newport harbor. This, the state's second-oldest Masonic temple, was once the town hall and, in 1803, Warren Academy.

Warren Baptist Church (e), 1844, NRHP, Main at Miller Street, is a Gothic designed by Russell Warren, king of Greek Revival. Stately in stone, the church has lancet windows and arched front door. The tower was demolished and rebuilt in 1855 by Rhode Island architect Thomas A. Tefft. The original tower bell was Paul Revere's thirteenth bell, recast in 1906. The 1767 parsonage was home of Rhode Island College (later Brown University). The Baptists chose this location for the college because Rhode Island represented religious freedom. The first commencement took place in 1769 in the first Baptist meetinghouse, built 1764. Sadly, both buildings were burned by the British May 25, 1778. Pastor Charles Thompson, valedictorian of that first graduating class, was captured the same day.

United Methodist Church (f), 1844, NRHP, Church Street, is Greek Revival with huge fluted Doric columns and full-height pilasters. The multilevel Georgian tower and steeple are 130 feet tall. Within, box pews are original. The swan's-neck pediment was a later addition. One of the oldest Methodist churches in New England, this is an important town landmark. The **Parsonage,** 1858, NRHP, 27 Church Street, is Italianate style. **Warren Commons** (g) was laid out before the church it faces. Here whaling ships filled water casks at the town pump. There are rock gardens and memorials to veterans and firemen. **Eddy-Cutler House** (h), 1806, 30 State Street, is a grand Federal with a Palladian window over the Victorian portico. It was built by Benjamin Eddy, a sea captain in West Indies trade. It was later owned by Charles Cutler, shipmaster, who made three whaling voyages to the Indian Ocean. He was also a mill owner and was lieutenant governor of Rhode Island in 1872.

Robert Carr House (i), c. 1787, 317 Water Street, is Georgian. Here Captain Caleb Carr kept a tavern. He operated a ferry to Barrington and built the *MacDonough,* which served in the War of 1812, and the *Chippewa,* sloop of war for Commodore Oliver Hazard Perry. **Peleg Rogers House** (j), c. 1765, NRHP, 15 Lyndon Street, a Colonial, is now the rectory of St. Mark's. **St. Mark's Episcopal Church** (k), 1830,

NRHP, Lyndon at Broad, is Greek Revival designed by Russell Warren. The broad portico is supported by massive fluted columns and has egg-and-dart molding, unusual canted enframement of front doors, shiplap facade, and stained glass windows.

2. GEORGE HAIL LIBRARY, *1889*, NRHP, 530 Main St. Open all year, no fee.

The library seems like a Gothic castle with Romanesque stone and rounded arches; the interior is Victorian with stained glass and prominent beams. This building and the Town Hall were designed by the architectural firm William Walker. The library grew from the 1871 Warren Public Reading Room Association. Upstairs, **Charles W. Greene Museum** is open all year, limited hours, no fee. The focus of the museum is the collection of relics from a Warren Indian burial grounds exploration in 1913. Featured also are ethnology, fire buckets, ship logs, and maritime documents.

3. FIREMEN'S MUSEUM, *1846*, NRHP, 38 Baker St. Open all year by appointment.

Fire Station Number Three was originally home to "Little Button," a hand engine of solid cherry that won fame in stream-throwing contests. Now center stage in the station museum is "Little Hero," the town's first fire engine, an 1802 hand tub. Also displayed in a glass case are silver megaphones, lanterns, and other fire fighting memorabilia.

4. SAMUEL MAXWELL HOUSE, *1753*, NRHP, Massasoit HS. 59 Church St. Open summer, limited hours, appointment, fee.

Samuel and his wife Hannah Maxwell bought the land to build a meetinghouse. He preached in his home until 1764, when Baptists erected their own meetinghouse. Son James Maxwell was born in Warren in 1752, was captured during the Revolution, survived imprisonment, and returned to become a leading citizen. He had two wives and thirteen children. For nine surviving daughters, he built homes as wedding presents, and five of these houses survive.

The Samuel Maxwell house is the oldest on the waterfront. The exterior has a steep gable roof, large central chimney, and ancient soft handmade bricks in Flemish bond. Inside, simple rooms with paneled fireplaces are furnished with period pieces. The herb garden flourishes. This is a working museum of the eighteenth century with demonstrations of crafts, fireplace and bake-oven cooking, and candle dipping.

BEACHES, PARKS, OTHER POINTS OF INTEREST

A. **Warren Town Beach.** Water St. Open all year. No fee. Parking for residents only in summer.

B. *The Bay Queen.* 461 Water St. Operates summer. Fee. Cruises of Narragansett Bay on 145-foot vessel.

BRISTOL

King Philip, Russell Warren, Ethel Barrymore, Samuel P. Colt, Nathanael Herreshoff, and the DeWolf family all left their marks in this town of architectural and scenic beauty. King Philip's War began at Mount Hope (Pokanoket Neck) in Bristol in 1675, and it was to Mount Hope that Philip retreated. Here he was killed August 12, 1676. The area around Mount Hope was one of the few places left to the Wampanoag Indians after Chief Massasoit sold land to the Plymouth Colony.

Settled in 1680 and possessing a deep harbor, Bristol became a flourishing commercial and maritime center. When Rhode Island entered the slave trade in the 1700s, Bristol ships took an active part. This was interrupted by the Revolution. October 7, 1775, the British frigate *Rose* bombarded Bristol, demanding supplies. Forty sheep were given as tribute; the British stole ninety more. Three years later, May 25, 1778, was an even darker day in Bristol history. Three hundred Continental soldiers, believing exaggerated estimates of British troops, deserted the town, leaving it to British troops who pillaged, burned, and took prisoners.

Determinedly Bristol rebuilt, reaching its peak commercially in the 1800s. The town added privateering and fur trading with the Northwest and China to its growing sources of wealth. Elegant homes were in demand, as was architectural genius Russell Warren, who designed many of the grand buildings. By the 1850s, however, some families had lost their fortunes, others moved west seeking greater opportunities, and the 1849 Gold Rush called others. Bristol's maritime economy declined. In later years her maritime fame revived with the building of famous Herreshoff sailing yachts and America's Cup defenders.

1. **COLT STATE PARK. Rte. 114 and Asylum Rd. Open all year, fee in summer. Outdoor chapel, gardens, magnificent views, rest rooms, bike and bridle trails, boat ramp, fishing, snowmobiling, picnicking, swimming at adjacent Bristol Town Beach, ferry to Prudence Island.**

Enter this beautifully landscaped park through an impressive marble gateway topped with bronze bulls sculpted in Paris in the likeness of two of Colonel Samuel P. Colt's prize bulls. The inscription, COLT FARM, PRIVATE PROPERTY, PUBLIC WELCOME, was Colt's way of sharing his beautiful 460 coastal acres in the early 1900s. He combined three farms, connecting them with a system of roads. The stone bridge over Mill Gut, once adorned with statues, remains as part of that roadway. Colt built a grand summer home (the Casino), guest cottages, a farmhouse, and barns. You can still see the stone barn, guarded by bronze lions, which housed his prize Jersey herd and elegant trophy room. Each summer his Jersey cows and Berkshire sows competed in county fairs. The

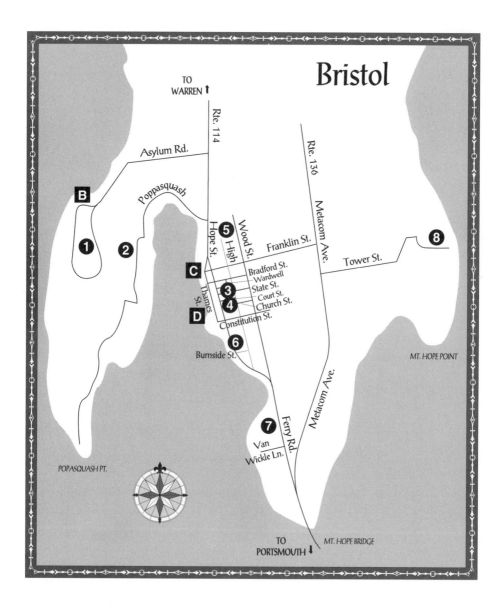

barn was so clean animals' reflections showed in shiny ceilings. Modern machinery was not allowed. Field work was done by Percheron draft horses, and produce raised was given to the employees.

Colt hosted gala parties here on his summer estate. When he died the Industrial Trust Company (Fleet Bank), which he founded (see 3), operated the farm. The state bought the property in 1965 and maintains its regional state park headquarters here.

2. COGGESHALL FARM MUSEUM, part of Colt State Park. Poppasquash Rd. Open all year, fee. Educational programs, craft demonstrations, harvest fair; produce, craft, and animal sales.

The Coggeshall Farm has been a working seacoast farm since 1680. Sheep and chickens wander the grounds as of old, greeting you with mild curiosity. Normal farm chores are done with tools and skills of the eighteenth century. Stepping back in time, you see an original 1700s farmhouse, replica blacksmith shop, barn, carriage house, sheep shed, weaving shed, and chick coop. Farm animals are similar to the original breed stocks of the eighteenth-century farmer. Herb and vegetable gardens, orchards, and hay fields are similar to original plantings. Chandler Coggeshall, who was born, lived, and farmed here, founded the University of Rhode Island's State Agricultural School.

3. LINDEN PLACE, *1810.* 500 Hope St. Open by appointment, fee. Tours, preservation, cultural and educational programs, conferences; Bristol Art Museum in 1906 ballroom, Wardwell St.; exhibit dates and times are announced.

Designed by Russell Warren, this Federal mansion welcomes you to Bristol's nineteenth-century society. General George DeWolf, wealthy from privateering, slave trading, and Cuban sugar, built this elaborate home for $60,000. When entertaining President Monroe, he bought a silver basin just for him to wash his hands in. Flamboyant, ambitious, and making huge profits, DeWolf encouraged others to lend him money. For years they enjoyed profits along with him. It all ended in 1825, when his sugar plantations failed. No longer able to pay creditors, he and his family escaped on a snowy night in December and sailed for Cuba. Because his empire had been built on town money, much of Bristol failed with him. When creditors found he had eluded them, they ransacked his home in fury. It was years before Bristol recovered. DeWolf returned secretly and died June 7, 1844, in Dedham, Massachusetts. The DeWolf name had been tarnished.

By 1828 the house was owned by William Henry DeWolf, George's cousin. He added the Gothic Revival octagonal sun room and Greek Revival billiard room, both designed by Russell Warren, plus a kitchen wing about 1840 and a wooden carriage house about 1850. He entertained President Andrew Jackson, whose portrait hangs in the house. William quickly spent his inheritance. Upon his death in 1853, his widow was forced to rent the sun room to a barber, take in boarders, lease the carriage house as a stagecoach stop, and later lease the whole building as a hotel, "The DeWolf House."

Linden Place, Bristol (Paul A. Darling/Linden Place)

Finally in 1865 the house was bought at auction for Theodora DeWolf Colt, General George's daughter. She was the widow of Christopher Colt, brother to the famous Colt 45 inventor and a silk manufacturer by trade. At last the house was in the hands of DeWolf descendants with enough money to restore it. Theodora planted linden trees on the grounds and named the mansion "Linden Place." High society returned, with visitors like Cornelius Vanderbilt and presidents Ulysses Grant and Chester Arthur.

Theodora's son, Samuel Pomeroy Colt, unlike his notorious grandfather, was Bristol's philanthropist and restored much honor to the DeWolf name. He built Colt Farm in 1903 and Colt Memorial School in 1906. He merged five local banks into today's successful Fleet Bank, was president of the United States Rubber Company, and served as a director of over forty companies. After his mother died, Samuel Colt built the brick carriage house, known as the ballroom, designed by cousin Wallis E. Howe in 1906. A son, Russell, married Ethel Barrymore, who spent many summers here. Scenes from *The Great Gatsby,* starring Robert Redford and Mia Farrow, were filmed here in 1974. Granddaughter Ethel Barrymore Colt Miglietta started an acting workshop at Linden Place and helped establish the Bristol Art Museum.

This most elaborate home in Bristol is a beautifully balanced Federal structure. Corinthian columns reach to the second floor, giving the impression that the front hall is two stories high. The exquisite entranceway is highlighted by an elliptical fanlight set within a two-story arch. Inside, the hallway greets you with crystal chandelier and stairway sweeping dramatically upward to a central skylight, adding fascinating shadows and light. In the high-ceilinged parlors and dining room, delicate ceiling medallions abound. The immense dining-room chandelier is from Buckingham Palace. Colonel Colt's symbolic colt statues, James DeWolf's famous carriage, an octagonal mid-1700s summerhouse from Charles DeWolf's mansion, and gracious gardens further enhance this historic home.

4. BRISTOL HISTORICAL AND PRESERVATION SOCIETY MUSEUM AND LIBRARY. 48 Court St. Open summer, limited hours, donation, fee for library research.

Built as a jail in 1828, the building was made from African stone ballast used on Bristol ships. It replaced a 1792 wooden jail, reusing some materials. Inside, displays relate to Bristol life. The first floor has portraits by itinerant painter Cephus Thompson, Benjamin Franklin's writing box and case, and Deputy Governor Bradford's writing desk. Upstairs is a dungeonlike cell, a room of children's toys, a DAR room, slave documents, ships' charts and accounts, and Indian and local artifacts. A rear jail section from 1859 is now a small museum. Displays in cells and corridor include documents, Civil War memorabilia, guns, ship models, and a key and brick from the dreaded Libby Prison.

5. HOPE AND HIGH STREETS. Walking tour, homes private.

Walk these streets to see the architectural variety of Bristol and the progression of architect Russell Warren's talents in the many homes he designed. North of Linden Place is the marble and bronze Classical Revival **Colt Memorial School** given to the town by Samuel Pomeroy Colt in memory of his mother. Notice its stately portico, intricate bronze work around windows, and open book motif. At 474 Hope is the 1792 **Norris–Abbott/Bradford House,** which replaced Deputy Governor William Bradford's home burned by British in 1778. Notice unusual three tiers of cutwork parapets in Chinese Chippendale style.

At Bradford and High streets is the **First Congregational Church,** an English Gothic–style building erected 1856. Its congregation, gathered in 1680, is the oldest Congregational Society in Rhode Island. **Number 281 High Street** was built as a barn for James DeWolf. Nearby is the 1817 **Bristol County Courthouse,** NRHP, topped by a wooden belfry tower supporting an octagonal cupola. Believed built by Russell Warren, the courthouse was one of five rotating sites for Rhode Island's General Assembly 1819–52. Now with limited use, it has been a courthouse since 1853.

The Federal home with added Victorian bays at 56 High was built for **James DeWolf** in 1793. James, uncle to George DeWolf, was a wealthy slave trader who not only sold slaves but formed his own company to keep commissions and, if prices were low, used his slaves on his sugar plantations in Cuba. He married Deputy Governor William Bradford's daughter Nancy and was speaker of the state legislative assembly and a U.S. senator. Four eagles atop parapet corners of the Federal at **341 Hope** were carved by seamen on the *Yankee* in 1812 and given to the *Yankee's* captain and the owner of this house, Benjamin Churchill, as a wedding gift.

The 1883 Richardsonian Romanesque building at Hope and Court streets is a **memorial to General Ambrose Burnside,** inventor of breech-loading rifles, Civil War General, state governor 1866–69, and U.S. senator 1875–81. He was known for his shaving style, "Burnsides," soon called sideburns. Across the street is **St. Michaels Episcopal Church,** organized 1718. The English-style dark wood in the chancel area, high arched ceiling, and pews create a striking contrast against light walls and a beautiful Tiffany window behind the altar. Near the entrance is a servicemen's memorial chapel.

Russell Warren built the house at **86 State Street** in 1807 and bought it in 1813. He took liberties with conventional design, creating something uniquely his own by combining the front entrance with the hall window above and using slanted quoins. He also built the 1810 house at **92 State** with its full porch, uncommon in that era, and the 1850 Italian villa at **89 State.** At 617 Hope Street is **Governor Francis Dimond's House,** designed by Warren in 1838 and set in a neighborhood of Colonial, Georgian, Federal, Greek Revival, and Queen Anne homes. At 956 Hope the 1698 house, NRHP, was once **headquarters for General Lafayette.** The Victorian house at **1200 Hope,** NRHP, designed by Russell Warren, was built for famous artist Charles Dana Gibson's grandfather and his wife, who was a DeWolf.

6. HERRESHOFF MARINE MUSEUM. 7 Burnside St. Open extended season, fee. Home of America's Cup Hall of Fame; gift shop, group tours, video room; special programs; Herreshoff family house, 142 Hope St.; plaque near house.

This museum is dedicated to the Herreshoffs, America's most successful boat-building family 1878–1924. Brothers John Brown and Nathanael Greene Herreshoff began what became a world-famous company with John handling the business and Nathanael ("Captain Nat") supervising engineering, design, and experimentation. They developed ways to increase sail volume, with the 1903 *Reliance* carrying the largest mainsail to that date. Nat's creative mind introduced cross-cut sails, web frames, lighter rigging and hull construction, and powerful light steam engines. His designs defended the America's Cup six times between 1893 and 1920. Every detail of each vessel was done at the Herreshoffs' plant, from design and engineering through building and equipping wood or metal vessels up to 160 feet in length. The results were superior ships. In

1890 the Herreshoffs built the first seagoing torpedo boat, U.S. *Cushing,* for the navy. During World War II they built one hundred naval vessels.

Here you see Herreshoff vessels of varying sizes, uses, and designs, including Captain Nat's skiff; the catboat *Sprite,* built by the brothers when they were teenagers; and *Trivia,* Harold Vanderbilt's yacht. A gasoline launch, a yacht tender, a cat yawl, experimental sailing sloops, and racing catboats add to the display. Photos, trophies, models, and paintings testify to the Herreshoffs' dedication to yachting perfection.

7. BLITHEWOLD MANSION AND GARDENS, *1907,* NRHP. 101 Ferry Rd. Grounds open all year, mansion open extended season and December, fee. Guided tours inside, self- or guided tours outside, gift shop, special horticultural exhibits and events, concerts, courses, lectures.

Thirty-three acres of manicured lawns, flowering shrubs, and flower gardens explode in carefully planned coordinating color. Exotic and native plantings include Chinese toon trees, a bamboo grove, and a 90-foot giant sequoia. All provide a perfect setting for Blithewold's forty-five-room mansion. Overlooking Bristol Harbor and Narragansett Bay, the original mansion, a summer home for Pennsylvania coal magnate Augustus Van Wickle, was built in 1895 as the result of a gift. Augustus surprised his wife, Bessie, with a $100,000 Herreshoff yacht. She was delighted but said they lacked a proper place to moor it. The search began, resulting in the purchase of this waterfront property as the "perfect" mooring site.

Several years after Augustus died in a hunting accident, Bessie married William McKee; but tragedy struck again when the original mansion burned in 1907. Within the year they built the present manor in the grand English seventeenth-century style, furnishing it with much that was salvaged from the first house. Over the years Bessie, an ardent traveler, brought furnishings back from all over the world. In the telephone room are Chinese teak fretwork and an inkstand made from a solid block of anthracite coal, a reminder of the source of the Van Wickle fortune. The living room has Tiffany lamps, an 1875 rosewood German Biedermeier secretary, and a mantel from the country house of Queen Victoria's nephew. The dining room boasts elegant paneling, a nineteenth-century barouche table and chairs, and a late seventeenth-century William and Mary cabinet inlaid with ivory. Chinese Rose Medallion vases greet you as you climb the stairs to the second floor. The master bedroom, with sleeping porch and sweeping views, displays nineteenth-century Dutch marquetry furniture.

Though spacious and grand, this home is a place where real people lived and exudes a feeling of warmth and welcome. After Bessie died, daughter Marjorie Van Wickle Lyon lived here and enjoyed Blithewold life to the fullest until her death in 1976 at age ninety-three. She willed the estate to the Heritage Trust of Rhode Island so that visitors might enjoy the gardens designed by landscape architect John DeWolf and vicariously experience the gracious life of an earlier time.

Blithewold, Bristol   (Dr. Stanley Summer)

8. HAFFENREFFER MUSEUM OF ANTHROPOLOGY. Tower St.
Open extended season, limited hours, fee. 500 acres, changing exhibits, gift shop, festivals, lectures, films.

This museum, a vital part of Brown University's Department of Anthropology, is located on land that was once a summer camp of the Wampanoag Indians. It is near Mount Hope, where their sachem, King Philip, was killed in 1676 during King Philip's War. In more recent years this land held the summer home of successful businessman and ardent collector of Indian artifacts Rudolph Frederick Haffenreffer, Sr. He began a museum of American native artifacts here on his property, called the Mount Hope Grant, in the early 1900s. Upon his death 500 acres, buildings, and the museum were given to Brown University. Today's museum has an unusually fine collection of more than 10,000 ethnographic and 100,000 archeological specimens and artifacts from peoples native to North, Central, and South America. Three galleries interpret their lifestyles and display their art along with art from Asia, Africa, the Middle East, and the Pacific Islands.

BEACHES, PARKS, OTHER POINTS OF INTEREST

A. Fourth of July Parades. Nationally known, celebrated since 1785; center lines on parade route painted red, white, blue.

B. **Bristol Town Beach.** Colt State Park. Open all year. Fee. Lifeguards, rest rooms, sandy beach, concessions, tennis, basketball; swimming.

C. **Independence Park.** Thames St. Open all year. No fee. Former railroad yard, now waterfront park and southern end of **East Bay Bicycle Path;** views, boat ramp; fishing.

D. **Rockwell Waterfront Park.** Thames and Church sts. Open all year. No fee. Pier, views, swings, benches, playground; **Prudence Ferry,** daily trips to Prudence Island, summer trips to Hog Island.

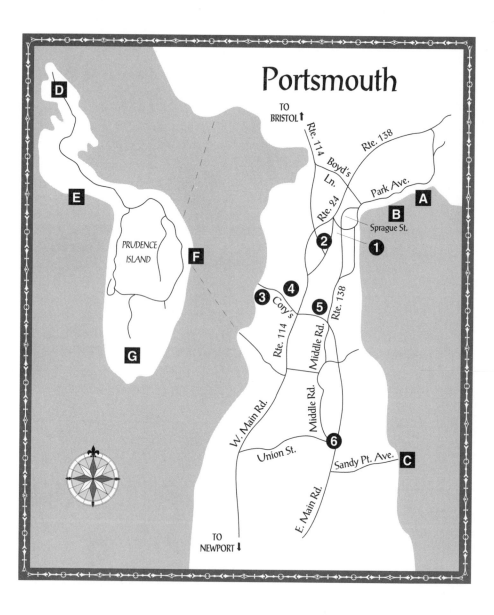

PORTSMOUTH

Portsmouth[12] is the site of the second settlement of Rhode Island. Founders were physician John Clarke and wealthy businessman William Coddington, both banished from Massachusetts Bay Colony in 1638 for agreeing with Anne Hutchinson. They and their group of twenty-three, including Anne Hutchinson's husband, William, signed the Portsmouth Compact for a theocratic government, which specified freedom of personal doctrine. Soon Anne Hutchinson and her family and followers joined them. Within a year, however, a struggle for leadership resulted in winner Anne Hutchinson and thirty settlers remaining in Portsmouth while Clarke, Coddington, and nine others left to found Newport. Less than a year later, Portsmouth and Newport united, calling their island Rhode Island, as had Florentine explorer Giovanni da Verrazano in 1524. Providence, Portsmouth, Newport, and Warwick formed the first General Assembly and the beginning of Rhode Island's history as a state in 1647.

During the Revolution Portsmouth was the site of the Battle of Rhode Island, August 1778. The British, who had occupied the island, pulled back to Newport, and American General John Sullivan moved more than 10,000 men to Portsmouth. They marched south to attack the British at Green End Fort in Middletown without the naval support of the French fleet, which had retreated to Boston to repair storm and battle damages. On August 29 a major battle was fought, and the Americans retreated from the island the next day. Though defeated, the colony won, as the British discovered they couldn't occupy and defend the whole Narragansett Bay area.

1. BUTTS HILL FORT, *1777.* Dyer St. off Sprague St. Open all year, no fee.

Here the British built a fort and earthworks in 1777 to defend their occupation of the island. A year later Americans used the fort in a major defense in the Battle of Rhode Island. Little remains. As you follow the path to the summit, you need your imagination to visualize the historic action of the past.

2. MEMORIAL TO FIRST RHODE ISLAND REGIMENT, "Black Regiment," NHL. West side of divided Rte. 114 North, immediately after Rte. 24 branches right. Open all year, no fee.

This quiet oasis is an historic site of the Battle of Rhode Island, 1778. The memorial honors the First Rhode Island Regiment, called the "Black Regiment" as it was the first black and Indian slave regiment formed in Rhode Island. Part of the American right flank, these soldiers won their freedom as they fought gallantly and well, with little loss of their own. Later the regiment protected the west passage to Narragansett Bay and marched with Washington to Yorktown.

3. GREEN ANIMALS, *c. 1860s*. PSNC (Preservation Society of Newport County). Cory's Ln. Open extended season, fee. Topiary gardens, small toy museum in main house, plant and gift shop.

Not your usual museum, Green Animals is dedicated to topiary gardening—the centuries-old technique of shaping living plants into figures or animals. Green Animals is the oldest topiary garden in the country, the farthest north, and considered the finest. Swan, unicorn, camel, donkey, dogs, bears, rooster, peacock, ostrich, giraffe, policeman, sailboat, horse and rider, and an elephant are among the eighty sculptured topiary pieces.

Thomas Brayton purchased the property in 1877. He and his superintendent, Joseph Carreiro, created the formal gardens and topiary: animals from California privet and yew, geometric forms from English boxwood and California privet. Trimming is necessary every two weeks in summer. After periodic removal of deadwood, plants take two to three years to reestablish. Gardens include an herb garden, gourd arbor, lily pond, rose garden, and vegetable and cutting gardens. The small summer estate, later permanent home to Thomas Brayton's daughter Alice, has a beautiful setting above Narragansett Bay. Alice remained unmarried, as her father assured her she needn't marry for the usual reasons of status or wealth.

4. PORTSMOUTH ABBEY SCHOOL. Cory's Ln. Open all year, no fee.

In 1926 Benedictine monks started a priory school here that has grown to today's abbey school. Five hundred acres of fields and woods bordering Narragansett Bay provide the setting for the beautiful modern campus. Central is the **Abbey Chapel of St. Gregory,** where stone, wood, and stained glass meet to provide a place for quiet reverence. From a metal crucifix suspended above the altar wire beams appear to radiate outward and upward to the vaulted ceiling—beams that in fact hold the cross. The sculpture was designed by Richard Lippold.

5. FRIENDS MEETING HOUSE, *1700*. 11 Middle Rd., near corner East Main Rd. (Rte. 138) and Hedley Ave. Open all year for services.

Hessian troops were quartered here when the British occupied Newport. Before the decade passed, the structure held a boarding school, which moved to Providence in 1819 to become Moses Brown School. Quakers dominated Portsmouth history for the first 150 years, and this was the only house of worship until the early 1800s. The building has been modified and is more elaborate than most.

6. PORTSMOUTH HISTORICAL SOCIETY/UNION MEETING HOUSE, *c. 1866*, NRHP; Southernmost School, *c. 1716*, NRHP. East Main Rd. (Rte. 138) at Union St. Open summer, limited hours, and by appointment, fee.

The sanctuary of the Union Meeting House is a museum of eighteenth-century costumes, radios, phonographs, and home and farm equipment of times past. The church is plain clapboard with eyebrow lintels over windows. Its front entry with double doors is surmounted by a round window under triangular molding. Here Julia Ward Howe, whose summer home was at 745 Union, often gave sermons on world peace and women's rights, including suffrage. In the barn the last horse-drawn mail coach, a wooden sleigh, carriages, and farm implements are displayed.

The old schoolhouse, Southernmost School, is on the grounds. Portsmouth's first school and one of the oldest still standing in the state had a stone end wall with bake oven for the schoolmaster to prepare his food. The arched plaster ceiling is more decorative than most. Antique student desks cluster around the central stove. Schoolbooks, bells, quill pens, lanterns, and teacher's desk are on view.

BEACHES, PARKS, OTHER POINTS OF INTEREST

A. Teddy's State Beach. Park Ave. Open all year. No fee. At old stone bridge abutment, Stone Bridge Marina; lifeguards; picnicking, fishing from stone abutment; limited parking.

B. Island Park Beach. Park Ave. Open all year. No fee. Walk-on beach.

C. Sandy Point Beach. Sandy Point Ave. Open all year. Fee in summer. Lifeguards, rest rooms, bathhouses; swimming.

D. Narragansett Bay National Estuarine Sanctuary. Prudence Island; ferry from Colt State Park (summer) or Thames St., Bristol (all year). Sanctuary open all year. No fee except for ferry. Part of state park system; outdoor research lab and education are sanctuary's focus; North Prudence has historic farm site, densest deer herd in New England, wayside exhibits, self-guided nature trails, rest rooms; picnicking, hunting, fishing, camping (fee); naturalist programs in summer; weather station, part of interpretive program; cars on access roads only.

E. Sandy Beach. Prudence Island. Open all year. No fee. State beach.

F. Sandy Point Light. Prudence Island. External view only.

G. South Prudence Bay Island Park. Open all year. No fee. State park; beach, dock, self-guided nature trail; picnicking, fishing, camping (fee).

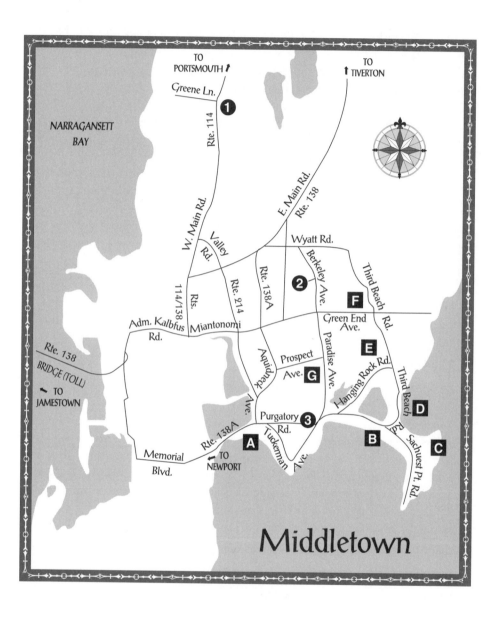

Middletown

MIDDLETOWN

Middletown separated from Newport plantation in 1743. While Newport went on to become a summer resort for the rich and famous, Middletown, with its fertile lands, grew as a farming community, proud of its agricultural accomplishments. During the Revolution Middletown lay at the doorstep of the British occupation of Newport. It was burned and pillaged on December 7, 1776, by British and Hessian troops, who went on to occupy Newport. For three years residents lived in fear of British attack. Some farmers fled the island, while others acted as invaluable spies for the colonial army. Today Middletown is a charming Rhode Island seacoast town.

1. PRESCOTT FARM, *c. 1715*, NRHP. 2009 West Main Rd. Open extended season, fee.

One of the most daring captures of the Revolution took place here July 9, 1777. Lieutenant Colonel William Barton, commander of the colonial forces at Tiverton Height (now Fort Barton), learned that General Richard Prescott, commander of the British troops at Newport, was here at Henry Overing's estate with only a small guard for protection. Barton knew if he captured Prescott, it would give the Continental Congress the opportunity to exchange Prescott for the popular General Charles Lee, captured by the British. With forty men Barton overcame sentries and burst into the Overing home, capturing the general in his bed. Via blackberry fields and small boats, Prescott was taken to Warwick. Later the exchange was made, and Barton received a hero's sword from the Continental Congress.

The c. 1730 Overing House is not open, but the wing in which Prescott set up summer headquarters is now a separate building open to the public. It is furnished as it might have been that night, including several 1600s furnishings from Plymouth. A British rifle with the Tower of London hallmark is mounted over the fireplace, and a copy of Prescott's uniform hangs by the door.

Geese and ducks greet you as you walk the grounds of this forty-seven-acre reconstructed farm. A beautifully restored c. 1812 English flock windmill still produces five to six bushels of cornmeal per hour. Gears once made of oak, now of metal, work with rhythmic precision. The whole process can be observed as you move from the entrance to the top bonnet area, which turns in order to bring the sails into the most advantageous wind. The resulting flour is sold in the c. 1715 Country Store (Earle–Hicks House) built by John Earle in Portsmouth, where it was the ferry master's home. The country store shows what would have been available during the 1700s; displays also include an apple press, early child's walker, a child's goat cart, and various bottles.

Prescott Farm, Middletown   (James E. Garman)

2. WHITEHALL MUSEUM HOUSE, *1729*, NRHP. 311 Berkeley Ave. Open summer, fee.

Dean, philosopher, and Anglican bishop, George Berkeley set sail for Bermuda in 1728 to establish a college to educate sons of colonists for the ministry. Six months at sea and well off course, he and his party, which included artist John Smibert and architect Sir John James, landed in Rhode Island. Berkeley bought this property from Joseph Whipple in 1729 with the expectation of raising food for his Bermuda college, though that dream never materialized.

The small house, which may have been the original lean-to section, was expanded to the early Georgian two-story, center chimney home with hip roof and unusual double door you see today. Dentiled roofline and front-door pediment add to the design. Inside furnishings relate to 1729–31, when Berkeleys lived here. During that time Berkeley established a philosophical discussion group that became the basis for the Redwood Library in Newport. He tried to reconcile science with Christian doctrine, saying matter does not exist, it is only perceived, while at the same time the laws of physics are true. When he returned to Ireland, he gave his lands to Yale University, with rental income to go for theological scholarships. Today there is a Berkeley College at Yale University.

Over the years Whitehall was home to various tenants, quarters for British troops during the Revolution, a tearoom, and a public house run by a Mr. Anthony, grandfather of portraitist Gilbert Stuart. By 1899 the house had become derelict. Three Newport ladies rescued it and in 1902 gave it to the National Society of Colonial Dames in Rhode Island as a memorial to George Berkeley.

Today original English tiles frame the fireplace in the Green Parlor, and a copy of Robert Burton's *The Anatomy of Melancholy* (1621) lies on the table. In the Red Parlor are maps of Bermuda and New England, sixteenth- and seventeenth-century Jacobean furniture, a Spanish missionary desk, and a copy of the deed to Berkeley. The dean's bedroom has a seventeenth-century English chair with scroll-and-tulip carvings, and a c.1630 Jacobean chest. The keeping room, with simpler woodwork, has a large fireplace and an unusual spice rack with butterfly hinges and bun feet.

3. PURGATORY CHASM. Purgatory Rd. and Tuckerman Ave. Open all year, no fee. Views.

This 160-foot-deep chasm has legends of its own. One tells of an Indian squaw who had two suitors. She would marry whichever one successfully jumped the chasm. One made it and one did not.

BEACHES, PARKS, OTHER POINTS OF INTEREST

A. **Atlantic Beach.** Aquidneck Ave. and Purgatory Rd. Open summer. No fee. Small sandy beach; swimming; public right of way and parking by restaurant.

B. **Second/Sachuest Beach.** Third Beach Rd. Open summer. Fee. Pavilion, bathhouse, 2-mile sandy beach, lifeguards; swimming; horses allowed at limited times.

C. **Sachuest Point National Wildlife Refuge.** Sachuest Point Rd., off Third Beach Rd. Open all year. No fee. Visitor center, small museum, trails, views, bird walks; St. George's Chapel seen across the cove.

D. **Third Beach.** Third Beach Rd. Open summer. Fee. Rest rooms, mobile vendors, gentle surf, sandy beach especially good for children, boat ramp, lifeguards; swimming.

E. **Hanging Rocks.** Hanging Rocks and Third Beach rds. Where Dean Berkeley may have written parts of *Alciphron*, defense of Christian religion against freethinkers; 50-foot overhanging rock.

F. **Norman Bird Sanctuary.** 583 Third Beach Rd. Open all year. Program fees. 450 acres, 7 miles of free trails, fields, swamp woodlands, cliff overlooks, museum displays, gift shop; educational programs, arranged tours, bird walks; cross-country skiing.

G. **Paradise School.** 1875, HS. Prospect and Paradise aves. Open all year by appointment. Restored Italianate schoolhouse; changing exhibits relate to Middletown life.

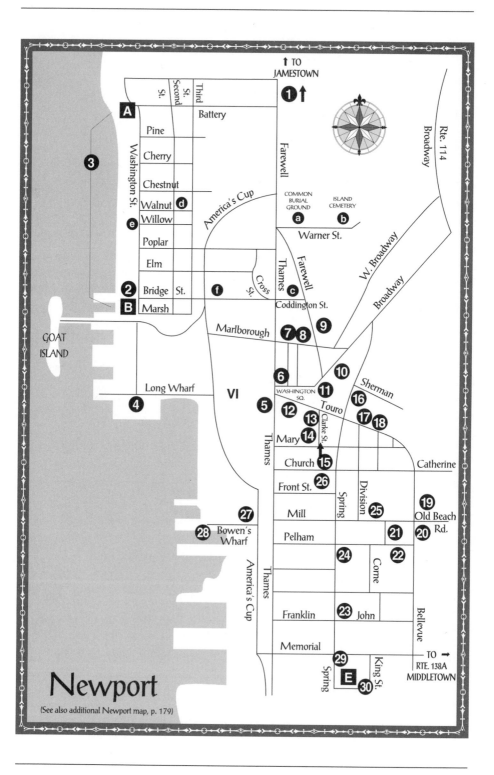

Newport

(See also additional Newport map, p. 179)

NEWPORT

The Newport story spans history. Legendary Vikings followed by colonists seeking religious freedom were succeeded by prosperous sea captains and merchants of the "golden era." Next the Gothic "age of innocence" was followed by the "gilded age" of giants who built castles and called them cottages.

Newport was founded in 1639 when Anne Hutchinson's leadership in Portsmouth, Rhode Island, caused dissenters to leave there and come to Newport. Church and state were separated from the beginning. The colony charter of 1662 included "full liberty in religious concernments." Newport, unlike most Massachusetts settlements, welcomed Quakers and Jews. Soon Newport was the principal colony for trade and became one of five rotating capitals of the colony. After statehood the General Assembly continued to take turns meeting here and in Providence until the early 1900s, when the new state house was built in Providence. British occupation in 1776 devastated the people of Newport and their economy.

Newport today is a fascinating combination of her fabulous past and present pleasures. Newport has eighteenth, nineteenth, and twentieth-century architectural treasures created by the country's major architects. Here you'll find one of the highest concentrations of Colonial architecture in America. There are more than 300 buildings dating from before the American Revolution and more public buildings survive from before the Revolution in Newport than in Boston, New York, and Philadelphia combined. These centuries of architecture and history are preserved by the Newport Historical Society (NHS), Newport Restoration Foundation (NRF), Preservation Society of Newport County (PSNC), Society for the Preservation of New England Antiquities (SPNEA), and concerned citizens.

1. **NAVAL WAR COLLEGE MUSEUM,** Founder's Hall, *1820*, **NHL. Coasters Harbor Island; exit off Rtes. 138 and 114 at Admiral Kalbrus Rd., West to Training Station Rd. to gate 1, Naval Education and Training Center. Open summer, limited hours. No fee.**

Founder's Hall was Newport poorhouse; in 1884 became first site of Naval War College, oldest in world. Exhibits focus on history of the art and science of naval warfare and on Narragansett Bay naval heritage.

2. **HUNTER HOUSE,** *c. 1748–54*, **NHL, PSNC. 54 Washington St. Open extended season. Fee.**

One of ten best examples of American Colonial residential architecture. Owned by

James Sheffield, deputy governors Jonathan Nichols and Joseph Wanton, and ambassador to Brazil William Hunter and his Quaker bride Mary Robinson; Nichols also prosperous merchant, privateer owner, proprietor of White Horse Tavern; Wanton was a Tory driven away by Revolution. Hunter House was headquarters of Admiral de Ternay, who died here; property included gardens, wharf, shops.

Beautiful Georgian; entrance modeled after Colony House, probably carved by Jim Moody, has segmented pediment-centered pineapple; Moody-carved entrance discarded when entries widened, added to Rectory of St. John's, finally returned to Hunter House; interior has noted floor-to-ceiling paneling, mahogany staircase. Pre-Revolutionary Newport furnishings include silver, china, paintings, and furniture by Townsend and Goddard, Newport cabinetmakers and furniture exporters to Charleston and West Indies; house interprets life of a very wealthy merchant during peak of Newport's golden era.

3. EASTON'S POINT AND CEMETERIES. Point bounded by Thames, Farewell, Washington sts.

Point and area beyond is treasure of well-preserved Colonial architecture. Point has waterfront homes of early craftsmen and sea captains since the first division of Quaker lands in 1725. Family homes remain from the famed Goddard and Townsend cabinetmaker families. Homes here included docks, warehouses, shops; now a living eighteenth-century neighborhood. Across water is **Goat Island,** used by British in Revolution and by U.S. military until recently; fine views of Newport Harbor.

Common Burial Ground ("a" on map), 1660s, Farewell St., is where early residents are buried; early stones are finest Colonial sculptors' art. Stone for John Ward Stone was carved 1698 by William Mumford; ledger stones by John Stevens II for Governor Samuel Ward and his wife, 1776, list their virtues; Stevens carved and signed stone for Pompey Breton in slave section. **Island Cemetery** (b), Warner St., contains monument to brothers Matthew and Oliver Perry; Standing Angel in Alfred Smith plot by noted sculptor Augustus Saint-Gaudens. **Coddington Cemetery** (c), Farewell and Coddington sts.; Coddington, first settler, governor, buried 1688; also five other governors.

Perry House (d), c. 1750, 31 Walnut St., private, Georgian with three dormers in gambrel roof, beaded clapboard; birthplace Matthew Calbraith Perry 1794; Perry was with brother Oliver Hazard Perry at Battle of Lake Erie 1813, signed treaty with Japan 1854 to open trade. **Sanford–Covell House** (e), 1870, 72 Washington St., was SPNEA, now bed and breakfast; lavish stick style, carved woods, stenciled ceilings, veranda, large windows on waterfront site. **Captain Peter Simon House** (f), c. 1727, 25 Bridge St., private, was scene of sad love story when dancing master Simon, Jr., brought Quaker bride, Hannah, here against her father's wishes; Simon deserted her; Hannah pined, was taken home on litter to die (see South Kingstown M).

4. LONG WHARF, *1685*. On waterfront.

Early Colonial trading center: ships brought molasses, spices, sugar, slaves from West Indies; brought manufactured goods, bricks for Britain; loaded tar, lumber, wool, cheese, butter, beef, pork, horses, furniture, clocks, silver, spermaceti candles; here Washington and Rochambeau reviewed French troops; still commercial waterfront, stacks of lobster pots, draggers tied at wharf.

5. THE MUSEUM OF NEWPORT HISTORY AT THE BRICK MARKET, *1762–72*, NHL. Thames St., parking at Visitor Information Center. Open all year. Fee.

Museum with exhibitions of 350 years of Newport history; plus decorative arts, artifacts of everyday life, graphics, historic photographs, ship models, paintings, colonial silver, a printing press used by Ben Franklin's brother James, a ball gown from the Gilded Age—all unite to show the exciting story of Newport. Interactive computer aids the exploration of the Newport National Historic Landmark District. Walking Tour leaves from Museum. Sophisticated audiovisual programs and exhibits also examine Newport's unique and diverse religious and ethnic mix and Brick Market history.

Structure is handsome brick Federal with classical motifs, two-story Ionic pilasters; Market designed by Peter Harrison, who adapted Inigo Jones's Old Somerset House to include market arcade; lower floor was market and watch house; upper floors were shops, later a printing office, then a theater; in 1842 top floor removed and arcade enclosed with large arched windows with fan lights, to use as town hall until 1900; 1930 rehabilitated by Norman Isham.

6. NEWPORT NATIONAL BANK/RIVERA HOUSE, *c. 1722*. Washington Sq. Open all year as bank.

Once home of Abraham Rodrigues Rivera, prominent member of early Jewish community, who helped start sperm oil industry, lay cornerstone for Touro Synagogue, and established Redwood Library, where Gilbert Stuart portrait of him hangs; residence of Governor John Gardner; 1803 Newport National Bank began here, lender toward Louisiana Purchase; classic Georgian Colonial exterior, gambrel roof, pedimented dormers and entry.

7. ST. PAUL'S METHODIST CHURCH, *1806*. Marlborough St. Open all year, limited hours and by appointment.

Oldest Methodist church with steeple in New England; original white Gothic has three-tiered tower at main entrance, pedimented facade; later, entry enclosed and building raised one story; interior elliptical arch, dentiled cornice; recessed paneling, pilasters in balcony.

8. WHITE HORSE TAVERN, *c. 1673*, NHL. 26 Marlborough St. Open all year as restaurant.

Said to be oldest operating tavern in country; liquor license acquired 1687 by William Mayes; son William Mayes, Jr., notorious pirate, granted 1702 license to sell "all sorts of strong drink"; pirate's sister married Robert Nichols, Nichols family kept tavern for more than two centuries; Lieutenant Governor Jonathan Nichols II first to hang sign of White Horse. Town Council met here, dining at town's expense; tavern was focus of town, gathering place for members of colonial legislature. Interesting clapboarded Colonial retains seventeenth-century exposed heavy-timbered framing, early R. I. "coves" where walls curve out to ceiling above fireplaces.

9. QUAKER MEETING HOUSE, *1699*, NHS. Marlborough and Farewell sts. Open summer and by appointment. Donations.

Quakers settled here 1657; together with Congregationalists and Jews formed basis of Newport's civic and commercial success; ancient Colonial is oldest religious structure in Rhode Island and country's oldest Friends' yearly meetinghouse. Original middle section—massive chamfered frame, hipped roof, tower—could hold 500 people; additions made 1726 and 1806 contain old Ship Room with curved ceiling timbers, materials from original Friends' Meeting House; nineteenth-century enlargements accommodated Newport Yearly Meeting.

10. WANTON–LYMAN–HAZARD HOUSE, *c. 1675*, NHL, NHS. 17 Broadway. Open summer. Fee.

Oldest remaining house in Newport; site of Stamp Act Riot 1765, when occupant burned in effigy for British sympathies. Colonial clapboarded with few inches exposed to the weather, steeply pitched roof raised in front for curved (coved) cornice, probably began with two-room plan; was remodeled early 1700s by Stephen Mumford; original seventeenth-century fireplace found behind paneling; exposed chamfered beams and gunstock corner posts, vertical boards marbled. House contains period furnishings, interprets life of upper-middle-class merchant of colonial Newport.

11. THE COLONY HOUSE, *1738–41*, NHL. Washington Sq. Open summer and by appointment. No fee.

Center of colonial Newport, second oldest capitol building in United States, replaced 1687 wooden building; was seat of colonial government (1739–76) and State House (1776–1900) along with Providence. From here in 1764 Governor Stephen Hopkins ordered cannons to fire at British warship *St. John,* an early overt resistance to British authority; in 1776 British used house as barracks, later French used as hospital; in 1781

Washington and Rochambeau met here to plan Battle of Yorktown; considered site of first Catholic mass in Rhode Island.

Stately detailed Georgian by Richard Munday built of bricks probably imported as ballast from Bristol, England; has rusticated belt course, window surrounds, quoins; emphasized central section capped by broken pediment with pineapple carved by Jim Moody; balcony with balustrade of twisted balusters; interior restored by Norman Isham 1917; row of Doric columns with entablatures and high pedestals on first floor; upstairs Council Chamber features elaborate floor-to-ceiling raised paneling with Corinthian pilasters on high pedestals, called one of the finest Colonial rooms existing; Washington portrait by Gilbert Stuart.

12. JOSEPH AND ROBERT ROGERS HOUSE, *c. 1790.* 33 Touro St.
Open all year as offices.

Federal with focus on doorway, leaded fanlight, broken dentiled pediment, Corinthian pilasters, faces Washington Square and statue of Perry.

13. CLARKE STREET MEETING HOUSE/SECOND CONGREGA-TIONAL CHURCH, *1735.* Clarke St. Private.

Hospital for British and French in Revolution; was lengthened and Greek Revival facade added 1847; has later Victorian added details. Pastor Ezra Stiles—writer, astronomer, president of Yale, friend of Ben Franklin—installed lightning rods still here. Now houses adaptive-reuse condominiums; on street of beautiful old structures, Colonials through Victorians, many NRHP.

14. NEWPORT ARTILLERY COMPANY ARMORY AND MUSEUM, *1835–36,* NHL. 23 Clarke St. Open summer or by appointment. Fee.

Newport Artillery Company 1639, chartered by General Assembly 1741, is oldest active company in continuous service in United States, took part in seven wars. Fine museum of military memorabilia has one of most complete collections of uniforms and weapons in United States, cannons cast by Paul Revere.

15. VERNON HOUSE, *c. 1708,* NHL. 46 Clarke St. Private.

Possibly began as smaller house owned by painter William Gibbs; major addition c. 1759 was for Metcalf Bowler, member of Assembly, chief justice of Supreme Court of Rhode Island, 1776 British Crown secret agent. House ironically became headquarters of General Rochambeau, who consulted with Washington here; after war home to Vernons, Patriot family of successful merchants. Now large, stately Georgian, design attributed to Peter Harrison; classical entrance, modillion-and-dentil cornice, balustraded hip roof; unusual Chinese frescoes within older section raise mystery of house's origin.

16. UNITED BAPTIST CHURCH, *1846.* 30 Spring St., behind Colony House.

Established 1638; charter from King Charles II, 1663, first gave "full liberty in religious concernments."

17. TOURO SYNAGOGUE, *1759–63,* NHL, NHS. 72 Touro St. Open extended season and by appointment and for services.

Oldest surviving synagogue in North America; designed by Peter Harrison, designer of King's Chapel, Boston, and Christ Church, Cambridge, from descriptions of synagogue in Amsterdam and after Inigo Jones's design. Contains Scroll of Laws c. 1492, brought here 1658, oldest Torah in United States; only the chairs are not from the eighteenth century or before.

George Washington was here twice; his pew reserved for heads of state and current officers of congregation; Washington letter reassured Jews that all are welcome; his early promise of religious freedom preceded Bill of Rights, is celebrated annually; Jews, settled possibly as early as 1650s, were allowed citizenship only after Revolution; tunnel under altar may have been for escape, as many founders had fled Spanish Inquisition. Twelve Ionic pillars stand for twelve tribes of Israel; balcony for women has twelve Corinthian columns that support domed ceiling; modified Georgian exterior is of coated brick with modillion cornice, portico with Ionic columns; quiet, cool appearance.

Across Touro Street is Russell Warren's grand Greek Revival, the **Levi H. Gale House,** 1833–38, 89 Touro St., with full-height Corinthian pilasters, now community building for synagogue; **Patriots Park,** adjacent, honors Jews outstanding in patriotism.

18. NEWPORT HISTORICAL SOCIETY AND MUSEUM. 82 Touro St. Open all year. No fee except for walking tours.

Exhibits of silver, pewter, clocks, portraits; collections of furniture by Job Townsend and John Goddard in Newport Room, eighteenth-century merchant's parlor. Research library, archival manuscript collection; changing exhibitions such as Vanderbilt family trains.

Attached is **Sabbatarian Meeting House,** 1729, NRHP; Seventh Day Baptists formed in 1671; oldest meetinghouse of sect in United States; architectural detail similar to Trinity Church (see 26); twisted-balustrated stairs, Union Jack paneled sounding board, raised paneling, wainscoting; original building was moved, enclosed in brick; Ezra Stiles preached here during Revolution.

19. REDWOOD LIBRARY, *1748,* NHL. 50 Bellevue Ave. Open all year. No fee.

Grew from 1730 Philosophical Club; oldest continuously used library building in United States; paintings by Gilbert Stuart, Rembrandt Peale, Robert Feke, John Smibert, Michel Felice Corne; Roman Doric temple, rusticated, with portico and wings, designed by Peter Harrison; exterior has portion of chain stretched across Hudson River during Revolution, statue of George Washington.

20. NEWPORT ART MUSEUM, 76 Bellevue Ave. Open all year. Fee.

Gift shop, classes, lectures, tours, performing arts, music. **Griswold Mansion,** 1864, NRHP, designed by Richard Morris Hunt for China trader and financier John Griswold; considered Hunt's finest work and most American creation; stick style, half-timber, steep pitched roof, bays, balconies; focus on skeletal "sticks" of structure; stable attached later; central octagonal hall gives access to rest of open interior space surrounded by porches.

Museum founded 1912 as Art Association of Newport; permanent collection and changing art exhibitions of contemporary and historical Newport and New England; Cushing Gallery in separate 1919 concrete structure; collection includes Sydney Burleigh, Winslow Homer, George Inness, Fairfield Porter, Red Grooms, Dale Chihuly, Howard Cushing, Edward Darley Boit, Julia Boit.

21. OLD STONE MILL, c. 1670. Touro Park on Bellevue Ave.

Once believed Viking, probably built by Rhode Island's first colonial governor, Benedict Arnold (great-grandfather of traitor Benedict Arnold), and referred to in his will as "my stone built windmill"; remarkably preserved stone foundation and walls of round arcaded structure; ruins once used to store powder and later hay; imposing, early example of seventeenth-century Rhode Island masonry.

Touro Park includes statues of Commodore Matthew Perry, with appropriate Japanese art, and Reverend William Ellery Channing, called "champion of human dignity."

22. CHANNING MEMORIAL CHURCH, 1881. 135 Pelham St.

Newporter William Ellery Channing founded American Unitarianism; exterior rough-cut granite; two John LaFarge stained glass windows, memorial plaque by Augustus Saint-Gaudens; Julia Ward Howe was member of this church of writers, artists.

23. BULL–MAWDSLEY HOUSE, c. 1680. 228 Spring St. Private.

Seventeenth-century four-room house of Jireh Bull and wife Godsgift, daughter of Governor Benedict Arnold; about 1750 Captain John Mawdsley added rooms and front facade, completely concealing original. Classic Georgian with dormers in neighborhood of historic homes along John Street.

24. NEWPORT CONGREGATIONAL CHURCH, 1855–57, NRHP. Spring and Pelham sts.

Gathered 1695; Romanesque Revival with rare intact 1880 interior by John LaFarge, Byzantine-flavored murals. Samuel Hopkins, pastor of First Congregational Church 1770–85, thundered against slavery, was hero of Harriet Beecher Stowe's *The Minister's Wooing.*

25. THE WARREN HOUSE, *1809.* 118 Mill St. Private.

Early brick Federal, summer home of Katherine Urquhart Warren, who founded the Preservation Society of Newport County, which headquartered here, now at 424 Bellevue Ave., corner Narragansett Ave.

26. TRINITY CHURCH, *1723–26,* NHL. Spring and Church sts.

Designed by architect Richard Munday after Old North Church of Boston and Christopher Wren's design; clock tower with arcaded belfry, lantern; soaring steeple with delicate detailed finials is one of few remaining fine pre-1740 Colonial spires; towers over prominent parklike setting above waterfront.

Within are galleries supported by superimposed piers, Tiffany stained glass windows, triple-deck wineglass pulpit (only one in United States), sounding board, box pews; Washington worshipped here, as did Queen Elizabeth II; tradition tells that 1733 organ given by Bishop Berkeley was played by Handel; keyboard now in NHS collection.

27. SEAMAN'S CHURCH INSTITUTE, *1919,* NRHP. 18 Market Sq. Open all year.

"Haven for men and women of the sea" since 1919. Some fees for services: rest rooms, washing machines, showers, light meals, day room, library, Chapel of the Sea. Beautiful Georgian Revival brick, designed by Whitney Warren, many dormers, Federal end chimneys.

28. BOWEN'S WHARF, off America's Cup.

Part of old harbor, held shops, wharves, bank, homes, ship chandlers, sailmakers, blockmakers; now shops, restaurants. Three reconstructed buildings survive; still visible are granite-walled quay, cobblestone street.

29. ST. MARY'S ROMAN CATHOLIC CHURCH, *1848–52,* Spring St. and Memorial Blvd.

Stone-block Gothic; oldest Catholic parish in Rhode Island; Jacqueline Bouvier and John F. Kennedy married here.

30. EDWARD KING HOUSE, *c. 1846,* NHL. King St., Aquidneck Park. Open all year as Senior Citizens' Center, gift shop.

Italianate villa designed by Richard Upjohn for Edward King, merchant and landowner; massive, asymmetrical red brick; sharp angles, heavy brackets; central entrance loggia, heavy detail in balconies.

(For all subsequent entries, see map page 179)

31. NEWPORT CASINO AND TENNIS MUSEUM AND HALL OF FAME, *1880*, NHL. 194 Bellevue Ave. Open all year. Fee. Grass courts for public use and tournaments, tennis museum, library, court tennis court, restaurant.

The now-restored shingle-style complex was designed by McKim, Mead and White as one of first country clubs; exterior of smooth brick piers with shingled upper floor is symmetrical, ordered; interior courtyard has shingled clock tower; piazzas' spindle-screen partial enclosures show Japanese influence; original plan included elegant areas for lawn games, court tennis, bowling alleys; theater by Stanford White has delicately detailed interior, hosted Oscar Wilde, ballerina Danilova.

Site of first U.S. national tennis championship, 1881–1914, now called U.S. Open; hosted Volvo Hall of Fame, Virginia Slims. Museum of tennis memorabilia has exhibit rooms devoted to Davis Cup, Dwight, Sears, women in tennis. Indoor court tennis court for medieval game on replica of castle courtyard, complicated parent of all racquet sports, is one of only nine in United States.

32. KINGSCOTE, *1839–41*, NRHP, PSNC. Bellevue Ave. at Bowery St. Open extended season. Fee.

Designed by Richard Upjohn for George Noble Jones of Savannah; Newport's first summer "cottage"; light, gentle, picturesque Gothic with asymmetrical mass, roofline, gables, dormers, porches, nestled within landscape. Dining room added 1880 by White of McKim, Mead and White—cork ceiling, Tiffany glass wall, metal fireplace detail, dark wood paneling, all linked by molding; Chinese export porcelains and paintings collected by second owner, China trade merchant William Henry King; furnishings from four generations of King family.

33. THE ELMS, *1901*, NRHP, PSNC. Bellevue Ave. Open extended season. Fee.

Horace Trumbauer designed stone French neoclassical chateau for Philadelphia coal magnate Edward J. Berwind; projecting central section, balustraded roof. Stands amid neighborhood of privately owned mansions; lavish interior; eighteenth-century furnishings and art, some on loan from museums and private collections; formal sunken gardens, balustraded terraces, statuary, fountains, gazebos.

34. SAMUEL WHITEHORNE HOUSE, *c. 1811*, NRHP, NRF. 416 Thames St. Open all year, limited hours and by appointment. Fee.

Beautiful, stately brick Federal, prominent delicate portico, denticulated cornice; eighteenth-century garden; museum of furniture, particularly from Newport Goddards and Townsends; Newport-crafted silver, pewter; Oriental rugs, Chinese export porcelain.

35. CHATEAU-SUR-MER, *1851–52*, NRHP, PSNC. Bellevue Ave. Open extended season. Fee.

Seth Bradford–designed opulent French Second Empire–style mansion built for retired banker and China trade king William S. Wetmore, enlarged 1872 by Richard Morris Hunt; granite ashlar block, high mansard roof, irregular mass; notable ballroom with sliding mirror doors; intricate carved woodwork by Luigi Frullini; appropriately opulent furnishings.

36. OCHRE COURT OF SALVE REGINA COLLEGE, *1888–91*, NHS. 100 Ochre Point Ave. First floor of Administration Building open all year. No fee.

Late Gothic French chateau expresses designer Richard Morris Hunt's feelings for beaux-arts style; built for Ogden Goelet of New York; dominates tiny site amid other mansions. Cold white limestone, mansard roof, Gothic pinnacles; within, three-story great central hall—rich, unconventional decor above cool, white marble of first floor.

37. THE BREAKERS, *1895*, NRHP, PSNC. Ochre Point Ave. Open extended season. Fee.

First Breakers, built for Pierre Lorillard by Peabody and Stearns 1877, sold to Cornelius Vanderbilt, was huge, imposing Queen Anne–style, burned 1892; replaced for Cornelius Vanderbilt II by Richard Morris Hunt, design based on Renaissance palaces of Genoa merchants. Considered height of American palatial mansions; imperial symmetry of alabaster, marble, mosaics, antique woods; seventy rooms; reception room was gift of Marie Antoinette to goddaughter. Interior emphasis is monumental size and rich decor—blue marbles, golden swags, festoons, cartouches, and gilt everywhere; two-story inner courtyard surrounded by rooms with Hunt's original designed furniture. Frederick Law Olmsted firm planned grounds; children's playhouse remains from first Breakers.

38. THE BREAKERS STABLE, *completed 1895*, PSNC. Coggeshall Ave. Open summer, limited hours. Fee.

Vanderbilts' original carriages, coaches, livery equipment; brick, gas lamps, wrought iron; large carriage room, twenty-six open stalls, two box stalls. Another interesting glimpse of life in Newport at turn of the century.

39. ROSECLIFF, *1902*, NRHP, PSNC. Bellevue Ave. Open extended season. Fee.

Designed by Stanford White for Mrs. Herman Oelrichs, daughter of one of Comstock Silver Lode discoverers; graceful white terra-cotta mansion based on Louis XIV's Grand Trianon at Versailles, with formal facade, Ionic columns. Has large central hall, focus on curving marble staircase; decoratively molded plaster, forty rooms, largest private ballroom in Newport; Court of Love believed designed by Augustus Saint-

Gaudens. Estate was central setting for film of *The Great Gatsby,* also for party scene in *True Lies,* starring Arnold Scwarzenegger.

40. THE ASTORS' BEECHWOOD MANSION, *1856,* 580 Bellevue Ave.
Open extended season. Fee.

Costumed actors welcome visitors as guests of "The" Mrs. Astor, once queen of American society; mansion was summer home of Caroline Schermerhorn, wife of William Backhouse Astor, who was grandson of fur trader John Jacob Astor. Mrs. Astor's New York ballroom's capacity of 400 created the "New York 400," first social register in United States. Original Italianate mansion designed by Andrew Jackson Downing and Calvert Vaux, duplicated when destroyed by fire; scale smaller than most others, white stucco with quoins, keystone-arched windows.

41. MARBLE HOUSE, *1888–92,* NRHP, PSNC. Bellevue Ave. Open extended
season. Fee.

Designed by Richard Morris Hunt for William K. Vanderbilt; height of grandeur with semicircular drive to two-story Corinthian-columned porte cochere; solid rectangle of marble has arched windows, giant pilasters, heavy entablature, balustrade; inside, marble-faced interior walls; gilded ceilings, pilasters, trim; gilt and mirrored ballroom; original furnishings; yachting memorabilia room; Chinese pagoda teahouse.

42. BELCOURT CASTLE, *1892,* NHL, NHS. Bellevue Ave. Open all year, lim-
ited hours in winter; tour includes tea. Fee.

Designed by Richard Morris Hunt, after Louis XIII hunting lodge, for Oliver Hazard Perry Belmont and former Mrs. W. K. Vanderbilt; combines house and stables; elaborately medieval and eclectic; exterior brick use suggests stick style; ballroom with stained glass windows, huge plaster castle over fireplace, trefoil gallery, distended vaults; replica of gold coronation coach; stained glass collection, antique treasures.

43. CASTLE HILL COAST GUARD STATION, Ridge Rd. Open all year
by appointment. No fee.

Where Atlantic Ocean meets Narragansett Bay; station building is beautiful classic Georgian; adjacent to Castle Hill, estate of forty acres, great views; park here or at Castle Hill Inn to walk to lighthouse (automated, not open).

44. HAMMERSMITH FARM, *1887.* Harrison Ave. Open extended season.
Fee.

On Narragansett Bay, gift shop, gardens, shingle-style house on 1640 farm, last working farm in Newport; twenty-eight rooms, fifty acres; summer home of Auchincloss family, scene of wedding reception of Jacqueline Bouvier and John F. Kennedy; original furnishings.

45. FORT ADAMS STATE PARK, *1776 site*, NHL. Fort Adams Rd. off Harrison Ave. Grounds open all year. Fee in summer.

Huge park on water-surrounded peninsula; strategic location now wonderful recreation site. Park facilities: fish piers, boat launch, fields, visitor center, Block Island ferry seasonally; picnicking, swimming.

Within park are Museum of Yachting and Fort Adams Beach; 1776 fort occupied and destroyed by British 1779; 1799 fort of 21.5 acres named to honor President John Adams; rebuilt under direction of Lieutenant Colonel Joseph Totten, completed 1857, of Maine granite; earthworks, cannon; modified for use through World War II; tunnels, powder magazines, three tiers of guns; fort itself closed to public.

Museum of Yachting within park, open extended season, fee; exhibitions of Newport's golden age of yachting; vintage sail and powerboats, models, photos; galleries of solo sails, America's Cup; visiting great yachts; museum's flagship, J-class sloop *Shamrock*, America's Cup 1930, anchored here; Classic Yacht Regatta annually; public sail and lessons program; *Providence*, Continental sloop, moored here and at War College Museum; 10-gun, 110-foot topsail sloop; reproduction of first American state navy chartered craft; now for charter; **Fort Adams Beach,** open, fee in summer; lifeguards, rest rooms, showers, concessions.

BEACHES, PARKS, OTHER POINTS OF INTEREST

A. **Battery Park.** Washington and Battery sts. Open all year. No fee. Was Fort Greene, occupied by British in Revolution; views, benches; picnicking, street parking; nice area to walk along gas lantern–lined street of buildings from colonial times. (See map page 166.)

B. **Storer Park.** Washington St. Open all year. No fee. Tiny green on boat-filled harbor, 50 feet of harbor viewing, benches. (See map page 166.)

C. **Easton's Beach/First Beach.** Off Route 138A Memorial Blvd. on causeway. Open all year. Fee. Open water beach stretches from Cliff Walk to Middletown; lifeguards, pavilion, bathhouses, concessions, carousel, arcade, picnicking; events, concerts.

D. **Cliff Walk.** Accesses: (1) Memorial Blvd., (2) Narragansett Ave. at Forty Steps, (3) Ruggles Ave., (4) Bellevue at Ocean Dr. Open all year. No fee. National Recreation Trail, 3-mile path along Atlantic; wild roses, some rugged terrain; access #2 at "Forty Steps" is restoration and memorial of steps made by early 1800s family for children to get to water.

E. **Aquidneck Park.** Spring St. Open all year. No fee. Small green, benches.

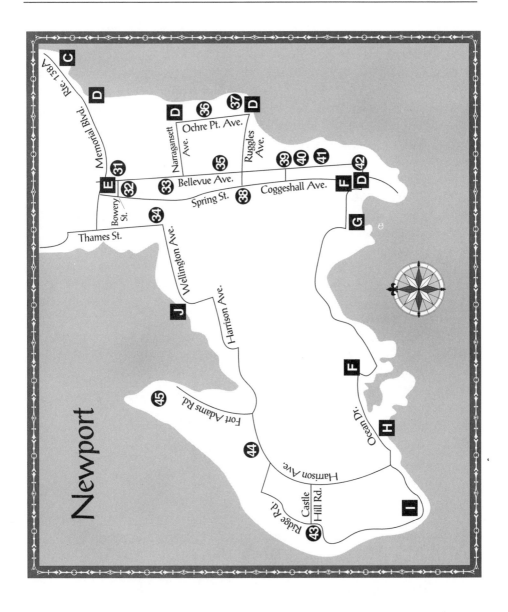

F. Ocean Drive. Open all year. No fee. About 9 miles along Atlantic Ocean passing Bailey's Beach, Almy Pond, salt marshes, ledge; limited areas to pull off road to enjoy views.

G. Bailey's Beach. Ocean Dr. Private beach with large gray pavilions; claims to be most exclusive beach club in country.

H. Price Neck Park. Ocean Dr. Kings Beach Fishing Area. Open all year. No fee. View of Brenton's Reef; fishing, scuba diving, picnicking.

I. Brenton Point State Park. Ocean Dr. view turnoff. Open all year. No fee. Rest rooms, panoramic vista of Narragansett Bay and Atlantic Ocean, peaceful landscaped park; fishing, picnicking; unusual granite representation of ancient Portuguese compass is memorial to early Portuguese explorers.

J. Kings Park Beach. Wellington Ave. Open all year. No fee. Small beach directly on Newport Harbor. View of Lime Rock Lighthouse, keeper's cottage, long pier, all now Ida Lewis Yacht Club, named for light keeper's daughter who also manned light. Rochambeau statue and monument memorialize landing of 5,000 French allies here, July 10, 1780. Lifeguards, playground, bandstand, rest rooms, concession; picnicking, concerts; street parking.

The Breakers, Newport

JAMESTOWN

Jamestown's geography—on Conanicut Island in Narragansett Bay—has helped maintain its character as a quiet pastoral community and pleasant summer sanctuary. Yet this peaceful site was an important location in early colonial history. Massachusetts Bay Governor John Winthrop asked Roger Williams to settle and fortify the island to protect Boston. In 1657 Conanicut Island, named to honor Narragansett Sachem Canonicus, was purchased by Benedict Arnold, William Coddington, and other people from Newport. The earliest settlers here were mostly Quakers, the only significant religious group until the mid-nineteenth century. They farmed and raised sheep, which they shipped through Newport. During the Revolution the British burned structures and occupied the town and fort. In August 1778, 4,000 French under Admiral d'Estaing landed and forced British and Hessians to retreat to Newport. Three forts guarding the bay's entrance, a historic lighthouse, and pleasant homes never far from water views are found on this 9-mile-long island in Narragansett Bay.

1. WATSON FARM, *1796*, SPNEA. 455 North Rd. Open summer, limited hours and by appointment. No fee.

Many centuries of farming continue on these acres. Narragansett Indians used slash-and-burn methods, providing English-style grass for first settlers to feed their sheep in the 1600s. Island farming was unique—no fences or predators—until bridges brought skunks and groundhogs and now, potentially, coyotes. By 1657 the area flourished, supplying sheep breeding stock shipped through the ready market of Newport. During the Revolution British occupiers devastated the community and countryside, burning 300 cords of wood a day. After the Revolution, Job Watson bought 400 acres. His son Robert built this plain Colonial farmhouse, which has been home to five generations of Watsons. You can hike the hill to fields, pastures, and bay views; witness planting, growth, and harvest; watch sheep and cattle; and listen to the story of the land as told by the knowledgeable farmers.

2. JAMESTOWN WINDMILL, *1787*, NHL, HS. North Rd. Open summer, limited hours and by appointment. No fee.

This weathered old mill was used continuously for more than one hundred years. The 30-foot octagonal tower has a dome or "bonnet" that can be turned to face favorable winds. The bonnet holds the wind shaft and the sweeps—25-foot wooden lattice arms. Called a smock mill, it was a style common in Rhode Island. The 5.5-foot-diameter

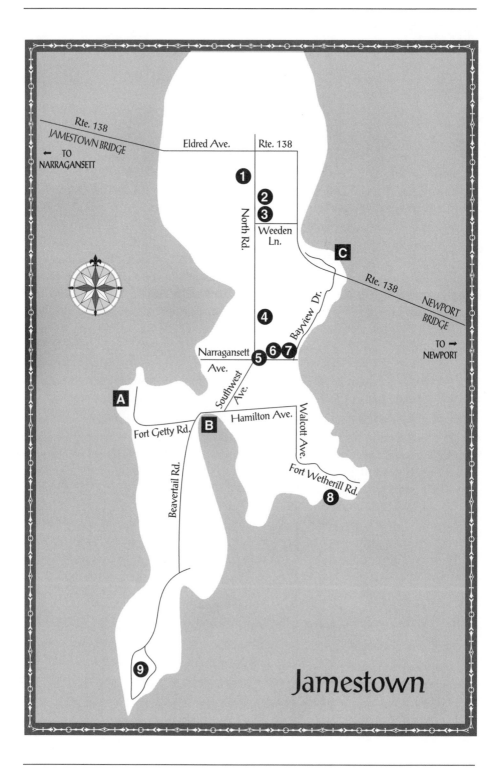

Jamestown

grinding stones weigh 3,500 pounds each. They are on the main floor, not the usual location. Grain is poured through a trapdoor on the second floor into the hopper. On the third floor you can see heavy beams, gears, wheels, and the huge solid white oak wind shaft. You can raise the top stone and discover that when it is lowered completely, the work of the mill comes to a grinding halt.

3. FRIENDS' MEETINGHOUSE, *1786–87*, NRHP. North Rd. and Weeden Ln. Open summer for worship and by appointment.

Simple and unadorned, this second meetinghouse typifies the history of conservative Quakers in Rhode Island. Two doors—one for men, one for women—and weathered shingles are the only ornaments of the exterior. Within are facing benches, wide floor boards, partitioning, and a wall that swings down from a central beam and fully divides the congregation. These dividing shutters allow independence in business meetings, say Quakers. Windows are large enough for light, but too high to permit distractions. The first meetinghouse, moved to this site, suffered from British possession and was replaced by this meetinghouse.

4. SYDNEY L. WRIGHT MUSEUM, NRHP. Jamestown Philomenian Library, 26 North Rd. Open all year, no fee. Award-winning playground created by volunteers.

A unique collection gathered from an archeological dig is beautifully displayed in a separate section of the public library. The source, an Indian burial site on Conanicut Island, is judged to be about 3,400 years old. The exhibition includes the only Narragansett Indian basket from the seventeenth century known to exist, soapstone pots, bowls, a pestle, spear points, a scraper, and an ax head from the ancient cremation site. English pots, thimbles, and sheet-brass breastplate were probably gained in trade with Roger Williams or other settlers.

5. ARTILLERY PARK, *1656*, NRHP. North Rd. and Narragansett Ave. Open all year, no fee.

This peaceful setting surrounded by stone walls was created as a cemetery in 1657. Later it was also an artillery garden, a practice ground for militia. In 1775 the British camped here.

6. JAMESTOWN MUSEUM, *1886*, NRHP, HS. 92 Narragansett Ave. Open summer, no fee.

The museum is truly Jamestown. The structure was built elsewhere as a school, moved here to be the town library, and now displays Jamestown's history. This small farming community had an unusual local industry—its ferry system, the focus of the museum's permanent collection. About 1675 Governor Carr began ferry service between

Jamestown and Newport. His descendants continued the service until 1873, when sailing ferries were replaced by steam. Steam ferries were replaced by the Jamestown Bridge in 1940 and the Newport Bridge in 1969. The ferry exhibition features pennants, name boards, lanterns, photos, maps, operating gear, and models including steamers *Beavertail* and *Conanicut*. Revolving exhibits highlight Jamestown history; a recent one presented fifty years of the Jamestown Bridge.

7. FIRE MUSEUM. 50 Narragansett Ave. Open all year through fire station, no fee.

Position of honor goes to the steamer, bought new by Jamestown for $3,300 in 1894. Refurbished and meeting class A tests, it still pumps water when taken to fires on occasion, drawing admiring crowds. The hand tub on display is one of Newport's first. Upstairs are wood fire mains, historic fire coats, awards, and a nozzle from Hitler's house in Berchtesgaden, given to a past fire chief by General Dwight D. Eisenhower.

8. FORT WETHERILL, NRHP. Fort Wetherill Rd. Open all year, no fee. Boat launch, rest rooms; picnicking, hiking, fishing, scuba diving.

Granite cliffs afford open views of approaches to Narragansett Bay, particularly the eastern channel. This site, fortified for centuries, now provides fifty-two acres of natural beauty to enjoy as a state park within the Bay Island Park system. Trails along the rocky peninsula lead to spectacular vistas of Newport's Fort Adams, Trinity's steeple, and Castle Hill Light, and on the other side across the bay to Point Judith, and farther to Block Island. The first earthwork fortifications were called Dumpling Rock Battery, begun in 1776 but captured by British before cannons were installed. A stone tower and fortifications of Fort Dumplings were begun in 1799 but never completed. A century later Fort Wetherill contained seven Endicott batteries of two or three weapons, each with concrete walls 15 to 20 feet thick and covered by more than 40 feet of sand and dirt topped by vegetation. Plotting rooms and ammunition vaults were below and adjacent. Forts here protected Newport Harbor in the Civil War, the War of 1812, and both world wars. Now the guns, which never fired at an enemy, have been removed, and traces of older forts are gone.

Legend tells of nearby Pirate's Cave, another story of pirate treasure of Captain Kidd, the British privateer who became a notorious pirate. It was said that Kidd was a friend of Jamestown resident Captain Thomas Paine, a celebrated privateersman. Paine's friendship with Kidd was investigated after Kidd's wife asked Paine for twenty-four ounces of gold in 1699, the year Kidd was captured and hanged. No charges were filed.

9. BEAVERTAIL LIGHTHOUSE AND STATE PARK, *1856*, NRHP.

Beavertail Rd. Open all year; lighthouse museum open summer; no fee. Scenic overviews; fishing, scuba diving.

Beavertail's fascination begins with its geology. It was once a separate island, which wave and wind erosion converted to a peninsula by piling sand at Mackerel Cove. Narragansett Bay is a drowned valley and islands were hills. The park naturalist program focuses on geology, marine life, and shipwrecks. Within the park the open rocky peninsula affords wide panoramic views. The lighthouse still operates. The keeper's cottage is a museum of Rhode Island lighthouse history. Fresnel lens, photos, lighthouse keepers' uniforms, and other lighthouse memorabilia tell their stories. The site was the first in Rhode Island to install a light and was mentioned in a letter from George Washington in 1790. The 1749 light was burned by the British October 16, 1779. Its rubble base was exposed in the hurricane of 1938. The present granite tower, built in 1856, is north of the original base. Here fog signals—the first air-compressor whistle and steam fog whistle—were developed and tested.

BEACHES, PARKS, OTHER POINTS OF INTEREST

A. Fort Getty, Conanicut Battery, NRHP. Fort Getty Rd. Open all year, fee in summer. Boat launch, small beach, covered picnic areas, playground; hiking, camping. Earthworks of Conanicut Battery or Prospect Hill Fort, battered sides and artillery trench built 1776; occupied by British, site enabled British to bottle Continental Navy in Providence; some remains of 1900 Fort Getty used during World Wars I and II; see abandoned lighthouse, wonderful views of Narragansett Bay.

B. Mackerel Cove. Beavertail Rd. Open all year. Fee in summer. Town beach, lifeguards, rest rooms, concessions; swimming.

C. Taylor Point. Bayview Drive at access to Newport Bridge. Open all year. No fee. Town beach, path; scuba diving, picnicking, fishing.

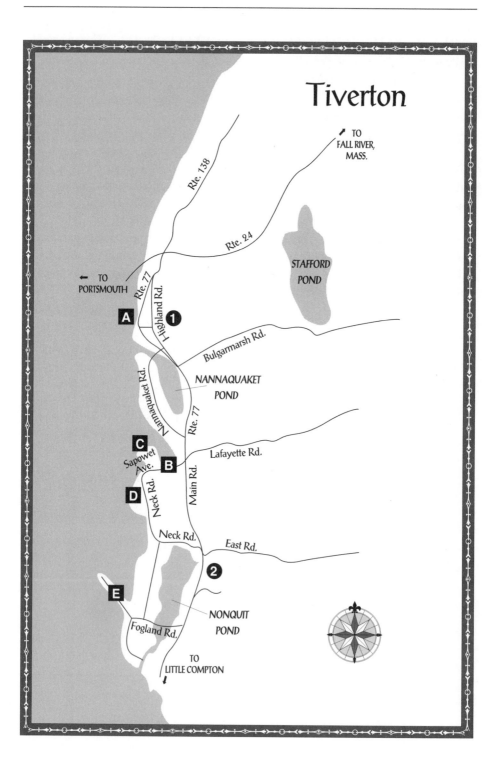

TIVERTON

T iverton is unusual. Though near Providence and Fall River, the village focus was on farming and fishing, being neither industrial nor heavily populated. The pastoral feeling remains in this quiet residential and summer resort community. Yet during the Revolution, Tiverton's location was strategic. The village was next to Aquidneck Island (originally called Rhode Island)—Portsmouth, Middletown, Newport—where the action was. In Tiverton Americans retreating from the British found a haven, gathered information from observations of the British across the Sakonnet River, and mustered in 1777 for the Battle of Rhode Island (see Portsmouth introduction). The following year the British warship *Pigot*—200 tons, with eight twelve-pound cannons—blocked Sakonnet River. The American sloop *Hawk*, commanded by Major Silas Talbot, with two three-pound cannons and sixty men, surprised the British. All British were captured with no loss of life on either side. In the next decade Captain Robert Gray of Tiverton became the first man to carry the American flag around the world, first to build a ship on the Pacific coast, and discoverer of the Columbia River. He named the river for the ship he commanded and claimed the land for his newly free country.

1. FORT BARTON, *1777* site, NRHP. Highland Rd. Open all year, no fee. Observation tower, marked history and nature trails.

Walk up a steep hill and you are immediately rewarded with a panoramic vista of the Sakonnet River, Narragansett Bay, and Rhode Island Sound. Sweeping views reveal why you don't drive far in Rhode Island without seeing water. You also appreciate the strategic location of Fort Barton, named for Colonel William Barton, leader of the successful raid in 1777 to capture General Prescott (see Middletown, 1). You can understand the logistics and picture the massing, a year later, of more than 10,000 men for the Battle of Rhode Island. General Sullivan commanded. Generals Varnum, Glover, Lafayette, and Nathaneal Greene were involved. Yet the twelve-day siege ended in retreat. Regular troops rejoined Washington, militia went home, and only a small force remained to man the guns of Fort Barton.

2. CHACE–CORY HOUSE, *c. 1730*, NRHP, HS. Main Rd. Open summer, limited hours, or by appointment; fee.

Weathered shingles face this simple, New England gambrel-roofed Colonial, which could be the oldest building in town. The kitchen is unchanged, with 7-foot-wide fireplace, huge parallel beams, elliptical beaded mantelpiece with open shelves, and vertical pine paneling. The Federal parlor has Victorian period furnishings. Treasures include a chocolate pot, a gift to his hostess and relative from Captain Robert Gray. The house is in Tiverton Four Corners Historic District, a village of shops and homes of whalers and China trade merchants. The Soule–Seabury House, on the northeast corner of Main and East roads, is a handsome Georgian.

BEACHES, PARKS, OTHER POINTS OF INTEREST

A. Grinnell's Beach. Route 77 at old bridge foundation. Open all year. Fee. Lifeguards, rest rooms, changing rooms, swings; swimming, picnicking, see Gould Island, fish from bridge abutment.

B. Ruecker Wildlife Refuge. Sapowet Ave. Open all year. No fee. 48 acres, 1.5 miles marked trails; woods, meadow, salt marsh, open water. Audubon refuge.

C. Jack's Island. Sapowet Ave. at Neck Rd. Open all year. No fee. Small peninsula of ledge; on-road parking. Audubon area.

D. Sapowet State Beach. Neck Rd. Open all year. No fee. Hunting, fishing, parking on beach.

E. Fogland Beach. Fogland Rd. Open all year. Fee. Lifeguards, rest rooms, swings, picnic tables, open peninsula of beach and marsh. Historic site: Fogland Ferry to Portsmouth with rates set by legislative acts; earthworks observation site for Patriots; July 8, 1765, Benjamin Church and militia company were attacked by Indians, retreated here, were rescued by sloop commanded by Captain Goulding.

LITTLE COMPTON

This tranquil country village was settled in 1674. Many settlers came directly from Plymouth, including Howlands and Aldens. Two decades later the Town House was both Congregational meetinghouse and town hall. About 1700 the first separate place of worship was built, the Friends' Meeting House. Little Compton's most famous son was knowledgeable Indian fighter Benjamin Church. Here he met with Squaw Chief Awashonks of the Sakonnet Indians August 1, 1675. She and her tribe agreed not to fight against whites in King Philip's War. One of her warriors, Alderman, killed King Philip, beheaded him, and paraded King Philip's hand and head before they were displayed in Plymouth for twenty-four years.

1. WILBOR (WILBOUR) HOUSE, *1680*; Barn Museum, 1860, NHS, HS.
West Main Rd. Open summer, limited hours, or by appointment; fee.

The Wilbors were Puritans who went from Boston to Portsmouth with Anne Hutchinson and then to Little Compton. Here they and their eleven children lived in the original two rooms. These rooms are furnished with Little Compton items based on the inventory of Samuel and Mary Potter Wilbor, who died in 1740. In the keeping room of the oldest section, where the family lived and parents slept, the basic structure remains. Furnishings include c. 1680 press bed, c. 1660 brass candlestick, and a Marshfield chest older than the house. The paneled inner walls and shell-plastered outer walls were common in early seacoast homes.

The 1740s addition rooms contain many rare furnishings and oddities such as birth pillows, wig caps, an early 1700s corset, and Little Compton chairs with split banister backs and distinctive finials and turnings. There are portraits of people such as John Simmons, who founded Simmons College because he felt women also needed education, and Sarah Soule Wilbor, who was active in women's rights. The 1860s addition rooms are furnished with Victorian treasures. The kitchen demonstrates modern developments with icebox, c. 1900 vacuum cleaner, and water supply from cistern and pump. Home to Wilbors and their descendants for three centuries, the farmhouse shows the evolution of architecture. Outbuildings are individual museums: the "Peaked Top" schoolhouse, cook house for chicken feed, and barn full of treasures with stories.

2. FRIENDS' MEETING HOUSE, *1700*, HS. West Main Rd. Open all year
by appointment.

The site is quiet—stone wall enclosure, austere unadorned exterior, and small graveyard with ancient stones, some bearing the name Howland. The usual separate doors lead to the simple interior. A fireplace at each end, basic wood benches, and partition-

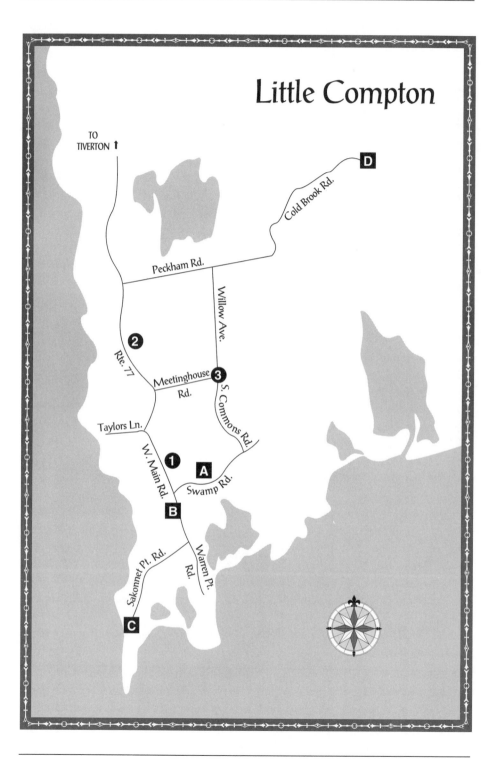

Little Compton

ing complete the white-walled, plain wood sanctuary. Original 1700s structure was rebuilt and altered in the 1800s.

3. LITTLE COMPTON COMMON HISTORIC DISTRICT, NRHP.
Meeting House Rd. Open all year, no fee.

The unspoiled triangular green is surrounded by structures from the seventeenth through twentieth centuries. The **United Congregational Church** still dominates the green. It was built in 1832 for a congregation organized more than a century before. Victorian changes began about 1872. The elegant church, once a small Greek Revival, has pilasters, door enframements, and a bracketed multiple-tiered tower and steeple. The **1675 burial ground** behind the church tells stories of early New England. The obelisk is for Elizabeth Alden Pabodie, daughter of John and Priscilla Mullins Alden and first white female born in New England. The set of ten raised gravestones are for Benjamin Church; his wife, Alice; and their children and grandchildren.

BEACHES, PARKS, OTHER POINTS OF INTEREST

A. **Wilbour Woods.** Swamp Rd. Open summer. No fee. Paths, some wide enough to drive; rock monuments; picnicking, hiking.

B. **Benjamin Church House Site.** West Main Rd. Open all year. No fee. Small stone with bronze plate marker on road (1 mile south of #1) tells where house and farm stood; Indian fighter and diplomat Benjamin Church also founded small mill business, wrote *Entertaining History of King Philip's War;* next house south belonged to son Thomas.

C. **Sakonnet Point and Sakonnet Light.** Sakonnet Point Rd. Active fishing village; fishing. See Inactive Sakonnet Light, restored, on tiny island of rock; open panoramic views of Sakonnet River mouth, Rhode Island Sound, Atlantic. Small village with working waterfront and breakwater is much as it was when President Chester Arthur visited, shook hands with all save a fisherman who refused, as had fish on hands; next day President in carriage tipped hat to that fisherman as he passed on his mule. Nearby, **Haffenreffer Wildlife Refuge and Fishing Area,** open all year, no fee; fishing, scuba diving.

D. **Rhode Island Red Monument,** in village of Adamsville. Only monument to a chicken in United States; breed established in 1854.

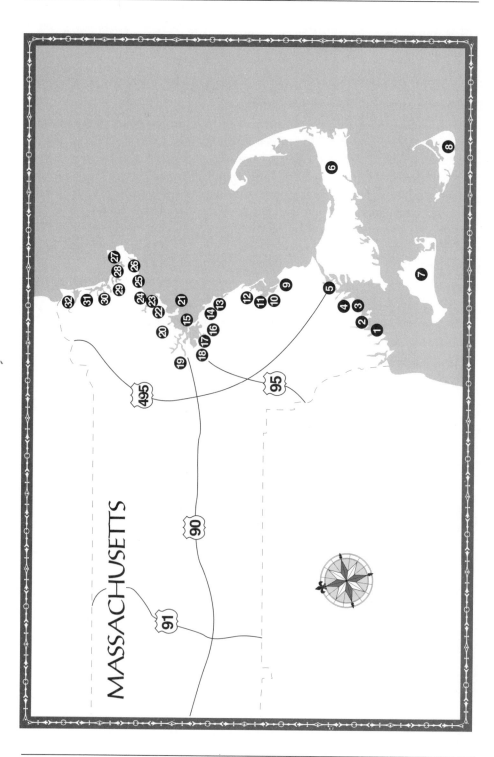

MASSACHUSETTS

(AT = Abbreviated Tour)

NEW BEDFORD

New Bedford is authentic. It is not a reconstructed town built to recreate the past. It is the past, intermingled with the present. When you enter a ship's chandlery you know seamen have entered the same doors for as long as anyone can remember. This is normal everyday life in a working New England seaport.

New Bedford evolved from a quiet pastoral and fishing community to the competition and excitement of being the whaling capital of the world. During that golden era prosperous sea captains and merchants lived on County Street, overlooking the busy harbor, where docks were lined with whalers and piled with barrels of whale oil. As whaling declined in the late 1800s, New Bedford became a leading cotton manufacturing center. At the same time fishing continued as the backbone of New Bedford's life. Today New Bedford has the largest fishing fleet in the country.

Thanks to history-oriented and preservation-minded citizens along with WHALE (Waterfront Historic Area LeaguE), the waterfront, in use since 1755, and many historic buildings have been restored in today's revitalized city. The **New Bedford Whaling National Heritage Park** includes parts of the city and the real-life active waterfront, interpretative museums, and visitor centers. All unite in telling the story of New Bedford and its people.

A walk along New Bedford's streets offers glimpses of fascinating architecture and interesting personages (homes private). **James Arnold's** 1821 mansion at 421 County Street illustrates Second Empire architecture. Arnold, one of New Bedford's merchant princes, was an early abolitionist, president of the New Bedford Port Society, and benefactor of Harvard's Arnold Arboretum. At 106 Spring, corner of County, is the unadorned 1828 Quaker Federal home of **Samuel Rodman, Jr.** A leading whaling merchant and textile pioneer, Rodman showed through many years of meteorological records that New Bedford was uniquely qualified for textile manufacturing. **Samuel W. Rodman's** c. 1842 home at 412 County is a rough-cut granite Gothic cottage, while **William J. Rotch's** 1846 home at 19 Irving Street is a Gothic Revival cottage. William J. Rotch was mayor, local Republican party founder, president of Friends Academy, and a director of almost every corporation in town.

Gilbert Russell's 1805 house at 405 County has a Federal core remodeled in 1868 to French Second Empire with Italianate brackets and Oriental flair. Gilbert Russell was son of New Bedford founder Joseph Russell III. **William R. Rodman's** imposing granite Greek Revival mansion at 388 County cost as much as any home in the country when built in 1833. Here lived whaling merchant Rodman, one of the wealthiest men in town; Abraham H. Howland, Jr. and Sr., both mayors of New Bedford; and Joseph F. Knowles, Thomas S. Hathaway, and Frederick Grinnell, textile merchants from old New Bedford families.

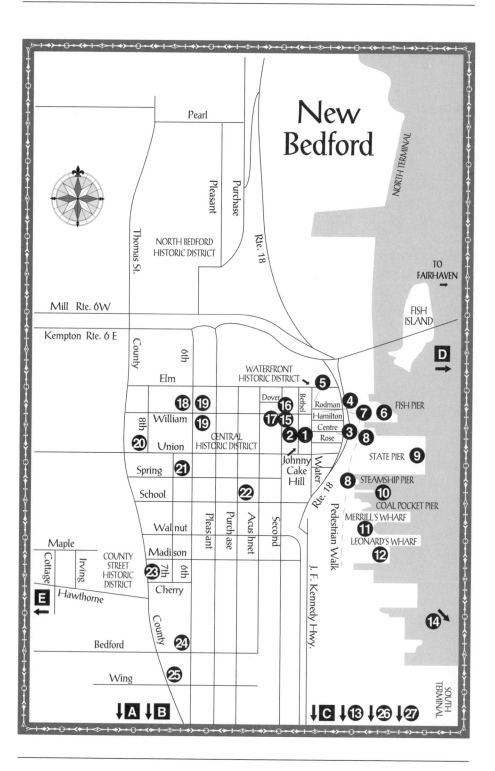

Joseph Grinnell's massive granite Greek Revival 1832 mansion at 379 County was designed by Russell Warren. President of Wamsutta Mills, U.S. representative, and Governor's Council member, Grinnell hosted John Q. Adams, Daniel Webster, and Abraham Lincoln here.

Few cities have preserved their past yet progress as well as New Bedford, which sought new avenues of economic prosperity before existing ones were exhausted. New Bedford's Waterfront District (NRHP, National Landmark District), its narrow, cut-stone streets and brick and cobblestone walks lighted by replicas from the past, has been a vital center since early days.

1. WHALING MUSEUM, Old Dartmouth Historical Society, *1904*. 18 Johnny Cake Hill. Open all year, fee. Conservation laboratory, research library, gift shop, theater, guided walking tours, programs.

The saga of the whale and of the men dedicated to hunting it comes alive at the Whaling Museum. Paintings, photographs, stern boards, figureheads, ship models, logbooks, and part of a ¼-mile panorama tell the story of whaling. Long voyages are reflected in the American folk art of scrimshaw and in paintings depicting whaling adventures in remote parts of the world. Supporting industries are presented in separate room displays. The *Lagoda*, half-scale replica of a square-rigged whaler, with humpback whale skeleton suspended overhead, provides a perfect background to relive days of whaling. The Bourne Building honors Jonathan Bourne, whaling merchant and owner of the *Lagoda* and of more whaling ships than anyone in New England at that time. You circumnavigate the globe as you follow the routes of the whalers.

2. SEAMEN'S BETHEL, *1832*. 15 Johnny Cake Hill. Open extended season, limited hours; donations.

The spirit of the sea is evident everywhere, from three-masted whaler weather vane to bowsprit-shaped pulpit and pew cushions covered with sailcloth. One pew in the Bethel was occasionally occupied by Herman Melville, author of the classic *Moby-Dick*. Below the chapel is the "Old Salt Box," named for the hold of a ship where fish were preserved in salt, possibly symbolic of preserving men's souls. In the early 1800s all levels of society existed in New Bedford, from socially elite to harlots, thieves, and murderers, with 5,000 sailors moving through the port annually. To counteract ills of society, local businessmen, led by Samuel Rodman, founded the New Bedford Port Society in 1830 and built the Bethel, which opened May 2, 1832. Over the years this nondenominational Christian service has counseled and supported seamen and their families and placed thousands of Bibles aboard ships. During the whaling era the society was an invaluable source, listing crews sailing from New Bedford. This simple gray clapboard building has inspired a world.

3. WILLIAM TALLMAN WAREHOUSE, *1790.* 13 Centre St. Open all year as business.

Historically important, across from the working waterfront, **Centre Street** was once lined with commercial buildings and had whaling try-pots at its foot. Today the area is restored, remaining a vital part of waterfront activities. The William Tallman Warehouse, one of the city's oldest buildings, was built in the Federal style by William Tallman, whaling pioneer and partner of New Bedford founder Joseph Russell III. Tallman served as New Bedford's first selectman 1787–1802.

WHALE (the nonprofit Waterfront Historic Area LeaguE) has offices in Tallman Warehouse. WHALE, dedicated to saving historically important structures and using them in adaptive ways, was responsible for the warehouse's preservation, as it has been for much of New Bedford.

4. DOUBLE BANK BUILDING, *1831–35.* Water St. Private offices.

This Greek Revival was designed by architect Russell Warren with massive Ionic portico and polished granite steps and facade. Housing two banks, the building was built when whaling was king and Water Street was known as the Wall Street of New Bedford.

5. RODMAN CANDLEWORKS, *1810,* NRHP. Water and Rodman sts. Open all year as offices and restaurant.

Samuel Rodman, Sr., whaling entrepreneur, built this candleworks, one of the first to produce superior spermaceti candles. The light of one such candle set the permanent standard for "candlepower." After the death of Samuel, Sr., the candleworks remained in the family under son-in-law Andrew Robeson. He was aided by Rodman's sons Benjamin and Samuel, Jr., and son-in-law Charles W. Morgan, owner of the famous whaling ship at Mystic Seaport, Connecticut. The building walled with 2-foot-thick rubble was restored by WHALE and the City of New Bedford.

6. FISH PIER. Open all year, no fee. Pier for Cuttyhunk Ferry *Alert II.*

Access is available via the Pedestrian Overpass, which, with its observation deck, can be reached from Rodman Street, east of the Candleworks (see 5). Fish Pier is on the water side of the overpass, and the walk continues to points 7 through 12.

The large open Fish Pier services New Bedford's fishing fleet. You will see ships tied up two and three abreast here and at wharves on both sides of the river. Vessels vary from $300,000 draggers to million-dollar scallopers, from rusty hulls with peeling paint to new steel-hulled ships with polished wood trim.

7. WHARFINGER'S BUILDING, *1934.* Fish Pier. New Bedford Visitors Center; open all year, no fee.

Wharfinger's, an unassuming brick building built for the harbormaster, was once the most important building on the waterfront. Here was decided the economic fate of every ship's catch. World prices for scallops and yellowtail flounder were set here each morning—scallop auction was 7:00 a.m., fish 8:00 a.m. At their appointed time fishing captains crowded into Wharfinger's, listing their catch on a board. A bell rang. In less than a minute, representatives from processing plants registered bids. Captains had fifteen minutes to accept them. Another bell. The auction was finalized. The outcome of seven to ten days' work at sea was decided in a few hectic minutes. Boats moved to processing plants. The catch was unloaded, processed, and shipped by truck, completing the vital cycle in the life of the fisherman.

8. LIGHTSHIP NEW BEDFORD. Not open. TONNESSEN PARK.
Open all year, no fee. Small waterfront pocket park.

Tonnessen Park is dedicated to Rasmus Tonnessen, founder of New Bedford Ship Supply, credited with helping many fishermen get their start in the fishing industry. He died in 1991.

Adjacent to the park is the lightship *New Bedford*, moored near vessels she once protected. In earlier days she was anchored as an aid to navigation in locations too difficult for lighthouses. Her powerful beacons, foghorns, and radio kept a lonely, vital vigil.

9. STATE PIER. South of lightship *New Bedford*. Open all year, no fee.

All foreign imports and exports for New Bedford pass through the State Pier, operated by the Commonwealth of Massachusetts. At this busy international terminal, local fishermen tie up long enough to sell shack fish (additional seafood brought up with the main catch) to truck buyers. State Pier is home port to U.S. Coast Guard cutters, which serve vessels in distress as well as patrol 200-mile offshore fishing areas from Canada to Florida on behalf of Uncle Sam. In 1876 a two-year training program for Coast Guard cadets began on the *J.C. Dobbin*, a converted schooner, which was replaced by the barque *Salmon P. Chase* in 1878. When the *Chase* wintered in New Bedford, the school held classes in a local sail loft. This school evolved into the U.S. Coast Guard Academy at New London, Connecticut.

The meticulously restored schooner *Ernestina* (NRHP), used for special cruises and educational tours, is moored here. The *Ernestina* was built in 1894 in Essex, Massachusetts, as the *Effie M. Morrissey*. She fished the Grand Banks for thirty years, explored the Arctic under Captain Robert Bartlett, and sailed the Atlantic in the Cape Verde packet trade. Cape Verde presented her to the United States for educational, cultural, and community use.

10. STEAMSHIP AND COAL POCKET PIER. Open all year, no fee.

Steamship Pier is aptly named. From 1891 to 1933 it served as a terminal for the picturesque white side-wheelers *Monnohansett* and *Martha's Vineyard*. These proud ferries, running between New Bedford, Nantucket, and Martha's Vineyard, brought special glamor to New Bedford. After World War II they were replaced by modern car ferries. With the excitement of the side-wheelers gone, however, people drove to Woods Hole, ending New Bedford's Nantucket ferry run by 1961.

Adjacent Coal Pocket Pier received and stored thousands of barrels of whale oil during the whaling era. By the late 1800s whale oil was replaced by coal stored in containers or "pockets" waiting to be shipped by wagon; thus the name Coal Pocket Pier. Today this municipal pier is a recreational window on a working waterfront.

11. BOURNE COUNTING HOUSE, *1847*, NRHP. Merrill's Wharf. Open all year as restaurant, inn, and business.

In this indomitable building Jonathan Bourne maintained counting rooms for over forty years. He was said to own more whaling tonnage than anyone in the country. When whaling declined, Bourne became a major adviser of the new textile industry. He was president and/or director of banks, mills, utilities, and railroads here and in Fall River; he was also alderman, state representative, and member of the Governor's Council. A restored part of New Bedford Heritage State Park, Bourne Counting House is located on Captain Edward Merrill's Wharf, where more whale oil was landed than anywhere else in New Bedford.

12. LEONARD'S WHARF. Open all year, no fee.

Leonard's Wharf was named for Samuel Leonard, who owned a wharf downriver, where he ran a prosperous lumber business from 1830 to the mid-1900s. Today Leonard's Wharf is a busy center for many members of New Bedford's active fishing fleet.

13. HURRICANE BARRIER, *1965*. Drive south on J. F. Kennedy Highway (Rte. 18) to end, turn left, go 1 block to Front St., turn right 1 block to Gifford St., park at end of street. Open all year, no fee. Views, fishing, walk along top of barrier.

Battered ships, broken bulkheads, and flooded waterfront buildings are a thing of the past. New Bedford's harbor is now protected by a 9,100-foot-long by 20-foot-high hurricane barrier from Fort Phoenix, Fairhaven, to Clark's Point, New Bedford. The disastrous effects of the 1938 and 1954 hurricanes and knowledge that New Bedford is in a flood plain forced the building of this multimillion-dollar barrier in 1965. Manned twenty-four hours a day, the barrier's opening is controlled by two 400-ton gates, each operated by a twenty-five-horsepower engine. When gates are open a strobe light flashes. If wind, tide, and weather conditions combine to threaten the harbor, strobe lights increase to constant flashing, an alarm goes off, radio announcements are made, and the gates close. Within twelve minutes the harbor is sealed off. Once inside sailors know they are safe—in one of the few truly sheltered ports in New England. On calm days the barrier looks like the Appian Way in Rome. You can see Sconticut Neck in Fairhaven, Cape Cod, Elizabeth Islands, and Martha's Vineyard on the horizon.

14. PALMER ISLAND AND LIGHTHOUSE, *1849*, NRHP. Accessible through Marine Park (D).

Palmer Island, named for William Palmer, who was scalped by Indians in King Philip's War, served as a detention camp for Indians and later as a garrison. In the 1800s this now unassuming island supported a summer home, hotel, dance hall, bowling alley, and amusement park. To protect seamen, the government built a light and light-keeper's house in 1849. During New Bedford's whaling era and prominence as a fishing port, Palmer Island Light welcomed mariners for over a hundred years. Automated in 1941, it was replaced by the Hurricane Barrier in 1965.

15. ANDREW ROBESON HOUSE, *1821*, NRHP. William and Second sts. Open all year as business.

This dominating Federal building is truly symbolic of New Bedford. Built by a prominent whaling and manufacturing entrepreneur, it was rescued and rehabilitated by the cooperative mountain-moving efforts of the city and WHALE. In spite of insurance snags, doubting experts, Christmas-shopping traffic, and the wild winter of 1978, the 550-ton mansion was painstakingly moved here from behind Pairpoint Glassworks on Second Street.

Original owner Quaker Andrew Robeson had interest in whale ships, a whale-oil refinery, and banks; he also managed Rodman Candleworks. His appropriately grand house was originally surrounded by gardens covering two city blocks. Chlorite rock forms the rubblestone walls faced with brick from Philadelphia. An unusual semielliptical fanlight and brick arches surmount the entrance and lower windows. The mansion has a Dutch cap roof.

16. NEW BEDFORD INSTITUTION FOR SAVINGS AND THIRD DISTRICT COURT OF BRISTOL, *1853*, NHL, NRHP. 33 William St. Open all year as bank.

When New Bedford Institution for Savings began in 1825, its aim was to serve those of moderate means when most banks were for the wealthy. Monies were invested in local commerce, mainly relating to whaling. The bank moved to this building in 1854, remaining for nearly half a century. The building housed Third District Court of Bristol from 1899 to 1914. In recent years the bank repurchased and revived the building, which now has limited teller operation in an 1800s setting amid handcrafted reproduction mahogany counters and cages. The structure combines Greek and Italian Renaissance Revival styles.

17. U.S. CUSTOM HOUSE, *1834*, NRHP. Second and William sts. Open all year, no fee.

Here sea captains enter to clear ships and cargos, and seamen from all over the world register. Largest and most elaborate of New England customhouses, it is the oldest building in the country continuously used only as a customhouse. The Greek Revival structure was designed by Washington Monument architect Robert Mills and (possibly) Russell Warren and was built at a cost of $32,000. The front facade is carefully hewn white granite with classical portico supported by four Doric columns of tooled granite. The interior features an unsurpassed cantilevered stairway.

18. FIRST BAPTIST CHURCH, *1829*, NRHP. 149 William St.

This white-steepled Federal and Greek Revival church stands as a monument to religious freedom. Early settlers in the area, mainly Baptists and Quakers, sought religious freedom from Puritan Plymouth. Reverend John Cooke, who came to the New World as a boy aboard the *Mayflower*, founded a Baptist Church in Tiverton, Rhode Island, in 1685. By 1813 some members wanted to have their own church in New Bedford. Meeting in the old New Bedford Town Hall, they incorporated in 1828 and a year later erected this building. The sky-reaching steeple has long served as a guide to mariners, thus its prominence on New Bedford's seal. As the steeple reached out to mariners, the church reached out to people, establishing missions for Portuguese, French, and Swedish members. A noteworthy member 1862–65 was Captain Henry Martyn Robert. One evening, while conducting a church meeting, he had so much trouble maintaining order that he later wrote *Robert's Rules of Order.*

19. CITY HALL, *1856*, and NEW BEDFORD FREE PUBLIC LIBRARY, *1837*. William St. Open all year, no fee.

The neoclassical City Hall bears a notable artistic frieze in the pediment crowning the front entrance. Industries of New Bedford are illustrated: fishing, whaling, textiles, shipping, and railroads. The motto on New Bedford's seal, *"Lucem Diffundo,"* "We light the world," is a living reminder of New Bedford's greatness as a whaling center whose whale oil in earlier days provided light for the world.

Across the street is the New Bedford Free Public Library, with a realistic whaling statue in front. The Greek Revival building, designed by Russell Warren, was originally the Town Hall and marketplace. The interior is Egyptian Revival. The library collections include books on whaling, plates from the original edition of Audubon's *Birds of America,* and a superb collection of nineteenth-century paintings and works by Albert Bierstadt, who lived in New Bedford.

20. FIRST UNITARIAN CHURCH, *1838*. Union and Eighth sts.

Looking as though it would be at home among the castles of medieval England, this rough-cut stone, early Gothic Revival church is unusual in that through its history it has included Congregationalists, Baptists, Quakers, and Unitarians among its membership.

The church body traces its history to the First Congregational Society of Acushnet in 1708. That early church was built under the auspices of the Puritan-minded General Court of Massachusetts, which taxed all colonists for church support. When New Bedford's selectmen refused to tax local Baptists and Quakers for a church foreign to their beliefs, the selectmen were imprisoned. Help was sought in England. As a result, in 1729 the General Court ruled that Baptists and Quakers were exempt from taxes levied to support town churches. A giant step for freedom of religion had been taken.

In 1796 thirty-five New Bedfordites separated from the Acushnet church and built their own Congregational church on the corner of Purchase and William streets on land given by Quaker William Rotch. When a division occurred in 1810, orthodox members formed the North Congregational Church. The liberal group retained the building and in 1824 became the First Congregational Society of New Bedford. That same year Dr. Orville Dewey, a leader in the Unitarian movement, was called as their minister. Soon afterward a group of influential Quakers, alienated from the Society of Friends, found a spiritual home in this intellectually open atmosphere, which ultimately became the First Unitarian Church.

The present building, designed by Alexander Jackson Davis and Russell Warren, was completed in 1838. In its three-aisle sanctuary, banners representing religions of the world are enhanced by a beautiful mosaic Tiffany window.

Pause for a moment to explore events that caused many Congregational churches to become Unitarian. As a reaction to years of strict Puritan discipline and strong Calvinistic convictions, a liberal wing developed in Congregational churches during the late 1700s. An early split came in 1805 when liberal thinker Dr. Henry Ware was appointed to the Hollis professorship of theology at Harvard College. Then in 1819 William Ellery Channing preached a sermon in which he set forth what would become Unitarian views (see Newport 22). With Harvard turning out liberal-minded ministers and Channing Unitarians taking hold, many Congregational churches split. Liberals formed Unitarian churches, and conservatives held to Congregational doctrines. Consequently, many of the first churches in New England's coastal area became Unitarian, though Congregationalism is considered the traditional church of early New England.

21. FRIENDS MEETING HOUSE, c. 1822. Spring St.

Quakers first came to the New Bedford area in 1664 seeking freedom from persecution. By the mid-1700s they were joined by Quakers from Nantucket, who brought invaluable whaling expertise. This practical asset, combined with the ethical, spiritual, and economic strengths of the Quakers, formed the foundation for New Bedford's greatness as the world's whaling capital and later as a leading textile center. In 1785 the first Society of Friends meetinghouse was built here on land given by Joseph Russell III. As the society grew, the present larger building became necessary. The old one

Whaleman's Statue, New Bedford   (Massachusetts Office of Travel and Tourism)

was moved to 17 Seventh Street; there it became the home of Nathan and Polly Johnson, close friends of famous black antislavery leader Frederick Douglass, who lived for a time with the Johnsons.

The present brick building has separate entrances for men and women. Its simple severity is broken only by a slight curve in the stair railing. Inside it is equally spartan, with hand-planed cushioned benches, simple glass fixtures, unadorned walls, and plain molding around curtainless windows. Quakers, who believe God's spirit is present in everyone, strongly opposed slavery, freeing their slaves by 1785. They established one of the early antislavery societies in 1834, and through the Underground Railroad helped hundreds of slaves to freedom.

22. ZEITERION THEATRE, *1923.* 684 Purchase St. Open all year as theater.

Built as a vaudeville house, it hosted silent movies. Recently it has been restored to its 1920s elegance. Marble columns and rich gumwood lead to the auditorium, which features a frieze of golden Grecian dancing figures and Czechoslovakian cut glass chandelier of 240 lamps and 6,000 pieces.

23. THE ROTCH-JONES-DUFF HOUSE AND GARDEN MUSEUM, *1834.* 396 County St. Open all year, fee. Gift shop, exhibits, concerts, program activities.

The William Rotch, Jr., estate is important for its beautifully preserved twenty-eight-room Greek Revival house and formal gardens, which show how a prominent New Bedford whaling merchant lived in the 1800s. William Rotch, Jr., born in 1759 on Nantucket, came to New Bedford after the Revolution and contributed mercantile talents to Rotch enterprises and New Bedford. Founder and president of New Bedford Institution for Savings, he contributed nearly half the money to build Friends Academy in 1811, and served the academy as an officer until his death in 1850. Following his death the house was sold to Edward Coffin Jones, whaling merchant, incorporator of the Marine Bank, and one of the richest men in New Bedford. In 1935 the house passed to the successful Mark Duff, of the New Bedford Hotel, Union Street Railroad Company, and Merchants National Bank. Later this home, once praised by John Q. Adams, was bought and preserved by WHALE.

24. NEW BEDFORD FIRE MUSEUM, *1867,* NRHP. Bedford and Sixth sts. Open summer and by appointment, fee.

Steam pumps, fire engines, buckets, models, awards, tools, logbooks, clothing, and photographs tell the history of New Bedford fire fighting. Working exhibits include clothing to try on, a pole to slide down, and bells to ring. The museum shares Fire Station Number Four, established in 1867, oldest active station in Massachusetts until decommissioned in 1979.

25. ST. JOHN THE BAPTIST CHURCH, *1913*. County and Wing sts.

This granite Romanesque church was the first Portuguese Catholic parish in the United States. In the mid-1800s Portuguese seamen from islands barely able to supply them with basic needs came to New Bedford aboard whaling ships. They first worshiped at St. Mary's Catholic Church but soon sought a church with their own language and customs. In 1871 this parish was established under the devoted leadership of Father Joao Ignacio de Azevedo. The present building has a domelike altar area highlighted by paintings depicting events in the life of Christ, Stations of the Cross done in relief, and brilliantly colored stained glass windows.

26. BUTLER'S FLATS LIGHT, *1898*, NRHP. Seen from East Rodney French Blvd.

Butler's Flats Light still glows its welcome to returning seamen. A 35-foot-diameter cylinder was filled with stone and concrete, putting the light 53 feet above mean low tide level. Living quarters 18 feet in diameter housed the light keeper; the wide balcony provided the only exercise space. Three generations of Captains Baker tended the light for eighty-two years. In 1942 the Coast Guard assumed control. The Coast Guard planned to destroy the light when a beacon was placed on the Hurricane Barrier, but local resistance prevailed. Deactivated in 1978, Butler's Flats is now owned by the city, has been restored, and once again sends out its guiding light.

27. FORT TABER PARK, *1860*, NRHP. End East Rodney French Blvd.

Clark's Point, where Fort Taber stands, has long served as guardian to New Bedford. There were earthworks here in the Revolutionary War. In 1846 Major Richard Delafield, father of American coastal defense, and Captain Robert E. Lee, who ultimately led the Confederacy against the Union, collaborated on the design of Fort Taber, named for New Bedford's Civil War mayor, Isaac C. Taber. Construction began in 1860, partly directed by Captain Henry M. Robert (see 18). By 1869 warfare had so changed that this fort was inadequate and work stopped. During the Spanish-American War the observation tower was built, the east bastions converted to mining casemates, and a searchlight unit installed. The fort was reactivated for the last time during World War I.

Clark's Point was an important navigational landmark for mariners during the Revolution. In 1797 town merchants financed the first lighthouse here, giving it to the government in 1800. In 1869 the light was moved to the fort's northeast corner. Fire destroyed it in 1965. Plans call for restoring the light and fort and for creating a large open park.

BEACHES, PARKS, OTHER POINTS OF INTEREST

A. West Beach. West Rodney French Blvd. near Valentine St. Open all year. No fee. Bathhouse, boat launch, concessions, lifeguards, pavilion, swimming.

B. Hazelwood Park. West Rodney French Blvd. Open all year. No fee. Fields, rest rooms, tot playground, views, picnicking, bowling on the green, basketball courts, tennis.

C. East Beach. East Rodney French Blvd. Open all year. No fee. Concessions, lifeguards, playground, views; swimming.

D. Marine Park. Popes Island, Rte. 6, Fairhaven side of bridge. Open all year. No fee. Fishing, picnicking, playground. **New Bedford Marina,** full marine services, boat rentals. Statue of **Prince Henry the Navigator** (1394–1460) given to New Bedford by Portuguese government and Prince Henry Society.

E. Buttonwood Park. Follow Hawthorne or Union St. west away from the city to Rockdale Ave. to the park. Open all year. No fee. Grounds designed by Frederick Law Olmsted; zoo, greenhouse, stage, ball fields, paddle boats, tennis, playground, rest rooms, picnicking, train rides, fishing, concerts, ice skating.

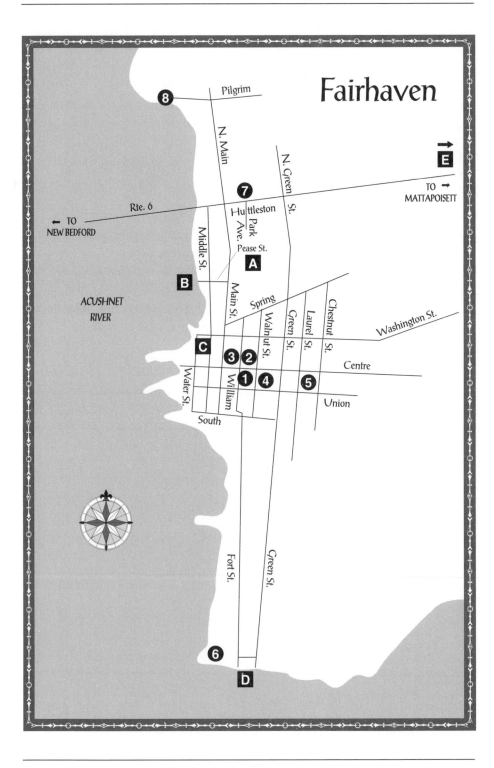

FAIRHAVEN

airhaven was inspired by the independent spirit of a Baptist minister, the compassion of a whaling captain, and the generosity of a capitalist. Reverend John Cooke, rejected in Plymouth for Baptist beliefs, was the strong leader of the early colonists who settled here along the Acushnet River. The settlement grew and expanded as a whaling and fishing center, ultimately becoming today's Fairhaven. Whaling Captain William H. Whitfield created a lasting friendship between Fairhaven and Tosashimizu, Japan, when, in 1841, he rescued Manjiro Nakahama, a Japanese boy of fourteen, from a China Sea island. He brought the boy to Fairhaven, where he educated and treated the boy, now called John Manjiro, like a son. Later Manjiro returned to Japan. During Commodore Perry's visit in 1853 he acted as interpreter, helping open Japan to world trade. The descendants remained close friends. In 1987 the Fairhaven/New Bedford–Tosashimizu (Manjiro's birthplace) Sister-City Committee was formed, resulting in a sister-city agreement between the two cities and countries, promoting international cooperation, friendship, and peace.

Henry Huttleston Rogers, born here 1840, spent his childhood at 39 Middle Street. In 1861 he went to Pennsylvania to learn the oil business. Following a series of partnerships and mergers, Rogers joined John D. Rockefeller and Standard Oil, becoming a vice president and director. He soon sat on boards of twenty-one major corporations, becoming a multimillionaire. His beloved Fairhaven, where he and his family lived in an eighty-five-room mansion on Fort Street, served as his sanctuary from business affairs. His generosity built Rogers Grammar School, 1885; Millicent Library, 1893; Town Hall, 1894; Cushman Park, 1903; the High School, 1906; Unitarian Memorial Church and Tabitha Inn, 1904; and a business block in Fairhaven center, including the George H. Taber Masonic Lodge, 1901. In New Bedford he gave the Bank of Commerce Building to the Whaling Museum, and to St. Luke's Hospital the Rogers Ward and White Home for nurses. Rogers was a benefactor and friend to Mark Twain, guiding him from financial ruin to financial security; he contributed to Helen Keller's Radcliffe education and helped her throughout her life, and he strongly supported Booker T. Washington.

Fairhaven remains an historic seafaring town with a busy waterfront servicing, repairing, and unloading fishing vessels.

1. MILLICENT LIBRARY, *1893*. 45 Centre St.

"Books are the liberated spirits of men, and should be bestowed in a heaven of light and grace and harmonious color and sumptuous comfort, like this, . . ."[13] So wrote

Mark Twain to library trustees in a letter that is part of the collection of his letters and manuscripts housed here. The library, built by Henry H. Rogers, was given in memory of Rogers's daughter Millicent. A masterpiece of Italian Renaissance, the building has rough-cut granite shaping the asymmetrical mass, with projected yet incorporated towers and conical forms. The interior is lavish and inviting. Marble statuary, paintings, and etchings are museum-quality treasures. Signatures of U.S. presidents are in a collection of papers and signed photographs begun by the Delano family, ancestors of Franklin D. Roosevelt. The libary is the first stop on the John Manjiro Trail (see introduction). Brochures and tapes are available. Begin by signing the guest book, signed by Emperor Akihito and wife in 1987.

2. FAIRHAVEN TOWN HALL, *1894*. 40 Centre St.

The Town Hall of French Gothic design was given by Abbie Palmer Gifford Rogers, wife of Henry H. Rogers. The asymmetrical exterior is composed of turrets and towers, hips and ridges, pillars and balustrades plus windows rectangular and arched, stained, leaded, and plain. This remarkable structure was created with ashlar and red beach granite, Delmonico brick, red slate, terra-cotta ornamentation, tile, and copper. The surprising symmetrical interior features polished carved oak, a great double staircase, and much brass and bronze.

3. FIRST CONGREGATIONAL CHURCH, *1844*. Centre and William sts.

This Gothic church has a central tower entrance flanked by hundreds of diamond-shaped windowpanes directing the eye heavenward. Inside are elaborately carved mahogany pews and pulpit, walls made to look like blocks of cut stone, and interior buttresses that appear to streak across the ceiling. The church, founded in 1794 as the Second Church of Christ in New Bedford, was located at Main and Centre streets in Fairhaven. Surviving a congregational split, which created Centre Congregational Church, the Second Church of Christ erected this brick edifice in 1845 and changed its name to First Congregational Church in Fairhaven. Its original 100-foot steeple was destroyed by the Great Gale of 1869.

4. UNITARIAN MEMORIAL CHURCH, *1904*. Walnut, Union, and Centre sts.

This church is a granite emblem of a man's dedication to his faith and devotion to his mother. Henry H. Rogers gave this fifteenth-century English Gothic–style complex as a memorial to his mother, Mary Eldredge Huttleston Rogers. The magnificent edifice, equal to many cathedrals in Europe, is in the perpendicular style. Its 165-foot bell tower holds eleven bells weighing a total of 14,000 pounds. The exterior is granite from Rogers's estate, with decorative elements in royal blue Indiana limestone. It is

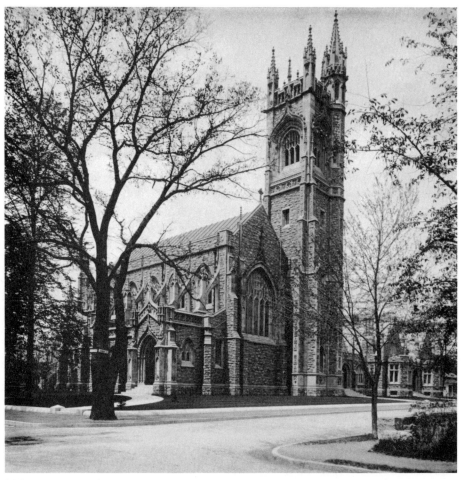

Unitarian Memorial Church, Fairhaven   (Millicent Library)

adorned with carvings by Italian artisans symbolizing scriptural events along with pinnacles and flying buttresses.

Interior walls are soft buff Indiana limestone, floors Italian marble, and woodwork bog oak from the Black Forest intricately carved by Bavarian craftsmen. The Tiffany windows by Robert Reid of New York illustrate teachings of Christ. Starting at the front with the "Nativity" Memorial Window, the emphasis is on light from the Christ child illuminating the deep blue of the night sky. The colors move through nine "Beatitude" windows, brightening until they burst forth in glowing brilliance in the "Sermon on the Mount" window. Here Christ appears to give His benediction to the congregation. This cathedral was one of Rogers's last major donations.

5. TABITHA INN, *1904*. **71 Centre St. Exterior view only; now Our Lady's Haven, a nursing home for the aged.**

In 1904 Henry H. Rogers began Tabitha Inn, named for his maternal great-grandmother. It flourished as a first-class resort hotel until 1942, when it housed Coast Guard trainees. It has been Our Lady's Haven since 1944. The Elizabethan design is reminiscent of a hostelry of Shakespeare's England, when U-shaped buildings formed inn-yard stages for traveling actors.

6. FORT PHOENIX, *1775–77*. **South end of Fort St. Open all year, no fee.**

Fort Phoenix commands the harbor with cannons still poised to defend Fairhaven. Near a fort that predated 1762, Fort Phoenix was built to protect New Bedford Harbor during the Revolution. It was made from granite quarried at the site on which it stands and was manned by thirty-eight officers and men. One of its eleven cannons was acquired from Castle Island, Boston Harbor; the cannon had previously been captured in 1777 by John Paul Jones at New Providence, Bahama Islands.

In 1778, under Major General Charles Grey, the British assaulted New Bedford harbor in retaliation for losses inflicted by colonial privateersmen. British ships and Hessian soldiers ruthlessly leveled much of New Bedford's waterfront and destroyed the fort. A daring rally led by Major Israel Fearing forced the British from the harbor. The fort was reconstructed in 1783 and named Fort Phoenix after the mythical bird. During the War of 1812, Fort Phoenix remained a tower of strength protecting the harbor. Reactivated and modified during the Civil War, it saw no action and was deactivated in 1876. The fort was purchased November 27, 1925, with funds from Henry H. Rogers's daughter, Lady Fairhaven, Mrs. Urban H. Broughton of England, and given to Fairhaven for a public park.

7. FAIRHAVEN HIGH SCHOOL, *1904*. **Rte. 6.**

Fairhaven High School is another boldly designed gift of Henry H. Rogers, who was deeply interested in education. He participated in planning the building, supplemented salaries to obtain the best educators, provided extensive laboratory equipment, and insisted on an attractive study hall to motivate upperclassmen, whose homeroom it was, to remain to graduate. Architecturally the structure is an Elizabethan-style masterpiece of granite-ashlar quarried from Fort Phoenix ledges, surmounted by limestone and brick and capped by a 35-foot turret with a four-face clock. Porches, archways, marble pillars, red-tiled floors, quartered oak paneling, stained glass, and elaborate ceilings abound. **Henry Huttleston Rogers Monument,** erected by citizens of Fairhaven in 1912, is appropriately on the grounds.

8. JOHN COOKE AND JOSHUA SLOCUM MEMORIALS. Pilgrim Ave. Open all year, no fee.

Cooke Memorial: Reverend John Cooke came to the New World aboard the *Mayflower* and grew up in Pilgrim Plymouth, where he surprisingly followed the Baptist faith. In 1652 he joined in purchasing land that ultimately included Fairhaven. As clerk he signed the deed with John Winslow and Chief Wamsutta. Settling here, he served as agent, magistrate, and representative to the General Court, and he built a garrison to protect settlers during King Philip's War. As a founder of Fairhaven, Cooke endeavored to plant seeds of moral strength and integrity deep in this fertile land.

Slocum Memorial: By the Acushnet River Captain Joshua Slocum rebuilt the 37-foot, nine-ton sloop *Spray*. On April 24, 1895, he left Boston Harbor to sail around the world on a three-year voyage, becoming the first person to circumnavigate the globe alone. The excitement of his courageous trip is told in his personal account, *Sailing Alone around the World*.

BEACHES, PARKS, OTHER POINTS OF INTEREST

A. **Cushman Park.** Access Park Ave. Open all year. No fee. Anna B. Trowbridge Memorial Shell, playground, green, rest rooms, tennis.

B. **Pease Park.** Fairhaven Harbor. Middle St. Open all year. No fee. Views, boat launch.

C. **Union Wharf and Water Street.** Explore the area to experience Fairhaven's active waterfront.

D. **Fort Phoenix State Beach.** Green St. Open all year. Fee in summer. Sandy beach, views, tennis; picnicking, swimming.

E. **West Island Beach.** East on Rte. 6 to Sconticut Neck Rd., turn right and follow it over Goover Island Causeway to Bass Creek Rd., beach off Bass Creek Rd. Open all year. Fee in summer. Views, swimming.

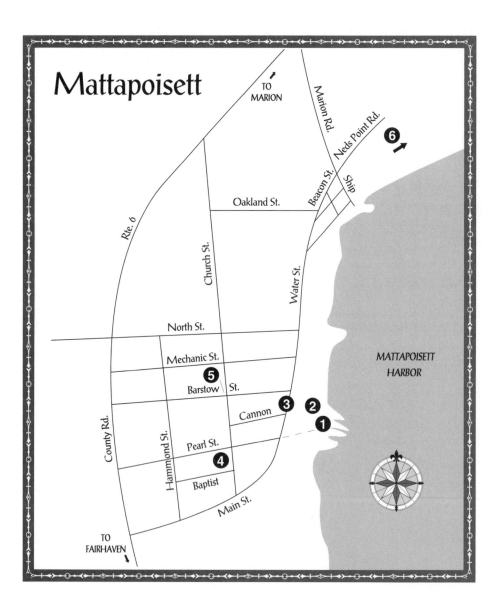

MATTAPOISETT

Mattapoisett and its neighboring towns, Marion and Wareham (profiled in the following two chapters), are three diamonds in the crown of Buzzards Bay. Each adds its particular radiance while sharing common ancestral bonds. From 1679 to 1682 proprietors purchased land between Plymouth and Fairhaven that they named Rochester for Rochester, England. In time their church grew and divided, creating the three parishes. Mattapoisett became a separate congregation in 1736.

Initially Mattapoisett's[14] economy was based on farming, lumbering, local fishing, and grist and fulling mills. By the mid-1700s the annual herring run added variety to farmers' tables, and shipbuilding along with coastal and foreign trade opened new horizons. As the shadows of the American Revolution drew closer, local sea captains, whose economy depended on open ports and unencumbered trade, entered the patriotic, prosperous, and dangerous world of privateering. Every captured British ship meant financial rewards for the privateersmen and help for the Revolutionary cause.

Following the Revolution and the War of 1812, the whaling era exploded with all its supporting industries. Some of the finest whaling ships in the world were built in Mattapoisett. Shipyards flourished. Beautiful ship captains' and merchants' homes were built. Mattapoisett was in its heyday. Luckily for today's visitor, few new buildings have been added. As you wander the streets of this quaint coastal village, incorporated in 1857, you can sense what life was like in the 1800s.

Following Mattapoisett's decline as a seaport, the town became a favorite place for summer visitors. It was also the birthplace of Francis Davis Millet, born November 3, 1846, in the house on the corner of Water and Cannon streets. Millet, a Civil War drummer boy, became a noted war correspondent, author, and artist. He was lost on the maiden voyage of the *Titanic,* April 15, 1912.

1. TOWN WHARF AND HARBOR, *1700s.* Water St. Open all year, overnight mooring fee. Rest rooms, boat launch.

This area was the site of many successive shipyards, starting with shipwright Charles Stetson's in 1752 and going through such well-known names as Barstows and Cannons. During the Revolution six yards were in full swing in Mattapoisett, and yards were active through the mid-1800s. The 650-ton *George Lee,* which slid down the ways at one of the numerous Barstow yards, was the largest ship built in Mattapoisett.

Take time to walk Mattapoisett Village, enjoy the many gardens, note the homes with historic dates, and be aware of the fact that the area was built in relation to its coastal trade and whaling industries. It is unique in that there has been little new construction since the heyday of whaling.

2. SHIPYARD PARK, *1752–1878*. Water St. Open all year, no fee. Bandstand, benches, summer concerts.

Shipyard Park commemorates shipbuilding days, when 400 men worked the yards and bowsprits reached over the roadways. Fifty whalers were launched between 1830 and 1840. Along Water Street craftsmen used broad axes, adzes, and whipsaws with surgical precision to turn rough-cut lumber into the finest of ships. Businesses along the waterfront included blacksmith shops, sail lofts, and ropewalks. Sawdust was in the air, and days were counted by ship launchings. Shipyard Park marks the site of several Holmes shipyards established in 1812 by Josiah Holmes, Sr. In 1878 Jonathan H. Holmes's whaling bark *Wanderer* was the last ship built in Mattapoisett.

3. MATTAPOISETT INN, *c. 1799*. Water St. Open as inn and restaurant.

Joseph Meigs, civic leader, shipyard owner, and master carpenter, built this as his home about 1799. Upon his death in 1846, the property passed to son Loring Meigs, state representative, captain of Mattapoisett Guards, shipbuilder and shipowner, and whaling vessel agent. The large old home has been an inn since about 1865. One long-time owner was Captain Charles Bryant, whaling captain and first governor of Alaska.

4. MATTAPOISETT HISTORICAL SOCIETY MUSEUM AND CARRIAGE HOUSE, *1821*. 5 Church St. Open summer and by appointment, fee. Special exhibits.

Mattapoisett's story is told in this museum, housed in the 1821 First Christian Meetinghouse, and in the Farm and Country Museum in the attached Carriage House. The preserved church is Federal in style, the Carriage House a replica of a 1700s post-and-beam barn. The society's collections include deeds, ships' papers, commissions, and photos as well as China trade treasures, half models, marine prints, paintings, scrimshaw, local Indian artifacts, a saltworks model, silver, and Sandwich glass. The barn exhibit focuses on the farm industry, including outdoor tools, threshing machines, a spinning room, carriages and wagons, carpenter's shop, and an 1890 kitchen.

5. FOURTH MEETING HOUSE, *1842*. Barstow and Church sts.

Mattapoisett settlers, tired of the long trek to Rochester, established a church in Mattapoisett in 1736. A year later they built their first building, which served until 1772, when Reverend Lemuel LeBaron was called. He served until a year before his death in 1836. During his pastorate the church's second and third buildings were erected. One was destroyed by the 1815 hurricane, while the other, built in 1816, NRHP, is still standing on Route 6 at Main Street. The records of that third building give the first mention of heat in meetinghouses in Mattapoisett. Possibly the ministers' sermons on love had kept the congregation warm for the first eighty years.

6. NEDS POINT LIGHTHOUSE, *1837*, NRHP, and Veterans Memorial Park. End of Neds Point Road. Open all year, no fee. Picnicking, fishing, swimming.

The whitewashed stone lighthouse was constructed by government lighthouse contractor Leonard Hammond, who was involved in coastal trade, shipyards, and saltworks. The light included a keeper's house until 1923, when the house was loaded on a barge and floated across the bay to Wings Neck. Apparently the move included the keeper, who cooked breakfast en route.

Clamshell Alley, Mattapoisett

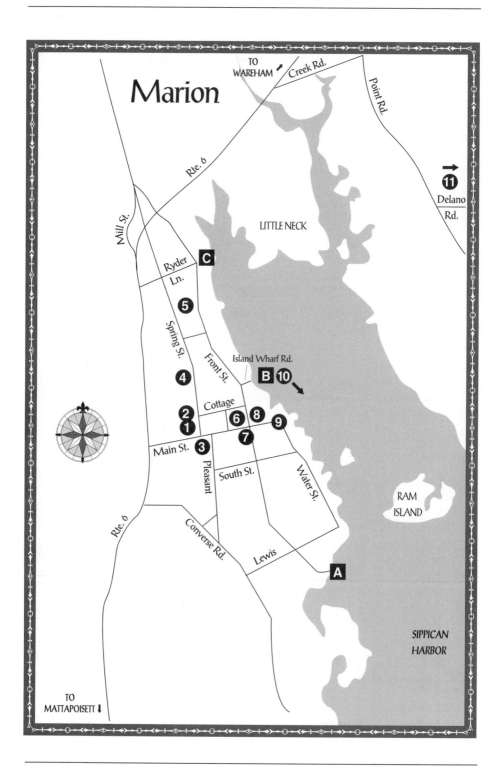

MARION

Buzzards Bay's second jewel, Marion, was incorporated in 1852, fifty-four years after it became a separate parish from the mother church in Rochester. This charming coastal town, originally named Sippican, was renamed Marion to honor General Francis Marion, the "Swamp Fox" of Revolutionary War fame.

Like Mattapoisett, Marion was influenced by the sea and affected by the Revolution and the War of 1812. Fishing and whaling formed the basis of its economy during the 1800s. At one time salt marshes were alive with windmills pumping seawater to saltworks, producing 20,000 bushels of salt in a year. The removal of duty on foreign salt, gold fever, railroads, Civil War, discovery of crude oil, and decline of whaling combined to undermine Marion's economy as well as that of Mattapoisett and Wareham in the mid- to late 1800s. With improved transportation, however, new lifestyles filled the economic gap as the towns became havens for summer residents. Along with beach lovers came people of the literary, artistic, and political worlds. Famous full-time and seasonal residents included Ethel Barrymore, Charles Dana Gibson, President and Mrs. Grover Cleveland, Richard Harding Davis, Richard Watson Gilder, Henry Hobson Richardson, and Henry James.

1. TOWN HOUSE, *1876*. Spring St.

Town House was created by eighty-four-year-old Elizabeth Taber, who wanted to "put some snap" into Marion. Born here in 1791, she returned a wealthy widow. The Town House was originally built as Tabor Academy (see 5). The spirited Mrs. Taber, though old and lame, purchased land, planned the academy, and supervised construction. The imposing Italianate has a bell tower, Greek-columned front portico, full-height corner pilasters, and ornamental brackets. The quill pen weathervane symbolizes Marion's concern for knowledge. In 1937 the building became the Town House when the academy was moved to the waterfront.

2. ELIZABETH TABER LIBRARY AND NATURAL HISTORY MUSEUM, *1872*. Spring St. Museum: by appointment, no fee.

This was the first gift of Marion's benefactress, Elizabeth Taber. She wanted children to value good books and education. She also provided for the Marion Museum of Natural History on the second floor. Virtually unchanged, the museum is a highly valued example of a nineteenth-century museum. Displays include birds, minerals, Indian artifacts, shells, and an American eagle brought down by a pitchfork. Corinthian pillars support the portico; corners combine quoins and pilasters; and brackets and dentils are featured at roof and pediment lines on this late Federal.

3. MARION ART CENTER, former Universalist Church, *1833*. Main and Pleasant sts. Open all year, fee for some events.

The building housing the Marion Art Center was originally the Universalist Church. Before 1833 Captain Noble E. Bates gathered friends who shared his views on a less Puritanical religion and the doctrine of universal salvation. Thus was born the Marion Universalist Church. After its decline the building became the art center. It serves Marion with art gallery, community theater, art classes, and special events.

4. OLD STONE STUDIO, *1820*. 46 Spring St. Open as businesses.

This ivy-covered building started as a saltworks and was later converted by Captain Henry M. Allen for refining crude oil and making charcoal. In the 1880s its aroma of oil and charcoal changed to one of perfume and lavish social gatherings: Richard Watson Gilder, editor of *Century Magazine*, restored it as an art studio for his wife. The Gilders attracted artists and writers, ushering in a new era. In this adapted salt and oil factory, the Gilders entertained Charles Dana Gibson, Ethel Barrymore, Henry James, Richard Harding Davis, and President and Mrs. Grover Cleveland.

5. TABOR ACADEMY, 1876. Front and Spring sts. Open all year as school.

On the shores of Sippican Harbor, Tabor Academy is a warm blend of old and new. In 1876 Elizabeth Taber founded Tabor Academy (spelled for Palestine's Mount Tabor) in what is now Town House. She selected the headmaster, and together they designed goals for the school. In 1880 she built Taber Hall, now at 13 Cottage Street, then on Spring Street, as the headmaster's home, where she lived in two rooms until her death in 1888. The school moved here in 1937. On Spring Street the focus of the modern chapel is the cross above an open altar. Themes of religion and science are boldly portrayed in stained glass windows and individually created needlepoint pew cushions. In summer, aboard the tall ship *Tabor Boy,* students go to sea—a tradition from the years when Marion's youth sailed on whalers, returning proud men.

6. MARION GENERAL STORE, *1794–99*. 140 Front St. Open all year.

This general store has been a focal point since 1794, when townspeople began the building as a meetinghouse, only to run out of funds. Captain George Bonum Nye agreed to complete it on condition he would own the property, making it one of the few individually owned meetinghouses in New England. By 1841 Nye had died, a new meetinghouse was sought, and this old one was bought by Deacon Stephen Delano for a social hall and store. Fifteen years later Andrew J. Hadley bought the building. He remodeled it, adding shops. It remains today a busy general store.

7. CONGREGATIONAL CHURCH OF MARION, *1841*. 28 Main St.

The founding members separated from the Rochester church in 1798. The present

Greek Revival building, with Christopher Wren–style steeple, was designed by Solomon K. Eaton of Mattapoisett, who designed all five churches that descended from the Rochester church. In 1872 donations were requested for the installation of a clock. When a church neighbor refused, Captain Henry Allen offered his share and an extra $50, providing there would be no face on the side viewed by the nondonating neighbor, thus a three-faced clock. As a memorial to Elizabeth Taber, a stained glass window was installed behind the pulpit in 1894. In 1915, when the present Hathaway Memorial windows of Mary and Martha were given, the Taber window was removed. Rediscovered sixty-one years later, it now beautifies the church's chapel.

8. SIPPICAN HISTORICAL SOCIETY MUSEUM, DR. ELLIS HOUSE, *1834*. 27 Main St. Open summer and by appointment, no fee.

The home of the Sippican Historical Society was Marion's second post office and home of Dr. Walton Nathan Ellis—physician, town clerk, postmaster, library founder, choir director, and poet. Later the house was owned by Dr. Ellis's daughter, Annie, who married Sylvanus Hall, appointed postmaster by Abraham Lincoln in 1860. Mr. Hall must have been a very formal man, for the story goes that he wore a starched shirt and collar night and day, changing only on Saturdays to be ready for Sunday church. It is hard to imagine how any starch could keep a shirt neat for seven days and nights unless the wearer slept standing up and rarely moved.

Inside the historic home are remembrances of bygone days: an old post office, early kitchen, Gerard Curtis Delano's Indian paintings, Charles Dana Gibson sketches, and paintings by Cecil Clark Davis. A *Mary Celeste* exhibit relates to sea captain Benjamin Briggs of Marion. Mystery surrounds his and his family's death. November 4, 1872, Benjamin sailed from New York as the *Mary Celeste* captain with family aboard. A month later his ship was a ghost ship—crew and longboat gone, water in the holds, cargo intact, and ship's papers gone. There were many theories, from extreme drop in pressure to possible fumes from alcohol cargo. Fear of explosion could have caused the captain to hurry family and crew to the longboat connected to the ship by a line, intending to return to the ship when the danger was over. But the line could have parted, allowing the ship to sail away, leaving them to perish.

9. MAIN STREET WALKING TOUR. Front St. to water. Buildings private.

In earlier times this area was called Wharf Village, and its wharves bustled with shipbuilding, sail making, ships' stores, and the excitement of docking whalers and coasters. **14 Main,** c. 1760, once contained a tiny dry goods shop and housed artist Charles Dana Gibson when he summered here. The small shed in back long ago served as town schoolhouse. Its fourteen-year-old teacher, Elizabeth Pitcher, later became town's benefactress, Elizabeth Taber. **9 Main,** c. 1780, is where Richard Harding Davis, worldwide adventurer-reporter-author, wrote while in Marion. Davis married artist Cecil

Clark in one of Marion's grandest occasions, for which Ethel Barrymore was maid of honor and Charles Dana Gibson an usher.

0 Main is the old "Watch-Out House" from where townspeople watched for returning whalers. The house was built so close to the water that ropes were attached to neighbors' houses to deter high tides from floating it out to sea. **1 Main** was a sail loft, and the small building across was a cooper's shop. At **99 Water Street** the Beverly Yacht Club was once the village inn, where shipbuilders lived, stagecoaches stopped, and churchgoers warmed up between services. Whaling ships docked where now pleasure boats tie up. Every other year the Bermuda Race starts from this club. The clubhouse was once the house of Admiral Harwood and is one of Marion's oldest houses.

10. BIRD ISLAND LIGHT, *1819*, NRHP. Sippican Harbor. Exterior view only.

According to legend the first light keeper of Bird Island, William S. Moore, was a former pirate. September 10, 1819, Moore lit the light that guided mariners for 114 years. Named for its many birds, the island must have been a dramatic change for an ex-pirate and his Boston bride. Possibly too much, for one day the minister crossed the frozen harbor to help bury the keeper's wife. Only once did the light go out, and that time purposely, to help a dying child. With a wrecked boat and a severe storm, the keeper's only hope was to extinguish the light and pray someone would come. Help came, but too late. The light was extinguished in 1933. In 1976 the Sippican Historical Society reactivated the light. The island is a breeding ground for roseate terns.

11. GREAT HILL ESTATE, *1909*. Delano Rd. House private, grounds open all year, weekdays, no fee. Paths, formal gardens. Directions: north on Rte. 6, right on Creek Rd., right on Point Rd., left on Delano Rd.

Wampanoag Indians camped here, leaving interesting artifacts such as a large rock hollowed into a bowl to grind corn. In 1860 the Marion House, a 300-guest hotel, was built near the present mansion. When visiting millionaire Albert Nickerson was asked to remove his contagious family, sudden victims of scarlet fever, he bought the hotel. Next sugar king John Searles owned the estate and later the Stone family, who in 1909 began changes culminating in today's estate. Though it is reduced in size, the buildings and 750 acres of splendor still create a vast estate in an era when few remain.

BEACHES, PARKS, OTHER POINTS OF INTEREST

A. **Silvershell Beach.** Front St. Residents only in summer.

B. **Island Wharf Park.** Island Wharf Rd. Open all year. No fee. Harbor views, bandstand, dock facilities, harbormaster; swimming.

C. **Old Landing.** Front St. opposite Ryder Ln. Open all year. No fee. Views, docking facilities, boat launching—residents only in summer.

WAREHAM

Wareham, the third jewel, became a separate parish and was incorporated in 1739. The rich maritime economy was enhanced by an abundance of natural bog ore, which formed the basis for important iron and nail industries. The first nail-manufacturing plant and rolling mill was founded in 1819, a forerunner of today's Tremont Nail Company. When local iron ore was depleted, old bogs became perfect locations for growing cranberries. Today they are a colorful and vital part of Wareham's world. Since the mid-1800s Wareham, with its beautiful Onset Beach area, has been a haven for summer residents and visitors.

1. FEARING TAVERN MUSEUM, *c. 1690*, HS. Elm Street. Open summer, limited hours and by appointment, donation.

Within the present tavern is an original two-story, four-room 1690s Cape. In 1765 extensive renovations were made with original timbers, walls, and fireplaces retained. An ell was added in 1835. Periods are preserved, with the 1690s public room adjacent to the 1765 taproom. Fascinating levels on the second floor provide secret passages through former windows into closets and tiny halls. Here a British soldier was successfully hidden.

The 1690s Cape was home to miller Isaac Bump, who sold to Israel Fearing. Son Benjamin Fearing inherited, making the 1765 renovations and becoming the first tavern keeper. The tavern was the center of town activity, where selectmen met and were served grog at town expense. Squire John Fearing held court in the 1800s, and rooms next to the public room were the town's first post office. Fearings retained ownership for nearly two centuries. During the War of 1812, more than 200 marines from the British *Nimrod* attacked Wareham, setting fire to a Fearing brig.

2. TREMONT NAIL COMPANY, *1819, 1867*, NRHP. Elm St. Open all year, no fee. Platform viewing of nail manufacturing. Company Store: hand-cut Tremont nails, reproduction hardware, paints, gifts, gourmet foods, explanatory film.

The Tremont Nail Company survives as a representative of the mills on this site and of many other Wareham mills. The first recorded mill here was the c. 1668–90 gristmill of Isaac Bump, builder of what became Fearing Tavern. Later, town minister Noble Everett augmented his income with a fulling mill on the east side of the river. Iron ore was discovered by colonists tilling the soil, and many households produced ironware and nails. In 1819 Tremont's predecessor began a nail-manufacturing plant and rolling mill on the site of Bump's gristmill. The Tremont Nail Company dates from

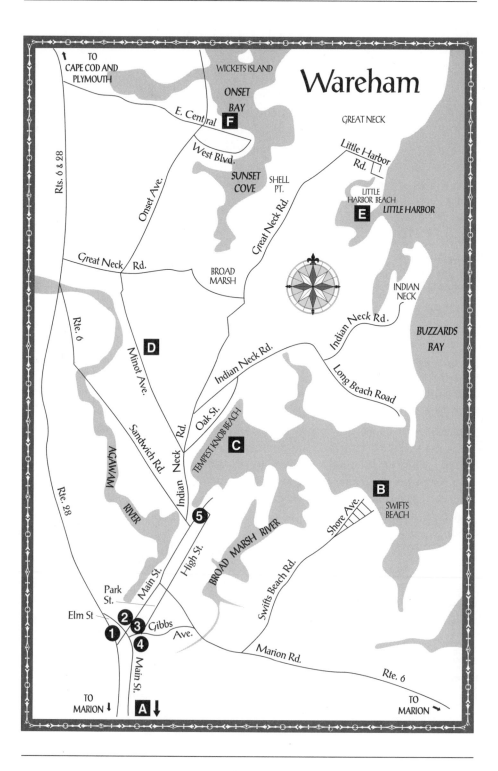

1858, the present buildings from 1867. This is one of two companies still making design-cut nails and is believed to be the oldest continuous nail manufacturing company in the country.

3. OLD TOWN SQUARE. Gibbs Ave. and Park and Main sts.

Starting on Main Street, moving clockwise, you come to the **Old Methodist Meetinghouse,** owned by the historical society. Built about 1825 on Tihonet and Carver roads and moved here about 1835, the building served until 1842 as a meetinghouse. Also moved to the square is the one-room **Indian Neck Schoolhouse** used in the mid-nineteenth century as a school and later as a parish hall for Union Chapel, on Indian Neck Road. Now owned by the historical society, it is open by appointment. The restored 1901 **Old Town Hall** houses town offices. At Park and Main streets is **Dr. Benjamin Fearing House** (private), built about 1825 by Israel Fearing's grandson. It became an inn in 1920, when stables and carriage sheds were converted to rooms. On Gibbs Avenue is **Everett School,** built in 1890 and named for Noble Everett, third minister of First Congregational Church.

4. FIRST CONGREGATIONAL CHURCH OF WAREHAM, *1914.*
Gibbs Ave. and Main St.

The church, organized in 1739, called Rowland Thacher as minister. In their first small wooden meetinghouse they worshiped, held town meetings, and met socially. That meetinghouse served until 1770, when a larger one was built. Beloved Reverend Noble Everett, a strong and industrious leader, came to Wareham in 1782 and served the church for forty years. Six years after his pastorate, a $10,000 steepled church was built where today's church stands. This building, beautiful but uninsured, burned in 1904. Undaunted, the congregation erected a new one in 1906, only to see it go up in flames in 1913. Again they built, but this time it was the present Gothic church made of stone.

5. CAPTAIN JOHN KENDRICK HOUSE AND MARITIME MUSEUM, *c. 1745,* HS. 102 Main St. Open summer and by appointment.

Many early New England sea captains and merchants owed their wealth to Captain John Kendrick of Wareham and his second in command, Captain Robert Gray (see Tiverton, Rhode Island). Kendrick and Gray left Boston September 30, 1787, aboard the *Columbia* (Kendrick), and the *Washington* (Gray), arriving in the Pacific Northwest a year later. After trading for furs they sailed for Canton, China, where they exchanged furs for tea, silks, and fine porcelain. On August 9, 1790, Gray, now commanding the *Columbia,* returned to Boston to a hero's welcome after 48,889 miles. This expedition began the lucrative China trade. Kendrick stayed in the Pacific, trading between China and the Pacific Northwest and opening the sandalwood trade between Hawaii and China. His was the first American ship to carry the stars and stripes to a Japanese

Fearing Tavern Museum, Wareham

island. In 1794 Kendrick was accidentally killed during a victory celebration at Pearl Harbor. His was the first Christian burial service in Hawaii. Gray's and Kendrick's discoveries established a legal basis for U.S. claims to Washington, Oregon, and Idaho.

Step inside Kendrick's home to see how a successful sea captain with wife and six children lived in the late 1700s. Wander through the furnished rooms and the maritime museum and relive the exciting days when independent adventurers were willing to navigate untried routes and knock on unopened doors.

BEACHES, PARKS, OTHER POINTS OF INTEREST

Parking stickers available free at Town Hall.

A. Tremont Dam Park. Left on Mill St., dirt road to dam. Open all year. No fee. Ruins of Tremont Nail Company from mid-1800s located here; 1919 design dam; gates, machinery restored to produce hydroelectric power; picnicking, canoeing, kayaking.

B. Swifts Beach. Swifts Beach Rd. Open all year. Sandy beach, views, concessions, lifeguards; swimming; sticker parking.

C. Tempest Knob. Oak St. Open all year. Sandy beach, views, moorings; picnicking, swimming; sticker parking.

D. Minot Forest. Minot Ave. Open all year. No fee. Park at school; trails, bird walks; picnicking.

E. Little Harbor Beach. Little Harbor Rd. Open all year. Six-acre sandy beach, lifeguards, rest rooms; swimming; sticker parking.

F. Onset Beach and Bluffs. Onset Ave. Open all year. Parking fee. Large sandy beach and park, bandstand, bathhouse, concessions, lifeguards, rest rooms, scenic tours from pier; picnicking, fishing, swimming.

CAPE COD

Shaped like a fishhook, Cape Cod was named for the many codfish caught off its shores. Only 70 miles long and 1 to 20 miles wide, the Cape attracts visitors every season of the year and is well loved by its many year-round residents.

Cape Cod has its own special ambience—weathered shingled homes, working windmills, lonely sentinel lighthouses, miles of open sandy beaches, marshlands teeming with life, dunes and low pines sculpted and resculpted by centuries of winds, and softly lapping waters of Nantucket Sound and Cape Cod Bay. There are also summer theaters, art colonies, historic buildings, and beautiful homes. Cape Cod offers something for everyone.

Named by Bartholomew Gosnold, Cape Cod holds its own place in history. At Provincetown, on the Cape's very tip, the Pilgrims first touched the shores of the New World on November 11, 1620. By 1627 Aptucxet Trading Post in Bourne was a center of commerce for English colonists, Indians, and Dutch settlers from New Amsterdam. Surrounded by water on three sides, Cape Codders early turned to the sea for their livelihood. Coastal packets connected Cape towns and mainland ports. Cape Codders captained and manned fishing vessels of all sizes and types and merchant ships and whalers on every ocean. Sandwich was the Cape's first settled town in 1637. International messages were sent directly from Orleans, Cape Cod, to Doelen, France, by transatlantic cable in the 1890s. In Wellfleet in 1903, Guglielmo Marconi sent the first two-way wireless communiqué between the United States and England—a message from President Theodore Roosevelt to King Edward VII.

Cape Cod was the birthplace of author Joseph C. Lincoln; Katherine Lee Bates, author of "America the Beautiful"; and well-known children's author Thornton W. Burgess, creator of Reddy Fox and the Old Mother West Wind stories. Other famous residents included Presidents John F. Kennedy and Grover Cleveland, Daniel Webster, and James Otis, plus myriad artists, musicians, authors, actors, and actresses.

As you enjoy the Cape, take time to meander the less-traveled back roads for a true feeling and insight into Cape Cod life. The beaches listed are open to the public either by direct fee or by purchase of parking stickers from local town halls. Cape Cod National Seashore accepts Golden Passes. See the map for general locations of listings.

BOURNE

1. CAPE COD SCENIC RAILROAD. Main St. and Academy Rd. Open summer. Fee.

Scenic and historic railroad, Bourne–Hyannis–Sandwich, refreshments served, special dinner train.

2. HERRING RUN VISITOR CENTER/ARMY CORPS OF ENGINEERS. Opposite Herring Pond Rd. (Rte. 6). Open all year. No fee.

Informative displays relating to construction and use of 17.4-mile-long Cape Cod Canal, widest in world, begun 1909; picnicking.

3. CANAL SERVICE ROADS.

Accesses at **Herring Run Visitor Center; Sagamore Recreation Area,** Canal Rd., Sagamore; **Sand Catcher Recreation Area,** Coast Guard Rd.; **Sandwich Recreation Area,** Freezer Rd.; **Midway Station,** Rte. 6 half way between canal bridges; **Bourne Recreation Area,** off Bourne Circle by bridge; **Tidal Flats Recreation Area,** Bell Rd., Bourne. Service road open to hike, bike, fish, no motorized vehicles; rest rooms, picnicking, and parking at access areas.

4. INDIAN BURIAL HILL. Off Herring Pond Rd. Open all year. No fee.

Ancient burial ground of Wampanoag Indians, site of First Meeting House for Indians in Plymouth Colony in 1637.

5. BOURNEDALE HERRING RUN AND CARTER BEAL CONSERVATION AREA. Herring Pond Rd. Open all year. No fee.

Herring run used since early settlers, alewives run April and May; picnicking.

6. PAIRPOINT GLASS WORKS, *1967*. Sandwich Rd., beneath Sagamore Bridge. Open all year. No fee.

Craftsmen demonstrate world-famous hand-blown glassware; gift shop.

7. APTUCXET TRADING POST AND MUSEUM. Aptucxet Rd. Open extended season. Fee.

Replica on original foundation of trading post built by Plymouth men; original income was used to repay Merchant Adventurers' Pilgrim loan. Saltworks, windmill, President Grover Cleveland's private railroad station, gift shop, guided tours.

BEACHES, PARKS, OTHER POINTS OF INTEREST

1. Buzzards Bay Beach. Electric Ave.
2. Queenswell Pond. Cherry St. Freshwater.
3. Bourne Scenic Park. Rte. 6 near Bourne Bridge. Open summer. Fee. Tidal pool, rest rooms; camping, picnicking.

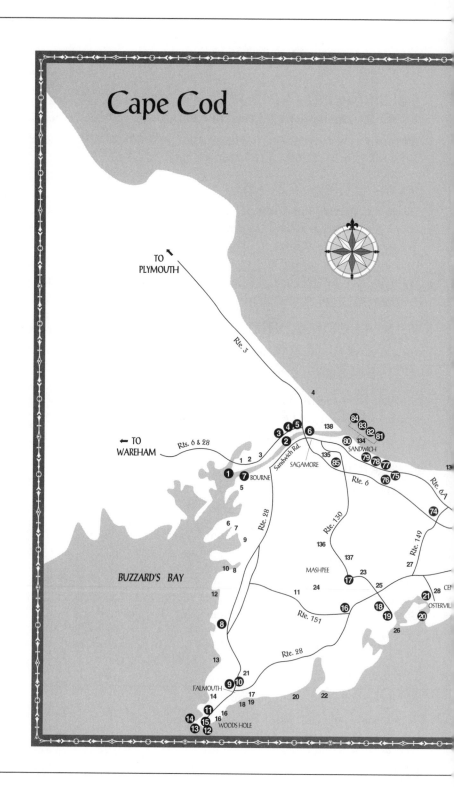

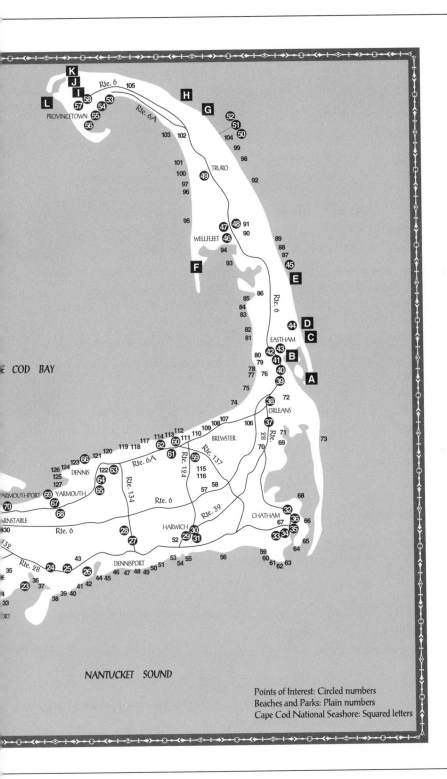

4. Sagamore Beach. Plymouth Rd., end of Clark Rd.

5. Monument Beach. Emmons Rd. off Shore Rd. Snack bar.

6. Barlows Landing Beach. Barlows Landing Rd.

7. Hen Cove Beach. Circuit Ave.

8. Squeteague Harbor. Megansett Rd. Clamming.

9. Picture Lake. County Rd. Fresh water.

FALMOUTH AND WOODS HOLE

8. FRIENDS MEETING HOUSE, *1775.* Main St. (Rte. 28A).

Quakers moved to the area in 1660s to escape persecution; meetinghouse still active.

9. HIGHFIELD OF FALMOUTH. Highfield Dr. off Depot Ave. Open all year. Fee.

500-acre estate, Cape Cod Conservatory, Beebe Woods Art Center for learning and performing arts, lectures; Conservatory's Light Opera and Falmouth Theater Guild open summer for performances.

10. FALMOUTH HISTORICAL SOCIETY WICKS–WOOD HOUSE, *1790.* Open summer. Fee.

Conant House Museum, 1770. Palmer St. **Bates House Museum.** 16 West Main St. Two-story Colonial; birthplace of Katherine Lee Bates, author of "America the Beautiful." Whaling, period furniture, paintings, china exhibits.

11. BRADLEY HOUSE MUSEUM OF WOODS HOLE. Woods Hole Rd. Open summer. Fee.

Model of village c. 1895, historic collections, third oldest building in town; walking tours.

12. CANDLE HOUSE, *1836.* Water St., Marine Biological Laboratory Administration Building.

Built as spermaceti candle factory, 2-foot-thick stone walls, whaling ship's prow on street side.

13. NATIONAL MARINE FISHERIES AQUARIUM. Open all year. No fee.

Exhibits of sea life from Cape Cod to Georges Bank, hands-on exhibits; observe work areas, harbor seals during summer.

14. ST. MARGARET'S GARDEN. **Millfield St. opposite St. Joseph's Church. Open all year. No fee.**

Quiet garden on bank of Eel Pond, view of St. Joseph's bell tower.

15. NOBSKA LIGHT, *1829.* **Church St. and Nobska Rd. Grounds open all year. No fee.**

Stationary blinking light, appears red if mariner is in dangerous waters; beautiful views; limited parking.

BEACHES, PARKS, OTHER POINTS OF INTEREST

10. Megansett Beach. Off County Rd., North Falmouth.

11. Ashumet Holly Reservation. North of Rte. 151 and Currier Rd., East Falmouth. Open all year. Fee. Self-guided nature walks. Massachusetts Audubon Society.

12. Old Silver Beach. Quaker Rd., West Falmouth. Bathhouse, snack bar.

13. Woodneck Beach. Slippewisset Rd.

14. Beebe Woods. Highland and Terheun drs. Trails.

15. Trunk River Beach. Oyster Pond Rd.

16. Shining Sea Bikeway, Falmouth to Woods Hole. Access Woods Hole Rd. and Steamship Authority parking lot at Woods Hole.

17. Full, year-round ferry service by Steamship Authority to Martha's Vineyard from Woods Hole. Parking Falmouth Heights Rd., Falmouth, and Woods Hole Rd., Woods Hole. Fee. Also seasonal passenger service from Falmouth to Martha's Vineyard on the *Island Queen.* Fee.

18. Surf Drive Beach. Surf Dr. and Shore St. Bird and wildlife reserve, bathhouse, snack bar.

19. Falmouth Heights Beach. Clinton Ave.

20. Menauhant Beach. Central Ave. and Menauhant Rd., East Falmouth. Snack bar.

21. Goodwill Park. Goodwill Park Rd. off Rte. 28. Fresh water.

MASHPEE

16. OLD INDIAN MEETINGHOUSE, *1684*. Rte. 28. Open extended season, limited hours. Donations.

Oldest standing church on Cape, originally used for Indian worship, meetings, and social activities.

17. MASHPEE WAMPANOAG INDIAN MUSEUM, *1793*. Rte. 130. Open extended season or by appointment. No fee.

Exhibits on Wampanoag life; Mashpee Indian reservation first one on country.

BEACHES, PARKS, OTHER POINTS OF INTEREST

22. South Cape Beach. Great Oak Rd.

23. Ataquin Park and Beach. Lake Ave. off Rte. 130, Mashpee Pond. Fresh water.

24. John's Pond Park. Hoophole Rd. Bathhouse, snack bar.

COTUIT, OSTERVILLE, CENTERVILLE, HYANNIS

18. COTUIT LIBRARY. Main St.

Ship models and Sydney A. Kirkman book collection.

19. HISTORICAL SOCIETY OF SANTUIT AND COTUIT. 1148 Main St. Open summer. No fee.

Restored c. 1790 Dottridge Homestead moved here from Harwich; changing exhibits.

20. CAHOON MUSEUM OF AMERICAN ART. 4676 Falmouth Rd., Cotuit. Open all year, limited hours. No fee.

Museum in 1775 Colonial farmhouse, marine paintings and work by American Impressionists and contemporary primitive artists Ralph and Martha Cahoon, museum shop.

21. OSTERVILLE HISTORICAL SOCIETY MUSEUM AND CAMMETT HOUSE. West Bay and Parker rds. Open extended season. No fee.

Crosby Boat Yard exhibits; Horace Crosby designed and built famous "Crosby Cat" boat; period rooms, majolica and Lowestoft pottery, antiques.

22. CENTERVILLE HISTORICAL SOCIETY MUSEUM. 507 Main St. Open summer. No fee.

Mary Lincoln House and Clark Lincoln Tin shop, 1850; fourteen rooms highlight Cape industries and home life; marine glass, period furniture, and clothing exhibits; Crowell birds, MacKnight paintings.

23. JOHN F. KENNEDY MEMORIAL. Ocean St., Hyannis. Open all year. No fee.

Circular fieldstone memorial in parklike setting.

BEACHES, PARKS, OTHER POINTS OF INTEREST

25. Lovells Pond. Santuit–New Town Rd., Santuit. Fresh water.

26. Loop Beach. Oceanview Ave., Cotuit.

27. Hamblin Pond. Rte. 149A, Marston Mills. Fresh water.

28. Joshua's Pond. Pond St., Osterville. Fresh water.

29. Craigville Beach. Craigville Rd., Centerville. Bathhouse.

30. Covell's Beach. Craigville Rd., Centerville. Bathhouse.

31. Orrin Keye's Memorial Beach. Sea St., Hyannis. Bathhouse, snack bar.

32. Kalmus Beach. Ocean St., Hyannis. Bathhouse, snack bar.

33. Veteran's Park Beach. Ocean St., Hyannis. Bathhouse, snack bar, play equipment, picnicking.

34. Full, year-round ferry service by Steamship Authority to Nantucket. South St. Dock, Hyannis. Also seasonal passenger service by Hy-Line Ferries to Nantucket and Martha's Vineyard. Ocean St. Dock, Hyannis.

35. Melody Tent. West Main St., Hyannis. Performance fee.

WEST AND SOUTH YARMOUTH

24. BAXTER MILLS, *1710*, NRHP. Rte. 28 near Mill Pond Rd. Open summer. No fee.

Rare underwater turbine-powered mill built by John and Shubael Baxter, ran for nearly 200 years; now restored and running.

25. ZOOQUARIUM. Rte. 28 west of Parker River Bridge. Open extended season. Fee.

Marine mammals, New England wildlife, local pond and sea life, domestic animals, petting zoo; shows.

26. JUDAH BAKER WINDMILL PARK, *1791.* Willow and River sts., South Yarmouth. Open all year. No fee.

Eight-sided windmill with conical cap, gristmill; Seth Baker ran mill until 1891; bought by Charles Henry Davis and made part of fifty-room house, where flag was raised atop mill to signal arrival of ships and barrel placed upside down to indicate departures; views; park on Bass River.

BEACHES, PARKS, OTHER POINTS OF INTEREST

36. Colonial Acres Beach. Standish Way, West Yarmouth.

37 Englewood Beach. Berry Ave., West Yarmouth.

38. Sea Gull Beach. South Sea Ave., West Yarmouth. Bathhouse, snack bar.

39. Thacher Park. Sea View Ave., South Yarmouth.

40. Seaview Beach. South Shore Dr., South Yarmouth.

41. Parkers River Beach. South Shore Dr., South Yarmouth.

42. Bass River Beach. South St., South Yarmouth. Bathhouse, snack bar.

43. Long Pond Beach, Wing's Grove. Indian Memorial Dr., South Yarmouth. Freshwater beach, cairn by entrance for last Indian in Yarmouth.

WEST DENNIS AND DENNISPORT

27. JERICHO HISTORICAL CENTER AND JERICHO HOUSE, *1801.* Old Main St. and Trotting Park Rd. Open summer. No fee.

Barn museum, household artifacts, driftwood zoo.

28. SOUTH PARISH CONGREGATIONAL CHURCH, *1835.* Main St.

Known as "Captains' Church"; 1835 Sandwich chandelier, 1762 London organ oldest pipe organ in continuous use in country.

BEACHES, PARKS, OTHER POINTS OF INTEREST

44. West Dennis Beach. Davis Beach Rd. Bathhouse, snack bar.

45. South Village Road Beach. South Village Rd., West Dennis.

46. Glendon Road Beach. Glendon Rd., Dennisport.

47. Sea Street Beach. Sea St., Dennisport. Bathhouse.

48. Haigis Street Beach. Haigis St., Dennisport.

49. Raycroft Parkway Beach. Raycroft Parkway, Dennisport.

50. Depot Street Beach. Chase and Depot sts., Dennisport.

51. Inman Road Beach. Inman Rd., Dennisport.

HARWICH

29. HARWICH HISTORICAL SOCIETY. Brooks Academy, Main St. and Rte. 124. Open summer. No fee.

Indian artifacts, antiques, dolls, tools, toys, maps, and cranberry industry exhibits; bound copies of *Harwich Independent* 1872–1958, publisher of vital records 1654–1850; first school of navigation in America held in building 1844.

30. BROOKS FREE LIBRARY. Main St. Open all year. No fee.

Large private collection of John Rogers, "the people's sculptor."

31. CRANBERRY BOGS. Along Bank St.

Can be observed all year; Harwich leader in cranberry production since 1840s.

BEACHES, PARKS, OTHER POINTS OF INTEREST

52. Sand Pond. Great Western Rd., North Harwich. Fresh water.

53. Pleasant Road Beach. Pleasant Rd., West Harwich.

54. Earle Road Beach. Earle Rd., West Harwich.

55. Bank Street Beach. Bank St., Harwich Port.

56. Red River Beach. Deep Hole Rd., South Harwich.

57. Long Pond. Long Pond Dr. Fresh water.

58. Wixon Memorial, Long Pond. Cahoons Rd. Fresh water.

CHATHAM

32. RAILROAD MUSEUM, *1887*, NRHP. Depot Rd. Open summer. No fee.

Housed in Victorian Depot active 1887–1937; several thousand railroad artifacts, some over 100 years old.

33. ATWOOD HOUSE HISTORIC MUSEUM, *1752*, NRHP, HS. 347 Stage Harbor Rd. Open summer. Fee.

Author Joseph C. Lincoln room; barn contains religious murals by Alice Stallknecht-Wight; art gallery with works by Harold Brett; Chatham twin light turret in garden; memorial for nearby unmarked grave of Squanto.

34 GODFREY WINDMILL, *1797*, NRHP. Chase Park, Cross St. Open summer.

Wind-powered gristmill still operates.

35. CHATHAM LIGHT, *1808*. Shore Rd. and Bridge St. Grounds open all year. No fee.

Earlier two lights were known as "Twin Sisters of Chatham"; Battle of Chatham Harbor marker, exceptional views.

36. CHATHAM FISH PIER. Shore Rd. and Bar Cliff Ave. Open all year. No fee.

Observation deck to watch active fishing fleet activities; headquarters for commercial and sport fishermen.

BEACHES, PARKS, OTHER POINTS OF INTEREST

59. Forest Beach. Forest Beach Rd., South Chatham.
60. Cockle Cove Beach. Cockle Cove Rd., South Chatham.
61. Ridgevale Beach. Ridgevale Rd., South Chatham. Snack bar.
62. Harding Beach. Harding Beach Rd., West Chatham. Trails, bathhouse, snack bar.
63. Oyster Pond Beach. Stage Harbor Rd., Chatham Village. Children's beach, bathhouse.
64. National Wildlife Refuge. Morris Island, Morris Island Rd. Trails; parking on Morris Island Rd.
65. Lighthouse Beach/Coast Guard Beach. Main St., by USCG Station.

66. Andrew Harding Lane Beach. Andrew Harding Lane.

67. Schoolhouse Pond. Sam Ryder Rd. Fresh water.

68. Fox Hill walk. Fox Hill Rd., park at town landing on Strong Island Rd.

ORLEANS

37. MUSEUM OF ORLEANS HISTORICAL SOCIETY. Main St. Open summer. No fee.

Was First Universalist Meeting House, now museum of sea, farm, and Indian artifacts and Orleans memorabilia.

38. FRENCH CABLE STATION MUSEUM, *1890*, NRHP. Cove Rd. and Rte. 28. Open summer. Fee.

International communications 1891–1959, messages sent by transatlantic cables directly to Doelen, France, original equipment on display.

BEACHES, PARKS, OTHER POINTS OF INTEREST

69. Pilgrim Lake. Herring Brook Rd. Fresh water.

70. Baker's Pond. Baker's Pond Rd. Fresh water.

71. Meetinghouse Pond. Barley Neck Rd. Fresh water.

72. Academy Playhouse. Main St. opposite Monument Rd. Fee.

73. Orleans/Nauset Beach. Beach Rd. Bathhouse, snack bar.

74. Skaket Beach. Namskaket Rd. Snack bar.

75. Rock Harbor. Naval encounter during War of 1812, packet ships between Boston and Cape.

EASTHAM

39. OLD COVE CEMETERY. Rte. 6 opposite Hay Rd.

Site of first meetinghouse shortly after 1644; *Mayflower* passengers buried here, other seventeenth-century graves.

40. EDWARD PENNIMAN HOUSE, *1876*. Fort Hill Rd. Open summer, limited hours.

Victorian built by whaling captain, whalebone gateway; continue short distance on Fort Hill Rd. for views.

41. 1741 SWIFT–DALEY HOUSE. Rte. 6 by post office. Open summer. Fee.

Nathaniel Swift of Swift meat-packing company lived here; antiques.

42. EASTHAM WINDMILL, *1793*. Rte. 6 and Samoset Rd. opposite Town Hall. Open summer. No fee.

Oldest windmill on Cape; hand-hewn machinery still operative.

43. EASTHAM 1869 SCHOOLHOUSE MUSEUM, HS. Nauset Rd. opposite visitor center of Cape Cod National Seashore (B). Open summer. Fee.

One-room schoolhouse used through 1905.

44. NAUSET LIGHTHOUSE, *1838*. Cable Rd.

Originally three lights known as "Three Sisters"; tower 114 feet, 25,000-candlepower light; present light brought from Chatham 1923. Parking at adjacent Nauset Light Beach.

BEACHES, PARKS, OTHER POINTS OF INTEREST

Cape Cod National Seashore (points indicated by letters):

A. Fort Hill. Fort Hill Rd. Bike and nature trails.

B. Salt Pond Visitor Center. Rte. 6 and Nauset Rd. Open extended season. No fee. Nature and history museum, nature and bike trails.

C. Coast Guard Beach. Doane Rd. Environmental education center in old Coast Guard Station, views, bathhouse.

D. Nauset Light Beach. Cable Rd. Bathhouse.

76. Herring Pond. Herring Pond Rd. Fresh water.

77. First Encounter Beach. Samoset Rd. Where Pilgrims first encountered Indians and exchanged fire.

78. Cole Road Beach. Cole Rd.

79. Great Pond, Wiley Park. Herring Brook Rd. Fresh water.

80. Salt Pond Beach. Rte. 6 before visitor center.

81. Kingsbury Beach. Kingsbury Beach Rd.

82. Campground Beach. Campground Rd.

83. Cooks Brook Beach. Silver Spring Beach Rd.

84. Sunken Meadow Beach. South Sunken Meadow Rd.

85. Thumpertown Beach. Thumpertown Rd.

WELLFLEET

45. MARCONI WIRELESS STATION SITE. Off Rte. 6, past Cape Cod National Seashore Headquarters. Open all year. No fee.

Guglielmo Marconi built telegraph towers here, in 1903 sent first two-way wireless message between United States and England, message from President Theodore Roosevelt to King Edward VII. Wayside exhibits; trails to White Cedar Swamp.

46. JOSEPH'S GARDEN. Main and East Commercial sts.

Symbolic of Reverend Joseph Metcalfe's dory; church would not allow him to fish, so he left dory in yard; storm filled it with soil, and flower seeds grew into a garden; symbolic dories found on Cape.

47. FIRST CONGREGATIONAL CHURCH, *1850.* Main St.

Church clock believed to be only one in world striking ship's time, installed 1952; Tiffany window depicting ship of *Mayflower* era; Hook and Hastings 1873 organ.

48. WELLFLEET HISTORICAL SOCIETY MUSEUM AND SAMUEL RIDER HOUSE, *c. 1800,* NRHP. Main St. Open summer. Fee.

Restored Cape farmhouse, Wellfleet memorabilia.

BEACHES, PARKS, OTHER POINTS OF INTEREST

Cape Cod National Seashore:

E. Marconi Beach. Off Rte. 6, enter by National Seashore Headquarters. Trails, bathhouse.

F. Great Island Trail. Chequesset Neck Rd. Trails along Bound Brook and Griffin Island, 8-mile trail to end of Great Island and back.

86. Wellfleet Bay Wildlife Sanctuary. Off Rte. 6 near West Rd. Open all year. Fee. Self-guided nature trails, gift shop, summer camp, Monomoy Island tours, classes, lectures.

87. Lecount Hollow Beach. Lecount Hollow Rd.

88. White Crest Beach. Ocean View Dr.

89. Cahoon Hollow Beach. Cahoon Hollow Rd.

90. Great Pond. Cahoon Hollow Rd. Fresh water.

91. Long Pond. Long Pond Rd. Fresh water.

92. Newcomb Hollow Beach. Northern end Ocean View Dr.

93. Indian Neck Beach. Pilgrim Spring Rd.

94. Mayo Beach. Kendrick Rd. past town pier.

TRURO

49. BELL CHURCH, First Congregational Parish of Truro, *1827*. Town Hall Rd.

Named for Revere bell; has Sandwich glass windows and miniature whale–shaped window latches.

50. TRURO HISTORICAL MUSEUM AT HIGHLAND LIGHT. South Highland Rd. Open summer. Fee.

Restored inn housing maritime and agricultural exhibits, artifacts back to Pilgrim days.

51. CAPE COD LIGHT (HIGHLAND LIGHT), *1795*. Coast Guard Rd.

Oldest light on Cape, present structure 1875; first light seen by mariners approaching Boston, most powerful on New England coast; path to scenic overlook, tours through National Park Service.

52. JENNY LIND TOWER. Seen from Highland Station parking lot.

In 1850 Jenny sang from top of tower, then part of Fitchburg Railroad Depot Hall; performed free as concert oversold and customers rioting. Tower was moved here 1927 by Harry Aldrich as memorial to his father.

BEACHES, PARKS, OTHER POINTS OF INTEREST

Cape Cod National Seashore:

G. Head of the Meadow Beach. Head of the Meadow Rd. Access to High Head Bicycle and Dune trails; glacial end of Cape; bathhouse.

H. Pilgrim Heights Area. High Head Rd. Interpretive shelter about spring discovered by Pilgrims; Pilgrim Land Sand Dunes, trails, rest rooms; picnicking.

95. Ryder Beach. Ryder Beach Rd.

96. Fisher Beach. Fisher Rd.

97. Pamet Harbor. Depot Rd.

98. Ballston Beach. South Pamet Rd. Trails to Pamet River on north side of parking area.

99. Longnook Beach. Longnook Rd.

100. Corn Hill Beach. Corn Hill Rd. Plaque for Pilgrims who found Indian corn here.

101. Great Hollow Beach. Great Hollow Rd.

102. Encampment Park. Pond Rd. Plaque commemorating Pilgrim camp.

103. Pond Village Beach. Pond Rd.

104. Coast Guard Beach. Highland Rd.

PROVINCETOWN

53. PROVINCETOWN ART ASSOCIATION AND MUSEUM. 460 Commercial St. Open extended season, weekends in winter. Fee.

Founded 1914 for artists, sculptors, art collections; across street is a saltworks windmill; museum shop, art classes, lectures, films.

54. PROVINCETOWN HERITAGE MUSEUM, *1860*, NRHP. 356 Commercial St. Open extended season. Fee.

Originally built as Methodist church; art gallery and museum, marine and Victorian artifacts, antique fire equipment, world's largest half-scale indoor model—schooner *Rose Dorothea*.

55. MACMILLAN WHARF, Rte. 6A and Lopes Sq. Open all year. No fee.

Boat rentals; annual Blessing of Fleet, over fifty fishing vessels, annually about ten million pounds of fish landed.

56. SETH NICKERSON HOUSE, *1746*. 72 Commercial St. Open extended season. Fee.

Built by ship's carpenters using some materials from shipwrecks; oldest standing house on Cape; excellent example of pre-1750 Cape architecture.

57. OLDEST CEMETERY IN PROVINCETOWN. Winthrop St.

Four *Mayflower* passengers who died during brief stopover in 1620 buried here.

58. PILGRIM MONUMENT AND PROVINCETOWN MUSEUM, *1910*. Winslow St. Open all year. Fee.

Tallest all-granite monument in United States, 252 feet, bas-relief at base commemorates Pilgrim's first landing, November 11, 1620; maritime, natural history, Provincetown, and Cape Cod exhibits; collections of arctic explorer Donald MacMillan.

BEACHES, PARKS, OTHER POINTS OF INTEREST

Cape Cod National Seashore:

> I. Beach Forest Trail and Picnic Area. Race Point Rd.

> J. Province Lands Visitor Center. Race Point Rd. Observation deck, displays, films; horse, bike, and hiking trails.

> K. Race Point Beach. Race Point Rd. Rescue Museum in old Coast Guard Station; bathhouse.

> L. Herring Cove Beach. End of Rte. 6. Bathhouse, snack bar.

105. Provincetown Dunes. Dunes parking sign just west of Provincetown/Truro line on Rte. 6.

BREWSTER

59. BASSETT WILD ANIMAL FARM. Tubman Rd. Open summer, Fee.

Unusual and familiar animals and birds, rides, picnicking.

60 NEW ENGLAND FIRE AND HISTORY MUSEUM. Rte. 6A. Open all year. Fee.

Diorama of Chicago fire; fire memorabilia, Brewster blacksmith shop; Ben Franklin Philadelphia firehouse, apothecary shop, working museum; world's only 1929 Mercedes Benz engine; Arthur Fiedler fire collection.

61. STONY BROOK MILL AND HERRING RUN. *1873*. Stony Brook Rd. Open summer. No fee.

Was gristmill, ice-cream plant, private home, now town-owned working gristmill; museum exhibits.

62. CAPE COD MUSEUM OF NATURAL HISTORY. Rte. 6A, West Brewster. Open all year. Fee.

Animal collections, ecological exhibits, saltwater aquarium, library, gift shop, trails, lectures, films, classes, and nature programs; 100 feet west is John Wing trail to Wing Island.

BEACHES, PARKS, OTHER POINTS OF INTEREST

106. Nickerson State Park. Rte. 6A. Flax Pond (fresh water), trails; camping, picnicking, fishing, swimming.

107. Crosby Landing Beach. Crosby Ln.

108. Linnell's Landing Beach. Crosby Ln.

109. Ellis Landing Beach. Ellis Landing Rd.

110. Point of Rock's Landing Beach. Point of Rocks Rd.

111. Breakwater Beach. Breakwater Rd.

112. Saint's Landing Beach. Robbins Hill Rd.

113. Robbins Hill Beach. Robbins Hill Rd.

114. Paine's Creek Beach. Paine Creek Rd.

115. Sheep Pond, Fisherman's Landing. Rte. 124. Fresh water.

116. Long Pond. Landing Dr. Fresh water.

DENNIS

63. SCARGO HILL OBSERVATORY. Scargo Hill Rd. Open all year. No fee.

Twenty-eight-foot tower highest vantage point on mid-Cape, given to town as memorial to Charles and Francis Bassett Tobey, 1929; overlooks Scargo Lake and across to Provincetown, named for Indian legend.

64. CAPE MUSEUM OF FINE ARTS. 60 Hope St. Open all year. No fee.

Exhibits, classes, lectures, trips.

65. CAPE PLAYHOUSE AND CINEMA, Main St. (Rte. 6A).

Open for performances; stage plays with name performers; old and new films; auditorium originally an 1838 Unitarian Church moved here in 1927, when playhouse and cinema began; cinema has one of the largest indoor ceiling murals (6,400 sq. ft.) in North America, designed by Rockwell Kent, assisted by Jo Mielziner.

66. JOSIAH DENNIS MANSE, *1736*, and OLD WEST SCHOOL-HOUSE, *1770*. Nobscuset Rd. and Whig St. Open summer. No fee.

Restored Colonial house museum with period exhibits.

BEACHES, PARKS, OTHER POINTS OF INTEREST

117. Sea Street Beach. Sea St.

118. Cold Storage Beach. Salt Works Rd.

119. Harbor Road Beach. Harbor Rd.

120. Howes Street Beach. Howes St.

121. Corporation Road Beach. Corporation Rd. Bathhouse, snack bar.

122. Princess Beach at Scargo Conservation area. Scargo Hill Rd. Fresh water, trails, playground, bathhouse.

123. Bayview Road Beach. Bayview Rd. Snack bar.

124. Horse Foot Path Beach. Horse Foot Path Rd.

125. Chapin Memorial Beach. Chapin Beach Rd.

126. Mayflower Beach. Rte. 6A. Bathhouse, snack bar.

YARMOUTHPORT AND YARMOUTH

67. CHURCH OF THE NEW JERUSALEM, *1870*. Opposite Strawberry Ln., Rte. 6A. Open summer for services.

Swedenborgian church with unusual Italianate architecture, outstanding organ.

68. CAPTAIN BANGS HALLET HOUSE, HS. 2 Strawberry Ln.. Open summer, limited hours and by appointment. Fee.

Greek Revival home of China trader Captain Thomas Thacher; 1740 kitchen; sea-oriented collections; lovely European weeping beech tree; park at post office. Trail leads to **Botanic Trail Gate House,** open all year, fee.

69. WINSLOW-CROCKER HOUSE, *c. 1780*, SPNEA. 250 Rte. 6A, Yarmouthport. Open extended season. Fee.

Shingled Georgian; seventeenth- to mid-nineteenth-century antiques with rare seventeenth-century wooden cradle.

BEACHES, PARKS, OTHER POINTS OF INTEREST

127. Bass Hole Beach. Center St.

128. Dennis Pond Beach. Summer St. Fresh water.

BARNSTABLE

70. CAPE COD ART ASSOCIATION. Rte. 6A. Open extended season, classes all year. No fee.

Exhibits by Cape Cod artists.

71. DONALD G. TRAYSER MEMORIAL MUSEUM, *1856*. Rte. 6A. Open summer. Donations.

Customhouse until 1913; Barnstable historic memorabilia, fishing and tool exhibits rear building.

72. STURGIS LIBRARY, *c. 1645*. 3090 Rte. 6A.

Oldest public building used as library in United States; original section served as home to Reverend John Lothrop 1639–53, also served as first meetinghouse; Henry Kittredge maritime reference collection, extensive Cape Cod genealogy.

73. OLDE COLONIAL COURT HOUSE, *1774*. Rte. 6A and Rendezvous Ln. Open summer, limited hours and by appointment.

Once King's Court, a church, now houses bicentennial memorabilia, flags; lectures.

74. WEST PARISH MEETINGHOUSE, *1717*. Rte. 149 just north of Rte. 6.

Outstanding example of Colonial ecclesiastical architecture; Revere bell, 5-foot rooster atop cupola; congregation gathered by Reverend Lothrop 1639.

BEACHES, PARKS, OTHER POINTS OF INTEREST

129. Millway Beach. Millway Rd. Bathhouse, snack bar.

130. Hathaway's Pond Beach. Phinney's Ln., West Barnstable. Fresh water, bathhouse.

131. Sandy Neck Great Marshes. Sandy Neck Rd. Trails 14 miles to Beach Point and back.

132. Sandy Neck Beach. Sandy Neck Rd. Bathhouse, snack bar.

SANDWICH

75. SANDWICH STATE FISH HATCHERY AND GAME FARM. Rte. 6A east of Pine Terrace Rd. Open all year. No fee.

Raises pheasant and quail; opportunity to observe life cycle of game birds.

76. BENJAMIN NYE HOMESTEAD, *1685*. Old County Rd. Open extended season. Fee.

Authentically restored with many family pieces; by Nye Pond, where six generations of Nyes ran mill until 1867.

77. QUAKER MEETINGHOUSE, *1810*. Gilman Rd. Open all year for services.

Oldest continuous Quaker meeting in America, established 1657.

78. STEVEN WING FORT HOUSE, *1641*, NRHP. Spring Hill Rd. opposite Juniper Hill Rd. Open summer. Fee.

Home has seventeenth- and eighteenth-century sections; Steven settled in Sandwich 1637, was member of first Friends Meeting in America, persecuted by Plymouth; house owned and lived in by same family for three centuries.

79. DAN'L WEBSTER INN, *1692*. 149 Main St. Open all year as inn.

Present inn rebuilt after fire destroyed most of original building, where Daniel Webster retained room year round.

80. YESTERYEAR DOLL MUSEUM. Main and River sts. Open extended season. Fee.

Outstanding collection of dolls displayed in old First Parish Meetinghouse, 1833; church clock gift of Jonathan Bourne of New Bedford whaling fame.

81. SANDWICH GLASS MUSEUM, *1907*, HS. Rte. 130 and Tupper Rd. Open extended season and by appointment. Fee.

Houses collections of Sandwich glass, 1825–88, and historic artifacts.

82. DEXTER GRIST MILL, *1654*. Grove and Water sts. Open summer. Fee.

Restored active gristmill built by Thomas Dexter, original Sandwich settler.

83. THORNTON W. BURGESS MUSEUM. Next to 82. Open extended season. Donation.

Memorabilia of Thornton Burgess, author of Mother West Wind books and other children's books; born in Sandwich, Burgess visited his Aunt Arabella Eldred Burgess in this home on **Shawme Pond,** where wildlife familiar in Burgess stories are ever present. Peaceful setting; pond dammed for early water power; **1683 cemetery** on Grove St. side; **Briar Patch Trails and Green Briar Nature Center and Jam Kitchen** off Discover Rd. near 4-mile marker on Rte. 6A.

84. HOXIE HOUSE, *1680s.* Water St. opposite School St. Open summer. Fee.

Classic saltbox, restored to 1680–90 period, furnishings by Boston Museum of Fine Arts; overlooks Shawme Pond.

85. HERITAGE PLANTATION, *1917.* Grove and Pine sts. Open extended season. Fee.

Property of Charles Dexter, who hybridized Dexter rhododendron. Seventy-six acres of Americana: Shaker Round Barn, windmill, carousel, antique and classic automobiles, art and military museum, extensive Currier and Ives exhibit, antique firearms, tools, arts, spectacular gardens, trails, picnicking.

BEACHES, PARKS, OTHER POINTS OF INTERESTS

133. Sandy Neck Beach. Sandy Neck Rd.

134. Sandwich Town Beach. Town Neck Rd.

135. Shawme–Crowell State Forest. Main St. Campsites, trails.

136. Snake Pond Beach. Snake Pond Rd. Fresh water.

137. Lowell Holly Reservation (Wakeby Reservation Sandwich Conservation Recreation Area). South Sandwich Rd., Wakeby Pond. Sandy beach, picnicking.

138. Scusset Beach. Phillips Rd. Bathhouse, snack bar.

MARTHA'S VINEYARD

(Full-service ferries to the Vineyard operate year-round out of Woods Hole on Cape Cod.
Seasonal, passenger-only ferries operate from Hyannis and Falmouth, also on the Cape.)

M artha's Vineyard is a land of history and hospitality. The island has been home to whaling captains, intrepid fishermen, and competitive anglers. It has been residence for prominent men and women and generations of Vineyard natives, as well as adopted home for those captured by its beauty and charm. Inhabited by Indians, named by Bartholomew Gosnold, settled by Thomas Mayhew in 1642, Martha's Vineyard has its own unique place in American history. Here from the very beginning, white settlers and Indians learned to live in peace. During the Revolution, this small island was blockaded by the British, whose raiding parties captured powder, livestock, and other goods until the island declared itself neutral land. From here Vineyard whalers plied the seven seas, and beautifully preserved captains' homes tell of those historic years. When whaling declined in the mid-1800s, Oak Bluffs became a popular place for religious camp meetings. First known as Cottage City, the area attracted thousands of visitors each year, opening the door for later tourism.

Today the Vineyard's main industry is summer visitors, for this is an island with unmatched coastlines and beaches, picturesque fishing villages, rolling hills and farmland, quaint weathered homes, stately captains' mansions, five guardian lighthouses, rose-covered fences, sturdy stone walls, and the ever-present wild grapes for which the Vineyard was named.

VINEYARD HAVEN

TISBURY TOWN HALL, *1844*. 21 Spring St. Open all year as town offices and Katherine Cornell Memorial Theater.

Built as Congregational-Baptist church, neoclassical architecture, restored for Vineyard Haven's 300th anniversary; in theater, wall murals of vineyard life.

OLD SCHOOLHOUSE MUSEUM, *1828*, HS. 110 Main St. and Colonial Ln. Open by appointment.

Built as school, used as Congregational church, was owned by DAR; now museum of Martha's Vineyard Historical Preservation Society: Scrimshaw, china, costumes, and artifacts relate to early island life.

WEST CHOP LIGHTHOUSE, NRHP. End of Main St. Closed to public.
Picturesque setting.

OAK BLUFFS

FLYING HORSES CAROUSEL, *1884*, NRHP. Oak Bluffs and Circuit aves. Open summer. Fee for rides.

Wooden horses carved by Charles W. F. Dare, New York, about 1876, now restored to that time; one has Coney Island #4 written on inside panel. Riders still grab for the brass ring and earn a free ride; one of the oldest operating carousels in country; excellent example of American folk art.

CIVIL WAR MEMORIAL STATUE, *1892*. Ocean Ave. Open all year. No fee.

Entitled *Chasm is Closed* and dedicated by Union soldiers and patriotic citizens, rare flesh-toned statue honors Confederate soldiers, believed to be only such one north of Mason–Dixon Line.

MARTHA'S VINEYARD CAMP MEETING ASSOCIATION, TRINITY PARK, TABERNACLE, NRHP. Access Circuit, Lake, Duke County, and Siloam aves. Area open all year. No fee.

Houses private. First camp meetings of Methodists 1835; land bought by Wesleyan Grove Camp Meeting Association 1839; group first pitched tents, built high fence; 1860s tents replaced by small gingerbread Gothic-type cottages; Gospel tent replaced by Tabernacle 1879. Illumination Night, traditionally held in August, begins with community sing at Tabernacle, then each building lights antique Oriental paper lanterns until entire campground is aglow.

EAST CHOP LIGHTHOUSE, NRHP. Highland Dr. Closed to public.

Also known as Telegraph Hill, site of earlier semaphore signal tower; now benches, beautiful views of Nantucket Sound.

STATE LOBSTER HATCHERY. Shirley Ave. off County Rd. Open summer, limited hours. No fee.

Interesting opportunity to observe egg-laden females and early life of young lobsters.

EDGARTOWN

OLD WHALING CHURCH, *1843*. Main St. Open all year as performing arts center. Fee.

Excellent example of Greek Revival architecture, reflects wealth of whaling era; large, beautifully restored interior with 160 box pews; 92-foot tower seen from ocean.

VINCENT HOUSE, *1672*. Pease's Point Way, behind Old Whaling Church. Open summer. Fee.

Oldest known house on island; original hardware, brick, and woodwork, clay insulation; fine example of early architecture; owned by Martha's Vineyard Historical Preservation Society along with Old Whaling Church and Dr. Fisher House.

DR. DANIEL FISHER HOUSE, *1840*. Main St., next to Old Whaling Church. Open all year as professional offices.

Large, impressive Greek Revival built by Dr. Fisher, physician and wealthiest man on island; house shows excellent adaptive reuse.

TOWN WHARF. Dock St. Open all year. No fee.

Earlier owned by Dr. Daniel Fisher and site of his whale-oil refinery, once believed to have supplied all lighthouses in country with whale oil. Today On-Time ferry leaves for Chappaquiddick, public access to island; observation deck; Cape Pogue Light, NRHP, on Chappaquiddick.

NORTH AND SOUTH WATER STS.

Lovely old captains' homes, white fences, and colorful gardens recall days of prosperous whaling era; Edgartown first settlement, county seat since 1642.

DUKES COUNTY HISTORICAL SOCIETY, COOKE AND SCHOOL STS., THOMAS COOKE HOUSE, *1765*. Open all year. Fee.

Francis Foster Museum; Gale Huntington Library, emphasis history and genealogy; Thomas Cooke was customs collector; twelve rooms furnished with Vineyard antiques, costumes, scrimshaw, ship models. Museum features "Vineyard and the Sea," Gay Head replica light tower and Fresnel lens used 1854–1952, whaleboat, 1854 fire engine, whale ship's tryworks on grounds; guided tours, special exhibits.

EDGARTOWN LIGHTHOUSE, NRHP. Starbuck Neck Rd. Beach open all year. No fee.

Light is on Lighthouse Beach at edge of harbor; views of Chappaquiddick Island, Nantucket Sound.

CHILMARK

MENEMSHA. End of North Rd. Open all year.

Quaint, picturesque working fishing village created when Menemsha Creek dredged 1905; center of Vineyard scalloping, lobstering, and fishing, both commercial and sport; Coast Guard base.

GAY HEAD

GAY HEAD CLIFFS AND LIGHTHOUSE, NRHP. End of Lighthouse and South rds. Open all year. No fee.

Mile-long cliffs of multiple layers deposited over millions of years, forming unique colors and revealing geological and archaeological past; cliffs NHL, no walking allowed on cliffs. Light built 1799, one of first revolving type. Spectacular views of Elizabeth Islands, Cape Cod, Nomans Land; restaurant and small shops, some run by descendants of Wampanoag Indians.

WEST TISBURY

MAYHEW CHAPEL AND INDIAN BURIAL GROUND. 1 mile in on South Indian Hill Rd. Chapel open all year, limited hours.

Small, well-preserved chapel built 1839; at one time school for Indians; religious services held here until 1903. Memorial to Reverend Thomas Mayhew, Jr., 1621–57, and community of Praying Indians he converted to Christianity. **Indian Burial Ground** of unmarked fieldstones; early pulpit rock behind; wildflower sanctuary, owned by Wampanoag Tribe of Gay Head (Aquinnah).

CHICAMA VINEYARDS, *1971*. Stoney Hill Rd. ¼ mile south of West Tisbury/Vineyard Haven line. Open all year as commercial vineyards.

Cultivates European and Vineyard grapes; first winery licensed in Massachusetts; wine tasting, tours.

BEACHES AND PARKS

Open, no fee, unless otherwise stated.

Vineyard Haven

Lake Tashmoo Town Beach. Lake Tashmoo off Herring Creek Rd.

Owen Park Beach. Main St.

West Chop Woods. Franklin Rd. Eighty-three acres, trails.

Oak Bluffs

Eastville Beach. Bridge between Oak Bluffs and Vineyard Haven.

Joseph Sylvia State Beach. Beach Rd.

Oak Bluffs Town Beach. Sea View Ave.

Edgartown

Felix Neck Wildlife Sanctuary. Vineyard Haven Rd. Donations. 350 acres, trails, visitor center and small museum bookshop, wildlife rehabilitation center, tours, classes.

Lighthouse Beach. Starbuck Neck Rd.

Sheriff's Meadow. Planting Field Rd. Sixteen acres, trails.

South Beach (Katama Beach). Katama Rd. on Norton Point.

Chappaquiddick Island

Cape Pogue Wildlife Refuge and Wasque Reservation (East Beach). Dyke and Wasque rds. Fee.

Chilmark

Menemsha Public Beach, North Rd.

Menemsha Hills Reservation and Beach. North Rd.

Gay Head

Lobsterville Beach. West Basin Rd.

Moshup Beach. Moshup's Trail, near Gay Head Cliffs. Summer parking fee.

West Tisbury

Cedar Tree Neck Nature Preserve. Indian Hill Rd. Trails through woods along beach, ponds, brook, views; no swimming or picnicking.

Long Point Wildlife Refuge. At Tisbury Great Pond. Fee. Out marsh plain, woods, marsh, salt and freshwater ponds, sandy barrier beach, trails with map.

NANTUCKET ISLAND

(Full-service ferries to the island operate year-round out of Hyannis on Cape Cod. Seasonal, passenger-only ferries operate from the same town.)

Once you have visited Nantucket Island, the Little Gray Lady of the Sea, it will beckon you back year after year. This picturesque island, 30 miles at sea, is 14 miles long, with endless beaches and colorful moors. Nantucket was settled by colonists who believed in living in harmony with one another. The island was nurtured by whaling, which set its destiny as the first whaling capital of the world. Though the golden years of Nantucket whaling prosperity were in the late 1700s and early 1800s, the aura of the whaling ship and the "Nantucket sleigh ride"—the wild ride in a whaleboat pulled by a harpooned whale—is still felt.

Nantucket offers a look into those whaling days when men challenged the mightiest of all mammals. Victory meant high financial rewards but failure meant severe loss or death, for there was little compromise with a 65-foot, 60-ton sperm whale. Here you will find whaling captains' mansions, cobblestoned streets, rose-covered homes with weathered shingles, and docks mooring pleasure and working boats from all along the east coast.

ABIAH FOLGER FRANKLIN FOUNTAIN, *1900*. Madaket Rd.
1 mile from end of Main St.

Site of the birthplace of Benjamin Franklin's mother, Abiah Folger, and the home of Franklin's grandfather, who was interpreter during the negotiations when Nantucket was purchased from the Indians in 1659.

FIRE HOSE CART HOUSE, *1886*. 8 Gardner St. Open extended season.
No fee.

Only survivor of neighborhood fire stations; fire-fighting equipment, century-old Siasconset pumper used by early volunteers.

FIRST CONGREGATIONAL CHURCH. Centre St. and Ash Ln. Open
extended season. Fee.

Climb to top of church tower for 360-degree panoramic view of island.

HADWEN HOUSE, *1845*. **96 Main St. Open summer. Fee.**

Greek Revival mansion of William Hadwen, wealthy merchant during Nantucket's golden years of whaling prosperity; appropriately furnished with Federal, Empire, and later revival styles.

MARIA MITCHELL BIRTHPLACE, *1790*. **Vestal, Milk, and Washington sts. Open summer. Fee. Observatory; Scientific Research Library and Hinchman House.**

Birthplace of Maria Mitchell, America's first woman astronomer and first professor of astronomy at Vassar College; early Quaker home shows Mitchell furnishings and memorabilia. Working observatory, open some nights for public viewing, lectures, classes. **Hinchman House** a natural science museum; library contains 9,500 volumes and research journals; Mitchell's notes, books, and correspondence; tours.

MUSEUM OF NANTUCKET HISTORY. **Straight Wharf. Open extended season. Fee.**

Housed in the 1846 Thomas Macy Warehouse, exhibits tell the story of Nantucket from early history through golden age of whaling and growth of summer residents to today's tourism; 13-foot diorama of Nantucket waterfront before Great Fire of 1846; demonstrations; special exhibits of Nantucket Historical Association.

NANTUCKET LIFE SAVING MUSEUM, *1874*. **Off Polpis Rd. Open extended season. Fee.**

Reconstructed Surfside Life Saving Station built 1874; lifesaving memorabilia.

OLDEST HOUSE, *1686*, **NHL, NRHP. Sunset Hill. Open extended season. Fee.**

Built for Jethro and Mary Gardner Coffin, it is a typical late seventeenth-century house in the Massachusetts Bay Colony.

OLD GAOL, *1805*. **Off Vestal St. Open extended season. No fee.**

Built of massive oak timbers and iron bolts; cells with fireplaces; stocks; it is said prisoners were allowed to go home at night.

OLD SOUTH CHURCH, UNITARIAN, *1809*, **NRHP. 11 Orange St. Open summer. No fee.**

Remarkable trompe l'oeil 1844 interior, historic Goodrich organ.

OLD WINDMILL, *1745.* **Mill and Prospect sts. Open summer. Fee.**

Built by mariner Nathan Wilbur, sails and wooden gears still transform wind power into mechanical energy.

PACIFIC CLUB, *1772.* **Main and Washington sts. Private.**

Built by whaling merchant William Rotch as warehouse and countinghouse; seamen's club organized 1854 for those who had sailed the Pacific.

PETER FOULGER MUSEUM/RESEARCH CENTER. Broad St. next to Whaling Museum. Open extended season for research by appointment.

Changing exhibits relate to Nantucket history; second floor houses Nantucket Historical Association Research Center and Edouard A. Stackpole Library, manuscript records of Nantucket island and maritime history, ships' logs, genealogical charts, audiovisual materials.

QUAKER MEETINGHOUSE, *1838.* **Fair St. Open extended season.**

Meetinghouse built as school for active Quaker community, later used for services.

THREE BRICKS, *1838,* **NRHP. 93–97 Main St. Private.**

Three identical mansions built during Nantucket's golden years by wealthy whaling merchant Joseph Starbuck for his sons.

WHALING MUSEUM, *1847.* **Broad and South Beach sts. Open extended season. Fee. Museum shop.**

Formerly the Hadwen (of Hadwen–Satler family) and Barney candle factory; now houses memorabilia of whale hunting, including harpoons and equipment used for processing whales during Nantucket's golden era; exhibits include scrimshaw and a 43-foot skeleton of a finback whale.

PUBLIC BEACHES

Open all year, no fee, unless otherwise stated.

Nantucket Town

Jetties Beach. Off North Beach St.

Children's Beach. Off South Beach St.

Coskata Coatue Wildlife Refuge. Open all year. Fee. 963 acres of sand dunes, salt marsh, wildlife sanctuary; surf fishing.

Brant Point Light, 1746, NRHP. End of Easton St. Grounds open all year. No fee. On site of second lighthouse built in Colonial America; friendly beacon to mariners and visitors.

Siasconset

Sconset Beach. End Sconset Rd.

Sankaty Head Light, NRHP. Sconset Rd. Red and white–striped tower on bluff warning mariners of dangerous waters.

Surfside

Surfside Beach. Surfside Rd.

Cisco

Cisco Beach. Hummock Pond Rd.

Madaket

Madaket Beach. Madaket Rd.

Dionis Beach. Eel Point Rd.

Great Point Light. Great Point. Present light replaced 1784 light that fell in storm of 1984; first and last thing people see as approach or leave island, vital navigational aid.

PLYMOUTH

ere during a cold New England winter, 102 ocean-weary, hungry, and
lonely colonists came ashore and laid the groundwork for the greatest
nation on earth. Many had been tried and tested through years of religious persecution in England, struggle in Holland to retain identity and faith, and
a sixty-six-day cramped, harrowing ocean crossing. They had the will not only to
survive but to grow, to build, and to create. On December 21, 1620, the voyagers,
including John Alden, William Bradford, Myles Standish, Elder Brewster, and
Edward Winslow, landed at what even then, on early maps, was called Plymouth.
That first winter took a gruesome toll. Only half lived to greet the spring. The survivors' spirits were lifted in March when Samoset, one of the feared Indians,
entered camp and said, "Welcome." He introduced the Pilgrims to Squanto and
Massasoit leader of the Wampanoag Indians, who helped the colonists. That summer they planted and harvested crops, filled empty larders, and improved living
conditions. Fall saw them so thankful that Governor Bradford declared a harvest
celebration, jointly shared by colonists and Indians.

As word of the Plymouth Colony's success reached England, craftsmen left to
seek land and possible wealth in the New World. They brought much-needed skills
to Plymouth Colony. During the 1630s settlers came to Plymouth and began towns
in the surrounding countryside. By 1645 the colony had grown to 2,500 and
included ten outlying towns. Through the years Plymouth has been a farming and
fishing community, mill town, and shipbuilding port. Today tourism is a vital part
of its economy. Exhibits, restorations, and reconstructions encourage you to go
back in time and understand the Pilgrim world.

1. PLIMOTH PLANTATION, HOBBAMOCK'S HOMESITE, CAR-
RIAGE HOUSE CRAFTS CENTER, *1947.* Route 3A. Open extended
season, fee includes *Mayflower II* (5). Museum, visitor center, gift shops, two
theaters; demonstrations, reenactments, workshops, special events; off-season,
special focus, hands-on tours by appointment.

At Plimoth Plantation, Pilgrims and the reasons for their first harvest celebration
(today's Thanksgiving) become real. This accurately recreated village is approximately
3 miles from the original Leyden Street (see 11), where the Pilgrims' first homes were.
Seventeenth-century reality is everywhere—from the buildings, furnishings, foods,
ways of cooking and tending crops and animals, to the very people themselves, who
speak with seventeenth-century English accents. In the timber fort and in more than
twenty homes and buildings made of wood and wattle-and-daub construction with
thatched roofs, you can see, feel, smell, and be part of life in 1627. The Fort/Meeting-

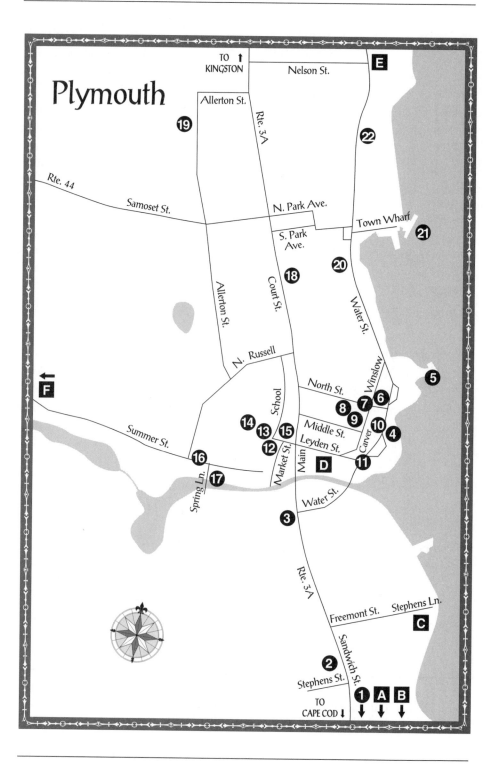

house with its plain benches and simple wooden pulpit speaks eloquently of a God-centered life. The cannon atop the fort reminds you of the hardships, dangers, and trials the Pilgrims met, accepted, and conquered. From this tiny settlement they looked out over village and harbor—their immediate small world, 3,000 miles from home and family. Talk with costumed interpreters, learn of their experiences as Separatists and Non-Separatists in England and Holland and of their survival in the New World, but remember they live in the world of 1627.

Walk along Eel River Nature Walk to the homesite of Hobbamock, a Wampanoag Indian from Pokanoket (now Bristol/Warren, Rhode Island) who lived with his family near Plimoth in the 1620s. Both Governors William Bradford and Edward Winslow wrote of how he helped the English settlers. Relive the Natives' way of life as you visit their bark-covered wetu's (houses) and hear Native staff in period costumes and non-Native staff tell the story of Hobbamock in 20th-century time.

At the Carriage House Crafts Center see how goods were made and international trade carried out in the early seventeenth-century. Craftsmen weave cloth and closely woven baskets, create redware pottery, and demonstrate the art of making fine furniture. The building is the original carriage house of Plimoth Plantation founder Ralph Hornblower.

Thanksgiving will never be quite the same after visiting Plimoth Plantation. You come away with a new pride in the founding fathers and mothers, a new understanding of their determination, sacrifice, and dedication, supported by an unalterable faith in the goodness and strength of their God.

2. HARLOW OLD FORT HOUSE, *1677*, NRHP. 119 Sandwich St. Open extended season, fee. Gift shop, classes, demonstrations.

The ancient Harlow House goes back to Old Fort Meetinghouse. When the fort was dismantled after 1676, its timbers were given to Sergeant William Harlow for his service in King Philip's War and later used in constructing this house. For 243 years Harlows, relatives, or in-laws lived here until the house was bought by the Plymouth Antiquarian Society in 1920. This working house museum depicts life as it was for the William Harlows, second generation Plymoutheans. William was a cooper, selectman, member of the General Court, and inspector of inns and ordinaries. His house has weathered shingles with gambrel roof and central chimney. The rustic interior rooms are furnished with seventeenth-century pieces similar to ones on Harlow's inventory.

3. HOWLAND HOUSE, *1667*, NRHP. 33 Sandwich St. Open extended season, fee.

In this weathered Colonial home, Pilgrims shared daily joys and concerns of Plymouth life in the 1600s. The house was built by Jacob Mitchel and sold in 1667 to Jabez Howland, son of John and Elizabeth Tilley Howland, who later lived here with Jabez. John

Plimoth Plantation, Plymouth   (*Courtesy Plimoth Plantation, Inc., Plymouth, Massachusetts*)

Howland had left England at age twenty-seven aboard the *Mayflower* as man-servant to Governor John Carver. He owned property in Kingston, Duxbury, and Plymouth; served on the Governor's Council; was one of the eight who assumed Plymouth's debts; and was agent for the Pilgrims' trading post in Kennebec, Maine. He died at age eighty and is buried on Burial Hill.

The original right side of this restored home began in 1666 with front room, fireplace, and room above. Its rooms are furnished with seventeenth-century pieces and a chest and Bible box believed to have belonged to Howlands. The beams, fireplace, and upstairs floor are original. Plaster would have been made of local goat hair, clamshells, and beach sand. The rear kitchen, fireplace, and borning room, plus two rooms above, now a minimuseum, were added about 1700. You advance fifty years as you step into the left side of the house, built about 1750. It has painted wood paneling, wood moldings, sash windows, and the more lavish furnishings of the eighteenth century, including pewter flatware.

4. PLYMOUTH ROCK, *1620*, NRHP. Water St. Open all year, no fee.

Though not the huge boulder your imagination expects, this small rock was a giant step for this country and the Pilgrims who landed here in 1620. It was first recognized as the Pilgrim landing site in 1742. Before the Revolution twenty yoke of oxen attempted to move it to Town Square. Unfortunately the rock broke in two, leaving the larger part on shore. In 1834 part of the rock was moved to Pilgrim Hall. Finally in 1880 it was returned and cemented to its original piece. The National Society of Colonial Dames of America gave the sixteen-Tuscan-pillared portico in 1921.

5. MAYFLOWER II AND PLYMOUTH STATE PIER. Water St. Open extended season, fee. Exhibits, gift shop, sightseeing boats.

Sixty-six days of rolling sea were marked with violent storms, poor sanitary conditions, limited food, seeping water, and a cracked main beam. One hundred two passengers were housed "tween decks," with no natural light or ventilation except when hatches were open. Yet undaunted Pilgrims knelt and thanked God for their deliverance when land was sighted November 9, 1620. Miraculously, of the 102 passengers who left Plymouth, England, September 6, only one died; and thanks to a birth on shipboard, 102 arrived in the New World.

Mayflower II, a reproduction ship of the period and tonnage of the *Mayflower,* lies at anchor next to State Pier. Aboard, costumed guides interpret in English dialect with knowledge only through 1620. When you stand "tween decks," feel the movement of the ship and imagine the pitching of the first *Mayflower,* the roar of waves and wind, and the darkness, dampness, and foul air with closed hatches. In 1954, to understand the first crossing, William A. Baker designed *Mayflower II,* later built by Stuart Upham of Devon, England. Handcrafted like the original, the three-masted square rigger, captained by Alan Villiers with experienced crew, left Plymouth, England, April 20, 1957. The ship proved seaworthy, but even the hardiest sailor suffered seasickness and found accommodations cramped for the thirty-three men, many fewer than the first *Mayflower's.*

6. PILGRIM MOTHER, *1920.* Water and North sts.

This statue, given by Daughters of the American Revolution on the 300th anniversary of the Pilgrim Landing, represents the *Mayflower* women. While Pilgrim men were the heads of families, the love, patience, and spiritual guidance of the women provided essential mortar for building this colony.

7. THE MAYFLOWER SOCIETY HOUSE MUSEUM, EDWARD WINSLOW HOUSE, *1754.* 4 Winslow St. Open summer, fee. Headquarters of General Society of Mayflower Descendants. Research library open all year, fee for non-members.

The mansion expresses living in both early Georgian Colonial and Victorian Colonial

The Mayflower II, *Plymouth*   (Massachusetts Office of Travel and Tourism)

Revival times. The Georgian front portion was built in 1754 by Edward Winslow, great-grandson of *Mayflower* passenger Edward Winslow (see Marshfield 1), third governor of Plymouth Colony. The fourth-generation Winslow's Tory views necessitated his rapid departure during the Revolution. Lydia Jackson, daughter of the next owners, married Ralph Waldo Emerson in the east parlor in 1835. In the same room in 1842, Lydia's brother, Dr. Charles Jackson, used himself in an experiment in which ether was discovered. In 1898 Chicago millionaire Charles Willoughby enlarged the estate, adding the rear Victorian addition. The home was doubled, moved back, and raised 5 feet. Notice elaborate tiers of balustrades, front portico, columned porch, and crowning cupola. Inside, the magnificent flying staircase is repeated to form a mirror image staircase linking the two periods. Woodwork of the Georgian period, traditionally painted, is complemented by the Victorian-era natural finish of Honduras mahogany, sycamore, and cherry. Many museum-quality furnishings are gifts of *Mayflower* heirs.

8. SPOONER HOUSE, *c. 1747.* **27 North St. Open summer, fee.**

In the Spooner House all furnishings are Spooner owned, accumulated over 200 years. The house provides insight into the daily life of a Plymouth family from pre-Revolutionary days to 1954, when the house became a museum. It is late Colonial–early Georgian style, with fireplaces and Oriental rugs in many rooms. Wallpapers are interesting, especially in the study, where paper once lined tea boxes from the Orient. Treasures from the China trade are displayed. Influence of the sea is throughout. The captain's bedroom window views the harbor, with neighboring houses slightly recessed so each has a harbor view.

Deacon Ephraim and Elizabeth Spooner moved here when Elizabeth inherited the right side of the house in 1763. Later they added the left side. Ephraim was merchant, town clerk, judge, and member of the colony's Legislature, Executive Council, and Committee of Correspondence. Son James, merchant and owner of Grand Banks fishing schooners, cut an east window to view the wharf. His son married a Spooner whose brother, Bourne, founded the Plymouth Cordage Company.

9. PLYMOUTH NATIONAL WAX MUSEUM. 16 Carver St. Open extended season, fee. Gift shop.

The Wax Museum is amazingly realistic. Twenty-seven detailed tableaus, reenacted from ancient records or paintings, depict early Pilgrim life. Sounds of crashing waves, driving rain, and cracking thunder bring extraordinary realism to the perfectly detailed wax figures.

10. COLE'S HILL, SARCOPHAGUS, STATUE OF MASSASOIT, *1620*, NHL. Carver, North, Water, and Leyden sts. Open all year, no fee.

This prominent hill offered security for the Pilgrims as a place from which they could oversee the harbor and surrounding area. Struck with the awesome hardships of that first winter, they all too soon used the hill to inter their dead. They dug unmarked graves secretly at night so Indians would not know of their heavy losses. In time they planted corn here, which helped turn questionable existence into survival. The hill was named for James Cole, who came from England in 1633 and lived and ran an inn or "ordinary" on this site until his death in 1692.

Today a granite sarcophagus, given by the General Society of Mayflower Descendants in 1921, bears the names of the Pilgrims who died that first winter. In close proximity stands the bronze figure of Wampanoag Sachem Massasoit, the Pilgrims' friend, who signed a mutual assistance pact that lasted more than fifty years. The statue, by Cyrus Dallin, was given by the Improved Order of Red Men in 1921. As you stand here, visualize one lonely ship of fearful yet determined settlers. At the same time, see today's harbor with its boats and reproduction of the *Mayflower*. Let the years slip away as the two visions intermingle.

11. LEYDEN STREET, *1621*.

Walk Leyden Street from waterfront to Burial Hill and walk the street of Pilgrims, the first street in New England. Here were the first Pilgrim homes—those of Bradfords, Brewsters, Winslows. Then the area was dirt surrounded by a stockade. Thatched-roofed, daubed-chimneyed, rough-cut wood homes looked up at the flat-roofed Fort/Meetinghouse with cannon atop.

12. 1749 COURTHOUSE, NRHP. Leyden and Market sts. Open extended season, no fee.

The 1749 Courthouse is the oldest wooden courthouse in the United States, yet its history goes back even farther. Probably about 1670 a court section was added to an existing "Country House" building. In 1749 that building was dismantled and probably laid out in the town square. Its timbers were used to construct the 1749 Courthouse, which kept the original courtroom. Spanning the times of both Country House and 1749 Courthouse, a Public Market, similar to Faneuil Hall in Boston, occupied the basement 1722–1858. In 1820 a new courthouse was built and the old building became the Town House. Restored in 1970, the 1749 Courthouse now has a museum on the first floor and the original courtroom on the second. Viewing the reproduction furniture, raised clerks' desks, formal witness stand, and jury benches, you can imagine the seven Pilgrim judges sitting at the raised bench facing the entrance to the courtroom, which is surrounded by portraits of American judges.

13. FIRST PARISH CHURCH IN PLYMOUTH, *1606*, building 1899. Leyden and School sts.

"The Lord hath more truth and light yet to break forth out of His Holy Word."[15] In 1620, guided by these words from Reverend John Robinson, ancestors of this First Parish Church set sail from Holland for the New World. Fourteen years earlier a small group, objecting to the rituals and hierarchy of the Church of England, broke with the established church and worshiped in secret at William Brewster's manor house in Scrooby, England. There, in 1606, they joined in a church body that has had a continuous fellowship from England to Holland to America to the present day. The first year here they held services under Elder Brewster in the Fort Meetinghouse. Their first settled minister, Ralph Smith, came in 1629. Two years later he was assisted by Roger Williams, who later founded Rhode Island. During the next one hundred years, from this church came sister congregations: First Church in Duxbury and First Church in Marshfield 1632, First Church in Eastham 1646, First Church in Plympton 1698, First Church in Kingston 1717, and the Second Church in Plymouth in 1738. In 1801 the minister, James Kendall, preached Unitarian ideas, and part of the congregation withdrew to form what is now Church of the Pilgrimage.

Today's beautiful Norman Gothic–style stone church is the congregation's sixth meeting place and fifth actual building. Its doorways, arches, and towers were fashioned after St. Helena's Church in Austerfield, England, where Governor William Bradford was baptized. The arched wooden interior is reminiscent of English castles. The choir loft window depicts Reverend John Robinson's farewell sermon. The building stands symbolically at the head of Leyden Street, where the first Pilgrims lived.

14. BURIAL HILL, FORT MEETINGHOUSE SITE, *c. 1621*. School St. Replica of early powder house.

Shortly after landing the Pilgrims fortified this hill with the help of the *Mayflower*'s crew, who mounted guns from the ship. Soon after, they built Fort Meetinghouse, mounting cannons on its barricaded roof. By 1637 the hill became a burial place, giving final rest to such famous personages as Elder Brewster; Governor Bradford; John Howland; General James Warren, president of the Provincial Congress, and his wife, Mercy Otis Warren, literary leader and author; and the American author Jane Austen.

15. CHURCH OF THE PILGRIMAGE, *1801*. Leyden and School sts.

In 1801 the Unitarian views of First Parish Church encouraged a group of parishioners to form the Church of the Pilgrimage. Here, keeping their Congregational heritage, members feel they have "adhered to the belief of the fathers"[16] and are the true successors of the first congregation, which began in Scrooby, England. That Separatist church, formed in England in 1606, became the basis of American Congregationalism, with each congregation having its own authority. The idea was a major contribution by Plymouth to American religion. This 1840 Tuscan building has a Greek Revival interior. The large, open sanctuary features Corinthian pilasters in an extensive colonnade reaching to an elaborate ceiling molding.

16. RICHARD SPARROW HOUSE, *c. 1640*, NRHP. 42 Summer St. Open extended season, donations. Pottery shop.

It is believed the left side of this clapboarded house was built by Richard Sparrow, making it the oldest house standing in Plymouth. It was originally built with one room downstairs and a sleeping room above. Inside, the focus of early settlers' home life was the large, light-giving fireplace. Here meals were prepared and heat given to warm occupants through cold New England winters. Later Richard Sparrow added the back rooms, creating a saltbox effect. In 1690 the next owners, the Bonum family, added the right side, tying into the central chimney. Following the Bonum years the house passed through several owners until 1932, when Katherine L. Alden bought and restored it. She lived in one side, using the other for a pottery school and museum. The pottery tradition continues as various potters form fine porcelain and stoneware clay into pots, which are displayed in the museum's craft shop.

17. JENNEY GRIST MILL, *1971*; Town Brook Park. Spring Ln. Open all year, no fee. Shops, benches, path to Brewster Gardens (D).

The Jenney Grist Mill is a reconstruction of a gristmill operated by John Jenny, possibly in 1636. The original mill was begun by Stephen Deane. When Deane died, John Jenny completed and operated it until his death in 1644; then his son Samuel took over. The mill operated for 212 years. Today there is a quaint weathered mill house, simple dam, waterpower controls, and a fish ladder where herring run in early spring. The mill grinds corn, wheat, and rye daily, as it did during colonial days and in the years when Town Brook supported many active mills.

Town Brook Park offers a pleasant place to relax and enjoy the scenery and many birds that land on the enticing pond.

18. PILGRIM HALL, *1824*, NRHP. 75 Court St. Open all year, except January, fee.

Pilgrim Hall, one of the oldest public museums in continuous service in the United States, was built by the Pilgrim Society. The solid Greek Revival structure was designed by Alexander Parris, architect of Boston's St. Paul's Church and Quincy Marketplace. The columned portico, originally wood, was recreated in granite in 1922. The cornerstone contains treasures, among them a 1621 sermon and a 1786 newspaper.

The museum houses the world's most extensive collection of Pilgrim possessions—books they read and wrote, tools, weapons, and furnishings they brought or fashioned. A video presentation tells the Pilgrim story. Paintings include Edward Winslow's portrait, the only actual painting from life of a *Mayflower* passenger. Swords of Captain Myles Standish and Governor John Carver; chairs of Carver, Brewster, Bradford, and Winslow; books by or about Elder Brewster; Bibles belonging to John Alden and Governor William Bradford are some of the priceless items in the collection. There is John Eliot's 1685 edition Bible, in which he translated phonetically the Indian language. Models of a Pilgrim house and Fort Meetinghouse and a section of the 1626 *Sparrow Hawk,* similar in construction to the *Mayflower,* are also here.

19. NATIONAL MONUMENT TO THE FOREFATHERS, *1859–89*, NRHP. Allerton St. Open all year, no fee. Gift shop.

From her impressive site above the harbor, the 36-foot figure of "Faith" surmounts the tallest solid granite monument in the United States. Faith is surrounded by seated representatives of Liberty, Law, Morality, and Education. The 81-foot-high monument was a prototype for the Statue of Liberty. It is dedicated to Pilgrims in remembrance "of their labors, sacrifices and sufferings for the cause of civil and religious liberty."[17] The creation of the monument was a primary goal of the Pilgrim Society, founded 1820 to perpetuate appreciation of the Pilgrims.

20 HEDGE HOUSE, *1809,* NRHP. 126 Water St. Open extended season, fee.

Major William Hammatt, desiring a unique home, built this basically Federal residence with unusual octagonal rooms. Hammatt was a successful young shipowner and merchant. He and his wife, a descendant of John Howland, entertained lavishly. The War of 1812 caused their move to Maine, where they founded the town of Howland. In 1830 Thomas Hedge, merchant shipper, purchased this house, and here his descendants lived for nearly a century. Hedge's Wharf was located where Plymouth Rock is today. The Hedges entertained with musicales in the drawing room. Daniel Webster was a frequent guest.

Inside this delicately proportioned Federal, a graceful staircase rises between octagonal formal front rooms. Marble fireplaces; bronze cornices; furniture of Hepplewhite, Queen Anne, and Chippendale styles; and china from Canton and Bristol complete the scene of a successful nineteenth-century merchant-shipowner. Upstairs, the master bedroom boasts a McIntyre bed, one of twelve made by the architect of Federal Salem. A pioneering 1863 bathroom is retained.

When the mansion was threatened in 1919, the Antiquarian Society formed to save it. Preservation included moving the building, and turning it to face the water. The Hedge House now also contains the Antiquarian Society's extensive collection of toys, costumes, and textiles.

21. TOWN WHARF, *1800s*, 1921. Water St. Open all year, no fee. Docking facilities, fishing, whale watching, charter boats.

Where you see Town Wharf and State Pier, in the 1800s you would have seen eight wharves serving whalers, merchant ships, and fishing vessels. Passengers traveled by steamboat from Plymouth to the Cape and Boston. Water Street bustled with cooper shops, countinghouses, blacksmith shops, sail and rigging lofts, and ships' chandleries. Today the harbor is alive with fishing boats, motorboats, yachts, and sailboats. Plymouth's fishing fleet still sails from here, as they have since the mid-1700s. At night Duxbury Pier Light and Plymouth Gurnet Light beckon, each flashing its own identifying sequence.

22. CRANBERRY WORLD VISITORS CENTER. Water St. Open extended season, no fee. Museum, views, free refreshments.

A special cranberry museum with actual working bog is offered by Ocean Spray Cranberries, Inc. Through their displays of antique and modern tools, photos, explanatory material, and cooking demonstrations you learn of the fascinating history and development of the cranberry industry.

BEACHES, PARKS, OTHER POINTS OF INTEREST

A. White Horse Beach. Taylor Ave. off Rte. 3A. Open all year. No fee. Sandy beach, swimming; limited parking.

B. Plymouth Beach. Warren Ave. off Rte. 3A. Open all year. Summer parking fee. 3.5 miles of sandy beach, views of Saquish Neck and Manomet Bluffs, lifeguards, bathhouse, concessions; swimming.

C. Stephens Field Park. Stephens Lane. Open all year. No fee. Small marshy beach, ball fields, concessions, playground, tennis; picnicking.

D. Brewster Gardens. Entrances Leyden and Water sts., Main St. near post office, and Jenney Grist Mill. Open all year. No fee. Paths, Plymouth memorials; location of Pilgrims' first gardens.

E. Nelson Street Park. Water St. Open all year. No fee. Views, marsh beach, ball fields; swimming, picnicking.

F. Morton Park. Summer St. Open all year. Summer fee. Freshwater inland park, bathhouse, lifeguards, concessions; picnicking, swimming.

KINGSTON

The Jones River, named for *Mayflower* Captain Christopher Jones, has been Kingston's essential artery from earliest settlement to today. In a 1627 land grant Governor William Bradford received river land, where he and his descendants built homesteads. By the 1700s grandson Major John Bradford owned most of what was the Precinct of Plymouth in 1717. He gave land for a burying ground, meetinghouse, school, minister's home, and training green for a new town, which would become Kingston, incorporated 1726. Today the Jones River is a peaceful stream, but in the 1700s wharves were busy with ships trading with England and Europe. The river's Landing ("b" on map), owned by Bradford, has hosted boat yards since 1765. Here the sixteen-gun brigantine *Independence* was built for the state navy in 1776. From 1806 to 1883 the renowned Joseph Holmes yard was in full swing. During those years the c. 1785 house at 51 Landing, built by shipbuilder Stephen Drew, was his sail loft.

Rocky Nook (a) was a busy marine center. Ships built on the river came here for final rigging at Delano's 1802 Wharf off Wharf Lane. Delanos were second to Holmeses in ownership of vessels in the mid-1880s. During this time the upper river supplied power to mills, forges, and factories—sustaining a dominant part of the Kingston economy from the 1820s to the 1900s. Today Kingston combines old-world traditions, well-preserved Colonial heritage, and modern-day small industry.

1. HOWLAND FARM SITE, *1638*. Howlands Ln. near Standish Ave., marker on right side.

This was the homestead of Pilgrims John and Elizabeth Howland (see Plymouth 3). On this seashore farm they raised nine children and John died in 1673.

2. FIRST PARISH CHURCH, *1851*. Main and Green sts.

Forty-eight families separated from the First Parish Church in Plymouth to establish this church in 1717. Many Pilgrim descendants rest in the adjacent Old Burying Ground. The first meetinghouse, 1721, was a small structure, large enough to hold the entire population for town meetings as well as worship. Men's and women's benches and rare family pews were separated from galleries where Indians and Negroes sat. Zephaniah Willis, who served as minister for sixty-seven years, was the town's first historian. During his ministry the second meetinghouse was built, 1798, with impressive twin towers flanking a columned portico. Today's 1851 church is Italianate and Greek Revival, combining dominating bracketed pediment, quoined corners, rounded-arch doors and windows, and shiplap facade. A two-manual tracker-action pipe organ

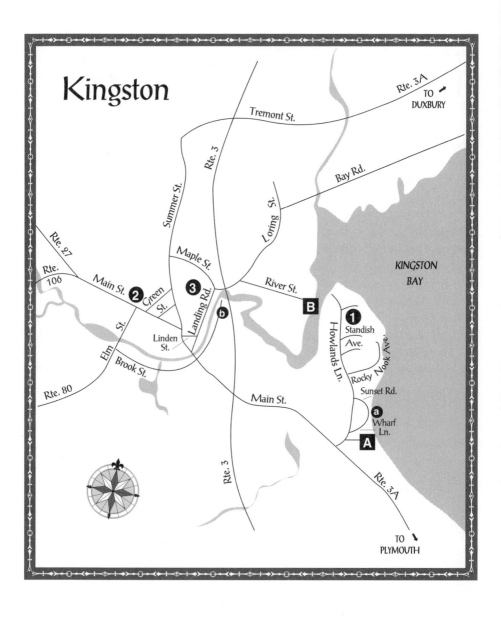

installed in the post–Civil War era by the legendary E. & G. G. Hook Organ Co. was restored in the 1970s.

3. MAJOR JOHN BRADFORD HOUSE, *1674*. **Landing Rd. at Maple St. Open seasonally and by appointment, fee.**

Major John Bradford, grandson of Governor William Bradford, was a prominent landowner, merchant, and gristmill owner as well as Plymouth deputy, state representative, selectman, town meeting moderator, and military leader in King Philip's War. In 1674 he built the west side of this home overlooking the Jones River, where he and wife Mercy raised seven children and lived for over half a century. In 1720 they built the east section. Here in later years a traveling priest celebrated the first mass in Kingston.

In 1920 historian George Francis Dow guided restoration, opening the house to the public a year later. Period furnishings recreate the image of family life of a seventeenth-century "principal inhabitant." At one time the manuscript of William Bradford's *History of Plimoth Plantation* was here. The irreplaceable treasure disappeared in the Revolution, reappearing fifty years later in a London palace library. Returned to its native land in 1897, it is preserved in the Massachusetts State House in Boston.

BEACHES, PARKS, OTHER POINTS OF INTEREST

A. **Gray's Beach.** Howland Ln. Open all year. Summer parking fee. Play area, bathhouse, lifeguards, tennis; picnicking, swimming.

B. **Ah De Nah.** End of River St., mouth of Jones River. Open all year. Boat launching fee. Harbormaster's office.

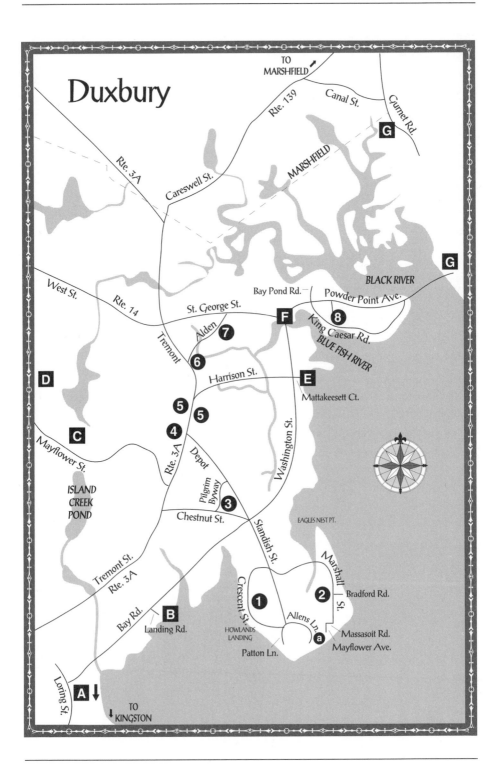

DUXBURY

Duxbury was home to Pilgrims John Alden, Myles Standish, and William Brewster and to shipbuilding merchants Ezra Weston and Ezra Weston, Jr. It began as a farming community, with the first recorded vessel built at Captain's Nook by Thomas Prince in 1719. Shipbuilding grew gradually, then flourished from the Revolution until the mid-1800s. Shipbuilding, coastal trade, and fishing touched every life. In winter seamen made shoes in home shops and did piecework for factories.

When larger ships were needed, shallow Duxbury harbor proved inadequate. Gold was discovered. Men's thoughts turned westward, and many left Duxbury. Soon, however, railroads opened a new era, bringing summer people to enjoy Duxbury's ocean and natural beauty. Today Duxbury is a picturesque New England coastal town with pride in its history and in its historic sea captains' eighteenth- and nineteenth-century homes.

1. STANDISH MONUMENT RESERVATION, *1872*. Crescent St. Open weekdays in summer, no fee. Views, picnicking.

Myles Standish's statue stands high above Captain's Hill, overseeing the area Standish spent the last thirty-six years of his life protecting. His strong military leadership in Plymouth resulted in mutual respect between Pilgrims and Indians, which helped keep the peace. Myles moved from Plymouth to a 120-acre seaside farm at Captain's Nook ("a" on map), where he and wife Barbara raised a family of seven. The picturesque house site on a bluff overlooking Plymouth Harbor can be seen at the end of Mayflower Avenue.

The 14-foot statue depicts Myles with sword sheathed, hand outstretched in a civil act—holding the colony's patent. Inside the 116-foot granite shaft are stones from New England states, with a keystone from President Grant. From the top you see to the east Clark's Island, named for John Clark, mate on the *Mayflower*. The island has held a salt-works and Plymouth's poorhouse and has been a bird sanctuary, grazing land, and home to hardy islanders. At the south end of Duxbury Beach are Saquish Neck (Indian word for clams) and the Gurnet (resembles a gurnet fish nose). Saquish Neck was the site of Civil War Fort Standish. On the Gurnet is the 1842 Plymouth Light, NRHP, and Fort Andrews, which was built during the Civil War. To the south is Plymouth, with old Plymouth Cordage. To the west across Kingston Bay is the Jones River. To the north is a sea of green sprinkled with church steeples, ponds, and beautiful countryside.

2. BREWSTER HOME SITE, *c. 1634*. **Marshall St. Open all year, no fee.**

Elder William Brewster struck a spiritual spark in Scrooby, England, which he sustained through persecution in England, exile in Holland, and tribulation on the high seas until it burst into flame in the New World. He inspired souls of Pilgrims in Plymouth and later in Duxbury. Widower Brewster built his home near Eagle's Nest Creek, near where you see lilacs and a historic marker.

3. OLD BURYING GROUND AND MEETINGHOUSE SITES, *c. 1635*. **Chestnut St. and Pilgrim By-Way.**

This was the center of Duxbury; here are sites of the first two meetinghouses and a historic cemetery. Myles Standish's grave is inside the stone enclosure, and John and Priscilla Alden's unmarked graves are in the Alden corner (by the intersection of Chestnut Street and Pilgrim By-Way), near son Jonathan's 1697 gravestone.

4. TOWN CENTER: FIRST PARISH CHURCH, OLD TOWN HALL, and DUXBURY TOWN OFFICES, *c. 1840*. **Tremont St.**

First Parish Church was built by ships' carpenters. Sturdy hidden framing supports one of the largest wooden-trussed assembly rooms in the country. It is the fourth building of the congregation, gathered 1632. Religion, education, and government have united here since the early 1840s, when a triumvirate of Greek Revival structures arose. White clapboard, wide pilasters, and dominating pediments are featured in all. First Parish Church is on the left with Mayflower Cemetery adjacent. Old Town Hall is in the center; and a modern replica of an earlier school, Partridge Academy, is on the right. Partridge Academy was established by the Honorable George Partridge, delegate to the second Provincial Congress, the Continental Congress, and United States Congress. After the academy burned, the Duxbury Town Office Building was built on its site. Partridge scholarship funds still aid Duxbury students.

5. CAPTAIN GERSHOM BRADFORD HOUSE, *1808*, NRHP, HS. 931
Tremont St. Open summer, limited hours, and by appointment; fee.

Captain Gershom Bradford House illustrates gracious living in this sea-oriented town. The house was built by a descendant of William Bradford and lived in by four Bradford generations. The delicate Federal entry retains original fan and side lights. The walk is of lava blocks brought from Sicily's Etna volcano by Gershom Bradford. The interior remains as in Captain Bradford's time, with original colors, delicately carved moldings, reproduced wallpaper, and Bradford furnishings. Across the street at 942 is **Captain Gamaliel Bradford House,** NRHP (private), built by Gershom's brother in 1807. The large wing, constructed in the 1700s, was attached to the 1807 house. The Captain Gamaliel House is similar to sister Jerusha's home, the King Caesar House (see 8).

6. ART COMPLEX MUSEUM, *1971*. 189 Alden St. Open limited hours and by appointment, no fee. Library, concerts, lectures.

This unique museum was initiated and is directed by the Weyerhaeuser family. It houses changing exhibits of contemporary art and permanent collections featuring ceramics, glass, Indian artifacts, and Shaker furniture, plus Oriental, European, and American paintings. There is an authentic Japanese tea house.

7. JOHN ALDEN HOUSE, *1653*, NRHP. 105 Alden St. Open summer and by appointment, fee.

Cooper, carpenter, and farmer, John Alden lived here with wife Priscilla until his death at about eighty-nine. They were immortalized by Alden descendant Henry Wadsworth Longfellow: In his poem Myles Standish asks John Alden to propose to Priscilla for him, and Priscilla replies ". . . speak for yourself, John."[18] Whatever the real story, it is known that the two young Pilgrims married in Plymouth by 1623 and developed into colonial leaders. They remained close friends with the Standishes, and daughter Sarah married Myles Standish's son Alexander. John was treasurer of Plymouth Colony and, like Myles Standish, became one of the "Undertakers" who paid off the colony's indebtedness. John and his sons built this Colonial house. The front portion, with central chimney, unobtrusive door, small windows, and steeply pitched roof, is separately formed from the older kitchen, buttery, and borning room. An archeological dig

John Alden House, Duxbury

unearthed Alden's first Duxbury house site, from about 1628, which is reached by a path behind the house. It is believed that after this 1653 house was built, the 1628 house was moved and attached to it. Ten Alden generations living here made modifications, such as the 1850 rear ell addition. Most of the structure, walls, floors, and fireplaces are original. Of special interest in the great room is the ceiling made from powdered oyster and clam shells, common in colonial times.

8. KING CAESAR HOUSE, *1808*, NRHP, HS. 120 King Caesar Rd. Open summer and by appointment, fee. Museum, gift shop.

From this imposing mansion King Caesar, born Ezra Weston, Jr., commanded his empire. His father, Ezra Weston, founded his shipbuilding firm, E. Weston, in 1764 at age twenty-one. Ezra Jr., established his own shipyard, Ten Acre Yard, at Bluefish River in 1834. The Westons created such a successful maritime conglomerate that each was known as King Caesar. Weston shipyards built ships using wood from Weston forests, sails from Weston sail lofts, anchors from Weston forge, and food from Weston farms. Weston-owned *Smyrna* in 1830 was the first ship to carry the United States flag to the Black Sea. Profits were invested in the Duxbury Bank, of which Ezra, Jr., was president. In the "Weston world" father and son were powerful yet generous employers. The empire dissolved after the death of Ezra, Jr., in 1841.

This Federal mansion provided an appropriate throne for King Caesar across from the wharf where his ships were rigged and fitted. Framed by a reproduction of the original fence, the house has rusticated corner boards grooved to resemble quoins, roofline trimmed with rope-carved molding, and front entry with elaborate leaded tracery and elliptical fanlight. Inside, front parlors feature wallpaper attributed to famous nineteenth-century French firms, Dufour et Leroy and Jacquemart et Benard. Furnishings are of the period. A small museum offers changing exhibits.

BEACHES, PARKS, OTHER POINTS OF INTEREST

A. **Bay Farm Conservation Area.** Loring St. at Kingston–Duxbury line. Open all year. No fee. Trails, views; picnicking.

B. **Landing Road Beach.** Landing Rd. Open all year. No fee. Small beach, views, boat launch; swimming; limited street parking.

C. **North Hill Marsh Wildlife Sanctuary.** Mayflower St. Open all year. No fee. 152 acres of oak and pine forest, freshwater marsh and pond, trails; birding, hiking.

D. **Waiting Hill Preserve.** Rte. 14 or Mayflower St. Open all year. No fee.

E. **Mattakeesett Court.** Town Landing. Open all year. No fee. Boat launch, harbormaster, moorings.

King Caesar House, Duxbury

F. Duxbury Rural and Historical Society, Charles Drew House, c. 1826. 685 Washington St. Open weekdays, limited hours and by appointment. Historical society office and library.

G. Duxbury Beach. Marshfield access from Gurnet Rd. off Canal St.; Duxbury access end Powder Point Ave. Open all year. Seasonal parking fee at Marshfield access. Boat launch, bathhouse, lifeguards, concessions; fishing, swimming, picnicking; limited Duxbury parking land side of bridge.

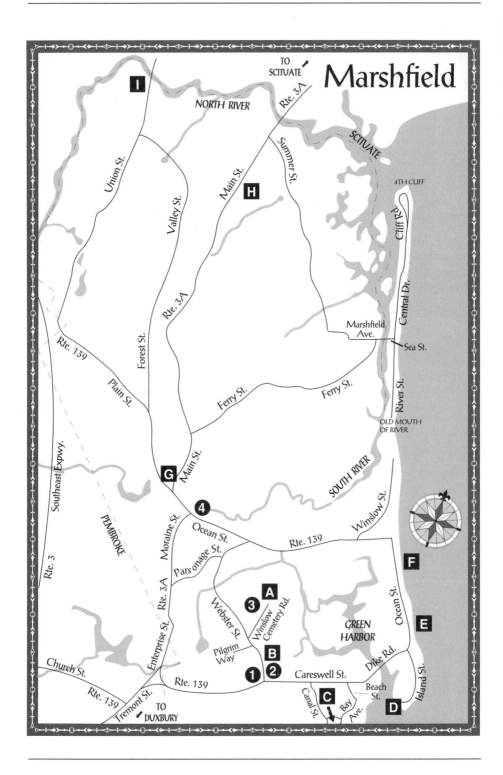

MARSHFIELD

M arshfield[19] has been home to two outstanding statesmen who played key roles in the country's history. In the 1600s Edward Winslow's diplomatic negotiations with the Indians and mother England helped strengthen and preserve Plymouth. In the 1800s Daniel Webster's brilliant oratory supported a strong federal government against the nullification acts and preserved the nation in a superb defense of the Compromise of 1850.

In 1632 Edward Winslow received a land grant at Green Harbor in what would become Marshfield. He began farming his lands summers, ultimately building his grand home, "Careswell," named for his ancestral home in England, and permanently moving here in 1636. The settlement grew and in 1640 was incorporated as the eighth town in Plymouth Colony.

The Revolution divided Marshfield, with some wealthy landowners, who held Provincial offices, remaining loyal to England. On January 31, 1774, the town carried by one vote a reaffirmation of allegiance to the Crown, becoming the only New England town to take such a stand. The "shot heard round the world"[20] could have been in Marshfield. Before the battle at Concord, Patriot General John Thomas sent troops to capture British forces at Marshfield loyalist Nathaniel Ray Thomas's home; but they arrived too late. The British had escaped. On June 19, 1776, Marshfield declared support for the Continental Congress. After hostilities, the town returned to farming, milling, fishing, and shipbuilding on the North River. Today, Marshfield is a cherished way of life.

1. 1699 ISAAC WINSLOW HOUSE, Daniel Webster Office, NHL, HS.
Blacksmith Shop, Careswell and Webster sts. Open extended season, fee.

Pilgrim Edward Winslow befriended Chief Massasoit and masterminded the vital treaty in 1621 between Wampanoag Indians and Plymouth Separatists. Losing his wife the first winter in Plymouth, he married Susanna White, mother of Peregrine, first white child born in New England. Their 1621 wedding was the first performed in Plymouth. Edward Winslow was also the first to bring cattle into the colony from England. In 1636 the Winslows came to Marshfield and built their home, "Careswell," between the present house and Duxbury marshes. Nothing remains, though it was one of the largest manorial farms in the colony. Edward served as governor of Plymouth Colony, member of General Court, and a New England Confederacy commissioner. His son, Josiah, chief military commander of Plymouth Colony and governor 1673–80, also lived in the original Careswell. Josiah's son, Judge Isaac, built the present house about 1699. Josiah's grandson, Dr. Isaac, a loyalist who died in 1819, was the last Winslow to live in the mansion.

This is one of the best-preserved homes of the leaders of Plymouth Colony. The common room shows seventeenth-century hand-hewn beams and large fireplace. In the old kitchen are buttery, root cellar, and walk-in fireplace. The front parlor is eighteenth-century, with small formal fireplace, wallpaper, plastered ceiling, and painted paneling and woodwork. Upstairs was Dr. Isaac's office, where Tory meetings took place. Across the hall was the bridal chamber of Judge Isaac's bride, Sarah Wensley.

Daniel Webster's law office is also part of the Winslow complex. In 1832 Daniel Webster purchased lands adjacent to the Winslows from the Thomas family and created an estate of over 1,800 acres. Daniel lived in the Thomas house, which had been rebuilt by Nathaniel Ray Thomas before the Revolution. The house, located off Webster Street, burned in 1878. Two years later Daniel's daughter-in-law built a Victorian mansion on the old foundation. Webster's beloved law office was restored and moved here in 1966. In his office are Webster's desk, photographs of his house, and personal memorabilia. Lawyer, orator, and congressman, Webster stood for strong federal government.

2. OLD WINSLOW SCHOOL HOUSE, *1857.* Careswell and Webster Sts.
Open limited hours in summer and by appointment, no fee.

The schoolroom remains as originally used, with dual student desks, covered glass inkwells, original clock, and organ. Additional collections have been donated by Marshfield families.

1699 Isaac Winslow House, Marshfield

3. WINSLOW CEMETERY, *c. 1641*. **Winslow Cemetery Rd.**

Enclosed by a wrought iron fence are graves of Daniel Webster and family. Above Daniel's grave symbolically flies the Stars and Stripes. Behind the fence is a monument to settlers of Green Harbor (Marshfield's first settlement). Nearby can be seen graves of Governor Josiah and other Winslows. The site of Marshfield's first meetinghouse is adjacent to the graves.

4. FIRST CONGREGATIONAL CHURCH, *1838*. **Ocean and Moraine sts.**

The present white-clapboard Greek Revival building is the church's fifth meetinghouse and its fourth building near this site. The first thatched-roof building was at Winslow Cemetery. Early in the 1800s the congregation, gathered in 1632, faced a critical decision—remain Trinitarian or become Unitarian. They decided in favor of Trinitarianism, remaining one of the few Old Colony churches to resist the Unitarian movement. Daniel Webster attended, as did Adelaide Phillips, musical idol of a century ago.

BEACHES, PARKS, OTHER POINTS OF INTEREST

A. **Daniel Webster Audubon Sanctuary.** Winslow Cemetery Rd. Open all year. Fee. Observation bird blind with displays to identify bird life, 2 miles of trails, exhibits, bird sightings listed, bird books.

B. **Cherry Hill/Webster's Wilderness.** Webster St. Open all year. No fee. Eighty-seven acres, trails, small pond, site of Webster's last speech, ball fields, playground; picnicking, hiking.

C. **Duxbury Beach.** Gurnet Rd. off Canal St. Open all year. Summer parking fee. 8-mile beach, boat launch, bathhouse, snack bar; fishing, picnicking, swimming.

D. **Green Harbor Marina and Town Pier.** Island St. Open all year. Launching fee. Snug harbor for boats, boat facilities; fishing.

E. **Brant Rock Beach.** Ocean St. and Dike Rd. Open all year. Fee. Half-mile sandy crescent, views, lifeguards; swimming.

F. **Fieldston Beach.** Ocean St. Open all year. No fee. Shingle beach, sandy at low tide, views; swimming; no parking.

G. **Veterans Memorial Park.** Rtes. 3A and 139. Open all year. No fee. Landscaped tiny park, benches.

H. **North River Wildlife Sanctuary.** 2000 Main St. Open all year. Fee. Natural history library, 150 acres, 2 miles of trails, riverside boardwalk trail; Massachusetts Audubon Society Shore Regional Office.

I. **Brooks-Tilden Shipyard Preserve.** Union St. by bridge. Open all year. No fee. Fifteen acres, woods and marsh on North River, canoe launch; fishing, picnicking.

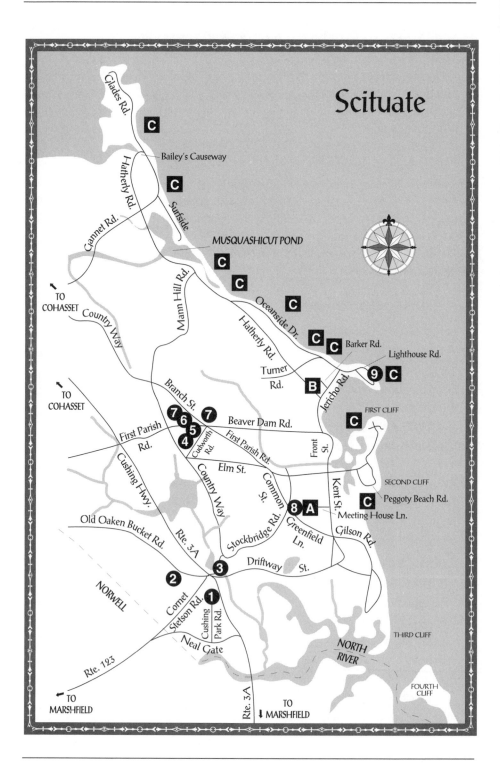

Scituate

SCITUATE

S cituate[21] is a town whose water tower looks like a fifteenth-century Roman tower and whose harbor is symbolically protected by picturesque Scituate Light. It is home of the "Old Oaken Bucket" made famous by poet Samuel Woodworth and was once saved from British attack by the courage and ingenuity of two light keeper's daughters. Here on lands already cleared by Indians, men from Kent, England, established homesteads before 1628. They organized their church, called Reverend John Lothrop, and became a town in 1636. The North River, with access to lumber, abundant shoreline, and protected waters, provided ideal location for shipbuilding—Scituate's main industry from 1640 to 1872. In 1773 James Briggs built the *Columbia,* later captained by John Kendrick (see Wareham, Massachusetts) and Robert Gray (see Tiverton, Rhode Island). Scituate still perpetuates the tolerant approach to life set by those first "men of Kent," who allowed Quakers to live in peace, opposed witchcraft trials, did not persecute Tories, and generally lived in peace with each other.

1. CUSHING MEMORIAL STATE PARK. Cushing Park Rd. Open all year, no fee.

The final resting place of Scituate's most famous son is the focal point of this lovely wooded retreat. An unbeaten path leads to the stone wall–enclosed Cushing family cemetery. Judge William Cushing succeeded his father as judge of the superior court of Massachusetts in 1772, where he was the only Patriot during the troubled period prior to open rebellion. In 1783 he made such a positive charge opposing the whole idea of slavery to the grand jury in the Quaco case that slavery was abolished in the state. He helped frame and interpret the constitution of the commonwealth, helped ratify and interpret the U.S. Constitution, and became a justice of the U.S. Supreme Court. He was asked by Washington to be chief justice of the Supreme Court, but he declined due to health. Much of his time was spent riding the circuit, accompanied by his wife—whose title, Madam, indicated a rank earned in her own right. Their travels, often in a one-horse shay, carried them as far as Portland, Maine, and Atlanta, Georgia. Madam Cushing remained a thrifty New Englander. She used White House dinner invitations and calling cards of famous people as winders on which to roll her embroidery thread. She carried on warm correspondence with Abigail Adams, Mercy Warren, and Mary Pinkney.

2. OLD OAKEN BUCKET WELL AND HOMESTEAD, *1675, 1835,* HS. Old Oaken Bucket Rd. Museum and house open in summer, limited hours, and by appointment; fee.

The old oaken bucket, symbol of Scituate, was made famous in verse by Samuel Woodworth, editor, author, and poet, in 1817. From New York he looked back fondly to his childhood home here on the Northey homestead with his father and his stepmother, Betsy Northey. He remembered that when he was a boy, working long, hot hours in the fields, nothing tasted as good as cool water drawn in an old oaken bucket from this well. Beside the house is the well and graceful sweep. The small attached 1675 building was moved to this location about 1835, when the present home was built, and has been restored as a museum. Artifacts of early Scituate and Northeys include original Currier and Ives and early engravings of the "Old Oaken Bucket," photos, song sheets, postcards, and other Woodworth memorabilia.

3. STOCKBRIDGE MILL, *c. 1640*, HS. Country Way. Open in summer, limited hours, and by appointment; fee.

The nation's oldest still-operating water-powered gristmill is the Stockbridge Mill. Framing rests on foundation stones laid in the mid-seventeenth century. Gate wheel, base millstone, and crane date to the 1600s. The grain chest is the only one found from this period. Isaac Stedman, a miller from England, dammed the First Herring Brook, which created the millpond immortalized in "The Old Oaken Bucket." The dam powered the gristmill Stedman built here about 1640, probably the first water-powered gristmill in Plymouth Colony. Some of the machinery still operating today he brought with him from England a mere two decades after the *Mayflower* landed. Stockbridges acquired the mill, expanded, built others, and handled much of the grist and lumber milling needed by the colony. This is one of the few mills to survive. Scituate's well-trained, well-armed militia successfully repulsed invading Indians during King Philip's War, held an important line of resistance, and saved the Stockbridge Mill.

4. LITTLE RED SCHOOL HOUSE, *1893*, HS headquarters. 43 Cudworth Rd. Open all year, no fee. Research library, books for sale, exhibitions, slide presentations.

The first high school built in town is now home to the Scituate Historical Society's fine library. The focus is genealogical and historical research. On permanent exhibition are carbon-dated Indian artifacts 8,000 to 10,000 years old, collected from Scituate and the North River area, and early documents, deeds, china, and decorative art. Changing exhibits have focused on Thomas Lawson, early tools of shipbuilding, and Christmas toys of early years.

5. CUDWORTH HOUSE, BARN, AND CATTLE POUND, *1797*, HS. 333 First Parish Rd. Open summer and by appointment, fee.

The first James Cudworth was a founding father of Scituate, captain of Scituate's first military company, and a commander of forces to the successful end of King Philip's

War. In 1658, when captain of militia, Cudworth urged tolerance for Quakers, proclaiming, "As I am no Quaker, so am I no persecutor."[22] For this Governor Thomas Prence had him removed. Fifteen years passed before Governor Josiah Winslow reinstated him as a general. James Cudworth's earlier Cape house was the first meeting place of the Scituate church until the meetinghouse for First Parish was built. Later the bench-lined shed of this 1797 Cudworth House offered warmth and hospitality to hardy members of First Parish Church between services. Beginning in 1821 the attic room hosted the fledgling Baptist Society for four years; later the same room welcomed Unitarians when their church burned.

The original Cape was removed and this gambrel built in 1797 by James's grandson, Zephaniah Cudworth. You enter a home of yesterday, walking by a working loom over 250 years old. The operator demonstrates and explains so well you finally understand how a loom works and what linsey-woolsey is (linen set up with cross threads of wool). The kitchen has an ancient fireplace and beehive oven surrounded by quaint though cumbersome utensils of old. Furnishings, pewter, china, and samplers, some as old as the house, are from Scituate. Featured are a Cushing room, a kettle forged by Mordecai Lincoln, a London piano more than 250 years old. The barn is a museum of tools and implements dating from early colonial times, including Lafayette's coach from Philadelphia and Judge Cushing's one-horse shay. The nearby cattle pound was built in 1671 and moved with careful regard for its original specifications, "Horse high, bull strong, and hog tight."[23]

6. FIRST PARISH CHURCH OF SCITUATE, *1881*. 330 First Parish Rd.

With its roots in England, its first building of chinked planks and board roof, its fifth church spire a landmark to mariners at sea, First Parish Church has long served its Scituate community. On January 8, 1635, the church was organized. The first regular minister was John Lothrop, who had earlier been imprisoned in London for his nonconforming ideas. Heated controversy over total-immersion baptism ended in 1654 when third minister Charles Chauncey left to become second president of Harvard College. He replaced Harvard President Henry Dunster, who in turn was called here to First Parish. Later the congregational split over Unitarianism divided families. Deacon Ward Litchfield took his five sons to the new Congregational Church while his wife, Betsy, and one son remained at First Parish. It is told that when the Deacon asked his wife to prepare a "light" supper for his hosting a meeting of "his" church, she complied by serving only twelve lighted candles. This, the sixth building, was dedicated in 1881.

7. LAWSON TOWER, *1902*, NHM, HS. First Parish Rd. Open summer, limited hours, and by appointment. DREAMWOLD, c. *1900*. Branch St. Private condos.

In the center of Europe's Rhine River stands a fifteenth-century Roman tower—the model for Scituate's most unusual, horizon-dominating water tower. The 153-foot structure was given to the town in 1902 by Thomas Lawson, who made his fortune when he cornered the copper market. An avid sailor, he built the yacht *Independence* to race for the America's Cup. She was not accepted for the race, so he destroyed her. He built the only seven-masted schooner then known—a ship used for coal cargo, then to carry oil from England, and finally sunk by a hurricane, because of that seventh mast, according to some.

Lawson had the tower built over the town water tower, which aesthetically offended him. The round, natural-shingled tower is capped by heavily bracketed overhangs, molded cone-shaped roof, and spire-topped dormers. As you climb the inside stairwell, you hear wind whipping but feel no sway. At the top, a ten-bell carillon is surrounded by a copper bell deck and cypress shingle–lined walls. The view over trees, church steeples, and endless water is spectacular.

Nearby is Lawson's estate, **Dreamwold,** the culmination of his dreams. The architecture is eclectic but balanced, featuring rambling Victorian styles. Chimneys rise from distinctively shaped roofs, and a modest columned portico frames the entry. The estate once included more than 500 acres and contained its own road and fire department system, grand racetrack, stables for more than 100 horses, prize livestock, pigeon-dove house, and even a hotellike housing arrangement for English bulldogs. Lawson wrote *Frenzied Finance,* an expose of the stock exchange that had been first the source of his riches and then, in 1922, the cause of his downfall.

8. MANN FARMHOUSE AND HISTORICAL MUSEUM, *late 1600s,*
HS. Greenfield Ln. Open summer and by appointment, fee. Wildflower garden.

This beautifully restored Cape spans three centuries. It is interesting architecturally, with its late-1600s foundation supporting the c. 1750s main house with attached 1825 ell. It is unusual, too, for having been home to only one family since the arrival of the first English settlers. Even a fascinating tale of pirate treasure unfolds within the walls. The first clue to treasure was the wearing of a huge old coin on his watch chain by the last Mann, Percy. He was an eccentric who allowed the house to fall to ruin to spite the town, which had taken his gravel pit by eminent domain. At his death distant heirs searched for gold coins with metal detectors, to no avail. The Scituate Historical Society, with Town Meeting approval, restored the house. During the process attic floorboards revealed two rusty cans filled with mid-1700s Spanish coins. Speculation has it that a pirate buried the treasure but was captured and that a Mann discovered the treasure on Third Cliff, then part of the family property.

The natural shingle Cape is pleasantly set amid three acres of old sycamore, horse chestnut, and black walnut trees, extensive crocus beds, and stone walls. Some furnishings date to the 1600s, and almost all are from the Mann family. A child's high chair marked "PW 1620 TM 1650" indicates the first user was Peregrine White (first white child born in New England), followed later by Thomas Mann. Other treasures are 1720 slat-backed chairs, Rodney Brace clock, and early Chippendale mirror. A sail loft is rigged and outfitted like the one that was here in 1821.

9. SCITUATE LIGHT, *1811*, HS. Lighthouse and Rebecca rds. Open in summer, limited hours and by appointment, fee.

In 1811 Scituate Light and its keeper's house were built at the entrance to Scituate Harbor. During the War of 1812, Rebecca (nineteen) and Abigail (fifteen), daughters of light keeper Simeon Bates, proved that two can make a difference. They watched while Colonel James Barstow and his regiment trained on the green near the light. On September 1, 1814, with militia absent and the girls alone at the light, two landing boats of British marines approached the harbor. Grabbing fife and drum, the sisters ran outside, hid behind a clump of cedar trees, and played with loud bravado "Yankee Doodle." Men in landing boats believed a regiment was waiting, reversed oars, and returned to their ship. The "Army of Two" had been victorious.

Unfortunately, captains often confused Scituate Light and Boston Light and ran full force into Minot's Ledge. A light was constructed on Minot's Ledge, and on November 15, 1860, Scituate Light was extinguished. Displayed within the keeper's home is the fife Rebecca used and Congressional documents about the light and the "Army of Two."

BEACHES, PARKS, OTHER POINTS OF INTEREST

A. **Men of Kent Cemetery,** 1628. Meeting House Ln. Monument lists names of founders, well-educated, wealthy, ambitious leaders directly from Kent, England; earliest grave 1628; site of first three meetinghouses.

B. **Barker Tavern,** c. 1634. 21 Barker Rd. Open all year as restaurant. Old section was garrison house of thick wood walls, rare handmade brick lining, porthole, massive central chimney.

C. **Scituate Beaches.** 18-mile coastline of three cliffs and many beaches. Parking for residents only in summer, except at Cedar Point, near the Lighthouse.

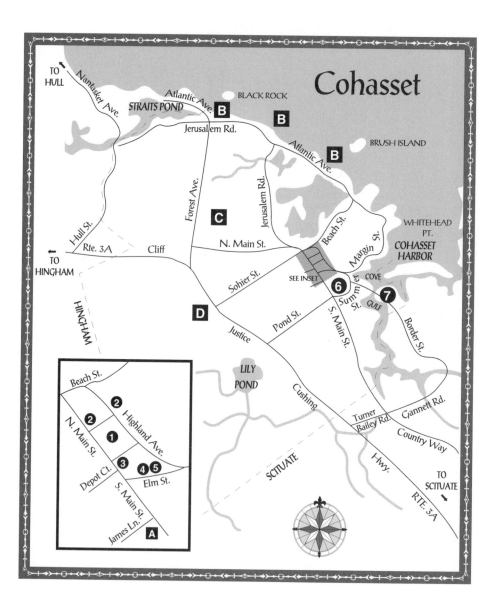

COHASSET

The glacial age left Cohasset literally standing on a rock and created rugged ledges, protruding granite fingers, and beautiful though treacherous rock-strewn coastline. Known for this wreck-causing shoreline, Cohasset is known also for daring, dedicated people. During the Revolution, when her husband was taken by the British, Persis Tower Lincoln skippered a boat to run the British blockade and obtained needed supplies from Gloucester. In 1807 the Massachusetts Humane Society stationed here the first lifeboat in the United States. In the War of 1812, militia Captain Peter Lothrop raced on horseback—without coat, hat, or saddle—to warn of the threatened arrival of eleven British barges and a sloop tender. Twelve hundred men responded, forcing the British into fast retreat.

Cohasset's picturesque Common has simple Colonials and more lavish eighteenth-century sea captains' homes. Fishing and shipbuilding served as mainstays of Cohasset's economy until railroads in 1849 aided the shift to a suburban economy. Beautiful homes and summer hotels were built along Jerusalem Road, still one of the most scenic drives in all New England.

1. THE TOWN COMMON, *1683*. North Main St. and Highland Ave.

Cohasset's Common is a jewel among picturesque New England commons. The broad green, complete with pond, is surrounded by historic homes (all privately owned), three churches, and the Town Hall. In the Colonial, Georgian, Federal, Greek Revival, Italianate, and French Second Empire houses lived the early ministers, sea captains, and merchants who conducted the affairs of historic Cohasset.

2. FIRST PARISH MEETINGHOUSE, *1747*. 23 North Main St. SECOND CONGREGATIONAL CHURCH, 1824. 43 Highland Ave.

First Parish Meetinghouse was built to accommodate a congregation growing since its 1713 commission. In 1799 the picturesque steeple was completed. In 1865 the clock was added, paid for by citizens' subscription, with the stipulation that it be forever under control of the town. The open sanctuary has box pews and Doric-columned gallery. The raised wooden pulpit, with ornate sounding board above, is flanked by pilaster-guarded windows. The first minister, Nehemiah Hobart, was grandson of Peter Hobart, first minister of Hingham, of which Cohasset had been part. Nehemiah Hobart wrote the basic covenant that laid the solid spiritual foundation for the infant church.

When Unitarianism split the First Parish Meetinghouse, twenty members left to build the Second Congregational Church, dedicating it in 1825. First Parish's seventh minister, Joseph Osgood, helped heal the breach, saying "We should be rivals only in Christian charity and good works."[24] Second Church congregation grew, and additions were made until fire struck in 1928. Within six months a service of rededication was celebrated in the larger, restored sanctuary. Today the two churches at the center of the Common stand in mutual support and respect.

3. ST. STEPHEN'S EPISCOPAL CHURCH, *1899.* Common, South Main St., and Highland Ave. Carillon concerts in summer.

St. Stephen's stands in beautiful compatibility with the granite ledges from which it rises. Its English perpendicular Gothic style, in massive granite, contrasts with and complements the New England white-clapboarded buildings of the Common. The peaceful sanctuary is smaller and warmer than you might expect, with boldly colored, biblical stained glass windows. Solid hand-carved oak pews face the carved, oak-paneled altar. The font shaft, a gift from Hingham, England, dates to about 1346 and is believed to have been damaged by Cromwell's men. The carillon in the bell tower, recently enlarged from fifty-one to fifty-six bells, was given in memory of Jessie Barron, wife of Wall Street's Commodore Barron, in 1924. St. Stephen's organist, Mrs. Edward Stevens, then became the first woman in the country to play a carillon. The array of bells ranges from the huge 5½-ton bourdon bell to the 12-pound ship bell.

4. CAPTAIN JOHN WILSON HISTORICAL HOUSE, *1810,* HS. 2 Elm St. Open summer, limited hours, and by appointment; donation.

Built right onto granite ledge and surrounded by neat fences and compact, cheerful gardens, the Colonial/Georgian-style house presents a way of life of the early 1800s. The house was built for Captain John Wilson, who commanded schooners to Malaga, St. Thomas, and other ports and who operated a ship's chandlery on the first floor. Wilson was captured during the War of 1812 while sailing his packet *Cohasset* to Boston. Fortunately, the *Cohasset's* cargo of fish didn't interest the British man-of-war, and Wilson and his ship were released to owner Levi Tower upon his payment of ransom.

Beautiful, exceptionally wide board wainscoting highlights the chandlery room; and near the fire, where the family gathered at night for warmth and light when the chandlery was closed, is an unusual settle. Paintings and furnishings from Cohasset families are here. Upstairs are the rooms where the family lived—quaint kitchen, cheery bedroom, doll-filled children's room.

5. MARITIME MUSEUM, *c. 1760,* HS. 4 Elm St. Open summer, limited hours, and by appointment; donation.

A fascinating museum of seafaring days is housed within the historic Bates Ship Chandlery built at the Cove. Here you find scrimshaw, ship models, weights and measures, photos, paintings, whaling implements, shipwright tools, wood from the original *Constitution,* and the quarterboard (the name plate on the stern) of the brig *Smyrna.* The

Smyrna, first American-flagged ship in the Black Sea, was owned by "King Caesar" Weston (see Duxbury). The plate washed off the brig while in Cohasset waters. The collection also includes a log pipe from Nathaniel Treat's saltworks, part of the lens of Minot's Light, and model of the pioneering ironworks of Mordecai Lincoln, with memorabilia of Abraham Lincoln, his descendant. The old ship chandlery, moved here in the 1950s, adds flavor to these relics of the sea.

6. CALEB LOTHROP HOUSE, *1821*, NRHP, HS. 14 Summer St. Open by appointment, donation.

This stately white-clapboarded Federal with its 12-inch brick ends is the only one of its kind in Cohasset. It reflects gracious living without the grand elegance of Salem Federals, marking a difference between the north and south shores in Massachusetts. It is decorated with period-painted original wainscoting, Dorothy Waterhouse wallpaper over original plaster, carefully coordinated draperies, and unique stenciling. Appropriate period furnishings include an Eli Terry clock and interesting brass plate fireplace fender. Caleb Lothrop, son of Peter Lothrop, Cohasset's 1812 Paul Revere, built this house where only Lothrops have lived. Caleb owned a ship chandlery, trading and fishing vessels, and a wharf within the Cove. He was bank treasurer, town treasurer, and selectman.

7. GOVERNMENT ISLAND, MINOT'S LEDGE LIGHTHOUSE. NRHP. Access from Border St. Open all year, no fee. Sail club, harbormaster, town docks, mooring, views; on island sticker parking only.

Here on Government Island, a small peninsula near the southern border of the harbor, Minot's Light was created. Disasters off Cohasset rocks led to the building of a lighthouse 2 miles offshore on Minot's Ledge. In 1847 the wildly hazardous job was begun. Three years later a 65-foot light and keeper's quarters rose above the support of nine iron pilings. Tragically, it took less time for the sea to destroy the light than for man to build it. In 1851 the tower plunged into raging seas, taking two keepers to their deaths.

Lightship replacement proved ineffective. Plans for construction of another Minot's Light began. On Government Island, 3,514 tons of granite were painstakingly hewn into 1,079 dovetailed blocks, matched to templates you see here, and transported by barge to Minot's Ledge. The tiny ledge was only above calm sea level 130 hours in 1855, the first year of construction. The 114-foot light was completed in 1860 and withstood the gale of 1888, when waves broke over the top. Its one-four-three pattern of flashes, now automated, is interpreted by many as "I love you."

Government Island is a living museum for the amazing lighthouse. The reconstruction here of part of the light, using blocks removed from the original, makes fascinating study. Here are the oil storage house, lighthouse bell, template patterns, old keeper's house, and Beacon Rock, from which the light was signaled.

BEACHES, PARKS, OTHER POINTS OF INTEREST

A. Red Lion Inn, c. 1704. 71 South Main St. Open all year as restaurant and inn. Originally a farmhouse, now an inn for nearly two centuries. Main dining room has ancient timbering, paneling, fireplaces, central chimney; wall cut shows clay brick insulation; third oldest Cohasset building.

B. Cohasset Beaches. Sticker parking only in summer.

C. Wheelwright Park. Entrances Forest Ave. and North Main St. Open all year. No fee. Peaceful wooded park, paths, riding ring; picnicking.

D. Whitney and Thayer Woods. Rte. 3A at Sohier St. Open all year. No fee. 750 acres, 12 miles of paths through woods, glacial boulders, views; skiing, hiking, picnicking. Trustees of Reservations.

HULL

Fishhook in shape, originally a storehouse for the Plymouth settlement, Hull was set aside as an early fishing station and incorporated in 1647. During the Revolution, gun batteries built on Telegraph Hill helped break the British blockade of Boston in 1776 and struck at British forces when they landed at Boston Light. In 1785 Massachusetts Humane Society began to aid rescue efforts in the many wrecks that happened off Hull. Most active member and most decorated lifesaver in U.S. history, Joshua James guided rescues of more than 600 people. In 1826 the Sportsman, Hull's first public house, was built, beginning the town's most prosperous era—gala summer hotels that flourished from mid-1800s to early 1900s. The silks and piazzas of the old hotel era are gone, as are the grand hotels and amusement park, but gracefully curved 4-mile-long Nantasket Beach still welcomes many each summer to enjoy sea breezes and escape city heat.

1. LIFESAVING MUSEUM, *1889.* 1117 Nantasket Ave. at Spring St. Open summer plus limited winter hours, fee.

This Lifesaving Museum is a monument to dedicated, courageous people. It began as "Old" Point Allerton Lifesaving Station, built by the federal government after unbelievable rescues by Joshua James and his lifesaving crews during the great storm of 1888. Again and again they set out that wild night to rescue crews of four different storm-stranded vessels. Nantasket Roads Channel, most often used, passes through Hull waters, where 70 percent of Boston Harbor's major wrecks occurred.

Over the years, lifesaving rescuers evolved useful equipment and team-spirited drill techniques similar to those of New England's volunteer firemen. Their success was their reward, as on the chilling February 1927 Sunday when the huge five-masted schooner *Nancy* foundered off Nantasket Beach. Led by Captain Oceola James, son of Joshua James, rescuers headed into monstrous waves after tying a rope to shore. Finally reaching the troubled ship, they timed waves and rescued the crew one by one. The museum features stories and activities to reenact rescues as well as a radio room, lookout, and surfboat *Nantasket.*

2. FORT REVERE MEMORIAL PARK, NHS. Farina Rd. Open all year, no fee. Paths, tower.

A most spectacular view of Boston Harbor is found at the end of Hull atop Fort Revere Memorial Park. You see stately buildings of Boston to the west. The island-studded harbor is at your feet. Nearest is George's Island and its Fort Warren, which held Southern prisoners during the Civil War. To the east are Brewster Islands, with Boston Light on

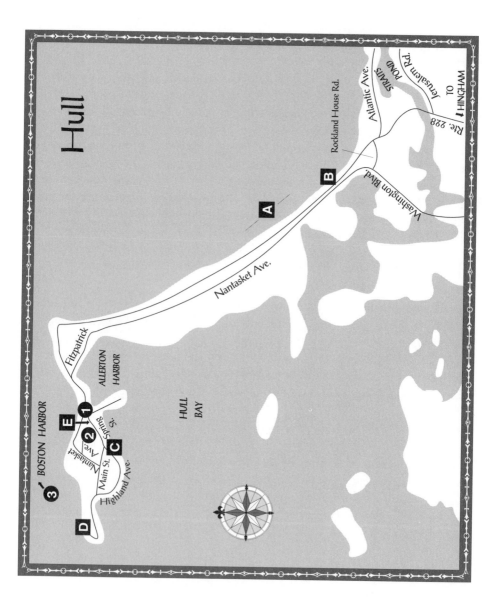

Little Brewster. Beyond Boston Harbor is the north shore, Cape Ann, and the two lights of Thacher's Island off Rockport. The total panorama emerges as you look back at Nantasket Beach and coastlines of Hingham and Cohasset to the south.

Commanding the harbor entrance, the elevation has been fortified since colonial times. In the 1600s beacons and a watchhouse were here. In the French and Indian Wars, Colonel Benjamin Church assembled 550 New Englanders and Indians here to assault the French in Maine and Acadia. The French garrisoned this headland with marines and sailors during the Revolution. In the War of 1812 the American *Chesapeake* and British *Shannon* fought a naval duel off Hull, during which the dying American Captain James Lawrence said, "Don't give up the ship!" In the 1800s this was Telegraph Hill: When an incoming ship was sighted, a wood signal on the tower indicated which ship, and the signal was relayed visually, via an island, to owners on Central Wharf, in Boston.

3. BOSTON LIGHT; *1716*, NHL. Boston Harbor. Exterior view only.

Boston Light dates to 1716, when a tonnage tax was collected to pay for the original light. Ironically, America's first lighthouse was a Revolutionary battlefield, attacked by both sides. When American attacks drove the British out, they mined the light. It was rebuilt in 1783 and remains undaunted.

BEACHES, PARKS, OTHER POINTS OF INTEREST

A. **Nantasket Beach.** Nantasket Ave. Open all year. Summer parking fee. Bathhouses, concessions, rest rooms; swimming.

B. **Carousel under the Clock.** Nantasket Ave. Marketplace, MDC Clock Tower Bldg. Open summer, fee.

C. **Hull Public Library,** c. 1888. Main St. Site was home to Reverend Marmaduke Matthews as unofficial parsonage in 1644; later occupant, Reverend Samuel Veazie, sued the town for back wages; present house built by John Boyle O'Reilly, patriot, poet, editor of the *Pilot.*

D. **View of Boston Harbor and Skyline.** End of Main St. Open all year. No fee. Fascinating water-level view.

E. **Historical Society Hall.** mid-1800s. Spring St. Open by appointment. No fee. Former Town Hall and fire station, houses artifacts of Hull history.

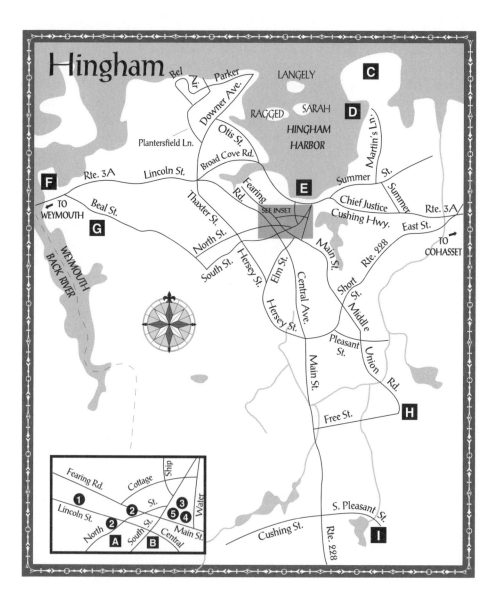

HINGHAM

Early settlers of Hingham, mainly from England's middle class, arrived in 1633. Edmund Hobard and Nicholas Jacob and families settled at Bare Cove, a shallow harbor bare at low tide. Two years later Hobart's son, Reverend Peter Hobart—tolerant of others' beliefs in a day when that was uncommon—arrived in Bare Cove with twenty-eight settlers from England.

In the 1600s Hingham was an agricultural community of self-sufficient homesteads, some local fishing, and limited shipbuilding. The next century saw the growth of mills, establishment of ironworks, shipyards along the harbor, and the beginning of commercial fishing. Hingham took a strong stand for independence during the Revolution. During the 1800s small industries manufactured nails, guns, woolen goods, leather articles, furniture, rope and sails, and coopering items such as the "Hingham Bucket." When railroads arrived after 1850 and industry grew elsewhere, Hingham's focus became more residential. Descendants of Hingham's early families brought inspired, dedicated leadership to the country: John Hancock, James Otis, General Benjamin Lincoln, President Abraham Lincoln.

1. THE OLD ORDINARY, *c. 1680,* HS. 21 Lincoln St. Open summer and by appointment, fee.

One of Hingham's greatest assets is the Old Ordinary, an original Colonial treasure that commands the hill above Lincoln Square. Warmly aged clapboards and white-trimmed twelve-over-twelve windows are capped by a wood-shingled roof whose interesting lines reflect modifications of many centuries. The prizewinning Colonial-style garden was designed by Frederick Law Olmsted, uncle of the then owner.

It all began in the 1680s when Thomas Andrews built a house, one room down and one up. By 1702 his son, also Thomas Andrews, was granted a license "to sell strong water. . . . provided he send his customers home at reasonable hours with ability to keep their legs."[25] Francis Barker—master mariner, captain of horse, and successful tavern keeper—bought the Ordinary in 1740 and made extensive additions. The spiced wine of a later tavern keeper was a favorite of frequent guest Daniel Webster. His portable writing desk and good-luck fishing cup are displayed here.

There is a sense of great age and history in the 1740s section, with its gleaming wide floorboards, chestnut summer beam, beautiful wainscoting, and Papillon wallpaper, one of the first continuous patterns. Period furniture, paintings, clocks, china, glass, pewter, and clothing are featured. Handwork, unique documents, a *Mayflower* treasure, and a Chinese tea chest containing some remains of tea from the Boston Tea Party are exhibited. Here is the keeper's note from the Minot's Light tragedy, found in

Old Ordinary, Hingham

a bottle in Massachusetts Bay by Gloucester fishermen. A collection of impressive tools is well labeled. The taproom has fascinating mementos of tavern keeping. Upstairs are cradles of both Hingham governors, Andrews and Long, and of an early Bradford. A closet reveals the exterior of the 1680s house—an original bracket of the overhang and wide clapboards.

2. NEW NORTH MEETING HOUSE, *1806*. 1 Lincoln St. General Benjamin Lincoln House, NHL. 181 North St. Private.

New North Meeting House was built from adapted plans of Charles Bulfinch; the plans are now at the Smithsonian. A beautiful, classic Federal, the church has delicate fanlights over entries capped by a Palladian window. Full-height plain pilasters grace the white-clapboarded facade crowned by clock tower, cupola, and banner weather vane. The church was formed by a group from Old Ship Meeting House led by "deacon in uniform" General Benjamin Lincoln.

The **General Benjamin Lincoln House** began as a small two-over-two-room home built on land granted cooper Thomas Lincoln about 1640. Large additions and changes were made in 1715, in Georgian style, and in 1790, in Federal style. General Benjamin Lincoln—local leader, aide to General Washington, secretary of war—received Cornwallis's sword as symbol of British surrender at Yorktown. Later, descendant Abraham Lincoln held the nation together through the terrible internal conflict of Civil War. Other Lincoln homes, private, are at 182 North Street (pre-1740) and at 172 North (pre-1700). This Lincoln Historic District neighborhood, where Lincolns have lived for more than three centuries, is rich in history and architecture—Colonial, Georgian, Federal, and classic vernacular Greek Revival.

3. HINGHAM CEMETERY, *1600s*. Entrances Main and South sts.

Three centuries ago a fort was built on the summit of this now peaceful hill during King Philip's War. The site is a good starting place for a walk through Hingham's history. Follow the upper of two roadways behind Derby Academy and Old Ship Meeting House. On the left, before the roadway bends away from the church, is a raised grave with granite slab inscribed to the first three ministers of Old Ship Meeting House, Reverends Hobart, Norton, and Gay, who served a total of 150 years. A short distance beyond is the fenced tomb of General Benjamin Lincoln. Pass under a magnificent beech tree, a natural temple, to the statue and grave of Civil War Massachusetts Governor John Albion Andrew. Across a side path is a monument to Massachusetts Governor John Davis Long.

4. OLD SHIP MEETING HOUSE OF FIRST PARISH, *1681*, NHL. 90 Main St. Open summer and by appointment, no fee. Bell concerts.

"Let the Work of Our Fathers Stand" is inscribed on the First Parish seal, and well the Old Ship Meeting House has stood for more than three centuries and fifteen generations. Old Ship was erected at a cost of 430 pounds, using lumber from the first church building. Inspired carpenters and shipbuilders combined skills to erect this oldest wooden church in continuous use in the country. The style is Elizabethan Gothic, after remembered churches in England. The commanding sweep of hip roof is capped by balustrades setting off the delicate lines of the spire.

Originally hard wooden benches faced a pulpit on the easterly side. By 1755 the first square pews were installed and the present pulpit built. In the mid-1800s Victorian additions were made—cushioned pews, carpeting, velvet hangings, organ, oil lamps, furnace. Today's beautiful meetinghouse combines the simplicity and strength of its seventeenth-century exposed naturally curved trusses and ceiling beams with the aroma and soft patina of its eighteenth-century wooden pews and pulpit. Adjacent to the church is the 1912 Hingham Memorial Bell Tower, housing eleven bells copied from ones in Norfolk, England. With one rope for each bell, eleven trained people combine talents to play.

5. OLD DERBY ACADEMY, school *1791*, building *1818*, HS. Main St. Open tour day and by appointment, fee.

Legend tells of Sarah Langley, a beautiful but ragged daughter of a fisherman living on Langley's Island, who met wealthy Dr. Ezekiel Hersey and captured his heart. Islands of Hingham Harbor perpetuate the story with their names: Ragged, Sarah, and

Langley. Actually, Derby Academy's founder, Madam Sarah Hersey Derby, did marry the dashing Dr. Hersey, who endowed a chair for anatomy that gave rise to Harvard Medical School. A Hersey family home remains at 229 North Street, a large Georgian with impressive Greek Revival entry, now housing community activities.

Following Hersey's death, widow Sarah married wealthy Salem widower Captain Richard Derby. Their pioneering nuptial agreement protected her holdings. Derby was a successful merchant in the triangular trade, a member of the General Court and Governor's Council, and father of Elias Haskett Derby, who developed the lucrative East India Trade (see Salem). In 1783, again a widow, now sixty-nine, Sarah returned to Hingham to make her dream a reality—creating what became one of the oldest coeducational private schools in the country. Here girls were to study classical subjects as well as needlework. In 1818 old buildings were removed and this elegant Federal built. The school has moved and now the building is home to the Hingham Historical Society.

BEACHES, PARKS, OTHER POINTS OF INTEREST

A. **Odd Fellows Hall,** 1829. 196 North St. Private. Was First Universalist Church in 1829; Reverend Phebe Hanaford, first woman minister in New England, ordained here 1868.

B. **Ensign John Thaxter House,** Hingham Community Center, c. 1695. 70 South St. Open all year for center activities. Thaxters lived here nearly two centuries; main room panels painted about 1785 by John Hazlitt, known English miniature artist.

C. **World's End Reservation.** Martin's Ln. Open all year. Fee. Paths and platforms through marsh, tree-lined meadows; 249-acre peninsula; views of Hingham, Boston Harbor; skiing, hiking. Trustees of Reservations.

D. **Martin's Lane Beach.** Martin's Ln. Small tidal beach (private), boat launching (public); parking allowed only while launching.

E. **Hingham Harbor Parks,** Grand Old Bandstand, Hingham Bathing Beach, Town Pier. Rte. 3A. Open all year. No fee. Open green on harbor, benches, boat docks; biking, fishing, picnicking, swimming. In summer, beach parking by sticker only.

F. **Stodders Neck Park.** Rte. 3A. Open all year. No fee. Paths along Weymouth Back River.

G. **Bare Cove Park.** Beal St. Open all year. No fee. 461 acres passive recreation on Weymouth Back River, trails; fishing, biking, picnicking.

H. **Wompatuck State Park.** Access Free St. Open all year. No fee. 2,700 acres, visitor center complex, self-guided nature trails, paved bike trails; camping (fee), hiking, biking, riding, picnicking.

I. **Fulling Mill Pond.** South Pleasant St. Open all year. No fee. Small pond; canoeing, picnicking; limited parking.

WEYMOUTH

Weymouth's first founder, wealthy London merchant Thomas Weston, was concerned with trade and financial return. In 1622 he set up a fishing station and trading post of men only and neglected to plant crops for food supply. The settlement became so desperate for food that some men stole food from Indians. It was soon abandoned. The next year Sir Ferdinando Gorges, who dreamed of establishing the most powerful settlement on the New England coast, obtained a grant that included Boston Bay. Learning from Weston's mistakes, he sent 120 men and women—including Church of England clergy, craftsmen, farmers, and traders—under the command of his son, Captain Robert Gorges. By next spring, Sir Ferdinando's power waned, and Captain Gorges returned to England. In 1624 families arrived from Weymouth, England, and joined the remaining community. With no governing head, settlers governed themselves and began the first American town government, which evolved into the familiar New England town meeting. Farming was the mainstay, with lumber, salt, mackerel, and iron ore as trade items for several centuries. During the 1800s shoemaking became an important industry, growing from family industries to huge industrial complexes by 1875.

1. ABIGAIL SMITH ADAMS BIRTHPLACE, *1685*, HS. 180 Norton St.
Open summer, fee.

This was the ell of the home of Reverend William Smith and Elizabeth Quincy Smith, where Abigail was born in 1744. The Smiths later added a large main wing, no longer on the site. Abigail enjoyed the warmth and security of this parsonage until her marriage. She learned religious and moral subjects; read Shakespeare and other classics; visited with Smith relatives, a socially prominent merchant family, in Boston; and visited her Quincy grandparents, where she heard lively political and legal discussions. For nearly three years John Adams traveled dusty roads to this parsonage, until Abigail agreed to marry him in 1764. As her husband, John Adams listened to and was influenced by Abigail's astute observations of the political scene. She handled the farm and the accounts and raised a family of four, often while John was away for political or national needs. She joined her husband in Paris, lived three years with him in London, was the first woman of the United States to be presented at the Court of St. James, lived in New York while John was vice president of the country, and was the first hostess of the newly built but unfinished White House in Washington while he was president.

This Weymouth house is the restored original ell of Abigail's childhood, with furnishings authenticated to the years she lived here, 1740 to 1760. As you walk through

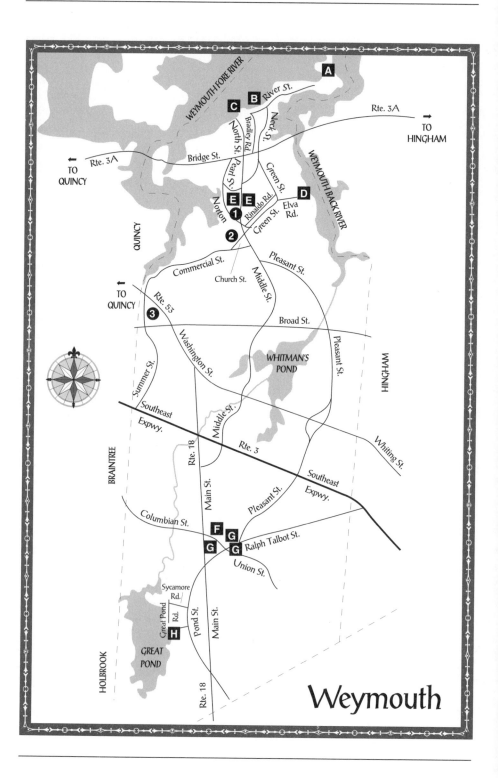

Weymouth

this historic home where Abigail grew up, you feel richer for having caught a glimpse of her life.

2. FIRST CHURCH OF WEYMOUTH, *1833.* 17 Church St.

In 1635 Anglican minister Joseph Hull brought definite religious activity, which blossomed into one meetinghouse and three dissenting ministers. In those unsettled times Puritans disputed doctrine among themselves, and Pilgrims and Church of England adherents added diversity. Reverend Samuel Newman was called in 1639, managed to unify the church, and created a scholarly concordance, probably the first of the English Bible and a basis of *Cruden's Concordance* still used today. Newman was followed by Reverend Thomas Thacher, physician, who wrote a lexicon of Hebrew and the first monograph on smallpox published in America. Next, Reverend Samuel Torrey became one of the few to decline the presidency of Harvard College. In 1833 the present meetinghouse was built—a beautiful example of New England church architecture, built by a committee following no particular form but selecting appealing features from many. Greek Revival and Georgian elements dominate.

3. TOWN MUSEUM, TUFTS LIBRARY, HS. 46 Broad St. Open all year by appointment, no fee.

A twentieth-century drought revealed a rare fifteenth-century American Indian dugout canoe in Weymouth Great Pond, which itself had been formed by a receding ice glacier over 12,000 years before. The dugout, one of only two known in North America, has been permanently preserved by an innovative use of polyethylene glycol. Tests indicate the 10-foot-long dugout was made from an eastern white pine approximately 150 feet tall about 1420, two centuries before the Pilgrims landed. The canoe is beautifully displayed in a mood-setting three-dimensional diorama of Great Pond so realistic you almost expect an Indian to emerge, retrieve the dugout, and paddle away. The museum also features collections from Weymouth's past—including an 1860s Elias Howe sewing machine, Civil War–era carpetbag, well-labeled surgical instruments, eighteenth-century kitchen utensils, and a shoe shop and tools.

BEACHES, PARKS, OTHER POINTS OF INTEREST

A. **Webb Memorial State Park.** River St. Open all year. No fee. Thirty-six-acre park, views of Boston Harbor, rest rooms, paths; hiking, picnicking.

B. **Wessagussett Beach.** Neck St. Sandy beach, views; sticker parking in summer.

C. **Great Hill Park.** Bradley Rd. Open all year. No fee. Small park, panoramic views, benches.

D. **Great Esker Park.** Elva Rd. Open all year. No fee. Natural gravel hill esker above marshes, miles of trails, nature walks; biking, hiking.

Abigail Smith Adams Birthplace, Weymouth

E. North Weymouth Cemetery, 1600s. North and Norton sts. Graves of Reverend William and Elizabeth Quincy Smith, parents of Abigail Adams, and other old Weymouth families; Thomas A. Watson, Alexander Graham Bell's assistant, believed buried here; Soldiers' Memorial on top of hill that was early Watch House Hill, also site of first meetinghouse.

F. Old South Union Church, 1854. 25 Columbian St. Was NHL, burned down 1989, reproduction built 1990; shiplap boarding, stately Corinthian pilasters, boldly denticulated pediment, clock tower, bell tower, graceful spire.

G. Columbian Square, 1800s. Columbian and Union sts. Oldest of public buildings is Fogg Shoe Factory from early 1800s; across is 1897 Italian Renaissance Fogg Library of Weymouth seam-face granite. Dramatic Richardsonian 1888 Fogg Building was once Opera House—turrets, towers, chimneys, spires rise in unbalanced glory above powerful core.

H. Great Pond Reservoir. Access at school off Pond St. or at treatment plant off Great Pond Rd. Open all year. No fee. Protected water supply, paths around pond.

QUINCY

Quincy[26] went from the frivolity of the maypole to the solemnity of the White House. In 1625 Captain Richard Wollaston left a small group of men here for the winter. The next spring Thomas Norton, London lawyer and adventurer, took over the group and created a trading post. He conducted his famous maypole escapades—erecting a flower-wreathed, antler-topped maypole around which the group danced and drank for days. Pilgrims and Puritan colonists tolerated him for a while but sent him back to England when they discovered he had sold more firearms to Indians than they possessed collectively.

In 1634 the uninhabited area was annexed to Boston and settlement began. Reverend John Wheelwright had a church here in 1636 but was shortly banished, along with sister-in-law Anne Hutchinson, for dissident religious activities. Among early settlers were the founders of the Adams and Quincy families of local and national prominence. In 1750 the first planned industrial development in the country began in what is still the Germantown section of Quincy.

Granite was important from colonial times. Quincy became known as "Granite City," supplying granite for the 1754 King's Chapel in Boston and for nineteenth-century Bunker Hill Monument, customhouses, and other important buildings. The Granite Railway, the country's first commercial railway, was built in 1826 to carry stone from quarries to tidewater, where it was loaded on sloops and schooners. Shipbuilding was a major industry here from 1600s to recent times, and "Quincy built" was a slogan known the world over. Many historic treasures remain in this modern city. Quincy Shore Drive provides an interesting, scenic coastline drive with fascinating views of islands and skylines, bay and industry.

1. JOHN ADAMS'S BIRTHPLACE, *1681*, part of Adams NHS. 133 Franklin St. Open extended season, fee.

John Adams, first son of Deacon John and Susanna Boylston Adams, was born October 30, 1735, in this early saltbox farmhouse. His father, a farmer, instilled two vital forces in young Adams' life: love and respect for the land together with a burning desire for knowledge. From here John Adams left for Harvard College, his graduation the first step in his career from unknown circuit lawyer to president of the United States. John inherited the adjacent saltbox with nine acres, where he moved with his new wife, Abigail, in 1764. John Adams was a leading Patriot, a signer of the Declaration of Independence, a diplomat, principal author of the Massachusetts Constitution, and first vice president and second president of the United States.

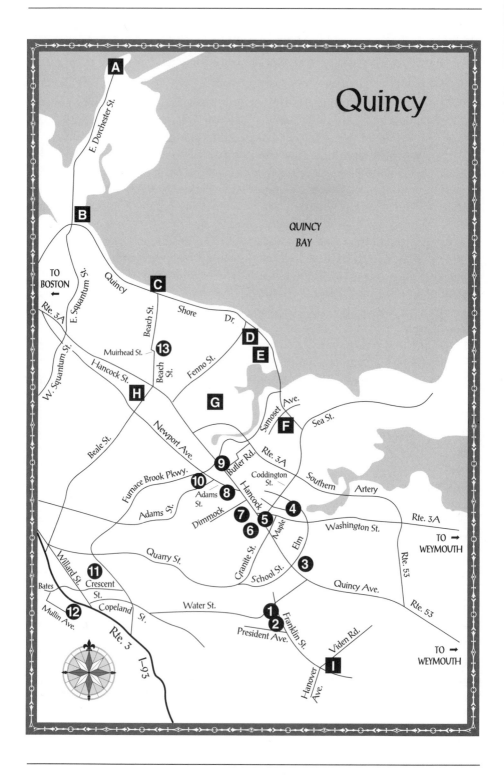

2. JOHN QUINCY ADAMS'S BIRTHPLACE, *1646 or earlier*, **part of Adams NHS. 141 Franklin St. Open extended season, fee.**

Here John and Abigail Adams lived for over twenty years and raised their children—Abigail, John Quincy, Susanna (who died in infancy), Charles, and Thomas. In this house lived the second and sixth presidents of the United States, the only father and son to so serve. Their birthplaces are the oldest and only adjacent presidential birthplaces in the country. John Adams, with his legal training, became embroiled in the defense of colonial rights, and this home became a political forum. Adams left for Philadelphia for the Continental Congress and to be minister to France and to England, but this was home, where his "dearest friend" and children were. On July 11, 1767, John Quincy Adams was born here. Before he was eleven, young Johnny sailed with his father to France, where he attended school. At fourteen he accompanied Francis Dana to Russia as secretary and interpreter before he graduated from Harvard. He became senator, ambassador, secretary of state, president of the United States, and representative.

This home—with central chimney, fireplace in every room, wide floorboards, period furnishings—shows life as it was when the Adams family lived here. In the kitchen Abigail melted down her pewter spoons to make bullets. Here she wrote most of her warm letters, which became excellent chronicles of the times. In his law office here in 1779, John Adams worked on the Constitution of Massachusetts, which was the pattern for the federal Constitution and other democratic constitutions. Authorities consider this to be his greatest contribution to history and one of the most important events in the chronology of democratic government.

3. CHRIST CHURCH, *1875.* 12 Quincy Ave.

Christ Church is the oldest Episcopal parish in Massachusetts—the oldest religious institution that was not an established town church. On School Street, a short distance west of the present church, is the old burial ground and site of the original church building of 1725. Through extraordinary lay leadership the parish survived the Revolution and kept its congregation, building, and glebe. The present fourth church building is a strong Victorian Gothic structure of Quincy granite, with 30-inch-thick walls. Because the founders of the church were political as well as religious dissenters, Jacobites, they received no silver from Queen Anne. More cherished is a silver chalice given by Caesar, a slave, in 1770. The church has the original books, some seventeenth-century, sent from England to the early congregation.

4. THOMAS CRANE PUBLIC LIBRARY, *1882*, NRHP. 40 Washington St.

A magnificent edifice dominates the main square of Quincy. It is considered architect Henry Hobson Richardson's "most perfect" Romanesque creation. Although it is not symmetrical, the arrangement of the mass still creates a balance of rugged strength.

The foundation is Quincy granite, the walls rough-hewn North Easton pink granite with horizontal accent bands of Longmeadow brownstone. The interior of the original Richardson building has elegant carvings around the massive fireplace. The room is rich in ornately carved North Carolina white pine of varying natural hues. Small stained glass windows add interest, particularly the "Old Philosopher" in the center, considered John La Farge's best work.

5. UNITED FIRST PARISH CHURCH (UNITARIAN) IN QUINCY; CHURCH OF THE PRESIDENTS, *1828, gathered 1639,* NHL. Quincy Square and Hancock and Washington sts.

This "stone temple" was designed by noted Greek Revival architect Alexander Parris, who was paid $500 for his work, which included supervising construction. The Doric portico features huge 25-foot columns supporting a massive front gable. Plain-cut blocks of Quincy granite form the facade and clock tower, topped by a gold-capped open belfry. The church was built of granite from John Adams's lands and was helped by a fund he established for it. The magnificent interior has high domed ceiling with plaster bas-relief, enclosed pews, and Santo Domingo mahogany pulpit. There is a small museum with models of earlier churches, photos, and pictures of Wheelwrights, Adamses, and Quincys. Under the church a black iron gate leads to the Adams crypt and the simple stone tombs of John and Abigail Adams and of John Quincy and Louisa Catherine Adams. Wreaths are given each year by the president of the United States.

The congregation's history goes back even farther to the "Chappel of Ease" begun in 1636, when Reverend John Wheelwright was delegated to preach here. Three years later the parish of the present church was gathered. The name has changed a number of times, and this is the fourth building. There have been many noted members and ministers, among them Reverend John Hancock, father of the first signer of the Declaration of Independence.

6. HANCOCK CEMETERY, *c. 1640,* Hancock St.

The grave of Henry Adams, great-great-grandfather of President John Adams, is the oldest identified grave, dated 1646. Colonel John Quincy, the man for whom the city was named and grandfather of Abigail Adams, is buried here. At nearly every turn along the paths of this peaceful sanctuary is a stone with a name you recognize, such as Josiah Quincy, "the Patriot," Reverend John Hancock as well as many fine examples of gravestone cutters' art.

7. CITY (TOWN) HALL, *1844.* Quincy Sq., Hancock St.

The Quincy granite City Hall was designed by Solomon Willard, father of the granite industry in Quincy. The facade is considered one of the finest in the country; the reflective glass addition provides remarkable contrast.

8. QUINCY HISTORICAL SOCIETY, ADAMS ACADEMY BUILD-
ING, *1872*, NHL. 8 Adams St. Open all year, no fee. Museum shop.

This schoolhouse of eclectic high Victorian Gothic was built of staunch Quincy granite and brick, with funds and materials provided by John Adams. He founded Adams Academy to provide the old-style classical education required for college entrance. He directed that the building be on the site of John Hancock's birthplace and the home of the Josiah Quincys to honor them. The academy was noted for high-quality school-masters, and it won the first known interscholastic football game in New England against Phillips Academy at Andover in 1875. Within, white walls contrast with dark, heavy timbers rising to the cathedral ceiling. The building is now the home of the Quincy Historical Society, which maintains a museum of Quincy and Quincy subjects and a fine historical research library and archive.

9. QUINCY HOMESTEAD, *1685*, NRHP, Colonial Dames. 1010 Hancock
St., entrance from Butler Rd. Open extended season, fee.

Judge Edmund Quincy III inherited this family home, which he renovated and enlarged in 1706 as the mansion house of a large estate. Here he lived with wife Dorothy Flynt and their children. The original house was built by Edmund Quincy II on land acquired by his father, Edmund I, about 1635. Edmund II was town moderator and a member of the General Court and of the Council of Safety that governed the colony after Governor Andros's removal.

In the house appropriate fine furnishings are from the seventeenth and eigh-teenth centuries. In the kitchen herbs hang from beams, and Dorothy Quincy Han-cock's spinning wheel stands in one corner. Duck your head to step into the hall and newer part done by Judge Edmund. The dining room has enclosed beams, paneled walls, a smaller Delft tile fireplace, and Oriental wallpaper. Behind the fireplace in the parlor you can see the earliest fireplace in the house. On a window pane in an upstairs room John Hancock is said to have scratched with Dorothy's engagement ring, "you I love and you alone." Dorothy, youngest child of the last Edmund to live here, married a leader of the impending Revolution, John Hancock, when he was president of the Continental Congress.

10. ADAMS NATIONAL HISTORIC SITE, *1731*, part of Adams NHS.
135 Adams St. Open extended season, fee.

When he returned from England, where he was minister to the court of St. James, and before assuming the office of vice president, John Adams supervised the revitalization of his new lands in Quincy. In 1787 he and Abigail had purchased this lovely house. In 1801 John returned here to Quincy to spend his final twenty-five years. Here he learned of his son's election as sixth U. S. president. Here Abigail died, and here, on

July 4, 1826, just a few hours after Thomas Jefferson's death, John Adams left this world, which he had spent his life serving.

John Quincy Adams inherited the estate. Though he rarely spent more than a few months at a time here, this was his oasis. It served as "summer White House" for both presidents. Then it passed to John Quincy's son, Charles Francis, ambassador to the court of St. James during the Civil War. His diplomacy helped keep England from openly supporting the South and prevented delivery of ironclad ships made by sympathizers for Southern use. Two of Charles Francis's sons, writers Henry and Brooks, lived on here after he died. The Old House was last lived in by Brooks Adams, who died here in 1927.

The historic Georgian Colonial is set amid well-landscaped grounds, including formal gardens designed by Mrs. Charles Francis Adams and a York Rose planted by Abigail Adams that still survives. When you enter the mansion you feel as if the Adams family has just stepped out. The house is just as it was when Brooks Adams died. Well-informed guides lead you through rooms and lives of four Adams generations, pointing out each family member's furnishings and their historical significance. All furnishings belonged to the Adamses. In the original seven-room house bought by John and Abigail is the parlor where Abigail shelled peas, folded laundry, and greeted guests. While John served as president, Abigail added six rooms, including a formal parlor for entertaining and a large study for John. Treasured furnishings include John

Adams Library, Adams National Historic Site, Quincy   (Courtesy National Park Service)

and Abigail's desk, Henry Adams's desk, John Quincy's globes, Daniel Webster's Napoleon sleeping bed, and Abigail's writing desk.

In a separate library building of slate-roofed Quincy granite and brick is the John Quincy Adams library and the papers of Charles Francis Adams. Fourteen thousand volumes in eleven languages fill floor-to-ceiling oak bookshelves. John Adams's writing desk, in which he had a pigeonhole for each department of government, is here, as is the desk John Quincy used in the House of Representatives. The whole site shares the heartbeat of the Adamses from 1787 to 1927.

11. JOHN WINTHROP, JR., IRON FURNACE, *1644*. Crescent St. Open all year, no fee.

Here are excavated remains of the furnace that produced the first commercial iron in the new country. The original construction is still evident—bellows, casting arches, even the marks of fires of the seventeenth century. Operations ceased by 1653 because of reduced supplies of bog iron ore and waterpower. From here skilled workers went on to found ironworks at Saugus and elsewhere.

12. GRANITE RAILWAY INCLINE, *1826*, NRHP. Mullin Ave. Open all year, no fee.

Railway machinery inventor Gridley Bryant built this granite incline to transport massive granite blocks from the quarry down to rail level to be carried to the Neponset River. You can see the lower half of the incline, where huge granite blocks were lowered on an ingenious endless chain mechanism from the quarry. This was the first commercial railway in the country. Its first contract was to carry granite for Bunker Hill Monument.

13. COLONEL JOSIAH QUINCY HOUSE, *1770*, SPNEA, NRHP. 18 Muirhead St. Open extended season, limited hours; fee.

Here stands the ancestral home of six Josiah Quincys. The first Josiah, brother Edmund IV, and brother-in-law Edward Jackson were Boston shipping merchant partners. In 1748 one of their ships, the *Bethel*, was surprised by a much larger Spanish treasure ship. The *Bethel* rigged her portholes with logs and spars to look like guns and ran lanterns and odd clothing and equipment up the rigging to present a ghostlike man-of-war appearance. It worked. The Spaniards gave up without a fight, and the captured treasure made each partner wealthy. Josiah returned to his native town. In 1770 he built this Georgian mansion, its balanced facade crowned with a monitor, on his inherited 200-acre farm. Josiah, Jr., was an ardent patriot and is known as "the Patriot" and "Boston Cicero." Josiah III continued to bring honor as president of Harvard, "great Mayor" of Boston, and in the 1820s, prime mover behind Quincy Market in Boston. His son, Josiah IV, was mayor of Boston, as was grandson Josiah, who became the third Quincy to be mayor of the city. Period furnishings, many belonging to Quincys, are featured. The elegant mansion is the proper setting for the wealth, prestige, and political power of the Josiah Quincys.

BEACHES, PARKS, OTHER POINTS OF INTEREST

A. Myles Standish Cairn, Squaw Rock Park. East Dorchester St. Open all year. No fee. Site of landing of Standish, Indian Squanto, and others on Sept. 30, 1621; paths through trees, water vistas; rest rooms.

B. Moswetuset Hummock, NRHP. East Squantum St. Open all year. No fee. Early 1600s seat of Massachusetts Indians, from whom name of state derived; unchanged Indian site, never used by white people; paths, view.

C. Wollaston Beach. Quincy Shore Dr. Open all year. No fee. Long gravelly sand beach, views; swimming.

D. Grossman's Park, Quincy Shore Dr. and Fenno St. Open all year. No fee. Named for Quincy-based family of building suppliers; paths along edge of marsh, benches.

E. Caddy Memorial Park. Quincy Shore Dr. Open all year. No fee. Named for World War II Congressional Medal of Honor winner; playground, bike path, trails.

F. Maypole Park. Samoset Ave. Open all year. No fee. Site of historic maypole also of cedar on Quincy seal; street parking.

G. Merrymount Park. Hancock St. (Rte. 3A). Open all year. No fee. Large park given by Adams; ball fields, playground, trails.

H. Site of beginning of Howard Johnson chain. Beale St. Quincy boy "Buster" Johnson had variety store 1925, added ice cream and grew; benches.

I. Abigail Adams Cairn. Franklin St. at Viden Rd. Open all year. No fee. Site where Abigail and son John Quincy witnessed the Battle of Bunker Hill, June 17, 1775.

BOSTON

Boston was founded in 1630 by Puritans led by John Winthrop. Through the centuries Boston has been a city of neighborhoods and people—families, builders, leaders, historians, artists, statesmen, politicians, preachers, presidents, philosophers, writers. Rich culture, history, and architecture are retained with pride amid the pioneering and powerful present. The Boston area is home to the first computer (MIT) as well as to America's first ferry boat (1631), public park (Boston Common 1634), still-existing free public school (Boston Latin), post office, public library (founded 1653), printed schoolbook, lighthouse, Board of Health (headed by Paul Revere), YMCA.

Boston is a walking city; driving can be a frantic blur except to points of interest beyond central Boston. Walk Boston's neighborhoods for the true flavor and character of this fascinating city.

DOWNTOWN

Here, in 1630, the first settlers founded Boston. Today, the Colonial-patterned streets wander through shopping areas, government center, and Chinatown and pass theaters and Faneuil Hall. Boston's Freedom Trail, America's first urban historic trail, which includes the seven sites of Boston National Historical Park, begins here. Follow the red brick line through the city to historic sites along the 3-mile round-trip walk. Freedom Trail points are marked "FT" in the following text.

Visitor information centers and tours are available:

- Boston Common Visitor Information Booth, Tremont St. at Boston Common, open daily all year.
- Boston National Historical Park Visitor Center, 15 State St., across from Old State House, open daily all year.
- Special Tours through Art Boston, Art New England, Boston by Foot, Horse Drawn Sightseeing Tours; harbor cruises, trolley tours.

1. BOSTON COMMON (FT), *1634*, NRHP. Tremont, Park, Beacon, Charles, and Boylston sts. Open all year. No fee.

Remains common land more than three centuries after purchase for common grazing land and militia training ground; oldest public park in country; includes small burial ground near Boylston Street and Shaw Memorial to first black regiment at Beacon and Park streets. Common begins "Emerald Necklace," chain of parks and green space designed by Frederick Law Olmsted extending from Common to Boston Public Gar-

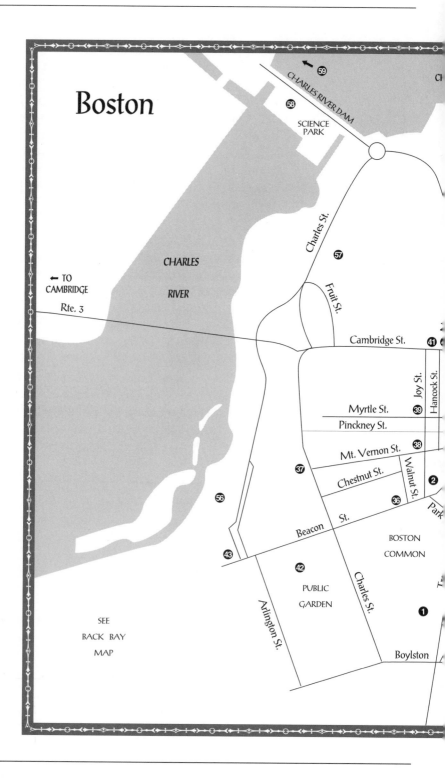

Boston

CHARLES RIVER

CHARLES RIVER DAM

SCIENCE PARK

Charles St.

Fruit St.

Cambridge St.

Joy St.

Hancock St.

Myrtle St.

Pinckney St.

Mt. Vernon St.

Chestnut St.

Walnut St.

Beacon St.

Park

BOSTON COMMON

PUBLIC GARDEN

Charles St.

Arlington St.

Boylston

← TO CAMBRIDGE
Rte. 3

SEE
BACK BAY
MAP

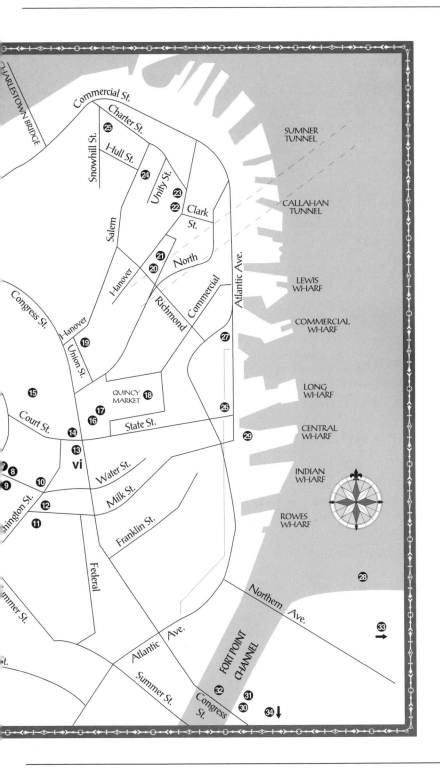

den, along Commonwealth Avenue, Fenway, Riverway, Jamaicaway and pond, to Arnold Arboretum.

2. MASSACHUSETTS STATE HOUSE (FT), *1795*, NHL. Beacon St. across from Common. Open all year. No fee.

Guided tours focus on architecture, history, legislature. Land belonged to John Hancock family; boldly impressive building designed by Charles Bulfinch, Boston's Federal architect and the country's first native-born architect; archives museum goes back to Pilgrims.

3. BOSTON ATHENAEUM (FT), *1847*, NHL. 10½ Beacon St. Open all year, limited hours. No fee.

Guided tours of elegant historic private library arts club; library access for research only.

4. ST. PAUL'S CATHEDRAL, *1819*, NHL. Tremont St. and Common. Open all year. No fee.

Massive Greek Revival by Parris and Willard, built by Boston's leading families of the time.

5. PARK STREET CHURCH (FT), *1809*. Park and Tremont sts. Open summers and by appointment.

Here William Lloyd Garrison gave first public abolitionist speech in 1829.

6. GRANARY BURYING GROUND (FT), *1660*. Tremont St.

Graves of Paul Revere, John Hancock, Sam Adams, Robert Treat Paine, victims of Boston Massacre, and parents of Ben Franklin.

7. KING'S CHAPEL AND BURIAL GROUND (FT), *1754*, NHL. Tremont and School sts.

America's first Church of England congregation, established 1686; now Unitarian; Boston's first burial ground adjacent, c. 1630, graves of *Mayflower* Pilgrim Mary Chilton and of Massachusetts Bay Colony leaders including Governor John Winthrop.

8. FRANKLIN STATUE (FT), *1856*. Old City Hall grounds, School St.

First Boston portrait statue represents native son with tablet of Ben Franklin highlights. Bold French Second Empire **Old City Hall,** NHL, is restored for adaptive use as restaurant.

9. SITE OF FIRST PUBLIC SCHOOL (FT). School St.

Plaque outside Old City Hall grounds; here was country's first public school in 1635, original site of Boston Public Latin School.

10. GLOBE CORNER BOOKSTORE (FT), *1712*, NRHP. Corner School and Washington sts.

Boston Globe office, now bookstore; here gathered literary heroes, among them Ralph Waldo Emerson, Nathaniel Hawthorne, Oliver Wendell Holmes; memorabilia and book collection.

11. BIRTHPLACE OF BENJAMIN FRANKLIN (FT). 17 Milk St. Private.

Bust of Franklin; plaque marks birthplace.

12. OLD SOUTH MEETING HOUSE (FT), *1729*, NHL. 310 Washington at Milk St. Open all year. Fee.

Exhibits, multimedia display, model of colonial Boston; explores role of Old South Meeting House in Revolutionary history of Boston; here a 1773 gathering turned into Boston Tea Party; poet Phyllis Wheatley worshiped here.

13. BOSTON NATIONAL HISTORICAL PARK VISITORS CENTER (FT), National Park Service. 15 State St. Open all year. No fee.

Good starting point from which to explore Boston: media presentation on Freedom Trail, knowledgeable guides and printed information, rotating exhibits, rest rooms.

14. OLD STATE HOUSE (FT), *1713*, NHL. 206 Washington St. Open all year. Fee.

Museum of Boston history from 1630 to twentieth century includes paintings, Revolutionary artifacts, tea from Boston Tea Party. Boston's oldest public building; was first British, then Massachusetts State House; here Declaration of Independence first read in Boston; John Hancock inaugurated as first governor in 1780.

15. CITY HALL PLAZA, *1975*. Government Ctr., Tremont St. Open all year. No fee.

Tours through massive concrete City Hall; open gathering spaces outside now host concerts, rotating exhibits, informal attractions; once Scollay Square area.

16 BOSTON MASSACRE SITE (FT). Near Old State House.

Here on March 5, 1770, violence erupted after a year of British occupation of the city; former slave Crispus Attucks was killed while leading mob assaulting British soldiers; Patriots fanned propaganda flames.

17. FANEUIL HALL (FT), *1742*, NHL. Congress St., head of Quincy Market. Open all year. No fee.

"Cradle of Liberty" was scene of Revolutionary meetings, was enlarged 1805 by Bulfinch. Now houses first-floor shops, meeting hall above, and third-floor museum of the 1638 Ancient and Honorable Artillery Company of Massachusetts; topped by famed pre-Revolutionary grasshopper weather vane, once stolen but rescued and returned to rightful place.

18. FANEUIL HALL MARKET PLACE, (QUINCY MARKET) (FT), NHL. Open all year. No fee.

Popular pedestrian mall; intriguing shops and eateries abound in preserved markets and warehouses designed by Greek Revival architect Alexander Parris.

NORTH END

Here is Boston's oldest residential neighborhood. Italian-American in flavor, it is busy and noisy with life. An open-air market provides local color as well as fresh fruit and vegetables.

19. CAPEN HOUSE, *c. 1713*. Union St.

Open all year as Union Oyster House, since 1826, Boston's oldest restaurant.

20. MOSES PIERCE–HICHBORN HOUSE, *1711*, NHL. 29 North Sq.

Open through Paul Revere House; restored 3-story brick house with period furnishings.

21. PAUL REVERE HOUSE (FT), *c. 1680*, NHL. 19 North Sq. Open all year. Fee.

Boston's oldest house; here Revere lived before and after Revolution; focus on people, architecture, furnishings of seventeenth and eighteenth centuries, Revere memorabilia; colonial herb garden.

22. ST. STEPHEN'S CHURCH, *1804*, NRHP. 401 Hanover St. at Clark St.

Only Charles Bulfinch–designed church remaining; impressive Federal with brick facade, white pilasters, ornate cornices, finials, bell tower, domed cupola.

23. PAUL REVERE MALL, *1933*. Hanover St. Open all year. No fee.

Includes famous Paul Revere statue by Cyrus Dallin; sidewalls have bronze plaques detailing Boston history.

24. OLD NORTH CHURCH (FT), *1723*, NHL. Salem St.

Oldest standing historic Boston church beautifully retains many original features; traditionally, here on April 18, 1775, signal lanterns sent Paul Revere on ride.

25. COPP'S HILL BURIAL GROUND (FT), *1660*, NRHP. Charter and Hull sts.

Originally North Burying Ground, Boston's second; here buried Cotton Mather, old Boston names, over 1,000 blacks since 1638; site of British fortifications during Battle of Bunker Hill.

WATERFRONT

Home of the Boston Tea Party, this area soon drew industries. Now wharves and warehouses have been revitalized and are used for shops, restaurants, condos, museums, and parks.

26. HARBORWALK. Begins at Old State House (14). Open all year. No fee.

Blue Harborwalk sidewalk symbols lead along State Street past Custom House Tower (with open-to-public observation platform), Quincy Market (18), to Waterfront Park (27), wharves along Atlantic Avenue, Aquarium (29), Children's Museum (30), Boston Tea Party Ship (32).

27. WATERFRONT PARK. Atlantic Ave. Open all year. No fee.

Peaceful place to walk, view harbor, appreciate restoration and adaptive uses. Waterfront scene includes 1710 Long Wharf; c. 1830 Gardner Building, once warehouse, now restaurant; 1845 Custom House where Nathaniel Hawthorne worked; 1858 Gridley Bryant–designed Mercantile Wharf; 1833 Commercial Wharf; 1836 Lewis Wharf with restored granite building.

28. BOSTON HARBOR ISLANDS.

Each island has its own personality—historic sites, rocky or sandy shore, wilderness and wildlife—in dramatic contrast with Boston skyline so near; islands created when glaciers ground bedrock, leaving drumlins and rock ridge that became the harbor islands; over 6,000 years ago Indians camped here; in 1614 Captain John Smith explored; colonial farming began by 1630; continent's first lighthouse (Boston Light) by 1713; important defense fortifications from colonial times through World War II. Sixteen of the 30-plus harbor islands are part of **Boston Harbor Island State Park,** some others are city controlled; most are open all year, no fee. Reach by ferry to **Georges Island,** from there free water taxi in summer to **Lovells, Gallops, Grape, Pumpkin Islands.** Facilities vary and include boat piers, historic fortifications, rest rooms; picnic, camp with permit, fish, walk, hike, swim; Georges Island has information desk, concessions, Fort Warren, NHL; Harbor ferry and other cruise lines.

29. NEW ENGLAND AQUARIUM. Central Wharf, Open all year. Fee.

More than 2,000 exotic fish and aquatic animals; world's largest cylindrical glass tank holds 180,000 gallons, viewable from all levels; hands-on tidal pool exhibit; separate marine mammal pavilion, pool, with dolphin show; benches, harbor views; whale watch cruises.

30. CHILDREN'S MUSEUM. Museum Wharf, 300 Congress St. Open all year. Fee.

Truly a museum for children; creative activities to see, touch, do, and think about include newsroom, Japanese house, climbing sculpture.

31. COMPUTER MUSEUM. 300 Congress St. Open all year. Fee.

Hands-on exhibits, giant walk-through computer, videos, recreations tell story of computer revolution.

32. BOSTON TEA PARTY SHIP AND MUSEUM. Congress St. Bridge. Open all year. Fee.

Hands-on museum and replica ship with presentations and costumed guides; recreates voyage, tax, dumping of tea.

33. FISH PIER. Northern Ave.

Pier before "no-name" restaurant; scene of Boston's active fishing industry; fish markets, harbor industry color.

34. FORT POINT CHANNEL AREA. Summer, Congress sts., east of Fort Point Channel. Open all year. No fee.

"Soho of Boston," area of artists and studios, scheduled open houses and festivals.

BEACON HILL

This residential area of hills has been fashionable since the late 1700s. It is a delightful study of historic architecture, particularly when highlighted by the sun at dawn or dusk. Louisburg Square is a fascinating example. The neighborhood—designated a historic district, NRHP, and NHL—is bisected by Charles Street and its myriad small shops.

35. CHESTER HARDING HOUSE, *1808*, NHL. 16 Beacon St. Open all year. No fee.

Once home of artist, now Boston Bar Association; ring bell to see Federal reception room.

36. APPLETON–PARKER HOUSES, *c. 1818*. 39–40 Beacon St. (Women's City Club). Open all year, limited hours. Fee.

Elegant double house on Beacon Street; here Longfellow married Fanny Appleton.

37. CHARLES STREET MEETING HOUSE, *1807*. Charles and Mt. Vernon sts. Open all year by appointment. Fee.

Antislavery headquarters; Garrison spoke here, also Harriet Tubman, Frederick Douglass. Outside retains Federal style dominated by clock tower, belfry.

38. NICHOLS HOUSE MUSEUM. 55 Mt. Vernon St. Open summer, limited hours rest of year. Fee.

See private life of privileged wealthy of old Beacon Hill; tour home designed by Bulfinch, owned by Rose Standish Nichols; Nichols furnishings.

39. AFRICAN MEETING HOUSE, AFRICAN-AMERICAN NATIONAL HISTORIC SITE, *1806*, NRHP. 46 Joy St. Open all year. No fee.

Restored simple Federal brick; first black church in New England; now oldest surviving black church building in country. William Lloyd Garrison founded New England Anti-Slavery Society here 1832; tours interpret importance of meetinghouse in past and present; **Black Heritage Trail** information through National Park Service (13).

40. OLD WEST CHURCH, *1806*, NHL. 131 Cambridge St.

Handsome Federal; British destroyed original building; time nearly destroyed this one. Once used as library, now Methodist church.

41. FIRST HARRISON GRAY OTIS HOUSE, *1796*, NHL, SPNEA headquarters, 141 Cambridge St. Open all year. Fee.

Well-informed guidance through Charles Bulfinch's classic Federal; once home to Boston mayor and congressman Otis; focus on history, people, antiques; Federal period furnishings of early 1800s.

BACK BAY

This neighborhood, created in the mid-1800s when marshland was filled, provides an interesting study of nineteenth-century American architecture and way of life. Streets are named alphabetically in this designated historic district, NRHP. Here are Boston Public Garden, shops, galleries, cafes, residences, skyscrapers, museums, and churches with Tiffany stained glass windows. (See Back Bay map, page 325.)

42. BOSTON PUBLIC GARDEN, NRHP. Arlington, Boylston, Beacon, Charles sts. Open all year. No fee.

Paths through beautifully landscaped grounds featuring statuary, flowers, shrubs, trees, pond, ducklings, and the famous Swan Boats (open summer, fee).

43. GIBSON HOUSE MUSEUM, *1859*. 137 Beacon St. Open extended season, limited hours rest of year. Fee.

Brownstone, only Victorian house open to public in Boston's Back Bay; furnishings of 1890s. Gibson Society also offers walking tours, special events. Headquarters of Victorian Society, New England chapter.

44. FIRST BAPTIST CHURCH, *1872*, NRHP. Commonwealth Ave. at Clarendon St.

First church designed by Henry H. Richardson; frieze by Frédéric-Auguste Bartholdi, creator of Statue of Liberty; huge stained glass rose windows by Louis Tiffany.

45. (NEW) OLD SOUTH CHURCH, *1877*, NRHP. Newbury, Dartmouth, and Boylston sts.

North Italian Gothic built when Third Church of Boston left Old South Meeting House.

46. BOSTON PUBLIC LIBRARY, *1895*, NRHP. Boylston St., Copley Sq.

Designed by Charles Follen McKim, magnificent Renaissance structure harmonizes with varied architecture of Copley Square; has low profile in granite with arched win-

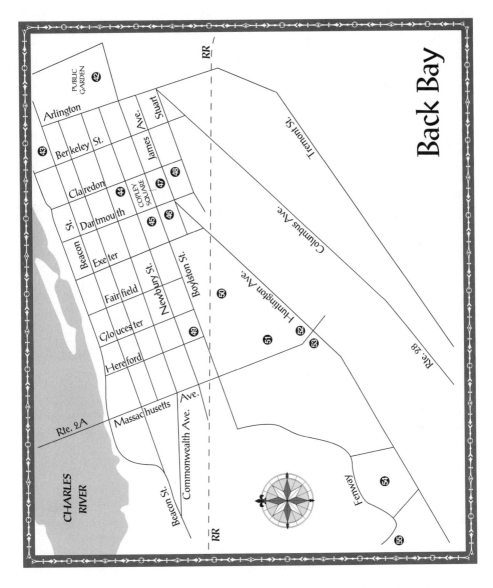

Back Bay

dows, bronze figures by Bela Pratt. Equally impressive interior is highlighted by murals by Abbey, Sargent.

47. TRINITY CHURCH, *1872–77*, NHL. Copley Sq.

Guided tours at limited hours and by appointment. Henry Hobson Richardson's masterpiece of Richardsonian Romanesque set in Copley Square; towers, turrets, pinnacles seem countless; rich interior is warmed by paintings and stained glass by John La

Boston Public Garden   (Massachusetts Office of Travel and Tourism)

Farge. Water levels below are regulated to saturate the 4,500 wooden piles supporting foundations. First minister, Phillips Brooks, wrote "O Little Town of Bethlehem."

48. JOHN HANCOCK OBSERVATORY. 200 Clarendon St., Copley Sq. Open all year. Fee.

Magnificently modern glass skyscraper, tallest in New England, has sixtieth-floor view plus multimedia exhibits.

49. INSTITUTE OF CONTEMPORARY ART. 955 Boylston St. Open all year. Fee.

Exhibitions present development of present-day art, selected modern masters plus innovative new talent. French Romanesque 1886 building was police station.

50. SKYWALK OBSERVATION DECK, PRUDENTIAL TOWER. Huntington Ave. or Boylston St.

Full 360-degree view from fiftieth floor. Prudential Center is convention center surrounded by pools, shops, restaurants, plazas.

51. CHRISTIAN SCIENCE CENTER. Huntington and Massachusetts aves. Open all year. No fee.

Nondenominational multimedia Bible exhibit "A Light unto My Path"; tour of Mapparium, glass globe of earth inside which you walk on glass bridge through equator; library, bookshop, news exhibitions; publishes *Christian Science Monitor*. Tour of 1894 "Mother Church" focuses on its Romanesque architecture.

52. MASSACHUSETTS HORTICULTURAL SOCIETY. 300 Massachusetts Ave. Open all year. No fee.

Major horticultural library.

53. SYMPHONY HALL, NRHP. Massachusetts at Huntington Ave. Open all year. Fee.

Magnificent hall has noted acoustics; home of Boston Symphony Orchestra, Boston Pops.

54. MUSEUM OF FINE ARTS, 465 Huntington Ave. Open all year. Fee.

One of world's best collections of fine and decorative arts from ancient to modern. Particularly notable are Asiatic art collection (world's largest); paintings from eleventh to twentieth century (especially French Impressionists); Egyptian old kingdom objects; actual rooms from old New England homes.

55. ISABELLA STEWART GARDNER MUSEUM, *1900*. 280 The Fenway. Open all year. Fee.

Italianate palace of Isabella Stewart Gardner, Boston's flamboyant hostess; priceless treasures and art; colorful gardens within. Classical music performed in Old World–style concert hall (fee).

56. ESPLANADE. Open all year. No fee.

A park along the Charles River. Summer performances (no fee) at Hatch Shell by Boston Pops Orchestra, Boston Symphony Orchestra, Boston Ballet.

57. MASSACHUSETTS GENERAL HOSPITAL BULFINCH PAVILION, *c. 1818*, NHL. Fruit St. off Charles St. Open all year, limited hours. No fee.

Guided tour of Bulfinch-designed building with Ether Dome, where ether first used in major surgery; slide presentation of hospital history.

58. MUSEUM OF SCIENCE, HAYDEN PLANETARIUM, OMNI THEATER, SCIENCE PARK. Open all year. Fee.

Extensive and varied displays, programs, demonstrations, some hands-on; all aspects and fields of science, fascinating to all ages. Separate shows in planetarium and Omni Theater, fees.

59. CHARLES RIVER RESERVATION.

From dams in Boston and Cambridge, along both sides of Charles River, to Newton Upper Falls; 961 acres; bike paths, riding trails.

POINTS OF INTEREST
OUTSIDE CENTRAL BOSTON

60. DORCHESTER HEIGHTS NATIONAL HISTORIC SITE, NHS. Thomas Park, South Boston. Open all year. No fee.

Monument to George Washington's victory when Henry Knox and men placed Ticonderoga cannons on heights and forced British to evacuate Boston March 17, 1776.

61. JOHN F. KENNEDY LIBRARY AND MUSEUM. University of Massachusetts, Boston Campus, off Morrissey Blvd. Dorchester. Open all year. Fee.

Exhibits relive career of JFK and politics; extensive archives available for research.

62. ARNOLD ARBORETUM, NHL. Arborway and Centre St. (Rte. 1), Jamaica Plain. Open all year. No fee.

Over 6,000 trees, shrubs, vines, many labeled; 300-acre park designed by Frederick Law Olmsted, funded by Harvard, established in 1880 by New Bedford merchant James Arnold.

63. MUSEUM OF THE NATIONAL CENTER OF AFRO-AMERICAN ARTISTS. Off Columbus Ave., 300 Walnut Ave., Roxbury. Open all year. Fee.

Changing exhibits of black American artists; housed in c. 1870 Gothic mansion of Roxbury puddingstone and sandstone.

64. CASTLE ISLAND. Gardner Way, South Boston. Yard open all year. No fee.

Entrance to Boston inner harbor; Fort Independence 1801.

CHARLESTOWN

Puritans came here in 1629 before settling Boston. Long a shipbuilding center, the town burned after the Battle of Bunker Hill. Restoration progresses, and streets meander by interesting old buildings to the Bunker Hill Monument and Charlestown Navy Yard, home of the USS *Constitution*.

65. CHARLESTOWN NAVY YARD, *1800*, NHL, National Historical Park. Charlestown. Open all year. No fee. USS CONSTITUTION, *1797*, NHL. Open all year, no fee.

USS *Constitution,* "Old Ironsides," oldest American ship afloat, in late 1700s blockaded pirates of North African Barbary states; defeated British Navy in War of 1812; now takes annual "turnaround cruise" in harbor July Fourth; tour historic ship with expert Navy guides. **Constitution Museum,** open all year, fee; history, construction, and life on board, multimedia presentation; building was 1832 engine house. **USS *Cassin Young,*** World War II destroyer; tours.

66. BUNKER HILL MONUMENT, *1826*, NHL. 43 Monument Sq., Monument Ave. off Warren Ave., Charlestown. Open all year. No fee.

Obelisk designed by Solomon Willard at redoubt site of fortification of Revolution's first battle; dioramas of battle; climb stairs to great view; living history programs.

67. CHARLES RIVER DAM. 250 Warren Ave., Charlestown. Open all year. No fee.

Explore and ride locks of Charles River Dam; exhibits and audiovisual history of dam and harbor.

CAMBRIDGE

Founded in 1630, Cambridge is home to Harvard College, the first school of higher learning, as well as MIT and Radcliffe. An academic, residential, and commercial center, Cambridge has college museums and walking tours. The wonderful old buildings that surround the Harvard Square area are best appreciated by walking.

68. LONGFELLOW NATIONAL HISTORIC SITE, *1759*, NHS, 105 Brattle St., Cambridge. Open all year. Fee.

Striking Georgian mansion with projected pedimented pavilion, built for loyalist Major John Vassal, became Washington's headquarters in 1775. Later Harvard Professor

Henry Wadsworth Longfellow and his wife, Fanny Appleton, created mecca for worldly greats including Charles Dickens; Longfellow lived forty-five years here, wrote most of his famous works; books and furnishings remain much as left by Longfellows in 1882. (While here plan also to see Harvard, MIT, Christ Church, historic and architecturally important houses.)

69. NEW ENGLAND SPORTS MUSEUM. Cambridgeside Galleria. Open all year. Fee.

Focus is history of sports in New England, professional and amateur; photos, trophies, videos, hands-on games; Ted Williams's locker, Marvin Hagler's boxing gloves, and life-size statue of Larry Bird.

LYNN

L ynn was settled in 1629. A meetinghouse was built, and the congregation gathered under the leadership of Reverend Stephen Bachiler. His lifestyle and beliefs were too liberal for early Lynn, however, and he was asked to leave. (Later he founded Hampton, New Hampshire—where in his nineties he was also asked to leave, for similar reasons.) In 1635 two shoemakers, Philip Kertland and Edmund Bridges, introduced the shoe industry that governed the economy of Lynn for nearly three centuries. The shoe industry grew: John Adams Dagyr improved quality and efficiency; Ebenezer Breed introduced morocco leather; the sewing machine and Jan Matzeliger's lasting machine were invented. The industry moved from small shoemakers' shops to large brick manufacturing centers. In another industry, Lynn's Thomson-Houston Electric Company merged in 1892 with the Edison General Electric Company and evolved into General Electric Company.

Women also played distinctive parts in Lynn's history. During the late 1700s many business ventures and ships' departures were scheduled based on the mystical and clairvoyant powers of Molly Pitcher. In the 1800s Maria Mitchell, an astronomer, became the first woman member of the American Academy of Arts and Sciences (see Nantucket, Maria Mitchell Birthplace). In 1873, Lydia E. Pinkham started the production of a patent medicine that became as familiar in households as today's aspirin. Called Lydia Pinkham Elixir, it was produced at 271 Western Avenue in Lynn until 1973. Also in Lynn, Mary Baker Eddy founded the Church of Christ, Scientist in 1879.

1. MARY BAKER EDDY HOUSE, *c. 1870s*. 12 Broad St. Open extended season and by appointment, no fee.

In a rocking chair in an attic room of this house, Mary Baker Patterson completed the final fourteen pages of her book *Science and Health* in 1875. It was the culmination of nine years of prayer, searching the Scriptures, and teaching and practicing metaphysical healing. Nine years earlier Mary had experienced what she was convinced was miraculous healing through reading and insight into the Scriptures. Her book set down her basic beliefs and proved to be the first step in the articulation of Christian Science doctrine. Here in her front parlor, she was ordained as a minister of her faith. Here she married Asa Gilbert Eddy in 1877. From here she preached in Boston and in 1879 received the charter for the Church of Christ, Scientist. A few of the furnishings belonged to Mrs. Eddy, and the colors and additional furnishings are of the type and period she would have used.

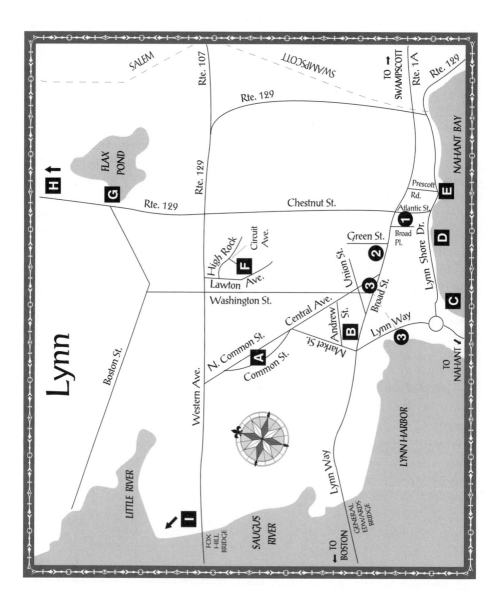

2. LYNN HISTORICAL SOCIETY, HYDE–MILLS HOUSE, *1836.* 125 Green St. Open all year, fee. Research library.

Lynn history unfolds as you walk through the museum within the Hyde–Mills House. The importance of the shoe industry in Lynn becomes obvious in displays of tools, methods, materials. A unique medallion of 234 different shoe soles has one for each manufacturer in Lynn in 1892. Early division of labor in the shoe industry found women working at home on uppers. Men attached uppers to the soles in small shoe shops like the one on display at Lynn Heritage State Park, on loan from Lynn Historical Society. The men worked amid lively discussions of politics and religion. In 1832 women began organizing trade unions; the home cottage industry was moving to small factories, and lines were being drawn between owners and workers. The museum has four period rooms tracing Lynn history and people from 1776 to 1876 through its extensive decorative arts collection. The museum wing features changing exhibitions.

3. LYNN HERITAGE STATE PARK, Visitor Information Center. 590 Washington St. Open all year, limited hours; no fee. Excellent introductory video. Waterfront Park. 154 Lynnway, via pedestrian overpass from Community College grounds. Open all year, no fee.

The Visitor Information Center features permanent state-of-the-art exhibitions of Lynn history—shoemaking, General Electric, and especially Lynn people. Included within this exciting modern museum is a separate 1830 early shoe shop, a "ten footer." Benches are set up, tools ready, the air full of the aroma of shoemaking, the apparent clutter just waiting for cordwainers to appear.

Five-acre Waterfront Park has boardwalk, marina, restaurants, and benches where you can enjoy views and picnic. There is an impressive Lynn mural on the side of a building past the boardwalk area. The goal of the multipanel mosaic mural is to celebrate Lynn and depict Lynn's past and present. It has nine panels with a total area of 650 square feet and is made of Venetian tiles and thousands of small ceramic pieces made by people of Lynn. It was created under the direction of artists Lillian and Marvin Killen Rosenberg.

BEACHES, PARKS, OTHER POINTS OF INTEREST

A. **Lynn Common,** NRHP. Shaped like sole of shoe; 1873 Civil War Monument. **Lynn Public Library,** 1900, classic Greek–Roman Revival stone structure with full-height Corinthian columns; interior stone, marble, tile floors; walls of ornate carvings, columns, pilasters, a huge mural, and elaborate ceilings. **Old West Burying Ground,** earliest settlers' graves. Central Green circled by different eras of history and architecture.

B. **GAR Building and Museum,** 1885, 58 Andrew St. Open all year by appointment.

Donation. Military museum and memorial to Lynn men and women who served in Civil War; Lynn's Post 5 was largest veterans' post in country; multiwar displays of photos, badges, histories, swords, guns, flags, uniforms; top-floor Grand Hall walls lined with 1,148 pictures of Civil War veterans from Lynn.

C. Nahant Beach. Causeway to Nahant, off Lynn Shore Dr. Open all year. Parking fee in summer. Long, open sandy beach, links with Lynn's beach (D); bathhouse, concessions, beaches, lifeguards, path, swimming.

D. Lynn Beach. Lynn Shore Dr. Open all year. No fee. Open sandy crescent, paved paths, benches, lifeguards; biking, picnicking, swimming; limited street parking.

E. Red Rock. Lynn Shore Dr. at Prescott Rd. Open all year. No fee. Small grassy promontory; a favorite meditation site of Mary Baker Eddy; benches, picnicking; no parking.

F. High Rock Park. End Circuit Ave. Open all year. No fee. Highest point in Lynn; crenellated, castlelike tower has 50-mile panoramic views; playground; limited parking.

G. Flax Pond. Chestnut St. (Rte. 129) opposite Boston St. Open all year. No fee. Pond where women soaked, washed, prepared flax in colonial times; bathhouse, benches, lifeguards, playground; limited street parking.

H. Lynn Woods. Access: Rte. 129 (Chestnut St.) to Great Woods Rd. Open all year. No fee. 2,000 acres woods, streams, ponds, hills, boulders, caves; stories of pirate deeds and treasures; nature classes, guided walking tours through Friends of Lynn Woods; picnicking, skiing.

I. Saugus Ironworks National Historic Site, c. 1650, NHS. 244 Central St., Saugus. Open all year. No fee. Reconstruction of first complete ironworks in country; Ironmakers House, iron furnace, forge, slitting mill; demonstrations.

NAHANT

Nahant, incorporated in 1853 as the smallest town in the state, began as common woodlots and pastureland for people of Lynn. By the 1820s summer hotels were welcoming Boston's aristocracy, who came by steamboat to enjoy silvery beaches and beautiful ocean vistas. Summer visitors to "Boston's Gold Coast" included Harriet Beecher Stowe, Daniel Webster, Henry Wadsworth Longfellow, John and Jessie Fremont, Oliver Wendell Holmes, and Elizabeth and Louis Agassiz. Cornelius Coolidge, architect and builder of some of Boston's Beacon Hill mansions, laid out roads and built substantial homes at East Point. Frederick Tudor arrived in 1824 and built a hotel, Maolis Gardens, and the Town Wharf. Steamboats once docked there; now the wharf is home to Nahant's active fishing and lobstering fleet and her summer flotillas of yachts, sailboats, and other small craft.

The best way to see Nahant is to cycle or drive, as there is no public parking beyond Nahant Beach, and the historical society has the only point of interest open to the public. Here you can learn Nahant's interesting past and imagine meeting Cabots and Lodges, poets and governors, judges, ambassadors, congressmen, cabinet members, Harvard presidents, tennis greats Sears and Dwight, and U.S. Presidents Taft and both Roosevelts, as well as people for whom cities were named, Lowells and Lawrences.

At 280 Nahant Road at Ocean Street is the Nahant Country Club and **Nahant Historical Society** headquarters and museum (open all year, limited hours; no fee). Intriguing special exhibits vary. The country club's old stone walls of Nahant granite were part of the c. 1824 summer home of Ice King Frederick Tudor. He persevered through scoffing, bankruptcy, and debtor's imprisonment to create and capture the ice market for Havana and Charleston, as well as icing English drinks as far away as Canton and Calcutta. He devised insulated boats for refrigeration, delivering New England ice in tropical lands in the 1830s.

The **Nahant Public Library,** on Nahant Road at the corner of Pleasant Street, began as the state's third public library in 1819. In 1895 this neo-Gothic structure of Weymouth seam-faced granite, Ohio sandstone trim, and green slate roof was built to house the library and town hall, now separate. Dark cypress woodwork in the main room is complemented by quartered oak in the impressive reading room. Both have intricately carved molding, panels, and fireplaces. Museum exhibits are displayed.

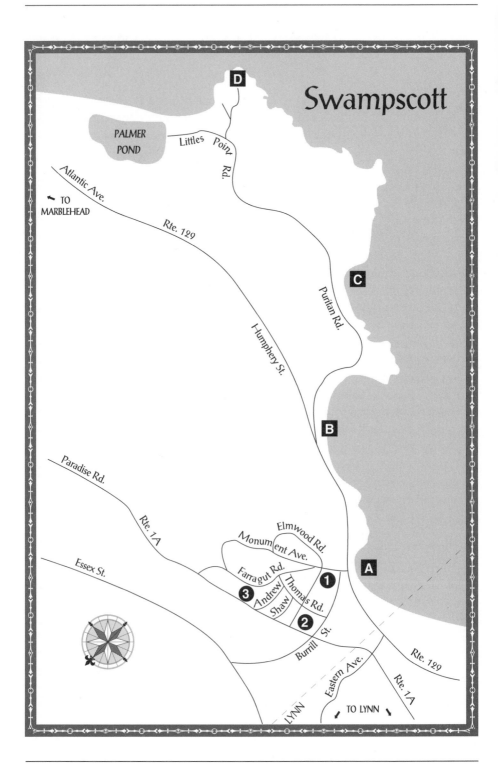

SWAMPSCOTT

Indians from Maine came south in summer to hunt and fish along the rocky coast that is now Swampscott.[27] They set up their headquarters on Black Will's Cliff, present site of Hawthorne-by-the-Sea Restaurant. They were followed by white settlers who established a fishing village. Here Theophilus Brackett invented the seaworthy Swampscott Dory in 1841, and here Ebenezer Thorndike adapted the lobster pot to a rectangular design (easier to stack). In 1852 the village seceded from Lynn to form Swampscott. Post–Civil War prosperity brought wealth to numerous Boston entrepreneurs, and these "captains of industry" began building hotels and summer estates in Swampscott. Here Elihu Thomson, cofounder of General Electric, built his home and laboratory. Frederick Law Olmsted designed the street layout, gardens, and park area along Monument Avenue. The town still fosters active fishing and lobstering activities and continues to draw summer visitors to its ever-changing, ever-beautiful coast.

1. ELIHU THOMSON HOUSE, TOWN ADMINISTRATION BUILDING, *1889*, NHL. Monument Ave. and Elmwood Rd. Open all year, no fee.

Swampscott may well be unique in the grandeur of its town administrative offices, housed within the manor house of General Electric cofounder Elihu Thomson. The red brick Georgian Revival mansion rose in 1889. The front facade has a Corinthian Palladian-style front portico, quoined corners, broken scroll pediments, and pink Vermont slate hip roof capped by balustrades repeated over the portico and crowned by urn finials. The greatest pleasure awaits within—probably the finest woodwork of its time found in New England today. Each molding, fireplace wall, window, and panel is hand carved of hard oak. Now town offices occupy the preserved elegance of the first floor's sitting, dining, breakfast, music, library, and billiard rooms. Upstairs the study dominates, with deep mahogany paneling and carved oak in Moorish flavor, a theme that carries even to the fireplace tiles. Speaking tube outlets are still present in this home, which was illuminated by electricity long before the public knew of such a possibility. The hall gave access to Thomson's laboratory above the attached carriage house. Thomson was an electrical engineer, inventor, and teacher and held more than 700 patents. He invented the first high-frequency generator and transformer, three-coil generator, electric welding by incandescent method, and watt-hour meter.

2. MARY BAKER EDDY HOUSE, *c. 1885*. **23 Paradise Rd. Open extended season, limited hours rest of year, and by appointment; fee.**

In 1865 Mary Baker Eddy (then Mary Patterson), an established writer with deep interest in church and temperance work, rented rooms in this bright, cheery home. It then had lovely gardens and lawns, a willow-shaded pond, and a meandering stream called the Jordan by its owners. On February 1, 1866, an event occurred that changed Mary's life. On her way to a temperance meeting in Lynn, she slipped, fell, and severely injured herself—to the extent that doctors felt she might not live and certainly would never walk again. On Sunday, February 4, while reading Matthew 9:1–8, she experienced a revelation of deep eternal truth. She left her bed and walked into the parlor, where friends were waiting in great sadness, fearing for her life. The joy of her miraculous healing started Mary on a nine-year search for an understanding of that healing and for insight into how she might impart this healing knowledge to others (see Lynn 1).

3. JOHN HUMPHREY HOUSE, *c. 1637*, HS. **99 Paradise Rd. Open all year, limited hours and by appointment; no fee.**

A gem of a house, with parts that may date to the 1600s, the John Humphrey House is the oldest in Swampscott. It is further distinguished by the people for whom it was named and probably built, Massachusetts Bay Colony's first deputy governor, John Humphrey, and his wife, Lady Susan. It has had many additions and alterations and was moved to this site in 1891. The small front hall has a seventeenth-century banister and narrow, steep stairway. The parlor leaps to Victorian times with furnishings and treasures from Swampscott's summer hotel era, including appropriate costumes. The back of the house shows its age, especially in the deep patina of unusual "king's boards," 2-foot-wide boards that line the stair wall. The king's mark, showing lumber meant only for the Royal Navy, is visible. That Humphrey dared to use this wood openly was sign of royal favor. Even in its most rustic state, this house was grand for its period. Some original Delft fireplace tiles remain and were probably brought to Swampscott by the Humphreys in 1634. The upstairs was finished, an unusual feature that early. In the oldest room, a cutout in the wall lets you see the hand-hewn beams, handmade bricks, and mortar mixed with seaweed. Records indicate the Humphreys brought timber and bricks with them to build their home.

BEACHES, PARKS, OTHER POINTS OF INTEREST

A. King's Beach. Humphrey St. Open all year. No fee. Lifeguard, wide sandy crescent; swimming; street parking only.

B. Fisherman's Beach (Blaney's). Puritan Rd. Open all year. No fee. Crescent of fine sand, **town pier; Fish House,** built by town 1896, only town-owned fish house in New England; **Chaisson Park** with memorials; lifeguard, benches, views; swimming; street parking.

C. **Whales Beach and Eisemanns Beach.** Puritan Rd. "Exedra," a semicircular stone seat, overlooks the beach and view; footpath to beach from parking lot off Humphrey St., sticker parking only.

D. **Marian Court Junior College, White Court,** 1895, 35 Littles Point Rd. Open as school, tour by appointment. No fee. Area of grand oceanfront mansions; White Court, a 30-room mansion, was summer White House for President Calvin Coolidge, 1925; lavish detail added after Coolidges by Falvey family; marble, pegged wood, inlaid parquet floors, hand-painted murals on canvas covering walls and ceilings, paneling in teak; mansion sold to Sisters of Mercy and renamed Marian Court 1954; expansive views of sweeping lawns and sea.

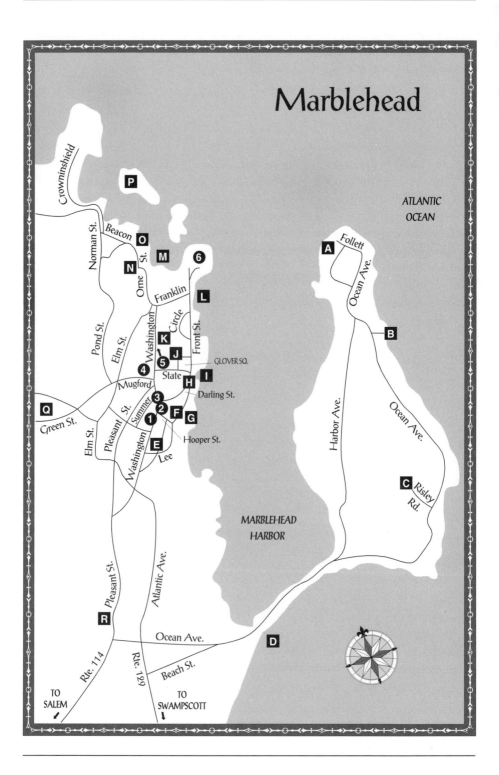

MARBLEHEAD

Marblehead was an early fishing station, part of Salem, where the first men came from Britain and Europe in spring to fish and returned home in the fall. By the mid-1700s Marblehead was a flourishing port with sixty merchants engaged in foreign trade and over eighty schooners plying the fishing banks off Newfoundland. This most prosperous period saw merchant greats Colonial Jeremiah Lee and "King" Robert Hooper build beautiful mansions. Hooper mansions still stand at 181 and 187 Washington Street, 8 Hooper Street, and 69 Pleasant Street; Lee mansions at 161 and 185 Washington Street.

The Revolution halted commercial enterprises. Colonial John Glover was ordered by General Washington to equip and man vessels for military use. The first commissioned privately owned vessel was Glover's *Hannah*, which sailed from Beverly Harbor September 5, 1775, claimed by both Marblehead and Beverly as the first naval ship in the country. Few towns gave as much to the Revolution in men, money, and livelihoods as did Marblehead.

Following the war merchants such as John Hooper, Sr., John Hooper, Jr., and Colonel William R. Lee reestablished their family fortunes and Marblehead's prestige in the world of trade. Fishing vessels returned to the Grand Banks. In 1846 disaster struck. Sixty-five seamen were lost in the Grand Banks during a brutal storm. In 1877 a devastating fire took seventy-six Marblehead buildings, leaving ninety families homeless and 1,500 people out of work. Marbleheaders rebuilt only to witness another disastrous fire in 1888, which basically ended the shoe industry. Yet a new industry was beginning. The beauties of Marblehead Neck and the magnificent protected harbor it created were discovered. In the 1860s summer visitors came to tents, then cottages, then grand summer hotels. The excitement of yacht racing—the joy of taut sails and salt spray—brought Marblehead the title "yachting capital of the world."

1. JEREMIAH LEE MANSION, *1768*, NHL, HS. 161 Washington St. Open extended season, fee.

Lee was a "codfish aristocrat" whose fleet of ships took cured Marblehead-caught fish to the West Indies and Europe and returned with salt, wine, iron, molasses, and sugar. Profits from this lucrative trade were lavishly dispensed to produce one of the finest mansions in colonial America for Jeremiah and Martha Swett Lee and their six surviving children. The pure Georgian three-story mansion features central pavilion with fanlight in pediment, quoined corners, prominent dentils, Ionic-columned portico, and cupola-capped hip roof.

The ten-panel Georgian door leads to pre-Revolutionary elegance. The spacious entry has a Santo Domingo mahogany true boxed staircase with stair-end carvings of rosette and leaf motif and intricate balusters of three alternate rope twist patterns. On the left is the Great Room where Washington, Lafayette, Monroe, and Jackson were received. There are full native pine panels, hand-carved woodwork, and Grinling Gibbons–style fireplace wall. Rare original handmade landscape wallpapers in three rooms have been traced to the London manufactory of paper stainer William Squire. Other treasures include fireplace tile work of John Sadler and Guy Green of Liverpool, nineteenth-century copies of John Singleton Copley portraits of Jeremiah and Martha Lee, Lee side chairs of Massachusetts Chippendale, American side chairs from John Hancock's Beacon Hill home, and other furnishings appropriate to the period and the social level of the Lees.

2. KING HOOPER MANSION, *c. 1728*, NRHP. 8 Hooper St. Open all year, limited hours; fee.

The mansion is a combination of two gracious homes. Greenleaf Hooper built a three-story gambrel-roof home about 1728. In 1747 his son, "King" Robert Hooper, added the front three-story Georgian mansion with its facade of quoined corners, wood grooved to resemble stone, and dentiled cornices. Robert Hooper was a leading merchant before the Revolution. His ships took the name Marblehead to nearly every port in Europe and the West Indies. He was called King for his benevolence and integrity as well as for his power and influence, a rare compliment from hardworking, independent fishermen. Torn between two loyalties, he left for Nova Scotia at the time of the Revolution. Years later he returned, but he never regained wealth or prestige.

The mansion demonstrates eighteenth-century prosperity, evident in the drawing room with its unusual double-dentil moldings, hand-carved paneling, and portrait copies of Washington, Lafayette, and Mrs. Hooper. (There were four Mrs. Hoopers and eleven children.) The borning room in the rear section has old stenciling and a curved ceiling of earlier Colonial style. The dining room has moldings, fluted pilasters, and Delft-tiled fireplace. Fine paneling of doors and fireplaces in bedrooms was curved by ships' carpenters to create the illusion of a ship's cabin. The third floor has an unusual ballroom with original chandelier in an eight-sided dome. It is now the Marblehead Art Association gallery.

3. ST. MICHAEL'S CHURCH, *1714.* NRHP. 11 Summer St.

St. Michael's Church is the result of a dream of early British and Marblehead sea captains who wanted to build a handsome church in which to worship as Anglicans. It was designed from captains' memories of a Christopher Wren church in London and constructed by American ships' carpenters. It was one of the first Anglican churches to arise, despite much strong Puritan disapproval. The second minister, David Mossom, officiated at George and Martha Washington's wedding in Virginia, where he moved after serving here. During the Revolution St. Michael's was forcibly closed. When American independence was declared, the historic bell was too exuberantly rung by Patriots who broke into the church. It had to be recast by Patriot Paul Revere, whose name is clearly marked on it.

In 1888, rescued from fire damage, decay, and subsequent renovations, St. Michael's again emerged as the handsome church dreamed of by her founders. Beautiful woods and stained glass windows of the Victorian Gothic sanctuary contribute to an air of warmth, dignity, and serenity.

4. TOWN HOUSE, *1727*, NRHP. Market Square, Washington and Mugford sts. External view, open for special events. GAR Museum, second floor, HS artifacts.

Marblehead's "cradle of liberty" is possibly the oldest American municipal building to serve its town continuously. Here Committee of Safety Patriots led Marbleheaders toward revolution, Vice President Elbridge Gerry began his political career, and men gathered to answer their country's call to the wars of two centuries. Built on an old jail site, this building housed public markets, town meetings, school, and town offices. It hosted Civil War GAR (Grand Army of the Republic) meetings, stored Fire Department equipment, and was Police Department headquarters. The stately Georgian appears Greek Revival, having been raised and placed on a high granite foundation in 1832.

5. FIRST CHURCH OF CHRIST IN MARBLEHEAD, OLD NORTH CHURCH, *1824*. 41 Washington St.

In early days missionary William Walton served as preacher and teacher, the town's only paid officer. In 1668 Reverend Samuel Cheever accepted the invitation of the "Church on the Old Hill" to become its new pastor. In 1715 two men were considered for his assistant: Edward Holyoke (home standing at 119 Washington) and John Barnard (home standing at 7 Franklin). When Barnard won, those strongly supporting Holyoke left to form a second church.

Reverend Barnard proved to be a dynamic leader not only of his church, which he served for fifty-five years, but of the community, doing much to help establish its early commercial prosperity. Today's beautiful stone and wood edifice was erected in 1824 and substantially remodeled in 1886. The cupola-topped bell tower proudly holds the 52-inch 1696 gilded copper codfish weathervane, a symbol both of Christianity and of the "sacred cod" of Massachusetts.

6. FORT SEWALL, *1742*. Front St. Open all year, no fee. Benches, rest rooms; picnicking; limited parking.

In defense of their settlement, Marbleheaders erected earthworks here as early as 1644. In 1742 much of what remains today was built with a fund of 716 pounds allotted by the

General Court. Sir Harry Frankland, collector of the Port of Boston, was retained to oversee the construction. When he arrived at Fountain Inn off Orne Street, he saw a ragged but beautiful sixteen-year-old girl named Agnes Surriage scrubbing the stairs. She captured his attention. With her parents' permission Sir Harry made her his ward and educated her in Boston. She traveled everywhere with him, much to the consternation of Massachusetts and London society, who ostracized her. It wasn't until 1755, when Agnes saved Sir Harry's life during an earthquake in Lisbon, that Sir Harry married Agnes. During the War of 1812, the fort, named for Chief Justice Sewall, was repaired and manned. British prisoners were held here. The fort was again manned during the Civil War. From this rugged promontory, a park since 1892, there is a panoramic view of Little Harbor, Gerry Island, Boston Bay, Cat Island, and Marblehead Neck.

BEACHES, PARKS, OTHER POINTS OF INTEREST

A. Chandler–Hovey Park. Follett St. Open all year. No fee. Rest rooms, picnic tables; small park with magnificent views of harbor, ideal for watching Race Week. Walk rocky ledges to **Marblehead Light;** white stone lighthouse was built 1835, replaced by steel tower 1895; one of few lights to show steady green light, now automated.

B. Castle Rock. Ocean Ave. Open all year. No fee. Just past mansion built by a Lydia Pinkham heir is public path to spectacular open headland; carefully climb rocky ledges for great ocean vista; limited parking.

C. Marblehead Neck Wildlife Sanctuary. Risley Rd. Open all year. No fee. Mortared stone gates lead from cul-de-sac to paths within sanctuary; bird watching, picnicking, nature study; limited parking. Massachusetts Audubon Society.

D. Devereaux Beach. Ocean Ave. at causeway to Neck. Open all year. Parking fee in summer. Gravelly, sandy crescent beach; covered picnic areas; lifeguards; rest rooms.

E. Abbot Hall, 1876, NRHP, Washington Sq. Open all year as Town Hall. No fee. Tall, massive Romanesque Victorian seen from everywhere in town or harbor is severely geometric with variety of brick patterns, windows, colors, dominating clock and bell tower. Selectmen's Meeting Room has *The Spirit of '76* painting by Archibald M. Willard of fifer, drummer, and drummer boy, given by General John H. Devereaux. Marblehead Historical Commission maintains small museum of Marblehead's proud history; displays include deeds, ships, maps, and memorabilia of fishermen and famous sons; gift shop.

F. Lafayette House, 1731. 2 Union St. Private. Marblehead legend says this Georgian has missing corner as Patriot homeowner chopped it off to allow Lafayette's grand coach to pass; or it could have been to allow passage of rum wagons, whose drivers tended to sample their loads.

The Spirit of 76, *Marblehead*   (Massachusetts Office of Travel and Tourism)

G. Crocker Park. Front St. Open all year. No fee. Rocky ledges, fantastic view of harbor, neck, causeway, Marblehead's roofline collage capped by Abbot Hall; benches, paths; swimming, picnicking.

H. Front Street. Walk from Washington Sq. down Lee, along Front St.; see amazingly adaptive architecture clinging to headland's ledges; move from more formal Georgian and Federal to older Colonials of Front Street, homes of landsmen and fishermen, shoemakers and ships' carpenters.

I. Town Wharf. Front and State sts. Open all year. No fee. Heart of great boating interests—builders, yacht brokers, marine supply, repair; stone wharf; always boats moving in for wharf services; rest rooms, benches; picnicking; limited parking.

J. General Glover House, 1762, NHL. 11 Glover Sq. Private. John Glover first marine general; he and his Marblehead men evacuated Washington's troops from Long Island by boat in almost total silence, carried Washington across the Delaware, led advance on Trenton. Glover was shoemaker, fisherman, successful merchant, built this Georgian; after Revolution went back to being cobbler to make ends meet.

K. Elbridge Gerry Birthplace, 1742, NRHP. 44 Washington St. Private. Born 1744, Elbridge Gerry was signer of Declaration of Independence; representative to Continental Congress, Provincial Congress, Constitutional Convention; governor of Massachusetts; vice president under President James Madison.

L. Screeching Woman Cove, Fort Beach. Front St. at Circle and Franklin sts. Open all year. No fee. Small rocky beach, best at high tide, views. Name comes from story of murder of sea captain's daughter by pirates; ghost of victim said to return with bloodcurdling screams.

M. Gas House Beach. Off Orne St. Open all year. No fee. Small sandy beach; at low tide can walk, with care, to nearby island.

N. Old Burial Hill. Orne St. One of highest points; site of first meetinghouse; intriguing old gravestones of churchyard amid rocky ledges, oldest stone 1681; 600 graves from Revolution, including General Glover's; views.

O. Fountain Park. Orne St. Open all year. No fee. Old fort site; headland views of islands, Marblehead, open sea.

P. Brown Island. Crowninshield Rd. Near end of Beacon St. Open all year. No fee. At low tide can walk, with care, to island, Trustees of Reservations.

Q. Old Powder House, c. 1755. 37 Green St. Exterior view. Powder stored for French and Indian Wars, Revolution, War of 1812.

R. Abbot Public Library, 235 Pleasant St. Open all year. No fee. Contains interesting art gallery, sculpture by Beverly Semans, ship models; Marblehead historical collection room.

SALEM

A small group led by Roger Conant founded Salem,[28] then known as Naumkeag, in 1626. John Endicott became colonial governor two years later. The following year six ships laden with 400 settlers and 140 cattle arrived. The people gathered their church and established a settlement. In 1630 the Crown appointed John Winthrop governor. He and a group of fellow Puritans arrived in force. Winthrop remained only a few weeks in Salem, moving the seat of government to Charlestown. Though Endicott was replaced as governor, he and Roger Conant and others continued to lead their settlement. It grew to be the successful trading and fishing village called Salem, from *shalom*, meaning peace. The year 1692 saw a dark moment in Salem's history: the infamous witch trials. The first people were accused of witchcraft on February 29, 1692. Twenty people were put to death and several hundred imprisoned, and all lived in fear. By May 1693 sanity returned.

In the late 1600s the first of Salem's many great merchants, Philip English, established prosperous trade with the West Indies, Spain, France, and Holland. In the mid-1700s, wealthy merchant and shipowner Richard Derby added to Salem's wealth and prestige as a seaport. During the Revolution Salem outfitted 158 vessels as privateers, building larger vessels for the purpose. After the war these larger ships were able to sail halfway around the world and open up new and lucrative trade routes. Merchants such as Elias Hasket Derby, William Gray, and Joseph Peabody kept Salem's docks alive and her harbor filled. Rugged Salem captains and seamen were maritime pioneers who opened trade with Calcutta, Bombay, Canton, Java, Sumatra, Madagascar, Zanzibar, Manila, Mocha, and Sydney between 1784 and 1800. They rounded the Cape of Good Hope, navigating rough, uncharted waters in sailing vessels dependent on wind and the mercy of currents and storms. They contended with sickness, death, hunger, loneliness, mutiny, and pirates. When they reached port, they faced possibly unfriendly cultures and the competition of British and European merchants. Nevertheless, treasures from foreign ports began to show in homes of successful sea captains and merchants. Federal architect and wood-carver Samuel McIntire created many beautiful mansions, a special wealth Salem preserves today.

Decline began with the War of 1812. Following the Civil War, competition from other larger, deeper ports and railroads brought further decline in Salem's maritime prosperity. Land enterprises began—tanneries and manufacturing of cotton, jute bagging, boots, shoes, lead—plus coastal trade in coal for mills here and in Lowell and Lawrence. Salem remains rich in beautifully preserved architecture, from early Colonials to the wonderful Georgians and Federals of the city's own Samuel McIntire.

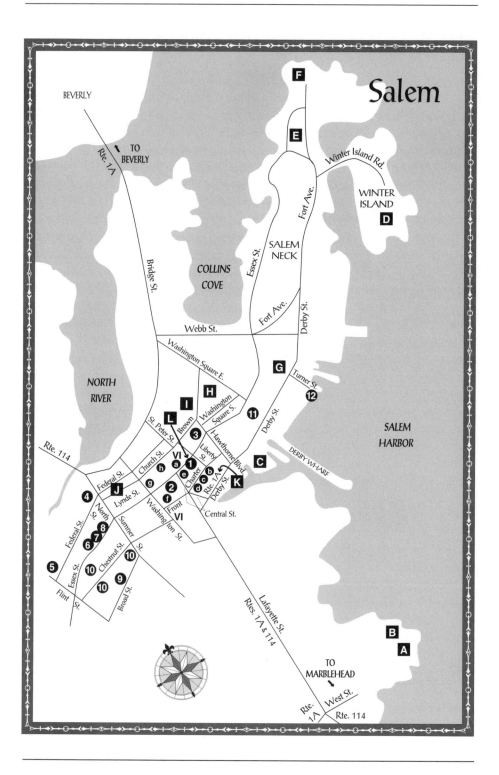

1. PEABODY ESSEX MUSEUM, *1824*, NRHP. Entrance on Liberty St. Open all year, fee.

This oldest continuously operating museum in the country is a maritime museum with special focus on worldwide ethnology and Essex County natural history. You are a captive the moment you enter and remain so through the many rooms of permanent and changing exhibitions. You sail historic ships with amazing men and women to unbelievable ports. Comprehensive collections include logbooks, documents, navigational devices, tools, and centuries of figureheads, including one carved by McIntire. There are portraits of ships, merchants, and captains of Salem and the Orient. You find over 700 ship models; extensive China trade collections, including export china; ships' furnishings; scrimshaw. Crowninshield family mementos feature a full-scale reproduction of the saloon of their yacht *Cleopatra's Barge.*

Salem ships returned from early coasting ventures and more exotic trade with China, India, Sumatra, the West Indies, and Pacific Islands. They opened the world, and Salem people were never the same again. The East India Marine Society was founded in 1799 to care for families should harm come to a seafaring member, to improve navigation for sailing trade adventures, and to form this museum of "natural and artificial curiosities." A two-stemmed pipe brought from Sumatra in 1799 was the first item of ethnology in the museum collection. Farsighted sea captains were America's first contact with unknown cultures. These cultures are now revealed here, where you learn about lifestyles of Pacific islands, India, Japan, China, and American Indians as they were before the influence of other cultures. The Polynesian collection is the country's finest, and the collection of Japanese household arts and crafts is the best in the world. The natural history section also began in 1799, with an elephant's tooth. Other "natural curiosities" followed—the first stuffed ostrich, peacock, penguin. Now the natural history department focuses on treasures of Essex County and coastal New England.

2. ESSEX STREET MALL. Pedestrian mall on Essex St. Open all year, no fee. Red line follows Salem's Heritage Trail.

East India Square Fountain ("a" on map). Symbolizes Salem's historic relationship to ocean and Far East.

Goult–Pickman House (b), c. 1660, NRHP. Liberty and Charter sts. Private. One of oldest houses in Salem; home of Judge Benjamin Lynde of Boston Massacre trial.

Charter Street Burying Point (c), 1637. Oldest graveyard in Salem; only known original stone of a *Mayflower* passenger (Richard More); Governor Simon Bradstreet's tomb at highest point; also Chief Justice Benjamin Lynde, Samuel McIntire, witchcraft judges Reverend John Higginson, Judge John Hathorne. Nearby is **Salem Witch Trials Memorial.** Liberty St. off Charter St.

Grimshawe House (d). 53 Charger St. Private. Peabody family home at time when Nathaniel Hawthorne successfully courted daughter Sophia.

Bulfinch Building (e). 1811. 11 Central St. Federal by Boston's Bulfinch; housed bank and insurance office where Nathaniel Bowditch presided and was first insurance actuary; 1899 Salem Fraternity established America's oldest boys' club here.

Old Town Hall, Derby Square (f), 1816, NRHP. Front St. Open all year. No fee. Was town hall and market, dedicated by President Monroe; brick Federal highlighted by delicately detailed windows with fan-arched heads, center Palladian window; upstairs formal hall, graceful chandeliers. Derby Square was site of McIntire's magnificent Elias Hasket Derby mansion, razed after Derby died.

City Hall (g), 1838, NRHP. 93 Washington St. Open all year. No fee. Greek Revival highlighted by wreath-decorated frieze and gilded McIntire eagle; second-floor Council Chamber remains as in 1838, lined with portraits, with royal blue wainscoting, ornamental gold.

Lyceum (h). 43 Church St. Open all year as restaurant. Began 1830, when lecture hall hosted speakers Webster, Lowell, Adams, Holmes, Thoreau, Mann; in 1877 Alexander Graham Bell made first public demonstration of telephone from here when he spoke to assistant Thomas Watson in Boston; wooden building replaced by brick before 1894.

3. PEABODY ESSEX MUSEUM, 1848, NRHP. Essex St. entrance 132 Essex St. Open all year, fee. Museum houses within grounds, publications, outstanding research library, museum shop, programs.

Here are the treasures of Salem. You see seven nationally significant historic houses beautifully and authentically furnished, a fascinating museum of history and art, and a one-of-a-kind research library. The central core is housed in two joined Victorian mansions, Plummer Hall, 1857, and John Tucker Daland House, 1851.

Plummer Hall, built as the Salem Athenaeum, has museum displays of priceless antiquity. Outstanding collections of historical artifacts, decorative and fine arts, and architecture reveal the lives of Salem's people from 1630 on. Three period rooms, among the country's earliest, were set up in 1907 by a pioneering preservationist of the Institute, George Francis Dow. There are interpretive displays of the seventeenth and eighteenth centuries and a special doll and toy world. The exhibits show the importance of Salem and Essex County in maritime trade, the resulting wealth, and how it was translated into artifacts and architecture.

The research library section of the Institute's central core is the **John Tucker Daland House,** designed by architect Gridley J. F. Bryant. Merchant Daland's regal drawing room is the reading room. Shelves of books reach toward tall ceilings; above twin ornate fireplaces are priceless urns on mantels topped with huge gilt mirrors.

On the grounds is a **Meetinghouse,** reconstructed in 1887 from seventeenth-century cut frame timbers thought to be from First Church of Salem. Nearby a "ten footer," the 1830 **Lye–Tapley Shoe Shop** from Lynn, is complete with all necessary tools for shoe workers in this early factory.

Historic houses are located on the grounds of the Peabody Essex Museum with access through the 132 Essex St. entrance. The c. 1684 **John Ward House**, NHL, is the oldest. It successfully creates the mood and appearance of the seventeenth century, with much framing and some floor sections from the original Colonial house. It was moved and restored by George Francis Dow and Essex Institute in 1910. Dow's front rooms and their furnishings interpret life and culture of the seventeenth century.

The Georgian **Crowninshield–Bentley House**, 1727, NRHP, 106 Essex St., is a rare example of Salem's interesting eighteenth century. Seafaring fish merchant John Crowninshield began the house in 1727. Additions and remodelings created a representative 1700s home in which the family lived until 1832. Crowninshields soon rivaled Derbys in their contribution to Salem's maritime supremacy. John Crowninshield's daughter, Elizabeth, married America's first millionaire, Elias Hasket Derby; and John's son, George, married Derby's sister, Mary. Reverend Dr. William Bentley—pastor, historian, naturalist, politician—lived here nearly thirty years, a boarder of widow Hannah Crowninshield. Bentley is best known as the writer of important diaries of New England, detailing the spirit as well as the facts of everyday life from his arrival in Salem as pastor in 1783 until his death in 1819.

The 1804 **Gardner–Pingree House**, NRHP, is at 128 Essex St. Considered by many to be Samuel McIntire's finest surviving work, it is everything a grand Federal mansion should be. The rhythm and balance of windows and string courses across the warm brick structure are crowned by a balustraded hip roof. The portico with beautifully carved Corinthian columns and pilasters draws the eye toward the delicately fan- and side-lighted classical McIntire door. Exquisite carvings and applied molded ornaments, McIntire's signature, accent the hall. Stairway balustrades and tread ends, detailed arch and door frames, and subtly elaborate cornices vie for your attention. The detail of fireplaces is unmatched—sheaves of wheat, rosettes, garlands, baskets of fruit, sprays of laurel, dentils, and reeded areas, are all deftly carved or applied. Furnishings, many items brought by captains from all over the world, demonstrate Salem's vast wealth before the War of 1812.

The 1818 **Andrew–Safford House**, NRHP, crown jewel of the late Federal period, at 13 Washington Square, is for external view only. Tall, monumental, vertical, this strong mansion features an elaborate Corinthian-columned and balustraded portico capped by a Palladian window. The smooth Flemish bond brick facade is ornamented by delicate keystone window lintels. A balustrade surrounds the whole house, with a smaller balustrade at the crest of the hip roof. On the south side four full-height off-center Doric columns attest to the wealth of first owner, John Andrew, shipowner and commission merchant in Russia.

4. PEIRCE–NICHOLS HOUSE, *c. 1782*, NRHP. 80 Federal St. Open by appointment through Peabody Essex Museum, fee. Gateway to historic houses along Federal, Essex, Chestnut, Broad sts.

Shipowner Jerathmiel Peirce hired twenty-four-year-old Samuel McIntire to design his grand home in the Georgian style of the time. Then, in 1801, he had McIntire update the right side in McIntire's own Federal style for daughter Sally's wedding. The result is a magnificent opportunity to understand architectural evolution and social history in seafaring Salem's prime. On the left is McIntire's classic Georgian parlor with heavy, bold paneling and molding. Across the hall is his remodeled 1801 Federal room, with lighter, more delicate woodwork. Here are six McIntire-carved and upholstered settees, with rosettes and acanthus leaves, designed for the recesses they still occupy. A McIntire eagle and four-post canopy bed are among the Peirce–Nichols family and Salem furnishings. The front facade has strong full-height corner pilasters, balustrades at roofline and roof crown, and fence with original flame-topped urn finials carved by McIntire. Outbuildings survive, including stable and countinghouse. The North River once reached the backyard, where the owner's ships docked.

5. COTTING SMITH ASSEMBLY HOUSE, *1782*, NRHP. 138 Federal St. Open by appointment through Peabody Essex Museum, fee.

Grand receptions for Lafayette in 1784 and Washington in 1789, gala balls, concerts, lectures, and other entertainments were hosted here. The Assembly House was built for those purposes by a small group of Salem elite. It was remodeled by Samuel McIntire about 1798 to become a private home. McIntire adorned the front facade with symmetrically placed windows, four pairs of second-story Ionic pilasters, a wide pediment with delicate fanlight, and a roof-crowning balustrade. His beautiful, elaborate doorway with rosettes and bellflowers is shadowed by the porch added after 1833.

Within, the Assembly House interprets Salem's rich, varied history in furnishings of different generations of the Smith family through the nineteenth-century. Trade with the Far East is evident in the east parlor with its furnishings from China, Zanzibar, India. The dining room of fine Salem Chippendale and the second-floor Victorian parlor provide interesting contrast. The privately owned **Cook–Oliver House** at 142 Federal Street is a more elaborate McIntire, c. 1802, with gateposts and wood finishing touches believed to be from his grand Derby mansion, which once commanded Derby Square.

6. ROPES MANSION AND GARDEN, *c. 1727*, NRHP. 318 Essex St. Open by appointment through Peabody Essex Museum, fee.

The magnificent formal garden of the Ropes Mansion features countless annual blooms, which provide continuing color and beauty. The large variety of plants includes rare shrubs from China, a gift of Arnold Arboretum. Garden, mansion, and all furnishings are gifts from the Ropes sisters, Mary and Eliza, the last of four Ropes generations to live here.

Each generation made architectural changes. The classic Georgian house, with balanced windows, dormers, and balustraded gambrel roof, was moved back from the street and raised. Fence, posts, and urn finials were added in 1894. The china and glass collection includes more than 300 pieces of Nanking-pattern Chinese export porcelain and possibly the world's largest single set of Irish cut glass, purchased in 1817. There is rare period furniture in Chippendale, Queen Anne, and Hepplewhite styles as well as Oriental rugs brought by Salem ships. Double parlors were remodeled in 1894 in Colonial Revival and contain mainly Empire furnishings. The 1835 dining room has original furnishings from its Greek Revival renovation time. Upstairs rooms were left as they were in 1842 and 1876. Sally Ropes Orne's wedding portrait was by Samuel F. B. Morse, of telegraph fame. Exploring the house is like visiting a prestigious nineteenth-century Salem family.

7. FIRST CHURCH IN SALEM, *1835*. 316 Essex St.

Organized in 1629, First Church was the first Colonial Congregational Society formally organized in America and still continuing. (First Parish in Plymouth was organized earlier, 1606, but in Scrooby, England.) In 1629 the ship *Talbot* arrived in Salem with three ministers aboard. Samuel Skelton and Francis Higginson remained in Salem, organizing their church; Ralph Smith traveled to Plymouth to become their first settled minister. Settlers of Salem cast ballots to determine who would be their minister—another first. Reverend Roger Williams served as third minister before he was driven from the colony for his views on religious freedom (see Providence, Rhode Island). Reverend Hugh Peters, fourth minister, did much to stimulate economic growth. He encouraged shipbuilding, fishing, planting and marketing of hemp, and the building of a water mill, glasshouse, and saltworks. He returned to England and supported Cromwell, for which he was hanged. In 1692 two church members, Rebecca Nurse and Giles Cory, were accused of witchcraft and harangued in church; one was hanged, the other crushed to death.

The castlelike English Gothic church was built of Quincy granite in 1835 by architect Gridley J. F. Bryant. Notice stained glass windows—two by Tiffany, one by La Farge, one by Reynolds. Rich woods form doored pews, altar, and quatrefoiled ceiling, symbolizing the cross.

8. WITCH HOUSE, *1642*. 310 Essex St. Open extended season, fee. NATHANIEL BOWDITCH HOUSE, NHL. 9 North St. Exterior view only; city offices.

On March 1, 1692, accused of witchcraft, Tituba, Sarah Osborn, and Sarah Good were examined in Salem Village (now Danvers) by magistrates John Hathorne and Jonathan

Corwin. The three were sent to jail in Boston to be held for trial. In June witch trials opened in Salem with Jonathan Corwin one of the judges. Trials were held at the courthouse on Washington Street, while meetings of judges and jurors—and possibly some pretrial examinations—were held in this house, Judge Corwin's home.

The house is restored to his time. Its open-beam keeping room and kitchen show life in the late seventeenth century, with large fireplace and built-in oven, colonial kitchen utensils, reversible 1690 table, pewter ware, and early one-hand George Clark clock. The "best room" has a 24-inch pine plank table, English slant-top desk, American banister chairs, and a cabinet with a secret drawer. Judge Corwin's bedroom was probably the room where frightened defendants were questioned. An ominous feeling still seems to prevail.

Around the corner on North Street (originally at 312 Essex), the **Nathaniel Bowditch House** was home to the famed navigator and mathematician. Bowditch wrote the *Practical Navigator* in 1802. Revised, his book is still used today.

9. PICKERING HOUSE, *1651*. 18 Broad St. Open all year, limited hours and by appointment; fee.

Join a ten-generation family tradition as your hostess, Mrs. John Pickering, welcomes you to their home, the oldest house in the country continuously occupied by one family. You sit in the living room, talk about Pickerings and their home, and see centuries of mementos. In a family scrapbook are letters from Presidents Washington, Adams, and Jefferson to ancestor Colonel Timothy Pickering. He was quartermaster general in the Revolution, President Washington's Indian negotiator, postmaster general, secretary of war, and secretary of state. For President Adams he was secretary of the navy and secretary of state. Colonel Pickering was also a farmer who won a plowing contest at age seventy-five.

There is a desk made by Reverend Theophilus Pickering, second minister of Essex; a portrait and needlework by Mary Pickering Leavitt, who died in 1805; a mirror from Portugal; a bonnet-topped highboy from Salem; china from all over the world; and a wine cooler that was a gift from President Washington. The house began in 1651 when the first John Pickering built a two-room half house on his farm. In 1671 the next John Pickering added the other half. By 1722 gables and back room were added to make the saltbox line. By 1842 Gothic peaks, trim, and fence created today's home.

10. CHESTNUT STREET. Stephen Phillips Trust House, early 1800s. 34 Chestnut St. Open summer, fee. Hamilton Hall, 1805, NHL. 9 Chestnut St. Open all year, no fee.

Many agree with Samuel Chamberlain that Chestnut Street is "the finest, best preserved and most aristocratic thoroughfare in America." Elegant Federals, with a sprin-

Chestnut Street, Salem

kling of Georgians and Greek Revivals, line both sides of the wide avenue. Salem's mighty sea captains and merchants lived here during Salem's most prosperous years.

A fence with delicately elaborate urn finials encloses one of the stately Federals, the **Stephen Phillips Trust House.** It is hard to believe this house was moved here from Danvers in the mid-1800s—in two sections, which were then linked by a central portion. The house was actually part of a grand estate called Oak Hill built for Nathaniel West and Elizabeth Derby West, daughter of Elias Hasket Derby. Believed designed by McIntire, the West mansion and its story are a feature at Boston's Museum of Fine Arts. Three rooms from Oak Hill are also there, containing many of Elias Hasket Derby's furnishings.

In 1914 Stephen Phillips bought this house. Family heirlooms and furnishings of five generations of Phillipses—a prosperous Salem sea captain and his descendants—are gathered here. Stephen's great-grandfather, China trade Captain Stephen Phillips, had built the Phillips ancestral home nearby at 17 Chestnut Street. His son, the Honorable Stephen C. Phillips, expanded the family mercantile efforts, served in Congress, and when mayor of Salem donated his salary to education. His son, Stephen H. Phillips, was state attorney general. It was his son who bought this house at 34 Chestnut Street.

Farther along is **Hamilton Hall** at 9 Chestnut Street. It was designed by Samuel McIntire, built in 1805, and named for Colonel Timothy Pickering's friend and frequent guest Alexander Hamilton. Here Lafayette was honored in 1824 at a gala occasion attended by 300. The grand ballroom is highlighted by large Palladian windows with fluted columns, simple entablatures, and ropelike dentils. Gilded Russian mirrors top twin fireplaces.

11. SALEM MARITIME NATIONAL HISTORIC SITE. Derby St. Open all year, no fee.

The heartbeat of Salem can be felt in this nine-acre historic site operated by the National Park Service. In the late eighteenth century, tied up at Derby Wharf might have been the 300-ton *Grand Turk* just back from China with cargo of teas and nankeens; or the *Mount Vernon* back from the Mediterranean full of silks and wines, reaping a profit of $100,000; or the *Revenge,* one of the fastest and most profitable privateers, unloading her captured prize. Between 1785 and 1799 Elias Hasket Derby, the country's first millionaire, sent his ninety-one vessels on a total of 180 voyages.

The building of **Derby Wharf** was begun by Richard Derby, Elias's father, about 1764. The wharf was lengthened in 1806 to serve more and larger vessels. Warehouses on the wharf held everything from tea, fish, lumber, exotic birds, rare wines, and imported porcelain to privateer-captured cargoes waiting to be auctioned.

Captains entered the **Custom House** (1819) to register their cargoes, obtain bills of lading, or pay import taxes. The Custom House collected over $25,000,000 between 1789 and 1879, listing 14,000 foreign entries. This dignified Federal-style building has granite steps, fanlight-topped doorway, classical pillars, and a hip roof with a cupola crowned by a golden eagle holding the U.S. shield. Inside is the surveyor's office made famous by Nathaniel Hawthorne in his book *The Scarlet Letter* and where Hawthorne worked from 1846 to 1849.

The **Bonded Warehouse** (1819) held goods waiting to be reshipped or to have duties paid. Here are samples of cargoes such as pepper from Sumatra, sugar from the West Indies, coffee beans from Arabia, and an old hoisting winch and a large model of the brig *Leander.* The 1829 **Scale House** stored measuring and weighing devices carried by the port's surveyor to measure incoming cargos on fifty different wharves in Salem.

The **Narbonne House,** built about 1670, shows architectural progression. It was originally a half house, the gambrel roof section was added about 1720, and there were further changes in the nineteenth century. As you leave the Narbonne House, observe a cross section of Salem architecture—the seventeenth-century Narbonne House, eighteenth-century Georgian Derby House, early nineteenth-century Federal Hawkes House, Custom House, Derby Wharf, and the harbor.

The **Derby House** was built in 1762 by Captain Richard Derby for son Elias Hasket Derby. Here Elias and his wife, Elizabeth Crowinshield Derby, and family of seven children lived until the end of the Revolution. From here he oversaw his early shipping business and sent his ships to open new trade routes throughout the world. The classic brick Georgian has beautifully balanced facade and windows, centered entry, strong dentils at eaves, and dormered third story. Georgian features within are paneled wainscoting and fireplaces, shutters, window seats, wide floorboards, and appropriate furnishings.

The **Hawkes House** (1774) was built by Derby to store goods brought back by his privateers. In 1801 it was bought by Benjamin Hawkes, who finished the Federal house. The **West India Goods Store** (1800) was built by Captain Prince to sell goods brought in on Prince ships. With its intriguing aromas of imported teas, coffees, and spices, it still resembles a store of the early days of trade in maritime Salem. **Derby Wharf Lighthouse** was built in 1871 and relit in 1983, using a modern solar panel as power source.

12. HOUSE OF THE SEVEN GABLES HISTORIC SITE; House of the Seven Gables, *1668*, Hawthorne's Birthplace, *c. 1750*, Hooper–Hathaway House, *1682;* Counting House, *1840;* NRHP. 54 Turner St. Open all year, fee. Museum shop in Retire Becket House (1665), introductory video, garden coffee shop.

Nathaniel Hawthorne was brought up in Salem, and both the city and his Puritan ancestry deeply affected his writing. He often visited his cousin, Susannah Ingersoll, and her adopted son, Horace, in her home—the house now called the House of the Seven Gables. Susannah filled his mind and imagination with stories of their ancestors and life in early Salem. Many of these ideas became part of his book *The House of the Seven Gables.*

The initial four-gabled house was built in 1668 by Captain John Turner, whose estate was valued at about 15,000 pounds. With a pound very roughly equivalent to $300, that made him one of the wealthiest men on the north shore. Turner's son added three gables about 1690, covered hand-hewn beams, papered walls of the parlor, and replaced small diamond-shaped windows with larger double-hung sash. Thus he created the present bright, cheery parlor room with its own special view of Salem Harbor. Captain Samuel Ingersoll, owner in 1782, had several gables removed. In 1908 Caroline O. Emmerton bought, restored, and opened the House of the Seven Gables to the public for a fee. Income was and is used to support the historic house and a settlement house to help people in the neighborhood.

Inside, the old kitchen fireplace has a crusie lamp on the hearth and a 1600s wine chest. The dining room, which in Hawthorne's story was Hepzibah's parlor, brings alive both the story and gracious living of the nineteenth century. The story and house are interwoven throughout the tour. There is a portrait of Susannah Ingersoll, a Simon Willard banjo clock, a Martha Washington chair, a Hepplewhite sideboard, and Hawthorne's checkerboard. The secret passageway to Horace's small gabled bedroom above is beside the fireplace, with a lever hidden within to open the special panel. Also in the house are portraits of Hawthorne and his wife, Sophia Peabody, and a desk and chair used by him.

In the **Hooper–Hathaway House,** three finished upright beams are believed to be part of Governor John Endicott's c. 1630s home. The seventeenth century is visible in the exposed beams, unfinished walls, and large fireplace of the kitchen. The eighteenth-century parlor has finished walls, moldings, and inside shutters. The **Counting House** is set up as a captain's office might have been in that time. In **Hawthorne's Birthplace** there is a painting of the ship *America,* on which Nathaniel Hawthorne's father sailed as first mate. This ship brought the first elephant to America. Upstairs is the bedchamber where Nathaniel was born July 4, 1804. Brick walks, gardens with varying colors and textures, flowering shrubbery, and large guardian trees unify this historic complex.

BEACHES, PARKS, OTHER POINTS OF INTEREST

A. Forest River Park. West St. Open all year, summer parking fee; parking for residents only on weekends. Paths along pleasant peninsula of fields, knolls, trees, ledges, natural beaches; ball fields, playground, benches, bathhouse, lifeguards, swimming pool; picnicking, beach swimming.

B. Pioneer Village. West St. Open summer, limited hours. Fee. Tiny early Colonial village, researched replica of c. 1630 Naumkeag (Salem), created 1930. Village clung to harbor for supply and communication; replica dwellings range from wigwams to thatched or shingled tiny cottages to the two-story replica of Governor John Endicott's "Fayre House"; crude yet ingenious facilities for fish drying, blacksmithing, brick making, woodcutting, evaporation of seawater for salt; demonstrates life in seventeenth-century Salem.

C. Pickering Wharf. Derby St. Popular, successful adaptive use of waterfront; specialty shops, restaurants, wharf, boat rental, cruises.

D. Winter Island Maritime Park, Fort Pickering, Fort Pickering Light, NRHP. 50 Winter Island Rd. Open all year. Fee in summer. Area was fishing village in 1626, site of Salem Inn about 1642, later commercial fishing port; boatbuilding developed, frigate USS *Essex* built and launched here 1799; point fortified since 1640s; shell of c. 1780 powder house, later used as fishing shack, remains. Fort Pickering, built 1799, was named for Timothy Pickering; ruins remain from Civil War era; five Coast Guard buildings remain. Fort Pickering Light, 1875–79, is built of brick and steel. Park has harbor and island views, pier, covered picnic areas, restaurant in summer, boat launch; sail boarding, scuba diving, camping.

E. Fort Lee. Fort Ave. Above first parking lot of Salem Willows. Open all year. No fee. Possibly Naumkeag Indian vantage point; fortified 1742; at top of hill see points of star where cannon stood; views, paths.

F. Salem Willows. Fort Ave. Open all year. No fee. Tidal beach, rolling grass areas, views; arcade, casino, restaurants, boat rides, and rentals, paths, benches, covered picnic areas, rest rooms, playground, tennis, ball fields, fitness trail.

G. Ye Olde Pepper Companie. 122 Derby St. Open all year as candy shop. Since 1806 "America's oldest candy company"; home of Salem "Gibralters," a sweet that wouldn't spoil on long sea voyages; on view is jar of Gibralters over 150 years old.

H. Salem Common. Washington Sq., Hawthorne Blvd. Impressive Common, octagonal bandstand, paths; size appropriate for surrounding dignified homes of Salem's most prosperous times. Common land since 1685, then training field; in 1802 Common was filled in and fenced, and McIntire designed gateways; his original carvings on triumphal arch are at Peabody Essex Museum; McIntire-designed house is at 74 Washington Square East, with classical entry and balustraded hip roof; nearby stands statue of Salem founder Roger Conant.

I. Salem Witch Museum. 19½ Washington Sq. Open all year. Fee. Formidable stone Romanesque church, now Witch Museum; gift shop, theater; multimedia scenes reenact story of witchcraft terror.

J. Witch Dungeon Museum. 16 Lynde St. Open extended season. Fee. Witch trials reenacted, tour of recreated dungeon.

K. Salem Wax Museum of Witches and Seafarers. 288 Derby St. Open all year. Fee.

L. National Park Service Visitor Center. New Liberty St. near Essex St.

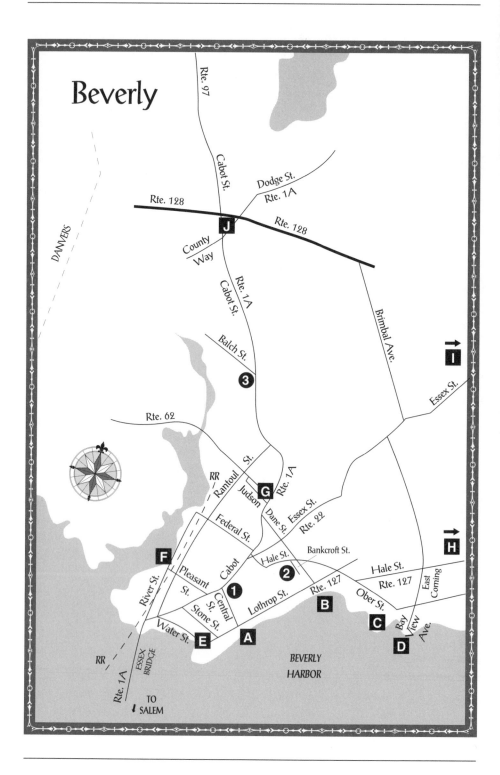

BEVERLY

Beverly, an agricultural and seafaring town, evolved from Salem. In 1636 Roger Conant, John Balch, and three others received 200 acres of land each. The settlement grew and established its first church under Reverend John Hale in 1667. By 1683 Beverly was a legal port of entry, its fine protected harbor setting the basic lifestyle for the next two centuries. In the 1690s Reverend Hale rejected his own early prejudices and almost single-handedly broke the witchcraft spell in Beverly. In the mid-1700s, merchants and Patriots George, Andrew, and John Cabot, Moses Brown, and Isreal Thorndike brought commercial prosperity. On September 5, 1775, the *Hannah,* owned by John Glover of Marblehead, sailed from Glover's wharf in Beverly, the first private vessel to be commissioned by General George Washington. After the Revolution, America's first power-driven cotton mill was built here. By the mid-1800s Beverly ships sailed to Spanish, South American, and West Indies ports, and the shoe industry began, becoming an important part of the economy. Beverly is a city of successful businesses, fashionable and pleasant residential sections, and well-preserved historic homes.

1. CABOT HOUSE, *1781,* NRHP, HS. 117 Cabot St. Open all year, fee.

You are invited to visit the Cabots, "by far the most wealthy in New England"[29] according to a 1780 source. The Revolution was just ending as John Cabot built this grand three-story mansion, the first brick dwelling in Beverly. Privateering during the Revolution had established the enduring Cabot fortune, and the Cabots' homes were showplaces. Andrew Cabot's c. 1783 mansion became the now-modified **City Hall** at 191 Cabot St.

The Cabot House here is a classic Federal brick with balanced facade, columned portico, dentiled cornice, and smaller third-floor windows. Within, early Federal features remain in paneled walls, simple dentils at ceiling and fireplaces, Dutch tiles, and box-enclosure staircase. Exhibits include many possessions of Captain Moses Brown, fellow merchant prince, Patriot, and friend of the Cabots. Furnishings, mostly from Beverly's historic families, date up to the 1830s. Pewter crafted by Israel Trask and Ebenezer Smith represents an important home industry. Portraits of pepper trade captains and merchants, primitives by Luke Prince, a military collection, a children's room, a maritime room, and a collection of mainly nineteenth-century textiles are exhibited. There are portraits of Lucy Larcom, an early writer who focused on concerns of Lowell textile working girls, and Hannah Hill, who began what is believed to be the country's first Sunday school. A first-floor room was the home of the Beverly Bank in 1802, tenth oldest bank in the country. Later, Beverly Savings Bank was formed here.

2. HALE HOUSE, *1694*, NRHP, HS. 39 Hale St. Open extended season, fee.

John Hale graduated from Harvard College and came to Beverly in 1664 as a religious teacher. Three years later he was called as first minister. Here he served with unusual courage and wisdom for forty years, leaving only briefly in 1690 as chaplain to a French and Indian Wars' expedition to Canada. In 1692 Hale became embroiled in witchcraft trials—until his own kind and gentle wife was accused. Then he reevaluated his thinking. He took a strong stand in support of her and other accused witches, ending the horrors of trials in Beverly, and wrote *A Modest Inquiry into the Nature of Witchcraft*. Hale descendants have lived here since 1694.

The earliest part of the house has a high peaked roof and original timbers and construction. The dining-room section, added by grandson Dr. Robert Hale in 1745, shows Georgian influence—recessed window shutters, decorative corner cupboard, and English hand-blocked wallpaper. Additions were made in the nineteenth and twentieth centuries as family size and fortune grew. Furnishings are from Beverly families, representing different furniture periods of nine generations. A clock and chest were left from the Hale family. Descendants include John Hale's grandson, Patriot Nathan Hale, and Edward Everett Hale, author of *The Man without a Country*.

3. BALCH HOUSE, *c. 1636*, NRHP, HS. 448 Cabot St. Open extended season, fee.

The ancient Balch House stands quietly on its one remaining acre above the traffic of Cabot Street. "Old Planter" John Balch built the two rooms of the right front gabled section about 1636 on his 200-acre grant. This early structure remarkably remains, now one of the oldest wood-frame houses in the country. Original beams are even older; they are English oak cut in England and shipped as ballast.

The Balch House has been restored to its classic early Colonial period, based on clues found in the structural elements. The 1600s furnishings replicate the 1648 inventory recorded at John Balch's death. The left side was added about 1650 by John's son Benjamin, whose birth after the charter was received made him the first male born in Massachusetts Bay Colony. Benjamin Balch lived here until the early 1700s with his three successive wives and thirteen children. When son David died mysteriously in 1690 at age nineteen, suspicions of witchcraft (unproven) became part of the trials and testimonies. In the left front room, the dominating loom and weaving arts displays represent the trade of many later Balches. The Balch family has owned the house for three centuries and continues to aid its support.

Together the three fine houses of the Beverly Historical Society span history and architecture—the c. 1636 early Colonial Balch House, the 1694 early Georgian Hale House, and the 1781 early Federal Cabot House.

BEACHES, PARKS, OTHER POINTS OF INTEREST

A. Independence Park. Lothrop St. (Rte. 127). Open all year. No fee. General Glover's Fourteenth Regiment was based at this only Continental Army post established by Washington north of Boston; here Glover read Declaration of Independence to his troops. Green expanse is dotted with benches and cannons; views of islands and sea; breakwater marks sandy/rocky beach; swimming; limited street parking.

B. Dane Street Beach. Foot of Dane through Hale sts. Open all year. No fee. Named for Nathan Dane, drafter in 1787 of Northwest Ordinance, which prohibited slavery in the Northwest Territory. Grassy fields lead to open beach, views of harbor islands, bathhouse, benches, playground; swimming; limited street parking.

C. Lynch Park. Ober St. Open all year. Parking fee in summer. Once-grand estate is now beautiful ocean park; fortified during Revolution. Summer White House for President William Howard Taft until owner, Mrs. Robert Evans, broke lease with Tafts and moved their cottage via barge to Marblehead to extend her rose garden; Tafts then summered at 70 Corning Street (private). Extensive beach, lawns, tree-lined paths, formal brick-walled gardens; former stable houses concessions; band shell, benches, paths, rest rooms, playground, lifeguards; swimming.

D. Hospital Point Light. Bay View Ave. External view. Home of commandant of Coast Guard covering the northeast; point fortified in Revolution; sixteen-gun British sloop of war HMS *Nautilus* engaged schooner *Hannah* off this point October 10, 1775; smallpox hospital here 1801; lighthouse part of residence built 1871, now automated; DAR monument.

E. Fish Flake Hill, NRHP. Water, Front, Davis, Stone, South Bartlett sts. Drive through. Listed on National Register as "unique cluster of Revolutionary War homes"; overlooks harbor where fish dried on flakes and houses led to wharves; General John Glover's wharf extended from Front Street to harbor, where he launched the *Hannah;* merchant/privateer Captain Hugh Hill's elaborate Federal (private) is at 50 Front Street.

F. Beverly Depot, c. 1897, NRHP. River and Pleasant sts. Open all year as restaurant. Modest brick and stone Richardsonian-style depot.

G. Cabot Street Cinema Theatre, c. 1920. 286 Cabot St. Open all year. Fee. Restored Art Deco movie palace noted for regularly featured stage magic spectaculars; also special films, oldies and modern.

H. Pride's Crossing, Beverly Farms. Hale St. (Rte. 127). Drive east on Hale Street along road of interesting houses; Henry Cabot Lodge's restored 1734 Widow Patch House at 269 Hale (private); at Pride's Crossing, c. 1879 railroad depot, now charming general store; Pride's Crossing was Newport-level Boston and New York summer colony; see $100,000 c. 1900 fencing of Henry J. Frick estate (mansion gone); on to Beverly Farms, another restored depot, and more elaborate estates along Hale and West streets.

I. Long Hill Reservation. 572 Essex St. Open all year. Fee. Peaceful 114-acre estate of fields, orchards, forests, wetlands; 400 varieties of plants; 1918 house, is reproduction of 1800s house in Charleston, South Carolina; was summer home of Ellery Sedgewick, author, editor of *Atlantic Monthly;* perennial garden by Mabel Cabot Sedgewick. Trustees of Reservations.

J. Site of First Powered Cotton Mill. Rte. 1A (Dodge St.), next to fire station; 1787 site marked by tall sign on busy corner. John Cabot a founder of this first powered cotton mill; President Washington made detailed description when visited, considered the mill a great early accomplishment in this new country.

GLOUCESTER

T he rugged granite promontory of Cape Ann, Massachusetts, has withstood pressures and movements of the glacial age and the constant buffeting of the ocean. Glaciers left the land rounded and rock strewn, not ideal for farming. It was the harvest of the sea that first brought early settlers to these shores and has since fed, employed, and made famous its inhabitants. Cape Ann was first named Cap aux Isles by Samuel de Champlain, who named Gloucester Harbor Beau Port in 1606. The cape was renamed for Queen Anne of England, consort of James I and mother of Charles I.

Gloucester is justifiably proud that its fishing industry is the longest continuously operating industry in the country. Fishing boats have sailed in and out of Gloucester's protected harbor since 1623. In early years, ships arrived laden with fish packed so tight that cargo had to be dug out by hand. Everywhere you looked, on wharves and even on rooftops, fish were drying on wooden racks called flakes and docks were piled high with salt. Today flakes and salt are gone—replaced by world-known processing plants. The Gloucester fleet, though greatly reduced in size, still brings in fish; but most comes by large, refrigerated oceangoing foreign ships.

1. STAGE FORT PARK, *1623*. Hough and Western aves. Open all year, parking fee in summer. Paths, two small sandy beaches, ball fields, lifeguards, tennis, concessions; swimming, picnicking.

Cape Ann's engrossing history began here when fishermen from Dorchester, England, landed in 1623. They set up fish-drying flakes, probably where the recreational fields are today. Fishermen from Plymouth joined them and, despite some heated discussions, learned to share the area and fish the waters in peaceful coexistence. The oldest defense fortifications in Massachusetts Bay Colony were situated here on Stage Fort and used during French and Indian Wars. Present earthworks were built during the Revolution, enlarged for the War of 1812, and fortified during Civil and Spanish-American wars.

High rocky ledges form the outer edge of Stage Fort Park. Climb paths for panoramic views of Gloucester Harbor and the promenade with the famous fisherman statue. Across the harbor is Fort Point, where breastworks were built in 1743 to protect the inner harbor. In the distance are fish-processing plants, Rocky Neck, Ten Pound Island with its lighthouse, and Eastern Point with picturesque light and unusual Dog Bar Breakwater (11).

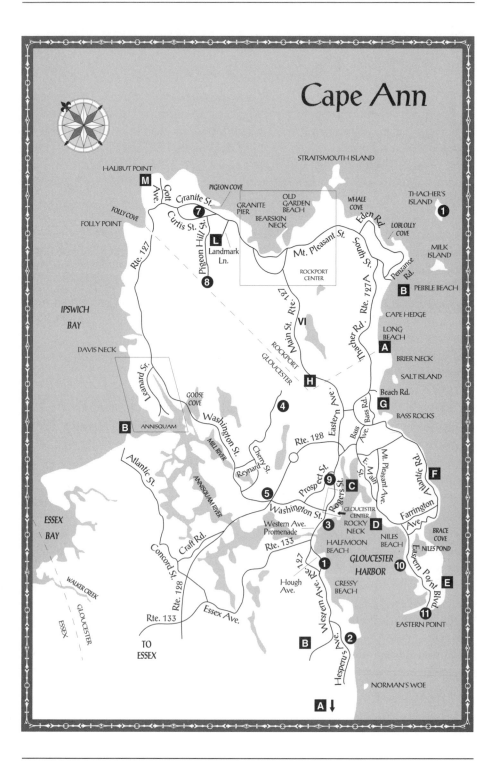

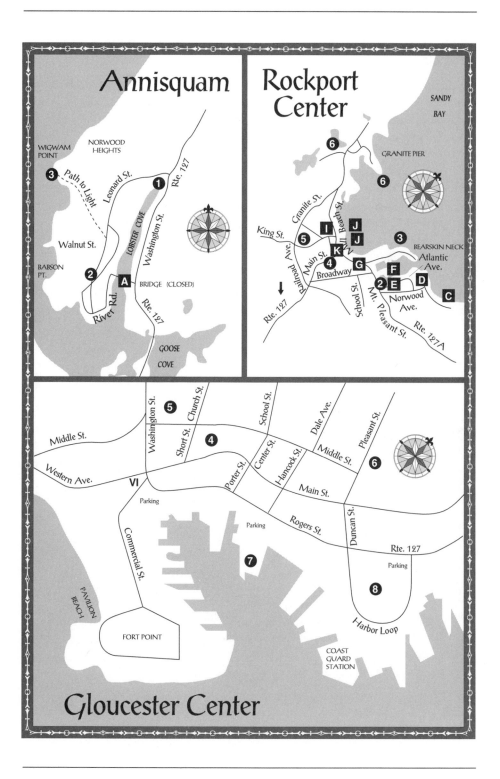

2. HAMMOND CASTLE, *c. 1928*, NRHP. Hesperus Ave. Open all year, fee. Museum shop; classes, concerts.

Hammond Castle is truly a castle—with massive stone towers, flying buttresses, Gothic windows, and an ancient-looking drawbridge. The Great Hall, a cathedrallike chamber, houses an organ with 8,000 pipes. The castle is eclectically furnished with rare and elaborate treasures such as floor tiles from a room in the palace of Christopher Columbus's son.

John Hays Hammond, Jr., (no relation to Hammond Organ Company) was an extraordinary and prolific inventor whose home was his hobby and workshop. He thrived on impressive entertainments and drew his guest lists mainly from the music and art worlds. Inspired by Thomas Alva Edison, Hammond worked with remote-control experiments that were predecessors to today's space probes. He delighted in his successful pilotless boat, which he ran in Gloucester Harbor and controlled from the castle—to the complete consternation of uninitiated fishermen.

Walk the grounds to appreciate views of Gloucester Harbor and of Norman's Woe, a rocky reef just offshore. Norman's Woe was made famous by Henry Wadsworth

Hammond Castle, Gloucester   (Massachusetts Office of Travel and Tourism)

Longfellow's poem "Wreck of the Hesperus," though the *Hesperus* was never wrecked at Norman's Woe and Longfellow had not even seen the reef when he wrote the poem.

3. MAN AT THE WHEEL, FISHERMEN'S MEMORIAL, *1923*, and Blynman Drawbridge. Western Ave. Promenade.

The dominant figure at the head of the outer harbor is the Gloucester Fisherman, constantly standing at his helm, seemingly aware of every change in weather and movement of the sea. This statue, sculpted by Leonard Craske, honors more than 10,000 Gloucester fishermen who have lost their lives at sea. It is a tribute to Gloucestermen who "go down to the sea in ships,"[30] descendants of more than 350 years of men facing gale winds, high seas, shipwrecks, and death.

Intriguing **Blynman Drawbridge** crosses the cut that connects Gloucester Harbor with the Annisquam River. If you are lucky, you will get to see this electric ratchet bridge grind its way open to allow a graceful mast to pass. Early fishermen realized a need for a safe inland water route between Massachusetts Bay and Ipswich Bay. Reverend Richard Blynman was not only the first minister of the settlement but a creative engineer. In 1643 he was commissioned to cut through marshlands and build a bridge over the cut. Tolls charged to nonresidents paid part of the salary of this enterprising minister. For 300 years Blynman Bridge supplied the only roadway to Cape Ann until the Route 128 bridge was built.

4. SARGENT–MURRAY–GILMAN–HOUGH HOUSE, *c. 1768*. 49 Middle St. Open extended season, limited hours, fee.

This dignified Georgian home with its beautiful paneled staircase has period and rare furnishings, paintings, ceramics, and glass. It is fascinating for the people it has housed. Winthrop Sargent was a successful merchant and influential leader of early Gloucester. He built this house for his daughter Judith, a talented writer and important force in her own right. When widowed, she married John Murray, who had come from England in 1770 with the idea of universal salvation. Murray found others in Gloucester, led by the Sargents, considering the same new thoughts. Together, overcoming much adversity, they began the first Universalist Church in America. Their perseverance in fighting payment of taxes to Gloucester's First Parish resulted in the setting of a far-reaching legal precedent by Massachusetts: the right of freedom of worship and voluntary church support. John and Judith Murray went on to lead the Boston Universalist Church.

Sargent descendants include John Singer Sargent and Governors Winthrop and Francis Sargent. Next in the house came Major Frederick Gilman, whose son Samuel wrote the song "Fair Harvard" for his alma mater and became a Unitarian minister. The house was next owned by the Honorable B. K. Hough, for forty years treasurer of the Independent Church (Universalist).

5. INDEPENDENT CHRISTIAN CHURCH, *1805.* **Middle St.**

The Independent Christian Church (Unitarian and Universalist) stands tall and proud—the historic culmination of dedication and adversity conquered. This is the mother church of Universalism in the United States. The church itself is impressive, with lofty four-story spire patterned after a Christopher Wren design. The sanctuary has been changed somewhat but retains much original beauty. The whale-oil chandelier, which had been abandoned, was found, electrified, and restored to its commanding position. The Willard clock is original. The Historic Room exhibits memorabilia and documents of the historic precedent set by John and Judith Murray and their Sargent-led supporters.

6. CAPE ANN HISTORICAL ASSOCIATION, *c. 1804.* **27 Pleasant St. Open all year, fee. Research library, museum shop.**

Gloucester's past glories can be relived and the city's present understood and appreciated in this museum of Cape Ann heritage. Large wings have been added to the original museum, which was the c. 1804 home of Revolutionary Captain Elias Davis. The Davis house has two floors of period furnishings. The many unique-to-Gloucester treasures exhibited in the museum include the largest collection of artist Fitz Hugh Lane's work and the Gloucester *Centennial,* a dory sailed to England in 1876 in one of the first recorded solo Atlantic crossings. The main maritime/fisheries gallery also features Howard Blackburn's *Great Republic,* built in 1900 for his second solo Atlantic crossing. Here you are aware of Gloucester's history and stories as told by Rudyard Kipling in *Captains Courageous.*

7. SEVEN SEAS WHARF. **Rogers St. Open all year, no fee. Tour boats.**

This is Gloucester! Walk around Gloucester House restaurant and look at myriad wharves, boats, warehouses—the atmosphere you expect from over 350 years of continuous fishing. Seven Seas Wharf was used by early settlers to dry and salt fish for export. Now fishing boats—usually five- to seven-man draggers—tie up, stow gear, mend nets. Some of the support beams of the wharf are old masts pegged together. History has been lived here—pirates outfoxed, British ships repulsed, and letters of marque issued to provide for a privateer navy. The wharf has witnessed the long evolution of fishing and processing and countless trading ships heading to and from foreign ports.

Hidden Park's entrance is hidden to the right of the parking lot. A short, shrub-lined path leads to a bench facing the water. This is the face of Gloucester, the artist's view.

8. FITZ HUGH LANE HOUSE, *1849*, NRHP. Not open to public. Captain Solomon Jacobs Park. Rogers St. and Harbor Loop. Open all year, no fee. *Adventure*, Gloucester schooner, NHL. State Fish Pier. Open all year, fee. Tours and by appointment; office in Lane House.

On a rise of land overlooking the harbor stands the seven-gabled granite house of Gloucester's famous son, marine artist Fitz Hugh Lane. Though crippled in body by polio at age two, he had an artistic genius that knew no bounds. Lane captured the moods, the successes and tragedies, and the pictorial history of Gloucester's waterfront during the mid-1800s. After Lane's death in 1865, the house was used as a jail, called Old Stone Jug.

Behind the house, on the waterfront, is **Captain Solomon Jacobs Park,** a "window on the harbor." It was named in honor of Captain Jacobs, "king of the mackerel killers." From the park you can see the nearby U.S. Coast Guard Station and, on the smaller building, the relief sculpture by Adio diBiccari from the painting *To the Rescue* by Anton Otto Fischer. Farther along the harborside is the square white-towered building in which Clarence Birdseye perfected his quick freezing techniques in 1925. Ten years earlier, when a trapper in Labrador, Birdseye discovered he could keep cabbages indefinitely by freezing them in brine. His successful quick-freezing of fish in bulk, along with refrigeration, caused a profound change in the Gloucester waterfront and in the lives of her people and those throughout the country.

The Essex-built 121.5-foot *Adventure* has mast and standard rigging of a schooner. After years of fishing followed by windjammer cruising, she returned to her home port—a live exhibit of an historic Gloucester fishing schooner. As you tour her deck, look out over the harbor at modern draggers, tuna fishers, and others—past and present maritime Gloucester. A video of fishing days and tours above and below deck are available. Sailing cruises for research, education, and pleasure are planned.

9. OUR LADY OF GOOD VOYAGE CHURCH, *1915*. 142 Prospect St.

High on the skyline of Gloucester are the two blue-capped, bell-shaped towers of the Portuguese National Church of Our Lady of Good Voyage. Framed by these towers is the dramatic figure of "Our Lady." The original statue, carved from fruitwood in the mid-1800s, is at the Cape Ann Historical Association (see 6). The imposing church was styled after a church on San Miguel Island in the Azores. A thirty-two-bell carillon was placed in the twin towers in 1922. The sanctuary is painted the deep blue of the ocean, and columns on walls hold models of ships that sailed from Gloucester. The central figure is the Virgin Mary holding baby Jesus in one arm and a Gloucester schooner in the other.

10. BEAUPORT, *1903–34*, SPNEA. Eastern Point Blvd. Open extended season, closed summer weekends, fee.

It all started as a small cottage! Then Henry Davis Sleeper, builder of the cottage, rescued the interior of a 1728 house in nearby Essex and had it installed here. From then on, Sleeper added rooms with their own names, personalities, and distinct features until he had added over thirty. He had studied architecture and gained recognition as an interior decorator. His goal at Beauport was to graphically display this country and her people. Each room is chock-full of treasures, many relating to the room's theme, usually patriotic. During World War I Sleeper helped form and operate the American Field Service in France.

11. EASTERN POINT LIGHT AND DOG BAR BREAKWATER. Eastern Point Blvd. Open all year (except light), no fee.

Eastern Point Light and Dog Bar Breakwater mark the entrance to a safe, snug harbor that was once the scene of shipwreck and disaster. Long ago these treacherous rocky headlands had a stand of oaks that sailors could sight as a landmark on clear days. But storm and time removed the trees. In 1829 a stone monument was erected, with lantern and lightkeeper added two years later. The present stone and iron light was completed in 1848 and rebuilt in 1890.

The Rockport granite Dog Bar Breakwater was constructed over a submerged sandbar in 1904. At the end is a smaller light, looking like a miniature New England church. At times storms have tossed huge granite blocks from the breakwater into the harbor. You can walk the half-mile-long breakwater to the light at the end; see the Boston skyline; look across at Hammond's Castle and Norman's Woe; watch ships and fishing, sail, and power boats enter and leave busy Gloucester Harbor.

BEACHES, PARKS, OTHER POINTS OF INTEREST

A. **Rafe's Chasm Park.** Hesperus Ave., .6 mile past Stage Fort Park (2). Open. No fee. Limited parking. Walk through woods, ocean-side shrubs to open ledges of exposed granite; 200-foot-long chasm, 60 feet deep, with spectacular sights and sounds at certain tides and storms.

B. **Ravenswood Park and Chapel,** 1889. Western Ave. Open. No fee. Five miles of marked trails, trail map at Chamber of Commerce Visitor Center (VI on map); unspoiled 500-acre park, gift of Samuel E. Sawyer; wild magnolia, glacial moraine evidence, old quarry, site of Revolutionary smallpox pesthouse.

C. **Reed's Wharf.** East Main St. Open all year. No fee. Galleries, shops, restaurants; view Gloucester's working harbor of yesterday and today; watch one-man draggers, line trawlers, gillnetting, lobstering, with processing plants in background; launching site in 1713 of first Gloucester schooner.

D. Rocky Neck. East Main St. Open extended season. No fee. Artists' galleries, shops, restaurants, homes, old Gloucester industries like Marine Railway and Copper Paint works; one of oldest art colonies on New England coast.

E. Eastern Point Bird Sanctuary. Eastern Point Blvd. Open all year. No fee. Twenty-six acres of coastal headlands, woods, marsh, paths, native wildflowers; migratory route for birds and monarch butterflies; parking at end of road. Massachusetts Audubon Society.

F. Scenic Drive. Atlantic Rd. Beautiful seacoast estates, rugged Cape Ann coastline, short paths to rocky ledges, ocean spray over tumbled rocks, view of Thacher's Island lighthouses; limited parking weekdays off-season.

G. Good Harbor Beach. Thacher Rd., footbridge from Beach Rd. Open all year. Parking fee in summer. Lifeguards, bathhouses, snack bar, open sandy crescent, footbridge across marshlands.

H. Whale Watching and Harbor Cruises. Many available in and around Gloucester; information at Visitor Center.

ROCKPORT

(On-street parking only. Suggest in season park at Visitor Information booth
(VI on map) and use bus/trolley. See locator map, pages 366–67.)

James Babson received a land grant in 1662 and established his farm and
cooperage in what is now Rockport. The village was mainly a fishing, lumbering, and farming community until Nehemiah Knowlton opened a granite
quarry in 1823. By 1840, when Rockport separated from Gloucester, more than
a thousand men were employed in the granite industry. Granite was shipped by
stone sloops, coastal schooners, and rail throughout the country and abroad. The
age of tourism also began in the 1840s. Summer residents came first by stagecoach, then by rail after the Boston to Gloucester line opened in 1847. Artists
came, too, for at every point and cove there was a picture to be painted. Paintings
by Cape Ann artists are valued throughout the country.

Roger Babson, born on Cape Ann in 1875, founded three colleges, including
Babson College; several museums; and the Open Church Foundation. He had moral
lessons carved on rocks in Dogtown (see Annisquam, 4) to provide lessons for all and
employment for stone carvers during the Depression. It is said that one of the earliest
homes in Rockport belonged to Elizabeth Proctor, who was convicted of witchcraft
in Salem in 1692 but saved from hanging by her pregnancy. From granite to artists,
Rockport has made its mark and draws tourists and artists to its rocky shores.

1. THACHER'S ISLAND, NRHP, and CAPE ANN LIGHTHOUSE, 1861. Off Land's End, best view from Eden Rd. Summer access via excursion/supply boat from town pier (T-Wharf, see F). Historic preserve and wildlife refuge (donation), trails, access to lighthouse.

Rock-strewn Thacher's Island was the scene of great tragedy in 1635. On August 14, a
small sailing vessel carrying twenty-three people left Ipswich headed for Marblehead.
The boat had anchored for the night in Sandy Bay (Rockport) when a crippling hurricane with 25-foot waves struck. The defenseless boat was driven onto rocky ledges
called Dry Salvages, later featured in T. S. Eliot's poem. Anthony Thacher and his wife,
the only survivors, were washed ashore on what is now Thacher's Island. Their four
children and their cousins, minister John Avery and his family, were lost. Massachusetts
Bay Colony authorized the building of two lighthouses and a keeper's house in 1771.
During the Revolution, however, the first keeper was removed by local Minute Men
because of his Tory leanings, and the lights were darkened until the war was over. In
1861 two new granite towers were built, each 124 feet tall with first-order Fresnel lenses.

The north light was extinguished in 1932. During the summer of 1967, racketeer Joe Barboza, his wife, and two-year-old child were hidden in the keeper's house by U.S. Attorney Paul Markham for protection while Barboza testified against the underworld.

2. HANNAH JUMPER HOUSE, *late 1700s*. 35 Mt. Pleasant St. Private.

This snug clapboard house was home to Hannah Jumper, early feminist. Long before Carry Nation and the rest of the country became interested in temperance, Rockport had its own temperance movement. Soon after the War of 1812, antiliquor feelings stirred, culminating in the "likker raid" on July 8, 1856, which was instigated and encouraged by Ms. Jumper. A large procession—mainly women armed with axes, mops, and brooms—invaded establishments selling "likker." They smashed barrels and bottles until streets actually ran with liquor. Their illegal actions were watched in horrified silence by government officials. The participants were twice tried and acquitted. Rockport remains a dry town to this day.

3. BEARSKIN NECK. Main St. Open all year, no fee.

This rocky finger of land evolved from a fishing, lobstering, and commercial center in the eighteenth and nineteenth centuries to the present-day mecca for artists, craftspeople, photographers, and tourists. There are two traditions behind the name Bearskin Neck. One says that during the early days of Rockport, bears were such a menace that men with dogs and firearms drove them to this point, killed and skinned them, and laid the hides on rocks to dry. Another legend tells about Ebenezer Babson, who in 1700 saw a bear attack his nephew here. Armed with only a knife, Babson rushed to the boy's assistance, lured the bear into the water, engaged in fierce battle, slew the bear, and laid the skin on rocks to dry.

During the 1700s fish shacks, ship chandlers, and sail lofts, along with local gossip and sea yarns, filled Bearskin Neck. The two-story building on the right at the entrance was built in 1808 and served as barracks for local militia, the Sea-Fensibles, during the War of 1812. A fort was erected at the end of the Neck and armed with a cannon to protect the harbor and fleet from the British. In 1822 William Hall started the first U.S. isinglass factory here. The tough, semitransparent, gelatinous ribbons, made from air bladders of fish, were used in clarifying alcoholic beverages. Today many of the old, weathered fish houses are renovated into art centers, gift shops, and restaurants. Partway out Bearskin Neck, a left turn takes you onto Old Harbor Yacht Club breakwater and a public cafe overlooking Sandy Bay. From the end of the Neck you can see Rockport Harbor, the Headlands, Straitsmouth Lighthouse, the Dry Salvages, Granite Breakwater, and north to Front Beach, Granite Pier, and Pigeon Cove.

4. FIRST CONGREGATIONAL CHURCH, *1803*. **Main and School sts.**

At the top of Main Street stands the church known as Old Sloop, whose steeple looks from the ocean like the mast of a great ship. In 1752 Reverend Ebenezer Cleaveland arrived to bring the gospel. He was a Patriot as well and served as a chaplain in the French and Indian Wars and the Revolution. He and Captain John Rowe led sixty-six townsmen to Bunker Hill. Before the war was over, forty men from this small village had lost their lives. On October 9, 1814, British ship *Nymph* attacked with three barges. The first took the fort on Bearskin Neck. The second was spotted by a parishioner, who rang the church bell to rouse the town. In an effort to silence the bell, men on the barge put such a charge of ammunition into their cannon that it sank the barge. The cannon can still be seen on the lawn of the church. Townspeople repelled the third barge, some even using stockings as slingshots to hurl stones at the invaders. A hole from one of the cannonballs is visible in the steeple.

5. SANDY BAY HISTORICAL SOCIETY AND MUSEUM, SEWALL–SCRIPTURE HOUSE, *1832*. **40 King St. Open summer, fee.**

Levi Sewall constructed this sturdy, impressive stone house with granite from his own quarry. Now a museum, it features a marine room, memorabilia of the granite industry, an Atlantic Cable exhibit, a special library with rare and unpublished works, and period furnishings. Other displays include ceramics, paintings, photographs, costumes.

6. GRANITE QUARRY, GRANITE PIER, AND BREAKWATER.
Granite St. Open all year, no fee except for car or boat on pier in summer.

As early as 1710 Joshua Norwood used slabs of granite for mooring stones, with an unusual twist. He drilled a hole in the center of a stone slab, through which he threaded the trunk of an oak tree with roots. Roots and the weight of the stone held the oak in place, while boats were moored to the top of the tree. Norwood also used granite for millstones. Soon the outside world discovered Rockport granite and the boom began. Steam engines greatly increased productivity in quarries, hundreds of men were employed, and stone sloops from Rockport sailed to many ports. Rockport granite built the Newburyport Custom House, New York's Holland Tunnel, and Salem's jail. In one month in 1874, 5,500,000 paving blocks for Boston streets were hand loaded onto 200-ton schooners.

Drive out the Granite Pier for excellent views of Rockport Harbor, Bearskin Neck, and Straitsmouth Light. From the pier a path leads under the arched Keystone Bridge (NRHP) into the quarry. Stone was moved by flat cars under the road from the quarry to the pier, where it was loaded onto stone sloops.

Waste rock was used by the government in 1885 to construct the offshore Breakwater, making Sandy Bay's deep anchorage a safe harbor for large ships, including

Teddy Roosevelt's Great White Fleet. Each summer until World War II the U.S. Navy filled the town's streets with sailors on shore leave from exercises conducted out of Sandy Bay Harbor. The Breakwater was to run 9,000 feet, though only 6,000 feet were built. Of that, only 900 feet showed above water level. Before work stopped in 1912, the total project had cost the government $1,750,000. The granite blocks were not permanently attached, and some have since slid into the ocean, creating submerged hazards.

Now the abandoned Granite Quarry is beautiful and peaceful. Colorful, stark cut ledges provide resting places for birds. There is restricted access to the quarry, as it is part of town water supply system. A high dam blocks off the far end, and a ground-level pool lies just inside, past the bridge.

7. OLD CASTLE, *c. 1715*, HS. Granite and Curtis sts. Open summer and by appointment, fee.

Obviously not a castle, this garrison-fronted saltbox was probably named from the sea. Its prominent and isolated location made it appear as an old European castle to fishermen of these shores. It was home to Jethro Wheeler and six generations of his descendants. Weathered shingles are in keeping with wide floor boards and dominating fireplace. The museum displays period furnishings and local memorabilia on the second floor. A blacksmith shop with forge and sling and granite workers' exhibits are on the first floor.

8. PAPER HOUSE, *1922–42*. Pigeon Hill St. Open summer, fee.

This unique house on Pigeon Hill is living proof of the strength and use of newspapers. In 1922 Elis F. Stenman and his family began to experiment with uses of newspaper without destroying the print. After twenty years of work and 100,000 newspapers, they created a house with walls of 215 layers of Boston newspapers. It is furnished with items made from rolls of newspapers looking much like bamboo. This project proved both practical and economical—and provided an unusual method of preserving history. The writing desk is made from newspapers covering Colonel Lindbergh's historic flight. The grandfather clock contains newspapers from the capitals of the then forty-eight states. All the newspapers could be unrolled and read today.

BEACHES, PARKS, OTHER POINTS OF INTEREST

Note: All parking lots are sticker parking only, except for lot at attraction A.

A. **Long Beach.** Thacher Rd. Open all year. Fee in summer. Footbridge from parking area to protected sandy beach, retaining wall. In 1895 trolley connected Gloucester with Long Beach, which then had pavilion, dance hall, theater.

B. **Pebble Beach and Cape Hedge Beach.** South St. Open all year. No fee. Beach of

Motif #1, Rockport

water-smoothed stones deposited by glaciers. Early fishing schooners used stones as ballast; when fish were loaded into hull, stones were thrown overboard.

C. **Old Garden Beach.** Norwood Ave. Open all year. No fee. Small grassy park, crescent of sand; **Cliff Walk,** public path from far end of beach, leads 3 blocks along cliff edge overlooking Sandy Bay, then connects with Marmion Way.

D. **The Headlands.** Atlantic Ave. Open all year. No fee. Path to Headlands (open ledges on ocean); harbor and ocean views; limited street parking.

E. **Star Island Park.** Atlantic Ave. Tiny park on harbor, benches; provides window on waterfront.

F. **T-Wharf.** Broadway. Open all year. No fee. Sandy Bay Yacht Club; views of harbor, breakwater, and **Motif #1,** colorful fishing shack on Bearskin Neck that symbolizes town, subject of many paintings; limited street parking.

G. **Rockport Art Association, The Old Tavern,** c. 1787. 12 Main St. Open all year. No fee. Exhibition galleries of paintings, sculpture, graphic arts; demonstrations, lectures, annual Christmas pageant, festivals, concerts, fairs, flower shows, tours. Housed in former tavern; one tavern keeper, Stephen Randall, drove local stage with top hat; later keeper, Caleb Norwood, added 1838 ballroom.

H. James Babson Cooperage. Main St., Rte. 127. Open summer, limited hours. No fee. Summer kitchen for an early farm displays barrel-making tools and gear; huge fireplace that seasoned two barrels at once; barrels used to pack dried fish to ship.

I. Old Parish Burying Ground. Beach St. Earliest graves: Richard Tarr, first settler; "Fighting Parson" Cleaveland; Rev. David Jewett; Hannah Jumper; plus honored dead of French and Indian Wars, Revolution, War of 1812.

J. Front and Back Beaches. Beach St. Open all year. No fee. Rest rooms, concessions; small sandy beaches, benches, bandstand; swimming; limited metered parking.

K. Millbrook Meadow Park. Across Beach St. from Front Beach. Charming small park along mill brook and original millpond; bridge, stairway memorials to original town granite workers, dam and sluice, children's play area, picnic benches.

L. Pigeon Hill Park. Landmark Ln. Open all year. No fee. Had watch house during Revolution; open fields, trees, views; park on summit of Pigeon Hill; picnicking.

M. Halibut Point State Park and Halibut Point Reservation. Gott Ave. Open all year. Summer parking fee. Walk through woods, low seacoast shrubs, heaths to open ledges; panoramic ocean views encompass three states; historic **Babson Farm Quarry,** now water filled. Old submarine spotting tower is park headquarters (limited hours) and possible future museum of quarry industry in Rockport; summer self-guided tours interpret marks on granite, tell how granite was hoisted, moved, loaded on schooners.

ANNISQUAM AND WEST GLOUCESTER

(See locator map, pages 366–67.)

The village of Annisquam was settled in 1631 as Planter's Neck. In colonial times it was a busy shipbuilding, fishing, and trading center and a thriving port with a fleet that reached other continents. Annisquam's people included many successful sea captains. These days are reflected in the charming present—narrow, winding streets with buildings remaining from those heady times mixing well with more recent construction of prosperous twentieth century.

1. ANNISQUAM VILLAGE CHURCH, *1830.* Washington and Leonard sts.

At the head of Lobster Cove stands the white village church with its bell tower, symbolizing the spiritual center of Annisquam. It was built in 1830, replacing the original meetinghouse of 1728. The quiet of that first meetinghouse was shattered by controversy in 1765, when John Wyeth became minister against the wishes of part of the congregation, then was dismissed three stormy years later. Four years later Obadiah Parson began a ministry that ended under a cloud of moral accusations. Though exonerated by church council, Parson departed, leaving the church without a regular minister for many years. In 1804, Reverend Ezra Leonard came and smooth sailing began. In 1811 Leonard accepted the views of Universalism and was so well respected that his entire parish joined him in his new allegiance.

2. THE VILLAGE CENTER: Annisquam Exchange and Art Gallery, Annisquam Historical Society, Village Hall. Leonard St. Open seasonally, limited hours; no fee.

The old Leonard School, topped by a large bell, is home to Annisquam Exchange and Art Gallery. The exchange features handcrafted works and antiques on the first floor and an art gallery on the second. Set back on the small green is the Annisquam Historical Society in the old firehouse. An historic stagecoach, photos, prints, and documents are on view in this museum of Annisquam's past. The Village Hall has seen many uses. Constructed in 1828 as a Baptist meetinghouse, it later became Mechanics Hall—a place for public gatherings. A store, post office, and sail loft were located here, followed by a club room and later a restaurant. Now the Village Hall contains the library and post office.

3. ANNISQUAM LIGHTHOUSE AND SQUAM ROCK. Access Walnut St. between stone pillars. External view only, no fee.

Follow the path through the stone pillars. Soon on the left is a path to Squam Rock. It was called Squaw Rock for a young Indian girl who fell or jumped to her death from this rock. Over the years it has become known as Squam Rock. Farther along the path, you come over a rise and see Annisquam Lighthouse. Continue the gentle descent to the shore and light, a quiet focal point for artists and photographers. The lighthouse is situated on rocky Wigwam Point, where Indians gathered in summer months for fishing and clamming. The first lighthouse was built of wood in 1800 and burned whale oil. Connected with it was a one-room keeper's house. By 1850 the present keeper's house was built. The picturesque lighthouse you see today, stark white with a black cap, was constructed on its solid rock foundation in 1897 and electrified twenty-five years later.

4. DOGTOWN, *c. 1719–75*. Off Cherry St. Open all year, no fee. Map or guide strongly advised. Hiking trails, berry picking, seasonal hunting.

Walking through fields, woods, and ruins at Dogtown, you find it hard to realize that this was the bustling residential and farming center of Gloucester from around 1719 until the Revolution. It was the crossroads of the cape, with easy access by road or water to Annisquam, Pigeon Cove, Sandy Bay, or Gloucester Harbor. Following the Revolution, however, many men never returned. Activities shifted from farming to the sea—fishing, trade, shipbuilding. The community became deserted; only a few old people and their dogs remained. Then only dogs were left.

Today there are interesting trails for historian, geologist, naturalist, and the curious. This was the southernmost terminal moraine of the glacial period, leaving interesting rock formations. The area is full of local bird and animal life as well as being on the natural flyway for migrating birds. Wild shrubbery—blueberry, bayberry, beach plum, viburnum, and laurel—add beauty and color to different seasons. Wildflowers abound; wild orchids are of special interest. Here are the stones Roger Babson had carved with mottos such as *Mother knows best.*

5. WHITE–ELLERY HOUSE, *c. 1703*. Poplar and Washington sts. Currently not open.

John White, minister of the church that stood on the Gloucester Green, was the first recorded owner of this oldest house still standing in Gloucester. Next owner was John Stevens, who ran a successful tavern. Much of the business of the early town was carried on by selectmen over a good meal and mug of spirits. In 1740 Captain William Ellery became tavern proprietor. The house remained in the Ellery family until acquired by the Cape Ann Historical Association in 1947. When the traffic circle was built, the house was moved from its site on the south side of the former green. The well-preserved house retains much of its early style as well as the flavor of this early colonial center.

BEACHES, PARKS, OTHER POINTS OF INTEREST

A. Lobster Cove Bridge, 1847. Bridgewater St. Open all year as footbridge. Fine view of Lobster Cove. Wooden bridge, built as drawbridge for busy port; until 1861 was toll bridge unless travelers going to church, school, or military duty or hauling coal; fares 1 cent for pedestrians to 12.5 cents for two-horse wagons.

B. Wingaersheek Beach. Atlantic St., West Gloucester. Open all year. Summer parking fee. Lifeguards, concessions, rest rooms. Mouth of Annisquam River opposite Annisquam Light; protected wide, gently sloping, sandy beach. Once called Coffin's Beach, was site of Revolutionary War skirmish when Captain Linzee of British ship *Falcon* sent landing party to Peter Coffin's farm for mutton; Coffin and others battled from behind dunes, sailors retreated; British next seized heavy schooner in harbor, cargo was sand.

Man at the Wheel, Fishermen's Memorial, Gloucester   *(Richard B. Kimball)*

ESSEX

The Chebacco Parish of Ipswich was settled in 1634 and incorporated as Essex in 1819. Settlers farmed, and some turned to the river and bay to supplement their livelihood with fishing, clamming, and shipbuilding. James II became king of England in 1685. He broke with Parliament, nullified New England's charters, and sent Sir Edmund Andros to govern the colonies. Harsh graduated property tax was imposed on freeholders. Coastal towns, poor after King Philip's War, sought leadership in opposing these unwanted taxes. In 1687 John Wise, the powerful minister of Ipswich's Chebacco Parish (later Essex), spoke out against the taxes and recommended resistance if necessary—the first definite stand against taxation without representation. For this statement of conscience, Wise was arrested along with others. Within two years, however, James II was overthrown and Andros imprisoned, Simon Bradstreet became governor, and John Wise became a representative from Ipswich.

By the 1850s busy shipyards along the Essex River turned out roughly a vessel a week, 60 in 1852 alone. Over 4,000 wooden vessels, built at more than 15 yards, have passed the delta of the Essex River, which also offers some of the world's best mud flats for clamming. Essex clams, still dug by hand, are enjoyed throughout New England. Now restaurants and antiques shops line the river.

1. EARLY SHIPYARDS AND ESSEX RIVER. Main St.

In 1668 Ipswich set aside one acre of common land here to be used for shipbuilding. The trade was carried on well into the twentieth century, making this the oldest shipbuilding site in continuous use in the western hemisphere. Local sawmills provided wood, local settlers had talent and leadership, and the river provided the place and means for launching ships with a 5-mile tidal path to the ocean. The earliest vessels were built for the builder's own use—generally for a season of fishing, and then sold. "Shallops" were built for local inshore fisheries and ranged from twelve to twenty tons register. By the late 1700s they had evolved into the "Chebacco boat" and the "pinky." The Chebacco boat, developed in Essex about 1770, had two masts and was fore-and-aft rigged; it had a pointed or "pink" stern and no bowsprit. The larger pinky added a bowsprit with headsails. Larger vessels for offshore banks and distant fishing, thirty to ninety registered tons, were rigged as schooners or brigs. Power was added to sail in 1905 when the *Thomas S. Gorton* was built for the Gloucester fishing fleet. Twenty-five years later the Arthur D. Story Shipyard launched the *Gertrude L. Thebaud,* last of the great schooners powered by sail and motor. The last Essex sawn-framed vessel was the schooner yacht *Eugena J.* in 1949.

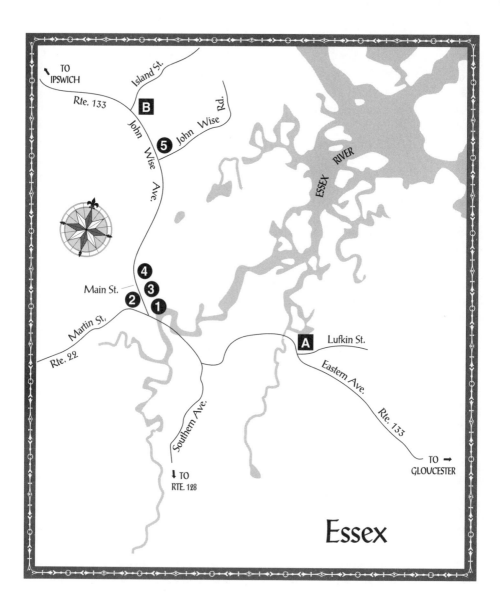

TO
IPSWICH

Rte. 133

Island St.

B

John Wise Rd.

John Wise Ave.

5

ESSEX RIVER

4
Main St.
3
2
1

Martin St.

Rte. 22

Southern Ave.

A Lufkin St.

Eastern Ave.

Rte. 133

TO
GLOUCESTER

↓ TO
RTE. 128

Essex

2. FIRST CONGREGATIONAL CHURCH, *1792–93*. Main St.

The peaceful appearance of this dignified old church, fourth built for this Essex congregation, does not hint of its fascinating and sometimes violent history. The congregation stirred ill feelings when it petitioned to separate from Ipswich and build its own church nearer home. Ipswich did not want to lose the revenue, so it forbade Essex men to erect their own church. Abigail Varney and a group of women met and decided to interpret the law that *men* were restrained but not women. The women arranged to have the church completed by neighboring men. Ipswich was furious! The women were arrested, but nothing came of it, and they had their own church.

Appropriately for this determined group, their first minister was Reverend John Wise, who served here from 1680 until he died in 1725. He was not only spiritual leader but farmer, author, chaplain during the French and Indian Wars, activist in community affairs, and a man deeply interested in wider causes affecting mankind. He supported the unpopular smallpox inoculation, was open in his dangerous disapproval of witch trials, and is best known as the source of the stirring words, "Taxation without representation is tyranny."[31] Thomas Jefferson said of him, "No other American Colonial author equals John Wise in breadth and power of thought."[32]

In 1797 members donated silver and jewelry to be used to cast a Paul Revere bell, giving it an unusual tone. The bell, one of the last three Revere made, hangs 60 feet above the road in the square bell tower. For years it marked the working life of Essex shipbuilders—called them to and from work, home to noon dinner, and back to work—and rang for fires and town meetings, tolled for the dead, and called all to worship.

3. ESSEX SHIPBUILDING MUSEUM, HS. 28 Main St. Open extended season, fee. Film, shop.

This large white building resembles the 1835 school it once was, yet the bell is not the usual school bell. It is from the USS *Essex*, the third vessel to carry the name. The bell from the later aircraft carrier USS *Essex* is on display within. The museum captures the spirit of the days of shipbuilding. A film and exhibits of tools, scale and half models, photos, documents, and artifacts display the lore and skills of shipbuilding. The "Frame Up" exhibit contains full-scale frames of fishing schooners, many built for Gloucester fishermen. The museum shop has model-making equipment, tools, books, and work of local craftspeople. Called the finest schooner museum in America, it features the Essex-built 83-foot fishing schooner *Evelina M. Goulart*. The schooner is located near the town ramp, on waterfront land where she was built in 1927. Late in 1990 she came upriver, though she draws 12 feet. The hull is for external view and shipbuilding research.

Caulker at Work, Essex   (Collection of Essex Shipbuilding Museum)

4. OLD BURYING GROUND, *1680,* and ESSEX HEARSE HOUSE, *c. 1840.* Main St. Open all year by appointment, no fee.

The Old Burying Ground has more than 300 headstones. Here are buried Reverend John Wise and his successors, Theophilus Pickering and John Cleaveland (brother of Ebenezer Cleaveland of Rockport), as well as the first schoolmaster, Nathaniel Rust, Jr. The stone marking the grave of John Wise refers to Wise as "a star of the first magnitude" and is raised above the rest. As you wander among interesting old stones with their subtle or obvious messages, you notice family names such as Story, Burnham, and Andrews that are still prevalent in Essex today, centuries later. The Essex Historical Society has an inventory of graves available for research at their museum (3). This serene site carries a story from 1818 of a village doctor's macabre theft of eighteen bodies for research.

The small building near the road is the Essex Hearse House, which housed the first hearse. It was built on the reinterment site of eighteen empty caskets. The hearse house contains an ancient sleigh hearse and a more modern 1860 horse-drawn dome hearse with Gothic windows. Preserving caskets that had iceboxes, used before embalming, are also displayed.

5. REVEREND JOHN WISE HOUSE, *c. 1701.* **John Wise Ave. Private.**

In 1680 John Wise came to Essex, a Harvard graduate, son of an indentured servant. He was at home here in Essex, yet his thoughts and words would affect the whole nation. In August 1687 Wise led the protest against Governor Andros and the unwanted property tax. He was jailed for his efforts. But he ignited the spark that would stir Americans for years and finally result in the Declaration of Independence. In addition, Wise was a physically strong man. A story is told of his challenge by the county's wrestling champion, who was promptly thrown to the ground. The second time the challenger was hurled over a fence. He conceded defeat and requested Reverend Wise to toss his horse over the fence, too, so he could go home. Behind a split-rail fence and shrubs is a Colonial saltbox house that was home to Reverend John Wise centuries ago.

BEACHES, PARKS, OTHER POINTS OF INTEREST

A. **Allyn Cox Reservation.** Eastern Ave. Open all year. No fee. Benches, field and water views; fields extending to marsh and Essex River; interesting plants with labels; hiking, exploring, picnicking, any use that doesn't harm environment; programs. Essex County Greenbelt Association headquarters.

B. **Stavros Reservation.** Rte. 133 and Island St. Open all year. No fee. Walking paths look out over Essex marshes and river to Crane Beach and Argilla Rd. Trustees of Reservations.

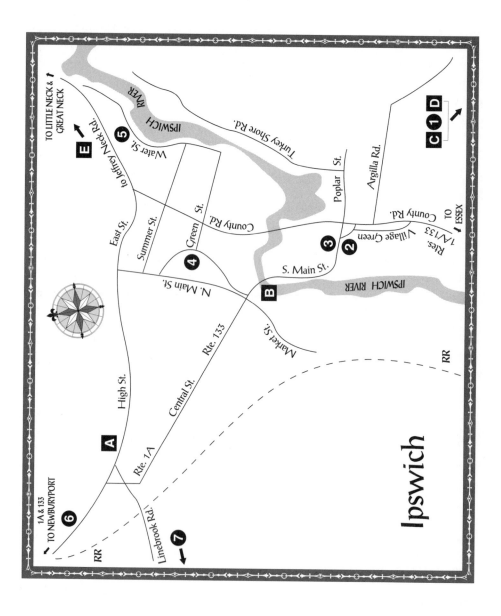

Ipswich

IPSWICH

Ipswich, which included Essex and Hamilton, was a hub of intellectual and cultural activity for Puritan Massachusetts Bay Colony from the town's inception under John Winthrop, Jr., until the Revolution. This area was a cradle of learning where students trained before Harvard; birthplace (Essex section) of the first stand against taxation without representation; and pioneer (Hamilton section) in the westward movement.

The Winthrops were an historic family. John Winthrop, Sr., a crusader of strong moral and religious commitments, was the driving force in the establishment of Puritan Massachusetts Bay Colony. His son, John Winthrop, Jr., established Ipswich with twelve men in 1633. Masconomet, an Indian sagamore, signed a pact with Winthrop, Jr., a year later. In exchange for protection, Masconomet sold land for twenty pounds, submitting authority to Massachusetts Bay Colony and agreeing to become Christian. To this settlement came people of learning and ambition. Richard Saltonstall served as deputy to the legislature. Nathaniel Ward, Ipswich's first minister, assisted in writing the "Body of Liberties" in 1641, which was the first civil code in New England, and wrote *The Simple Cobbler of Aggawam*, the first important prose in the colonies. Anne Bradstreet, first female poet in colonial America, had a book of verses, *The Tenth Muse*, published in London in 1650. Her father, Thomas Dudley, as well as her husband, Simon Bradstreet, and her brother, Joseph Dudley, were governors of the colony. Ipswich grew as a cultural center, second only to Boston, and fine quality, First Period houses were built, many of which remain along High, County, and South Main.

Ipswich was in economic trouble by 1750, when the harbor silted up, a result of erosion from too many trees being cut. The harbors of Newburyport and Salem grew in importance, and people there built fine Georgian and Federal period houses. Ipswich was also hit hard by the Revolution its people so strongly supported. The economy was depressed, fishing was limited, trade ground to a standstill, many intellectuals left, and returning veterans looked for greener pastures. These problems produced Ipswich's greatest treasure today, for resources were not available to tear down old houses and build new stylish ones. Early houses were repaired, preserving the greatest number of pre-Revolutionary houses to be found anywhere in the United States. The economy moved to production of fine lace and hosiery, which had been made from earliest times. The recorded census of 1790 shows people actively employed in making lace by hand, creating 41,979 yards of lace that year in Ipswich. These statistics were gathered by Alexander Hamilton in his efforts to encourage the new country's industries and reduce imports. In the late 1800s tourists were drawn to summer hotels, now no longer standing. American Impressionist Arthur Wesley Dow established an artists' summer colony, which flourished from the 1890s to the 1920s. The largest collection of his work is on display at the Heard House (3). Now visitors and residents appreciate beautiful beaches and historic houses.

1. RICHARD T. CRANE, JR., MEMORIAL RESERVATION, CASTLE HILL, *1925–27*, NRHP. Argilla Rd. Open all year, limited hours, fee. National-level concerts, programs, tours, special exhibitions.

Richard T. Crane, the Chicago millionaire who did for plumbing what Ford did for cars, built this spectacular mansion. Once an Italian-style mansion stood here, but Crane's wife desired a different style, so the first mansion was removed to make room for this one. The present Wren-style mansion is built of brick with two similar wings off an imposing central core. The beautiful, intricate woodwork in the library was brought intact from the castle of the earl of Essex, in England, and contains rare examples of wood carving by Grinling Gibbons. Walk out on the terrace overlooking the ocean or down the steps of the Grand Allee lined with Greek statues by nationally known sculptor Paul Manship, of Cape Ann. From high atop this tree-lined drumlin, you see Plum Island, Crane Beach, Ipswich River, and colorful marshes and coastline. The grounds total 1,326 acres, including beaches, dunes, and wide expanses of grass to picnic on during summer concerts.

2. WHIPPLE HOUSE, *c. 1655*, NHL, HS. South Main St. and County Rd. Open extended season or by appointment, fee.

The home of Elder John Whipple and his family is a national treasure, one of the oldest houses to survive in New England. The left side was built by Whipple c.1655 in the post-medieval style—steeply pitched, shingled roof and leaded glass casement windows. About 1670 the grander section was added by son Captain John Whipple, whose wealth created the mansion effect. His son, Major John, expanded the rear lean-to about 1700, now the earliest standing integral lean-to to survive. The house was moved here in 1927 from across the Ipswich River. Whipples were one of the wealthiest families in town, and descendants lived here nearly 200 years. Original summer beams, girts, and posts show the ancient heritage of the house. Massive hand-hewn beams dominate; the earliest, of tamarack, are on both levels on the left side. On the right, cross summer beams of chestnut have unusually fine ogee molding, which extends to the outside, displaying the wealth of the owner. You can stand erect in the huge fireplaces and see open sky above.

Displays include seventeenth- and eighteenth-century period furnishings and other rare objects. Ipswich's unique collection of lace includes fine linen pillow bobbin lace and machine lace. Whipple House gardens were designed by Arthur Shurliff, landscape architect of Williamsburg. Ann Leighton, author of *Early American Gardens:*

Whipple House, Ipswich

for Meate or Medicine, authentically recreated and planted the gardens using seventeenth-century documents. She was first to do so in the country.

3. JOHN HEARD HOUSE, *1795,* HS. 40 South Main St. Open extended season, fee.

This grand Federal home is set amid lovely old trees, and an attached ell, barn, and formal gardens complete the picture. The Heard family made their fortune in the exciting days of West Indies trade and later the China trade. The house is Federal, with the Palladian window and commanding height of the period. The covered portico was added to the pure flat facade in the 1880s. The interior is adorned with many treasures from the Orient, American period furnishings, and special collections. In the barn is the impressive art of Authur Wesley Dow and a notable collection of restored carriages.

4. FIRST CHURCH IN IPSWICH, *1971;* Meetinghouse Green, 1634. North Main St.

On this rocky hill above the Ipswich River settlers built their meetinghouse on Meetinghouse Green. In the 1600s the Green was the center of colonial life. Each month all males aged eighteen or older participated in military training here. Homes of distinguished settlers surrounded the Green—Nathaniel Rogers, minister to the meetinghouse; Richard Saltonstall, deputy to the General Court; Samuel Appleton of Appleton Farm; schoolmaster Ezekiel Cheever; and Reverend Nathaniel Ward. Later the Green also held the prison where some accused of witchcraft during Salem trials were held. Stocks and a whipping post for local offenders of Puritan laws were in evidence.

Here, too, was the Town House where, in 1687, Reverend John Wise (of the Essex section) and the people of Ipswich took the first public stand against taxation without representation. Nearby was the courthouse where John Adams tried cases as a young circuit lawyer. The original meetinghouse of First Church was built in 1634 here on Meetinghouse Hill, surrounded and protected by a fortlike stone wall. The first minister was Nathaniel Ward, assisted by Thomas Parker, founder of Newbury. Next came Reverend John Norton, credited with writing the first book in Latin in colonial America, followed by Reverend Nathaniel Rogers, scholar and patriarch of four generations of ministers who served a total of 137 years.

Ipswich didn't escape the witchcraft scare—or the evangelistic ardor of Reverend George Whitfield. Supposedly Whitfield preached such a fiery sermon that he aroused the anger of the devil, who fought with him all the way to the top of the steeple, where Whitfield overcame him. From the steeple, the story goes, the devil jumped onto rocks below. One cloven foot mark can be seen in the rocks on the eastern side of the church, and the other foot was said to have landed in Gloucester, an amazing feat even to imagine.

The cornerstone for today's sixth meetinghouse was laid in 1971. The commanding white brick structure combines modern architecture and craftsmanship and testifies to the dedication of its parishioners. In the open sanctuary with its wooden arches and ceiling are unusual windows made from geometric pieces of colored glass set in epoxy.

5. TOWN WHARF. Water St. Open all year, no fee.

In earlier centuries the scene at Town Wharf was very different. In the 1700s coastal fishing boats and trading ships from the West Indies and Europe tied up here. In the 1800s barges brought lumber, lime, and coal upriver from the sea. The early 1900s saw the wharf busy with steamers loading up to one hundred people at a time for regular trips on the river and along the coast to Little Neck and Plum and Grape islands, where there were summer hotels. In 1919–33 small boats went out as rumrunners to meet European and Canadian ships anchored offshore. Eventually the river channel filled with sand, making passage for large ships impossible, but fishermen and tourists still enjoy this wharf.

6. MERCHANT–OSBORN–LORD HOUSE, also called Austin Lord House, c. late 1630s. 97–99 High St. Private.

This house is of special architectural interest. Using careful detecting methods, expert Abbott Lowell Cummings declares it the oldest house in Ipswich. Within the visible Colonial exterior is hidden a tiny, one-and-a-half-story, one-room-deep Plimoth Plantation–style cottage, probably here since the late 1630s. Some time after that date, the roof was raised and another planter's cottage brought here and attached. Additions and a new facade complete the present impression. Proof of the early cottage can be seen in the attic and in what were once exterior walls of the first-floor front room.

7. 1640 HART HOUSE. Linebrook Rd. and Kimball Ave. Open all year as restaurant, no fee for informal tour.

The facade hides a fascinating collection of beautifully maintained rooms relating to the 1680s and 1840s. The two 1680s rooms are reproductions. The originals were entirely removed, including their whole external skeletons, and reside in museums— the Metropolitan in New York and Winterthur in Wilmington, Delaware. It is believed the original two rooms in the museums contain very fine paneling from the Saltonstall House. The accurate reproduction of the old parlor in the 1680 section has massive oak beams, huge fireplace, and pumpkin paneling. In the guest room above, a section of wall is open to allow a view of brick-filled construction, which included powdered clamshells and salt marsh hay. The 1840 section has attractively furnished guest rooms used when Hart House was an active inn. Harts were political and military leaders in early Ipswich. Lieutenant Thomas Hart, tanner, joined Reverend John Wise in the tax protest. Hart's son, Thomas, also a tanner, was representative to the General Court and fought in the French and Indian Wars.

BEACHES, PARKS, OTHER POINTS OF INTEREST

A. **Old Burial Ground,** 1634. High St. Founder John Winthrop, Jr.'s wife and child first to be buried here 1634; interesting stones of Ipswich historic families; portrait stone for Reverend Nathaniel Rogers shows details, even to the fourteen buttons on clerical robes.

B. **Choate Bridge,** 1764, NRHP. South Main St. Double-arched stone bridge, one of the oldest of this type in country, replaced earlier 1641 wooden one.

C. **Argilla Farm,** 1637. Argilla Rd. Private. Farmland of John Winthrop, Jr., granted 1636; next belonged to deputy governor of Massachusetts Bay Colony, Samuel Symonds; Symonds house replaced in 1800 by great-grandson Allen Baker with today's handsome Federal house.

D. **Crane Beach.** Argilla Rd. Open all year. Fee. Lifeguards, bathhouse, concessions; 4 miles beautiful wide sandy beach backed by acres of dunes; low pine and brush shelter deer and birds; ocean, Essex River, Castle Neck River border peninsula.

E. **Great Neck.** Jeffrey Neck Rd. area. Homes private. Was common pastureland, low marshes, plus two glacier-rounded drumlins; area overlooks Plum Island and sound; fed by Plum, Rowley, Parker, Eagle Hill rivers; Indian artifacts found; end of Clark Pond Road is small beach between Great Neck and Little Neck.

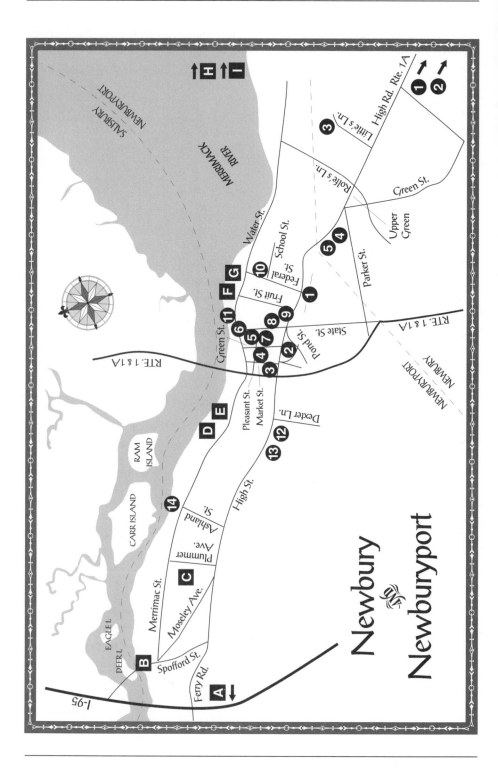

Newbury *&* Newburyport

NEWBURY

Reverend Thomas Parker and a group of farmers and herdsmen sailed from England aboard the *Mary and John,* arriving in Ipswich in 1634. The next year Parker and twenty-three families traveled up the Parker River, carved homesteads from the wilderness, and created the town of Newbury. Farming and cattle raising continued to be the main occupations as the settlement spread westward and others moved to settle Newburyport at the mouth of the Merrimack River. Many of the early homes still exist along High Road. The home where Parker and his cousin Reverend James Noyes lived until they died still stands at 7 Parker Street (private). Newbury is a treasure of seventeenth-century houses.

1. OLD TOWN HILL RESERVATION. Newman St. (first street north of lower Green). Trustees of Reservations. Open all year, no fee. 370 acres; hiking, skiing, picnicking.

A short, steep climb to the top of Old Town Hill affords a sweeping panoramic view of marshes, Plum Island, Isles of Shoals, and Newburyport. Samuel Sewall enjoyed wandering this land and described views in his journals, and John Greenleaf Whittier wrote a poem based on Sewall's observations.

2. DOLE-LITTLE HOUSE, *early 1700s,* SPNEA. 289 High Rd. Open all year by appointment, fee.

Set on a crest rising above the river, this house once shared the site with old ferry operations and a tannery run by Richard Dole. Dole probably purchased the property from Nicholas Easton, who moved to Rhode Island, where he became lieutenant governor. Dole was not only a tanner, but a merchant and patriarch of six generations. The steep pitched roof and tiny diamond panes of the restored house suggest earlier construction.

3. SPENCER-PIERCE-LITTLE HOUSE AND FARM, *c. 1700,* SPNEA, NHL. Little's Ln. Open summer, fee.

John Spencer arrived in Newbury in 1635 with Reverends Parker and Noyes. He soon became Newbury's representative to the General Court and a militia captain. Condemned as a follower of Anne Hutchinson and John Wheelwright, who were outlawed for their ideas of religious freedom, Spencer probably returned to England. He left land and possessions to nephew John Spencer, Jr. In 1651 Spencer, Jr., sold the place to his uncle Daniel Pierce; Daniel built or added to this house, where many generations of Pierces lived. Later, half the land was purchased by Nathaniel Tracy, prosperous Revolutionary privateersman and owner of many grand houses. He died in 1796 at age forty-five.

A most unusual house, the center was built of stone and brick on a cruciform plan, with two wooden wings added early in the nineteenth century. The stone was probably rafted down the Merrimack River and the brick shipped from England, as it is smaller than the size decreed by the Massachusetts General Court. Interpretation is multilayered, allowing looks through walls to earlier construction and times past. The barn is eighteenth century. Much of the 230 acres is still farmed, continuing 300 years of agricultural history.

4. TRISTRAM COFFIN HOUSE, *c. 1651*, SPNEA. 16 High Rd. Open summer, fee.

The original ell, with side door facing south, was built about 1651. The front addition soon followed, made by Tristram Coffin, Jr., for his extensive family. The porch is believed to be much later. The steep pitch of the wood-shingled roof, narrow clapboards, and simple lines mark this early Colonial. Newbury's Colonials provide interesting contrast with the later Federal and Georgian mansions on High Street in Newburyport.

Tristam Coffin, Sr., ran a ferry to Salisbury. He later moved to Nantucket, where he was the driving force behind its purchase in 1659. His son Tristram, Jr., was a deacon in Newburyport for twenty years and representative to the General Court for years, as was his son Nathaniel. The Coffins produced two Harvard graduates per generation until Joshua, who wrote the *History of Newbury,* graduated from Dartmouth in the early 1800s. He was a teacher and the subject of the poem "To My Old Schoolmaster" by John Greenleaf Whittier. Treasures of eight Coffin generations are found here. Of particular interest are the seventeenth- and eighteenth-century kitchens, the buttery, and the parlor with early nineteenth-century wallpaper.

5. SWETT–ILSLEY HOUSE, *c. 1671*, SPNEA. 4 High Rd. Open all year by appointment, fee.

This interesting old Newbury Colonial was occupied by craftsmen, tradesmen, and tavern keepers—another contrast with the impressive Federals and Georgians occupied by Newburyport's sea captains and merchants. The oldest section was probably two rooms and two stories, with later extensive additions. Solid, massive cellar walls, heavy oak frame, and immense chimney are early features. This was home to Captain John March, who led a company in an attack in Canada in 1690, and to Dudley Colman, an officer on Washington's staff at Valley Forge nearly a century later. The house was a Post Road tavern under Oliver Putnam. His son Oliver, Jr., left a handsome endowment to start a free high school.

NEWBURYPORT

(See locator map, page 394.)

Beautifully preserved houses of world-traveling sea captains, wealthy merchants, shipbuilders, and talented and artistic people document Newburyport's past. Here lived William Moulton and Anthony F. Towle, famed silversmiths; John Lowell, a framer of the Massachusetts Constitution; Theophilus Parson, a lawmaker and Massachusetts chief justice. Here were Rufus King, a statesman who signed the federal Constitution, and Mayor Caleb Cushing, U.S. attorney general. Newburyport's William Lloyd Garrison, journalist, was a leading abolitionist, and John Marquand was a Pulitzer Prize–winning novelist.

The first meetinghouse, built in 1725, began the waterside settlement that became independent Newburyport in 1764. The Revolution, then the depression of Jefferson's embargoes and the War of 1812, followed by a sweeping fire, brought disaster. But work began again. The romantic era of clipper ships—graceful, sleek hulls with tall masts and billowing sails—brought a new identity to Newburyport. Donald McKay, who started his ship designing at Currier Shipyards on Merrimac Street, went on to Boston to build the *Lightning*, fastest clipper ship ever built. The famous packet *Dreadnaught*, called "Flying Dutchman," was built in Newburyport by Currier and Townsend in 1853. In all, 317 ships—clippers, three-masters, merchant ships—slid down the ways between 1831 and 1892. One of the busiest shipbuilding and trading ports on the coast, Newburyport became birthplace of the U.S. Coast Guard (E). But again winds changed, and aging docks were quiet until historical restoration rescued the city. Now tourists visit revitalized downtown shops and admire restored Georgian and Federal-style homes of captains and merchant kings.

1. FEDERAL HOUSES OF HIGH AND GREEN STREETS.
Private.

High Street affords an interesting study in both architecture and geology. It traces the slope of an esker, a long gradual hill of gravel, boulders, and sand deposited by an ancient glacier. The street's architecture tells a more recent history. From the early Colonial Newbury end of High Street, stately Federals march in grand rows, physical reminders of the height of Newburyport's glory between the Revolution and the War of 1812. Green Street illustrates the transition from Georgian to Federal-style houses. Across High Street along Pond Street are examples of later architecture: Greek Revival and Victorian styles.

2. FROG POND, *1635*; BULFINCH-DESIGNED COURT HOUSE, *1805*; OLD STONE JAIL, *1824–25* (private). High and Pond sts.

On the upper side of Frog Pond is Old Hill Cemetery, with graves from pre-Revolutionary days and views of the Newburyport skyline. From here, picture the pond as it was in the early 1700s. A windmill stood across from a long ropewalk that provided ropes for ships' rigging. A potash house and grazing cows and sheep completed the scene. When shadows of the Revolution darkened the sky, a powder house was built at the foot of the cemetery hill, a training field was laid out, and a saltpeter manufactory built where the potash house stood. After the Revolution the ropewalk was gone, and Nathaniel Tracy planted trees in its place.

In 1805 the Court House was built, designed by Charles Bulfinch, and is still used as a courthouse. The side facing the pond shows Bulfinch influence. The front had an open portico of brick pillars and arches supporting the second floor but was remodeled to its present design in 1853.

On the northern side of Frog Pond, behind a high spiked stone wall, stands the Old Stone Jail of Newburyport. Built to last, it was constructed of 3- to 5-foot granite blocks hauled from Rockport. The warden's house (also private) is on the corner of Vernon and Auburn streets. Its rough-cut fieldstone contrasts with the more formal cut stone of the jail. Behind is the carriage house and cobblestone entrance to the jail and yard.

3. ST. PAUL'S EPISCOPAL CHURCH, *1922*. 166 High St.

The first church of this unusual Episcopal parish was built in 1738. A prudent decision taken during the American Revolution makes this the oldest Protestant Episcopal parish in Massachusetts. As the Revolution approached, it seemed as if Reverend Edward Bass would have to choose between serving his parishioners and retaining allegiance to the Crown. Instead, he excluded from all his prayers and liturgy any reference to England or the Crown. The dedicated minister, never discussing politics, served such Patriots as Patrick and Nathaniel Tracy, Rufus King, and Tristram and Michael Dalton. In recognition of his efforts to revive the Episcopal Church in America, Bass was made the first Episcopal bishop in Massachusetts in 1797. He continued to serve here until his death in 1803. In 1800 a new St. Paul's church building was erected with a carved wooden bishop's mitre surmounting the bell tower, signifying a cathedral. The building was destroyed by fire, and the present stone church was built in 1922. Historic memorabilia are displayed in the entranceway.

4. BROWN SQUARE, *1802*; CENTRAL CONGREGATIONAL CHURCH, *1826*; GARRISON STATUE, *1893*. Pleasant and Titcomb sts.

Moses Brown—manufacturer of carriages, importer of sugar and molasses, owner of a rum distillery, bank director, proprietor of a 1794 woolen factory, selectman—was born in Newburyport in 1742. He planned Brown Square in 1802 as a block of brick offices and commercial buildings. The only building completed, however, was the large Federal brick on the northwest corner, once a private residence, now Garrison Inn.

At the head of the square stands the Central Congregational Church, second on the site. It was gutted by fire and rebuilt in 1861. In the center of the square is the William Lloyd Garrison statue, honoring the journalist-abolitionist. He apprenticed on the *Newburyport Herald* at age thirteen. In 1826, when he was twenty-one, he published his first newspaper here, the *Free Press,* which included John Greenleaf Whittier's first poem. Garrison later edited papers throughout the East Coast, returning to Boston and the *Liberator.* He founded the first society for the abolition of slavery and led the abolition battle.

5. UNITARIAN CHURCH, *1801.* 26 Pleasant St.

Visible from the Merrimack River and most of Newburyport, the impressive steeple of the Unitarian Church represents the first parish, established here in 1725. At that time the meetinghouse was built at the foot of State Street in Market Square. John Lowell was called as first minister (see 13). In 1801 the old church was torn down and this larger one built here on Pleasant Street. The most notable feature is the beautiful steeple, its four tiers ranging from simple to ornate. The weathercock, 159 feet above ground, originally graced the steeple on the first meetinghouse.

6. MARKET SQUARE, *1725, 1811,* NRHP. State, Merrimac, and Water sts.

Here at the river's edge, Indians once made camp for the summer; they were followed by earliest white fishermen. The first wharf along the Merrimack River was built near what is now the foot of State Street. In 1725 a meetinghouse was built. Countinghouses and warehouses rose in the vicinity, and the square became the market area for farm and craft products. In 1811 fire struck. Rebuilding in solid brick and stone, Newburyport created Market Square, one of the finest examples of homogeneous Federal commercial seaport architecture in the country. In the twentieth century the square declined with the rest of the local economy and was slated for urban renewal. Fortunately, however, many buildings were spared and are now restored and filled with appealing shops.

7. NATHANIEL TRACY HOUSE, *1771,* Public Library. 94 State St.

This commanding brick was built by Patrick Tracy and given to his son Nathaniel as a wedding gift. Nathaniel was to know the heights of great wealth and influence and the despair of bankruptcy. During the American Revolution, his twenty-four privateers captured 120 British prize ships, which sold for $3,950,000. Tracy was also the principal owner of 110 other ships. He donated huge sums of money to Newburyport. By the end of the Revolution, however, he had lost most of his ships, and in 1786 he faced bankruptcy. He was forced to sell his properties, including the Longfellow House in

Cambridge. He lost his home here, in which he had entertained Thomas Jefferson and Benedict Arnold. Later the house hosted Governor John Hancock; George Washington, during his triumphant visit to Newburyport; and Lafayette in 1824.

The house was remodeled as the town library in 1865, and the exterior acquired its Victorian look in the 1880s. The interior retains many early Federal features. The Directors Room, open on request, has furnishings of the early American republic and paintings by Gilbert Stuart and Mather Brown. Throughout the library are displays of paintings, chromolithographs, and a collection of rare Audubon prints.

8. DALTON HOUSE, *1746.* 95 State St. Private.

Michael Dalton, captain and prosperous merchant, built this handsome Georgian for his son Tristram. Tristram Dalton was active in the reformation of public education in Massachusetts and served as speaker of the General Court and state senator. After firmly supporting the adoption of the new U.S. Constitution, he became one of the first senators from Massachusetts. Like his father, he was a pillar of St. Paul's Church. He graduated from Harvard with John Adams and often entertained Adams's son, John Quincy Adams, as well as George Washington here. Another frequent visitor was Theophilus Parsons, law teacher of young Adams and of Robert Treat Paine's son and Rufus King. Parsons advocated the Bill of Rights, managed Massachusetts' adopting the Constitution, and was chief justice of the state supreme court.

When Washington was declared the new capital, Dalton sold his interests in Newburyport, invested the proceeds in the fledgling city—and lost his investment. A gentleman of the old school, to support his family he went to work in the customhouse in Boston. The house is a beautiful formal Georgian with wood facing cut to resemble stone. The slate gambrel roof is capped by two chimneys, and the facade is highlighted by a decorative front entry.

9. CUSHING HOUSE, *1808,* NHL, HS. 98 High St. Open extended season, and by appointment, fee. Library, garden.

When John Newmarch Cushing bought this impressive Federal mansion, he had no idea how important his son and this house would become. It was in the dining room here that son Caleb Cushing and Jefferson Davis decided on Franklin Pierce as the Democratic candidate for president. President Pierce subsequently appointed Cushing attorney general. Cushing was a member of Congress, a general in the Mexican War, Newburyport's first mayor, a judge, and minister to Spain. As first ambassador to China, he negotiated a difficult situation into a treaty that effectively opened the door of China to full-scale American trade. His home was a center of society, where he entertained Jefferson Davis, Franklin Pierce, and John Quincy Adams.

Appropriately, this tall brick classic Federal is now the museum of historic Newburyport. Real treasures are here—the house museum memorializes a grand family and contains an outstanding collection of paintings, furniture, needlework, clocks, toys, silver, china, and glass. There is a genealogical library of important books, manuscripts, and other rare records. The grounds beautifully display how space was used in city lots in the nineteenth century. The 1840s garden reflects Caleb Cushing's interest in botany with plantings of native wildflowers. Rare roses of the 1840s are featured in a formal Renaissance garden. Outbuildings include a nineteenth-century barn and a shed used as shop or laundry.

10. OLD SOUTH PRESBYTERIAN CHURCH, *1746.* Federal St.

Fiery evangelist George Whitfield (see Ipswich 4) first arrived in Newburyport in September 1740, in a raging snowstorm. According to Ben Franklin, Reverend Whitfield could reach 25,000 people at one time and caused Franklin to empty his own pockets by his eloquence. Whitfield returned many times. His revivalism stirred New England as no one else has. Whitfield died at the home of his friend Jonathan Parsons, first minister of this church. Whitfield was buried under the pulpit at his own request. A memorial cenotaph was given by Honorable William Bartlet.

Old South's Reverend Parsons was Patriot as well as pastor. He called so passionately for Revolutionary volunteers that a whole company was formed in these aisles, said to be the first volunteer company in the Continental Army. Parsons was followed by John Murray, such an ardent Patriot and commanding speaker that the British put a price on his head. The third minister, Dr. Daniel Dana, was called to the presidency of Dartmouth.

11. CUSTOM HOUSE MARITIME MUSEUM, *1835,* NRHP. 25 Water St. Open extended season or by appointment, fee. Marquand Library.

The sea and the Merrimack River have always been the lifeblood of Newburyport. Indians were followed by white fishermen, then shipbuilding began as early as 1639. Water-based trade soon developed to the point where citizens resented British taxes. At the time of the Revolution, the focus was on building Continental Navy frigates and outfitting privateers. With independence came an interest in upholding the new nation's trade laws. The first revenue cutter, the *Massachusetts,* was launched in 1791, giving birth to the U.S. Coast Guard. Jefferson's embargoes, the fire of 1811, and the War of 1812 succeeded in bringing this proud and prosperous port to a standstill. Yet Newburyport rebuilt Market Square and reestablished enough trade to build the new Classic Revival Custom House in 1835. Then came the days of grand clippers and square-riggers. When these were replaced by steam, the harbor still was busy with local boats, and the Custom House remained open until the 1920s. Built of enduring granite, it was designed by Robert Mills, architect of the Washington Monument, and of the U.S. Patent Office and Treasury building. It is constructed entirely of granite and masonry, with no wood cross timbers. In an upstairs room the vaulted brick construction is exposed, and in the basement you see the vaulted foundation.

The museum brings alive Newburyport's days of sail. There are extensive collections centering on the Coast Guard, shipbuilding, customs collection, the China trade—more than 300 years of maritime history. Treasures brought home by Newburyport seamen mingle with art and furnishings crafted by skilled local artisans. The Marquand Library houses documents, books, paintings, and furnishings.

12. LORD TIMOTHY DEXTER HOUSE, *c. 1771*. 201 High St. Private.

Jonathan Jackson built a magnificent mansion on land he bought in 1771. He had graduated from Harvard; there he had met his friend and fellow Patriot John Lowell, who built the house next door at 203 High. Jackson was a member of the Committee of Safety, Provincial Congress, and Continental Congress.

In 1798 the mansion was purchased by Timothy Dexter, called by some the clown of Newburyport but by himself "the greatest philosopher in the Western world"[33] and about whom Pulitzer Prize–winner John Marquand wrote two books. Dexter worked and invested his way from a job as a leather dresser at age twenty-three to a position as eccentric entrepreneur and philanthropist. He transformed his sedate Federal home into a museum and built a fence with huge ornamental fence posts topped by statues of famous men and himself. Picture this mansion in "Lord" Timothy's day—surrounded by larger-than-life statues of George Washington, Thomas Jefferson, John Adams, Ben Franklin, John Hancock, Alexander Hamilton, carved animals, and even Adam and Eve! Only one of these statues has been found. Dexter built his own tomb and sponsored an elaborate mock funeral for himself. He made money in extraordinary ways, as when he sold bed-warming pans in the warm West Indies—to be used as cooking ladles for molasses. Later the Dexter house became an inn, then a boarding-house, finally a restored home. Tragically, it was nearly destroyed by fire, but it was recreated in the early 1990s. The beautiful replica Federal is embellished by columned portico, quoined corners, a six-sided cupola, and an ornamented chimney.

13. LOWELL–JOHNSON HOUSE, *c. 1774*. 203 High St. Private.

John Lowell, son of Reverend John Lowell, first minister in Newburyport, built this house about 1774. He was an ardent Patriot, judge, and member of the Provincial Assembly, Continental Congress, and General Court. In his role as a framer of the constitution of Massachusetts, he suggested the words, "all men are born free and equal," paving the way for abolishment of slavery in the state. He was also a force behind the idea of representation according to population. Lowell, Massachusetts, was named for his son Francis Cabot Lowell, founder of Lowell Institute in Boston. Another descendant, James Russell Lowell, was a poet and ambassador to the court of St. James. Later Patrick Tracy purchased the house and his son John lived here. An entertainment by successful merchant John Tracy was described by a French royal guest as "magnificence accompanied with simplicity."[34]

14. CURRIER–TOWNSEND SHIPYARD SITE, *1843*. **Merrimac and Ashland sts.**

The Currier–Townsend Shipyard was one of the main yards on the Merrimack River in the 1800s. Here the famous clipper ship builder Donald McKay began his designing career. In 1853 the legendary *Dreadnaught* was launched from this yard. This record-breaking Atlantic packet was built for speed and was so well designed and constructed that she once sailed 200 miles backward without rudder or wheel and still made it safely to port. Deep-water sailors affectionately called her the "wild boat of the Atlantic" or "Flying Dutchman." The last square-rigged ship built in Massachusetts, the *Mary L. Cushing*, was launched in 1883 from John Currier, Jr.'s, yard on this site.

BEACHES, PARKS, OTHER POINTS OF INTEREST

A. **Maudslay State Park.** Ferry Rd. Open all year. No fee. Extensive acreage of former estate on Merrimack River; woods, gardens, trails, fields, rolling hills; hiking, skiing, picnicking, programs.

B. **Chain Bridge and Conservation Sanctuary on Deer Island.** Spofford St. Open all year. No fee. In 1810 first chain suspension bridge in country replaced 1792 wooden drawbridge; collapsed 1827 but was rebuilt; charged tolls until mid-1800s. Conservation Sanctuary has nature paths leading to river; bald eagles sighted.

C. **Atkinson Common,** 1873. High and Plummer sts. Open all year. No fee. Fields, playground, tennis, reflecting pond, war memorials.

D. **Towle Silver 1690 House.** 262 Merrimac St. Open all year as Towle store. No fee. House built 1738 by Morse family, who lived here two centuries.

E. **Birthplace of U.S. Coast Guard.** Merrimac St. Open all year. No fee. Ship's bell and nun buoy mark entrance; here on Merrimack River first U.S. Coast Guard cutter, *Massachusetts,* launched 1791.

F. **Range Light.** Water St. Private. Four-sided brick lighthouse, used by ships' captains to line up with beam of another light; smaller white wooden range light at adjacent Coast Guard station; neither light now in use.

G. **Newburyport Art Association.** 65 Water St. Open all year. No fee. Building was workshop and loft of a spar maker; changing exhibits, classes, programs.

H. **Parker River National Wildlife Refuge.** Water St. to Plum Island, right after bridge. Open all year. Fee. 4,662 acres, wide sandy beach 7 miles long; dunes, marsh, wild berries, birds, wildlife; self-guided nature trail, observation tower; lifeguards, rest rooms; swimming, hiking, fishing, skiing, limited hunting.

I. **Plum Island Lighthouse,** 1787. Northern end of island. Parker River National Wildlife Refuge headquarters; state built two lights here, one burned 1856; lights moved many times because of shifting sands; lighthouse rebuilt 1898.

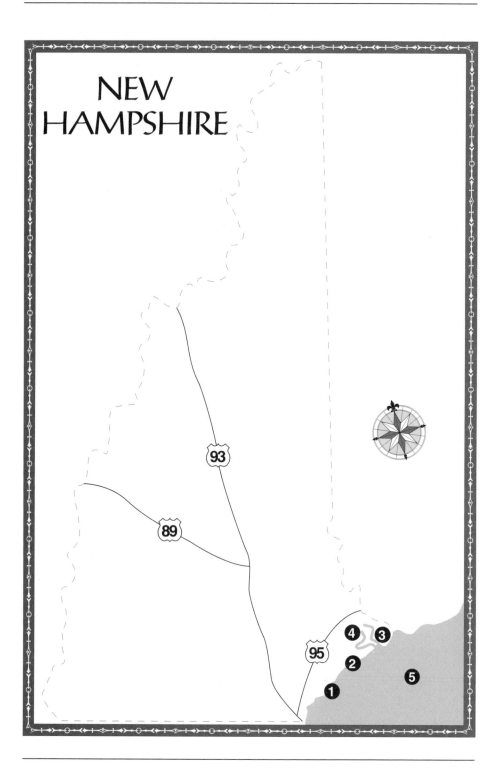

NEW
HAMPSHIRE

NEW HAMPSHIRE

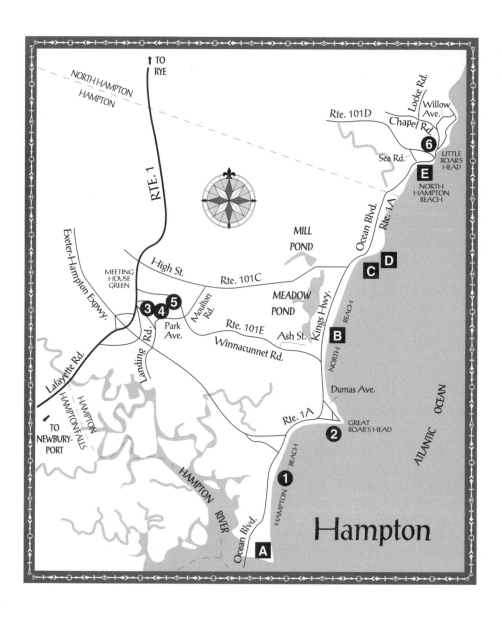

HAMPTON AND HAMPTON BEACH

Hampton has been home to many interesting people. It was founded by settlers from Newbury, Massachusetts, who sailed up the Hampton River and laid out their settlement on what is now Meeting House Green, once a flourishing Indian village. They were led by New England's answer to Ponce de Leon, minister-explorer Stephen Bachiler, who was in his seventies. Two of Bachiler's famous descendants were John Greenleaf Whittier and Daniel Webster. More than a century later, Hampton General Jonathan Moulton served in the French and Indian and Revolutionary wars and was town moderator and a state constitution delegate. A wealthy landowner in Moultonboro and New Hampton, Moulton was the focus of wild stories. In his poem "The New Wife and the Old," poet John Greenleaf Whittier portrayed the general as too frugal to buy his second wife a wedding ring; instead, he gave her his first wife's ring. Thus the ghost of his first, now very angry wife took up residence in their home, causing imaginable conflict. Another ghost, Goody Cole's, is also part of Hampton's eerie past (4).

During and after the Revolution, Hamptonite Meshech Weare guided New Hampshire as its first president. A century later Franklin Pierce summered in Hampton at 366 High Street with his wife, the former Jane Appleton, whose father was minister of the First Congregational Church and later president of Bowdoin College. In addition to fascinating people, Hampton has long been known for summer visitors and scenic coastal grandeur. Along Route 1A are magnificent views of the Atlantic Ocean and, on the horizon, the Isles of Shoals.

1. HAMPTON BEACH. Rte. 1A. Open all year, parking meters in summer. Extends 5½ miles along Atlantic; pavilion, lifeguards, swimming, concerts, special events.

John Greenleaf Whittier expressed its beauty in his poem, "Hampton Beach." Before summer visitors discovered it, the beach was home to fish houses, where fish were processed for trade with townspeople and fishmongers from as far away as Vermont. Today, in summer, the beach's Sea Shell Stage features nightly concerts, talent shows, fireworks, and other events. Across Route 1A is the casino, a center of entertainment since the big band era. One highlight is the annual Miss Hampton Beach Pageant. Past the pavilion on the beach is the **New Hampshire Marine Memorial** dedicated to New Hampshire's service personnel lost at sea.

2. GREAT BOAR'S HEAD. Off Rte. 1A on Dumas Ave. Short scenic drive.

For centuries this prominent land formation, with beautiful views, has been an identifying landmark guiding sailors safely home. From the ocean it appears as a great boar's head.

3. FOUNDERS' MEMORIAL PARK. Park Ave. Open all year, no fee.

This Green holds many reminders of Hampton's founding fathers and dedicated sons. The green oasis of **Founders' Memorial Park** is marked with stones of Hampton's founding families placed here by descendants. The central Founders' Stone is dedicated to Stephen Bachiler and the 1638 settlement. The larger stones on the perimeter recognize the original towns: North Hampton, Hampton, Hampton Falls, Seabrook—all once parts of "Old Hampton."

4. MEETING HOUSE GREEN AND TUCK MEMORIAL MUSEUM.
40 Park Ave. Open summer and by appointment, no fee.

Treasures from early Hampton are proudly displayed in the Tuck Memorial Museum, which also includes a Farm Museum and Seacoast Fire Museum. The Tuck family dates to original settler Robert Tuck. After six generations of prominent church and town activity, the Tuck family moved to Parsonsfield, Maine, where the Honorable Amos Tuck was born in 1810. Politician, abolitionist, and lawyer, Amos helped establish the Republican party. He was a friend to Abraham Lincoln and John Greenleaf Whittier and headmaster of Hampton Academy. His son, Edward, a financier, contributed much to Hampton—Tuck Athletic Fields, Tuck Memorial Museum, Founders' Memorial Park—as well as the Tuck Historical Building in Concord, Amos Tuck School of Administration and Finance at Dartmouth College, and the college's presidential residence.

The unmarked erosion rock **Goody Cole Memorial** is dedicated to the "Witch of Hampton." In the late 1600s Hampton gave in to dark fears of witchcraft. Eunice "Goody" Cole, an undoubtedly cantankerous woman who made a few well-placed threats, was perfect for the part. She was tried and convicted in 1656 for having a "familiarity with the devil," and sentenced to prison in Boston until 1671. Later she was again charged with witchcraft, but because of her advanced age, she remained as the town's ward in Hampton, where she was avoided by most. When she died, legend says some residents, to be sure her witchcraft days were over, drove a stake through her heart and quickly buried her. Being a town with a conscience, on its tricentennial, Hampton reinstated Goody Cole as citizen, burning condemning records. The ashes were to be buried, but this was decided against in an effort to encourage her spirit's restless wanderings. There are still rumors of a strange old lady wandering the streets at night.

Nearby is c. 1003 **Norseman's Rock,** whose markings many experts believe to be runic inscriptions dating to Norsemen's eleventh-century explorations. One of the most-documented theories is that the stone marked the burial place of Leif Ericson's brother, Thorvald, mortally wounded by Indians while exploring Great Boar's Head. Thorvald's final request, the theory goes, was to be buried in this beautiful land. Great Boar's Head being too full of angry Indians, Thorvald's men quietly buried him near present-day Ash Street (the rock was moved to the Green to protect it from vandals). Later, Indian legend said the area was taboo, referring to a white god buried under a rock. This may explain Hampton's relatively fewer attacks during Indian wars.

5. FIRST CONGREGATIONAL CHURCH, *c. 1843*. **Winnacunnet Rd.**

"They came to worship" is the simple statement that eloquently describes the purpose of Hampton's earliest settlers. Whereas many settlements began for commercial or territorial reasons, the founders of Hampton came to build homes and a meetinghouse where they could worship according to their own dictates. Begun by Reverend Stephen Bachiler and his followers in 1638, this is the oldest continuous Congregational society in New Hampshire. The present 1843 building is the sixth meetinghouse. The first four, from mid-1600s to 1796, were located on Meeting House Green. The fifth building was across the street, where it later served as town hall until destroyed by fire in 1949. Two treasures remain from the 1796 church: the ancient bell displayed on the front Green and the fine octagonal pulpit within the church. The pulpit had been discarded and left on a beach, where it was rescued and restored to its rightful purpose.

6. FULLER GARDENS. **10 Willow Ave., North Hampton. Open extended season, fee.**

Here former Massachusetts Governor Alvan T. Fuller had these beautiful two-acre gardens created for his wife, Viola Davenport Fuller. Designed in the 1920s in the Colonial-Revival style, the gardens' plants are artistically set amidst fountains, statues, reflective pools, and inviting pathways. More than 1,500 rose bushes, colorful beds of annuals and perennials, flowering shrubs, sculptured hedges, a Japanese garden, and tropical and desert plants in a conservatory provide a constant array of color from May through October.

BEACHES, PARKS, OTHER POINTS OF INTEREST

A. **Hampton Beach State Park.** Rte. 1A. Open all year. Parking fee in summer. Lifeguards, bathhouses, snack bar; swimming.

B. **Hampton North Beach.** Rte. 1A. Open all year. Parking meters in summer. At high tides waves crash on the seawall, sending spray over the wall onto Ocean Boulevard; rest rooms; swimming.

C. **Bicentennial Park.** Rte. 1A opposite High St. Open all year. No fee. Memorial to 270 men who signed original test papers supporting Revolution.

D. **Ruth G. Stimson Seashore Park.** Route 1A north of (C). Open all year. No fee. Fish houses have been in this area since 1638; around 1641 Massachusetts Bay Colony exempted fishermen from paying taxes on houses used for fishing; system worked until 1940s, when owners started using the houses for other purposes and town sued for taxes; Supreme Court ruled only the ones used for fishing could remain. Picnic benches.

E. **North Hampton State Beach.** Rte. 1A. Open all year. No fee, but parking meters in summer. Small beach nestled against Little Boar's Head, views of Isles of Shoals; scenic path runs 2 miles from beach north to Sea Road in Rye; swimming.

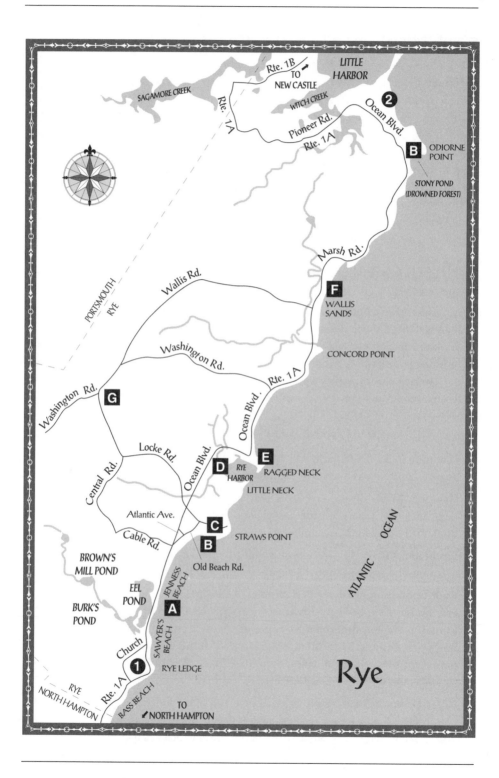

RYE

As you walk the quiet, orderly streets of Rye, with white houses, seacoast charm, and church steeple reaching to the sky, you relive the earliest days of colonial New Hampshire. It was here, in 1623, that David Thomson and a few men from Plymouth Company of England landed from the ship *Jonathan* and established New Hampshire's first settlement. They built a "great house" and trading post at what is now Odiorne Point. This was the headquarters for the later 1630 settlement of Strawbery Banke (Portsmouth) and New Castle. Early Rye was inhabited by rugged individualists, mainly self-sufficient farmers and fishermen. With the building of the railroad in 1842, tourism arrived. Five large Victorian-style hotels and twenty-five smaller ones were built. Today Rye is a New England seacoast town of sandy beaches and rock promontories and wonderful views of the Isles of Shoals.

1. SCENIC WALK AND VIEWS. Ocean Blvd. (Rte. 1A). Open all year, no fee.

Parking for visitors hoping to enjoy the beauty of coastal Rye is limited, but you can park at the North Hampton State Beach (meters in summer) and walk north in front of fish shacks on a 2-mile path along rocky ledges and seawalls. Magnificent estates on the land side vie for your attention. There are also several areas along the northern coast where you can park to view islands and ocean or explore rugged promontories.

2. ODIORNE POINT STATE PARK. Ocean Blvd. Open all year, fee in summer. Visitor information center, exhibit hall of science and history of locale, nature center, programs; small-boat launch at Creek, fee in summer; paths through fields, low brush, marsh, along open ledges; hiking, skiing, picnicking.

When you enter Odiorne Point State Park, take a little imagination with you, for here is land that has gone full-circle. The seacoast marshland of the first settlement in New Hampshire has progressed through homesteading, resort hotel and cottages, military fortifications, and now back to seacoast marshland. In 1623 the first settlers built a "great house," probably of stone, and a trading post. In 1660 John Odiorne began homesteading. Here his family and descendants fished, farmed, cut lumber, milled grain, and tended livestock for 282 years. After the Civil War a hotel and summer cottages were built. Soon after Pearl Harbor, Fort Dearborn was installed to protect Portsmouth Harbor. Four batteries of 155-mm guns and concrete gun casemates camouflaged with mounds of dirt to hold huge 16-inch guns were built. It is said that the day the 16-inch guns were fired for practice, the repercussion was so great that windows were broken on New Castle in Wentworth-by-the-Sea (see New Castle 1). It was strongly suggested by residents that guns not be fired again unless absolutely necessary. Now the land has returned to a natural state, with a few reminders of the former estates. The Science Center is a hub of scientific exploration and has an interesting history exhibit.

BEACHES, PARKS, OTHER POINTS OF INTEREST

A. Jenness Beach State Park. Ocean Blvd. (Rte. 1A). Open all year. No fee, but parking meters in summer. Extensive beach good for walking, swimming.

B. Drowned Forest. Old Beach Rd. to water right-of-way just past Atlantic Rd. Open all year. No fee. Remains of 3,600-year-old white cedar forests, drowned when sea rose as glaciers melted; low tide and winter storm currents sometimes reveal; another immediately south of Odiorne Point (see 2) is exposed every low tide.

C. Atlantic Cable and Old Cable House. 20 Old Beach Rd. Private. Site of first Atlantic cable direct to Europe, 1847–1921. **John Locke Memorial,** near Cable House: daring Indian fighter, slashed Indian canoes, hindered retreating war party; Indians ambushed and killed him two months later.

D. Rye Harbor State Marina. Ocean Blvd. Open all year. Summer parking fee. Public dock, launching ramp, boat rental, active commercial fishing wharf. **New Hampshire Seacoast Cruises** (fee).

E. Rye Harbor State Park. Ocean Blvd. Open all year. Fee in summer. Rest rooms, picnic tables, fireplaces; swimming at adjacent **Foss Beach,** small rocky beach.

F. Wallis Sands State Park. Ocean Blvd. Open all year. Fee in summer. Lifeguards, bathhouses, rest rooms, concessions, wide sandy beach, swimming.

G. Rye Town Hall, HS. Washington Rd. Open all year, limited hours. No fee. Museum displays of artifacts and photos.

NEW CASTLE

Earthworks reminiscent of a castle were built to defend the harbor after this area was settled, 1623–30. When King William and Queen Mary declared the settlement a separate township in 1693, it was named "New Castle." It served as the first capital of the province, home of royal governors, and busy social and political center prior to the Revolution. After the government moved to Portsmouth, New Castle was a prosperous fishing community for more than 200 years. It is now a peaceful community of restored cottages of craftpeople and fishermen along with summer and permanent homes. The impressive structure in the harbor was Portsmouth's naval prison, which once housed 83,000 inmates.

1. WENTWORTH-BY-THE-SEA, *1874*. Rte. 1B. Exterior view only.

In 1905, the Wentworth Hotel attracted worldwide attention during the negotiations of the Treaty of Portsmouth, which ended the Russo-Japanese War. President Theodore Roosevelt arranged to have the delegates and deliberating sessions housed here, though the actual treaty was signed at the Portsmouth Naval Shipyard. Over the years such dignitaries as Admiral George Dewey, Mrs. Jefferson Davis, Charles Evans Hughes, Thomas E. Dewey, Earl Warren, Hubert Humphrey, and Presidents Chester A. Arthur, Franklin Roosevelt, and Richard Nixon have stayed here. The hotel was named not for one of the Wentworth governors but for Samuel Wentworth, first innkeeper of New Castle. The hotel will be undergoing major renovations in the 1990s.

2. FORT CONSTITUTION, *1632*, NRHP; WALBACH TOWER, *1814*; FORT POINT LIGHTHOUSE, *1877*; Portsmouth Coast Guard Station. Walbach St. Open all year, except Coast Guard Station, no fee.

Since the 1630s, when earthworks made up the first fort, this point of land has protected the harbor. In 1694 the early fort was rebuilt and named for William and Mary of England. On December 14, 1774, the first open hostility with England occurred here. The preceding day Paul Revere had brought letters from Boston indicating British troops were en route to reinforce Fort William and Mary. Before they arrived, Sons of Liberty made plans to seize the fort's munitions. Royal Governor John Wentworth ordered the fort captain, John Cochran, to arm his five men and prepare for trouble. On December 14 drums beat in Portsmouth, calling men to attack the fort. By three o'clock 400 colonials approached the fort. Cochran ordered a round fired. Before his men could reload, the fort was taken, the king's colors lowered, and powder magazines broken into. Nearly one hundred barrels of gunpowder were taken upriver and hidden for later use by colonial troops at Bunker Hill. During the next two nights,

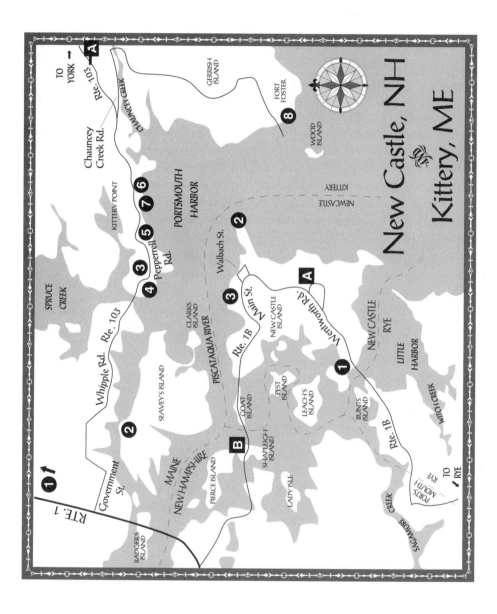

Fort Constitution and Fort Point Light, New Castle   (Courtesy U.S. Coast Guard)

Captain John Langdon and Major John Sullivan led raids removing cannons, muskets, and other stores. Governor Wentworth requested help from General Gage in Boston, who sent the armed sloop *Canceaux* and frigate *Scarsborough*, blockading Portsmouth Harbor until August 1775, when Royal Governor Wentworth and Captain Cochran sailed for England. The fort, renamed Fort Hancock, was placed under Patriot Captain Titus Salter and never again garrisoned foreign troops.

In 1791 New Hampshire turned the fort over to the United States government, naming it Fort Constitution in honor of the new Constitution. In 1806–08, Napoleon Eugene Henry Charles LeBrun, a French engineer, was hired to rebuild it. Ruins of his renovation are still seen. During the Civil War the wall by the point was replaced with blocks of granite, cut and fitted so mortar was not needed. In the 1900s new fortifications were added, including a mines building, now a museum. The harbor was mined in the Spanish-American War, and both world wars. Fort Constitution is probably the only fort in the United States that garrisoned soldiers during every national conflict from the American Revolution through World War II.

To the right of the parking area are remains of Battery Farnsworth, a concrete battery dating from the 1898 Spanish-American War. Near it are remains of Walbach

Tower, about which there is a widely told legend. During the War of 1812, New Castle was in danger of British attack. Overnight, a brick Martello tower, 30 feet high with 2-foot base walls, was constructed by the fort's garrison and frightened townspeople led by Brevet Colonel Walbach. The attack was thwarted.

In 1771, after a molasses ship grounded near Fort Point, Governor John Wentworth was persuaded to build a lighthouse. The present light, third structure at this location, dates to 1877. The Portsmouth Coast Guard Station and its ships stand as symbols of constant service to all mariners. Their primary duty is search and rescue from Cape Porpoise, Maine, to Hampton, New Hampshire.

3. PRE-REVOLUTIONARY CEMETERY, *1732.* Main St.

The oldest grave (that of the Honorable John Frost, Sir William Pepperrell's brother-in-law) dates to 1732.

BEACHES, PARKS, OTHER POINTS OF INTEREST

A. **Great Island Common.** Rte. 1B. Open all year, Fee. Was Frost Field summer estate, then Camp Langdon during World War II, then Naval Disciplinary Command; now park with tennis, playground, rest rooms, rocky and sandy beaches; picnicking, swimming.

B. **Harbor Islands.** Follow Rte. 1B over bridge system to Goat Island, then to Shapleigh Island, used to dry fish; on left largest island is Leach's, where Governor Benning Wentworth kept slaves; smaller islands are Snuff-box, Clampit, Blunts, and Pest, where smallpox victims were housed.

PORTSMOUTH

Succulent wild strawberries along the banks of the Piscataqua River were the perfect welcome for the eighty ocean-weary settlers who landed here in June 1630. The settlement was appropriately named Strawbery Banke, later Portsmouth. It was ideally located, for the river served as its communication line with other colonies and its avenue to trade and life-sustaining fishing. By the late 1700s Portsmouth shipyards turned out fifty vessels a year. The eighteenth century was a time of prosperity, high fashion, and elite social life in Portsmouth. One of the colonies' ten wealthiest towns, it had a flourishing aristocratic society and a profitable trade with the West Indies and Europe. This prosperity supported magnificent homes built in Georgian and Federal styles. Many remain.

On December 14, 1744, Patriot leaders in the Portsmouth region took the first military step for independence from England (see New Castle 2). A little more than a year later, on January 5, 1776, these Patriots issued their own declaration of independence, six months ahead of the official one. May 21, 1776, the first warship of the Continental Navy slid off its stocks in Portsmouth, christened the *Raleigh*. In 1800, the first United States Navy Yard opened on Dennett's Island in Portsmouth Harbor. Waters and wharves of the Piscataqua River were busy and prosperous in the nineteenth century, with the Navy Yard the major employer. Between 1845 and 1860 some of the most beautiful clipper ships in the world were built here. Then the advent of railroads and steamships brought to an end this period of maritime supremacy and prestige.

Today Portsmouth has an updated Navy Yard, Port Authority, and improved channel, and sailors still walk the city's streets. Uniforms and equipment have changed, but the aura of the sea remains alive in this seaport city, with its graceful metamorphosis from the era of proud clipper ships to today's nuclear submarine.

1. WENTWORTH-GARDNER HOUSE, *1760*, NHL. 50 Mechanic St.
Open extended season, fee.

This perfect Georgian was the magnificent wedding present of Madam Mark Hunking Wentworth to her son Thomas, brother of Governor John Wentworth. Because John represented the family in England and received many royal honors, Madam Wentworth wanted something special for Thomas. Restored under supervision of Wallace Nutting, the house retains much of its grandeur and charm. The front facade has quoined corners and wood blocks cut and fit to resemble stone ashlar. Master craftsmen worked fourteen months creating impressive paneling, arches, pilasters, and an elaborately carved central staircase. The house was later owned by Major William Gard-

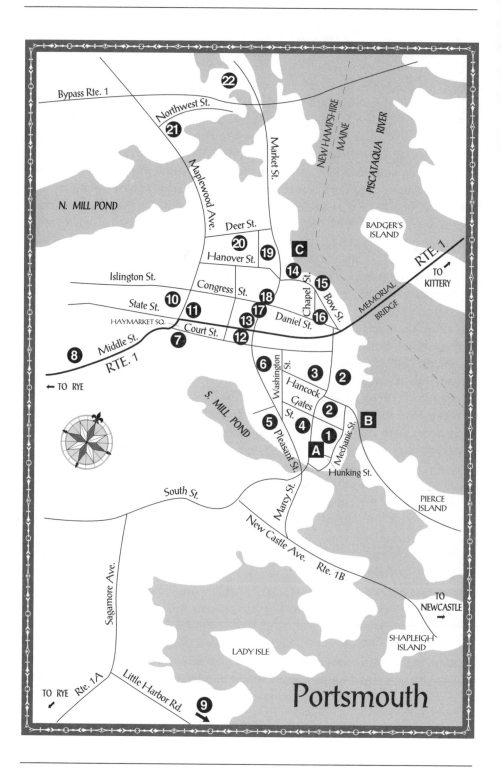

Portsmouth

ner and then by New York's Metropolitan Museum of Art, which wanted to move it to Central Park in New York City but was unsuccessful.

2. PRESCOTT PARK. Between Hancock and State sts. Open all year, no fee. Arts Festival July and August, plays, concerts, food festivals, classes.

Prescott Park, with formal gardens and detailed historic markers, offers a pleasant place to learn of Portsmouth's fascinating past. **Sheafe Warehouse Museum** (1705), in a beautifully preserved example of early eighteenth-century waterfront architecture, has massive beams and wooden knee braces similar to those used in ships' construction. Its design is registered in the Library of Congress. The museum contains folk art and wood carvings, including models of "gundalows," Portsmouth's distinctive craft designed to carry freight and passengers along the swift Piscataqua River without disturbing its many bridges. **Point of Graves Cemetery** (1672), across Hancock Street, is Portsmouth's earliest burying ground. **Liberty Pole** and **Shaw's Warehouse** (offices) relate to Revolutionary times.

3. STRAWBERY BANKE MUSEUM, NRHP. Marcy and Hancock sts. Open extended season, fee. Exhibits, orientation film, guides, crafts, concerts, special festivals.

Strawbery Banke is a unique achievement, a tour through time from earliest Portsmouth to the present. It is hard to believe that this section of Portsmouth had degenerated into substandard housing, with Puddle Dock a working junkyard, and was earmarked for urban renewal. Public-spirited citizens and local, state, and federal governments united to save and restore Strawbery Banke. The more than forty buildings range in time from the seventeenth to the twentieth century and in architecture from modest to pretentious. Included are the 1811 Governor Goodwin Mansion, 1762 Chase House, and 1780 Captain John Wheelwright House. Though a few buildings were moved here to save them from extinction elsewhere in the city, most are indigenous. Many are authentically restored and carefully furnished; others are for external viewing only or are partially restored to house crafts and special exhibits. Craftspeople demonstrate boat building, woodworking, coopering, eighteenth-century cooking, and much more. Costumed role players reenact lives of Captain Keyran Walsh (1810), writer Thomas Bailey Aldrich (1880s), and tavern owner John Stavers (1776). A floating exhibit of the *Piscataqua Gundalow,* a shallow-draft sailing vessel unique to the area, shows how lumber and other goods were transported to the port of Portsmouth during colonial times.

One restored building is the **Nutter House,** home of Thomas Bailey Aldrich. Though known for his children's stories, he also wrote *An Old Town by the Sea,* in which he captured Portsmouth with love and understanding. He grew up in this seacoast town and used it and the house he lived in, built by his grandfather, to give background and moral substance to his stories. As you tour the home where Thomas

Aldrich spent his childhood, you are in the world of his *Story of a Bad Boy*. Climb the staircase to the garret where Tom spent rainy afternoons rummaging through curiosities of a New England attic. Stand in Tom's bedroom, with the famous many-colored patchwork quilt and the wallpaper with its innumerable birds. Look through the window that allowed Tom a quick exit to get to the bonfire the town boys set before every Fourth of July. When you leave the Nutter House, Portsmouth will mean more to you than it did before you entered the world of Thomas B. Aldrich.

4. CHILDREN'S MUSEUM OF PORTSMOUTH IN SOUTH MEETING HOUSE, *1866*. 280 Marcy St. Open all year, fee.

This is the site of South Meeting House constructed in 1731. The present building, with Doric porch and elaborately bracketed tower, dates from 1866. The clock's heavy hand-wound iron weights extend to the basement. The meetinghouse has been a church, school, site of official city meetings, and now a museum. Here children can take part with hands-on enthusiasm in art, nature, and computer activities, as well as learn through intriguing exhibits such as "Reach for the Stars," a special on space, and even explore a Yellow Submarine.

5. GOVERNOR JOHN WENTWORTH HOUSE (MARK H. WENT-WORTH HOME), *c. 1763*, NRHP. 346 Pleasant St. Private.

If you graduated from Dartmouth in its first class, you received not only a degree but a land grant from Governor John Wentworth. Dartmouth College owes much to this early friend of education, who encouraged the earl of Dartmouth to create the college in 1769 and to endow it with 40,000 acres of land. To be present at the first commencement, Wentworth had College Road built from his summer home in Wolfeborough to Hanover, New Hampshire, a distance of 75 miles.

Governor Wentworth's tenure in office was a time of public improvement and prosperity as well as revolution. Able and conscientious, he tried to maintain the delicate balance between mother country and headstrong offspring. Even though a son of Patriot Mark Hunking Wentworth, to the colonists Governor Wentworth represented the Crown. He further angered his constituents when he gave refuge to a Tory member of the Exeter Convention. A mob collected and demanded the Tory be taken to Exeter for trial. The governor complied but considered it a personal insult. He gathered his family and sought refuge at Fort William and Mary. The colony's last royal governor, in 1775 he sailed for England.

6. GOVERNOR JOHN LANGDON MANSION, *1784*, NRHP, SPNEA. 143 Pleasant St. Open extended season, fee.

Governor John Langdon was one of the leading political figures of New Hampshire, 1775–1812, and one of Portsmouth's most prosperous shipbuilders and merchants. He

Governor Langdon Mansion, Portsmouth   (Douglas Armsden)

was influential in obtaining the Continental Navy's commission, in 1775, to build one of its first frigates, the *Raleigh*, in Portsmouth. The image of that ship is a prominent part of New Hampshire's state seal. Langdon put his fortune, reputation, and life on the line for independence. As General Burgoyne's army headed for Vermont, Langdon, presiding officer of the New Hampshire Assembly, made the following statement—and backed it by financing the New Hampshire forces that defeated Burgoyne at Bennington, Vermont, August 16, 1777.

> I have one thousand dollars in hard money. I will pledge my plate for three thousand more and I have seventy hogshead of Tobago Rum, which will be sold for the most they will bring. They are at the service of the State. If we succeed in defending our firesides and our homes I may be remunerated; if we do not then the property will be of no value to me.[35]

Langdon was a delegate to the Continental Congress, signer of the U.S. Constitution, U.S. senator, and New Hampshire governor. As first acting president of the United States Senate, he notified George Washington and John Adams of their election as president and vice president, and he launched the ship of state of the new nation as he administered their oaths of office.

Langdon's Georgian mansion is an elaborately decorated example of fully developed early American architecture. The entrance and portico are among the most beautiful in New Hampshire. The interior is noted for delicate wood carvings, window arches, and moldings. Furnishings reflect the mansion's and Portsmouth's pinnacle of glory. Extensive gardens complete the picture.

7. PEIRCE MANSION, *1799*. 18 Court St. Open all year for services and through church office.

John Peirce introduced a new form of architecture, his adaptation of Boston's Federal, when he built here on the outskirts of Portsmouth in what is now Haymarket Square. It proved an ideal location, for in the early 1800s three fires destroyed a large part of Portsmouth. After the fires many new buildings copied Peirce's style of architecture, adding a new dimension to building in Portsmouth. This mansion was occupied by Peirce descendants until 1965, then sold to Middle Street Baptist Church. A mahogany settee built to fit the curve of the staircase is on display at Winterthur Museum in Wilmington, Delaware. Outside, notice four Doric pilasters framing the front facade, elliptical entrance fanlight, carved medallions on the front, and large cupola atop the mansion.

8. RUNDLET-MAY HOUSE, *1807*, SPNEA. 364 Middle St. Open extended season, limited hours, fee.

James Rundlet built this Federal mansion for his family of thirteen children. He owned most of the land he could see to the south and west. Daughter Louisa married George May, and their descendants lived in the house until the 1970s. The house is significant for retention of its exterior surroundings—old fencing, walks, stable, gardens, coach house, outbuildings, and for its summer and winter kitchens with original Rumford Roasting Oven. This house shows the life of a prosperous merchant in the early 1800s.

9. WENTWORTH-COOLIDGE MANSION, *early 1700s*, NHL. Little Harbor Rd. Open extended season, fee.

The history of this rambling forty-two-room edifice parallels that of Portsmouth. Both reached heights of wealth and fashion before the Revolution. The mansion was the seat of government and the town social center as well as home to Benning Wentworth. Benning, son of the first Governor John Wentworth, was born in Portsmouth and graduated from Harvard. In 1741, as a native-born royal governor, he helped create a strong government and vital economy in New Hampshire. He strengthened inland areas by issuing 75 town grants for New Hampshire and 129 in Vermont. A less-popular practice was his keeping for himself 500 acres of each town grant.

The Wentworth–Coolidge House is described by Longfellow in his poem "Lady Wentworth." Built in segments beginning in the early 1700s, the house, as the governor knew it, was finished in 1760. The old formal dining room is guarded by a huge, heavy oak door. The ballroom, with individual dressing rooms, sustains the feeling of the high-spirited style of Benning Wentworth. In later years the home was purchased and restored by the J. Templeman Coolidge family, who presented it to New Hampshire in 1954.

10. PORTSMOUTH PUBLIC LIBRARY, *1809*, NRHP. Islington St.

An excellent example of a brick Federal, this building was first used by the Portsmouth Academy, a school for boys. It became a public school in 1868 and in 1896 was adapted as the town library. It was built and perhaps designed by Portsmouth's finest joiner, James Nutter, at a cost of $8,010.68. The master carpenter was John Miller, who is believed to have worked on the Peirce Mansion. In 1954, a special wing was built connecting the library and the 1810 Benedict House next door.

11. THE PORTSMOUTH HISTORICAL SOCIETY AT THE JOHN PAUL JONES HOUSE, *c. 1758*, NRHP, HS. Middle and State sts. Open extended season, fee.

John Paul Jones spent less than two years in Portsmouth, yet his presence at Purcell's boardinghouse is still felt. To this day it is known as the John Paul Jones House. The charming gambrel-roofed house was built by Captain Gregory Purcell for his bride, Sarah Wentworth, Governor Benning Wentworth's niece. After Purcell's death his widow opened her home to boarders, her most famous being John Paul Jones. Jones, having been commissioned as captain of the sloop *Ranger,* arrived in Portsmouth to oversee its final fittings, directing workmen at Sheafe's Warehouse. On November 1, 1777, the *Ranger* sailed proudly out of Portsmouth Harbor, bearing the first American flag flown at sea. This flag received its first foreign salute as the *Ranger* sailed into Quiberon Bay, France, with news of Burgoyne's surrender.

The restored home features period furniture, ceramics, costumes, fireplaces with tiled or carved mantels, paneled rooms, and a carved balustraded stairway. Walk through its historic rooms and fine museum and recall the early days of Portsmouth's past.

12. UNITARIAN CHURCH, *1824–28*. State St.

This church traces its lineage to the original South Meeting House. In 1821 the congregation left its Trinitarian heritage and adopted Unitarianism. The building, designed by Alexander Parris, was one of the first major works of popular granite architecture. The Rockport granite exterior with huge Tuscan portico is a good example of early nineteenth-century Greek Revival. A Paul Revere bell still hangs in the square tower. The interior has been restored to the 1850s era.

13. UNITED STATES CUSTOMS HOUSE, *1857–60*. State and Pleasant sts. Open all year as business.

The customhouse was designed in Italianate style and patterned after fortresslike Italian Renaissance city palaces, but the materials were from the rich resources of New Hampshire.

14. BOW STREET WAREHOUSES, *early 1800s*. Bow St. Open all year as businesses.

In the early 1800s these warehouses stored merchandise brought in by trading vessels. The Olde Harbour Association was organized to restore and preserve the warehouses for commercial use as small shops, restaurants, and apartments.

15. ST. JOHN'S CHURCH, *1807*. Chapel St.

High on Chapel Street stands the oldest church building still used as a church in Portsmouth. First built in 1732, it was called Queen's Chapel in honor of Queen Caroline, consort of King George II. The queen gave many gifts; her communion silver is still used Easter and Christmas. After the Revolution the parish was renamed St. John's Church. Following a Christmas Eve fire in 1806, the present brick structure was erected. In 1848 sanctuary walls were covered with shadow painting, giving an interesting three-dimensional effect. The bell was given by Colonel John Tufton Mason, who acquired it at the capture of Louisbourg in 1745. Damaged during the fire of 1806, it was recast by Paul Revere.

In this church, where New England and Anglican traditions are gracefully interwoven, worshipers included Presidents Washington and Monroe, Benjamin Franklin, and Jeremiah Mason. Funeral services for Admiral David G. Farragut were held here, and the credence table was given in his memory, the wood coming from Farragut's flagship, *Hartford*. Be sure to see the famous "Vinagar Bible," one of four such Bibles in the United States. The word "vineyard" was misprinted to read "vinigar" during a printing in 1717. The beautiful music of the church comes from a Brattle organ, one of the oldest pipe organs in the country. Governor Benning Wentworth's grave is in the adjacent cemetery.

16. MACPHEADRIS–WARNER HOUSE, *1716–23*, NHL. Chapel and Daniel sts. Open extended season, fee.

For anyone who has read Kenneth Roberts's *Northwest Passage,* the Warner House will have special significance, as it played an important role in his historical novel of

Portsmouth. Restored murals referred to in the book can still be seen in the hallway. If you use your imagination, you may picture Ben Franklin, hair blowing in the sea breeze and eyeglasses on the end of his nose, supervising the placement of his lightning rod on this three-story house in 1762, probably the first lightning rod used in New Hampshire.

Captain Archibald Macpheadris, born in Scotland, was a successful merchant, fur trader, and shipmaster. He built this home to be worthy of his bride, Sarah Wentworth, sister of Governor Benning Wentworth, and to suit his position on the King's Council. After Macpheadris's death in 1729, Governor Wentworth rented the house as his home from 1742 to 1759. In 1760 Captain Macpheadris's only daughter, Mary, married Jonathan Warner and returned to the magnificent mansion. One of the first urban brick Georgian houses in New England, it is recognized as the best surviving example of its period. It has spacious living rooms, fireplaces with old Dutch and English tile facings, fine paneling developed in Sir Christopher Wren's style, and fine Portsmouth furniture from these and other local families.

17. NORTH CHURCH, *1854*. Market Sq., Congress St.

North Church, with white steeple reaching into Portsmouth's sky, is a prominent landmark. Built here about 1712, the original church was later the scene of Portsmouth's Tea Party protesting Britain's hated import tax on tea. Notable churchgoers included Daniel Webster, Governor John Langdon, and William Whipple (see 19).

18. PORTSMOUTH ATHENAEUM, *1803*, NRHP. Market Sq., Congress St. Open all year, limited hours, no fee; tours.

The Portsmouth Athenaeum was chartered in 1817 as a fee-supported library, which served the area until Portsmouth's free Public Library was established. Today it serves as an outstanding research library with collections of rare volumes, eighteenth- and nineteenth-century newspapers, magazines, literature, and nonfiction—totaling more than 25,000 volumes. The present home of the Athenaeum was built, after a disastrous fire in 1802, as the central building of a composite of Federal period office buildings.

19. MOFFATT–LADD HOUSE, *c. 1763*, NHL. 154 Market St. Open extended season, fee. Changing exhibits. Museum shop in 1830s Counting House; original Coach House.

The Moffatt–Ladd House, built by John Moffatt, interprets the home of a wealthy merchant of the late 1700s and his descendants, who lived there until the early 1900s, when the house was turned over to the New Hampshire Colonial Dames. John Moffatt, born in England and captain of a British mast ship, settled in Portsmouth, where as a merchant he dealt in the West Indies molasses and rum trade, in luxury goods for prosperous Portsmouth families, and in pine trees for masts on British ships. He married the grandniece of John Cutt, first president of the Royal Province of New Hampshire. The first occupants of Moffatt's magnificent home were son Samuel and his bride Sarah Catherine Tuftson Mason, descendant of Captain John Mason, whose land grant from the king became the State of New Hampshire. In 1768 Samuel fled to the West Indies to escape creditors in a bankruptcy suit that was personally disastrous but resulted in records that have aided in the accurate refurbishing of the house. John Moffatt lived here with his daughter Katherine and her husband, William Whipple, delegate to the Provincial and Continental Congresses, signer of the Declaration of Independence, and brigadier general during the Revolution. Following the war, Whipple was an associate justice of the state supreme court. After his death, in 1785, and John Moffatt's in 1786, Katherine lived in the house until it was willed to Samuel's son Robert, who sold to brother-in-law Nathaniel Haven. His daughter Marie married Alexander Ladd and they and six children moved to the house in 1819. Their son was responsible for the elegant terraced garden, with grass steps, fruit trees, and multiple tulip bulbs—a quiet oasis behind the house overlooking the family wharf on the busy Piscataqua River.

This imposing three-story Federal house has an unusual architectural plan, which focuses on a Great Hall containing an elegant stairway and rare, early French wallpaper. Fine paneling, molding, rare English wallpaper, and fireplace details provide the perfect setting for period imported English and Portsmouth furnishings, many original to the house.

20. THE HILL AT PORTSMOUTH PARADE. Deer St. Open all year as businesses.

Five of the houses at Portsmouth Parade are on original sites. The rest were rescued from nearby urban renewal locations and moved to this adaptive preservation area. Exteriors have been restored and interiors remodeled.

21. JACKSON HOUSE, c. 1664, NHL. 76 Northwest St. Open extended season, limited hours and by appointment through SPNEA. Fee.

The oldest house still standing in New Hampshire was lived in by ten generations of Jacksons and has weathered more than 300 years. John Jackson, from Dartmouth, England, built the central part about 1664. With North Pond directly in front, the family had a convenient location for their shipyards. The house is a rare survivor of Colonial architecture. Clapboards are weathered and stained, doorway plain with nail trim. The roof is steeply pitched, reaching to ground level in the rear. The unfurnished interior is restored, with exposed beams, sheathed or roughly plastered walls, wide-board flooring, and unfinished rear lean-to. The five leaded casements were restored in the 1920s. The main impression of the house is one of function and solidity.

22. ALBACORE PARK AND PORT OF PORTSMOUTH MARITIME MUSEUM. **500 Market St. Extension. Open extended season, fee. Visitor center, gift shop.**

Here you can explore the original experimental submarine, USS *Albacore*, built in 1953 at the Portsmouth Naval Shipyard. The development of this craft revolutionized submarine history by proving for the first time that a submerged sub could travel for long periods of time at fast speeds. The ship also was important for its innovative sonar, propeller, and controls testing. A museum and a film show the *Albacore's* accomplishments and give further background.

BEACHES, PARKS, OTHER POINTS OF INTEREST

A. **Tobias Lear House,** 1740. 51 Hunking St. Plans call for future access through 1. Plain yet stately Georgian Colonial built by Tobias Lear III. Grandson Tobias, born here, was private secretary to George Washington and tutor to his stepchildren, also diplomat during presidencies of Jefferson and Madison; his second and third marriages were to nieces of Martha Washington; house in Lear family until Civil War.

B. **Four-Tree Island Recreation Park.** End of Hancock St. Open extended season. No fee. Views, picnicking.

C. **Cruises.** Harbor area. Leave throughout extended season. Fee. Visits to Portsmouth Harbor islands, Isles of Shoals, Great Bay; whale watching; inland river cruises.

ISLES OF SHOALS

(Ferry from Portsmouth, N.H.)

The Isles of Shoals[36] have been uniquely important since colonial times. It is believed fishermen from Europe fished these waters and probably landed on the isles long before John Smith charted them in 1614. In those early days the area teemed with seafood. Cod shoaled like bait fish—thus the name, Isles of Shoals. These beckoning isles consist of nine islands at low tide and eight at high tide. Rye, New Hampshire, has jurisdiction over Lunging, Seavey, Star, and White islands, while Kittery, Maine, includes the islands of Appledore, Cedar, Duck, Malaga, and Smuttynose. Portsmouth, New Hampshire, serves as lifeline to all the islands.

Soon after John Smith published his discovery, fishermen established a settlement on Appledore (then called Hog) and Smuttynose islands, naming the village Appledore. By 1640 there was a small church, a courthouse, and the first boys' academy in New England. Appledore boasted a settlement of more than 600 by the 1670s. Massachusetts, which held control over Maine, decided around 1680 to tax Maine islands, including Smuttynose and Hog. The islanders saw no reason to pay taxes. They simply moved across the state line to Star Island.

Thanks to special fish-curing techniques developed at the Isles of Shoals, Star Island dunfish were in demand throughout Europe before the Revolution. With the war's outbreak, islanders were ordered to the mainland. A majority complied, many floating their houses across to the mainland; one house still remains in York, Maine. This ended the Isles' prestige as a fishing center.

Following the war Captain Sam Haley brought new life to the Isles. He settled on Smuttynose, setting up a ropewalk, bakery, windmill, cooper's shop, and gristmill. He opened a small tavern and planted orchards. After his death in 1811, son Samuel continued his work. Samuel, Jr., received unexpected help when he uncovered bars of silver, believed to be pirate treasure. Before his death in 1839, Samuel, Jr., sold his beloved Hog, Smuttynose, and Malaga to Thomas Laighton.

Laighton, a successful businessman and politician, left Portsmouth with his family to become the light keeper on White Island in 1839. In 1847 they moved to Hog Island, which Laighton named Appledore. There he built Appledore House, one of the first large summer hotels in New England. The hotel, later run by Laighton sons Oscar and Cedric, was a haven for New England authors and artists and other sea-loving guests for more than sixty years. Thomas Laighton's daughter, Celia Thaxter, well-known poet and protégée of John Greenleaf Whittier, was a main attraction on Appledore Island from the 1870s to her death in 1894. Her cottage parlor was the center for many pleasant gatherings of writers, painters, and

Chapel, Isles of Shoals   (Douglas Armsden)

musicians. Famous visitors to Appledore were Franklin Pierce, James Russell Lowell, Thomas Bailey Aldrich, Nathaniel Hawthorne, Harriet Beecher Stowe, William Morris Hunt, Childe Hassam, and John Knowles Paine.

In 1873 John R. Poor built the Oceanic Hotel on Star Island. Four years later he sold to the Laightons, who operated the two islands until the early 1900s. Appledore House and Celia Thaxter's cottage burned in 1914. In 1916 the Oceanic and Star Island were bought by Star Island Corporation, a group of Unitarians and Congregationalists who had been meeting there for summer conferences since 1897. They continue to sponsor religious and educational meetings. Their facility includes the hotel, a stone chapel dating from 1800, and several houses from the eighteenth- and nineteenth-century village of Gosport. Appledore Island is also the site of the Shoals Marine Laboratory, a summer school and research laboratory for Cornell University and the University of New Hampshire.

Since the early days, light has shone forth from the Isles to guide and protect fishermen. Wives took whale oil lanterns and placed them in the meetinghouse at night to guide returning husbands. When Captain Haley moved to Smuttynose after the Revolution, he placed a lamp high in the window of his home. His son kept up the lifesaving practice until 1820, when the first lighthouse was built on White Island. If you attend a church conference today, you can join others in reenacting the tradition. Every evening guests take candle lanterns and walk the familiar path to the church, hanging the lamps on timeworn wall brackets. As the light shines out to sea, you realize the mainland is just a dark line on the horizon. The peace of the Isles enfolds you and you feel you are indeed on a "stepping stone to serenity."

MAINE

With its more than 2,500 miles of coastline, Maine expands beyond the realm of this book. To introduce you to the beauties of this coast, here are abbreviated tours of the first six towns along the coast of Maine.

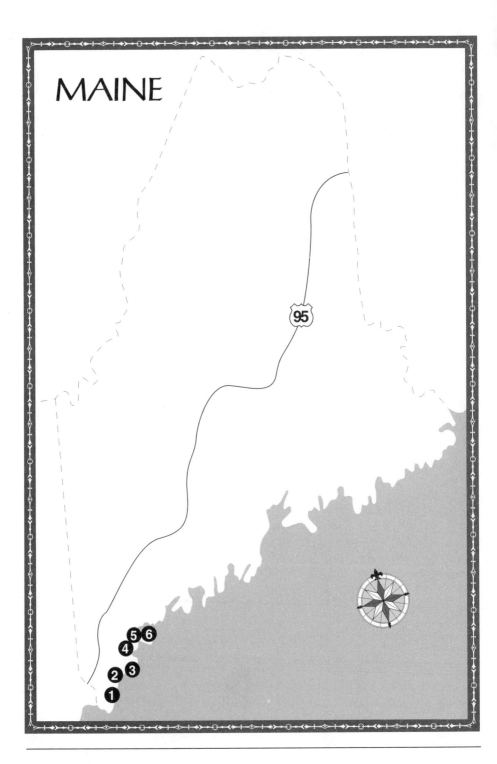

MAINE

KITTERY

(See locator map, page 414)

1. KITTERY HISTORICAL AND NAVAL MUSEUM. Rogers Rd., north of Rte. 1 rotary. Open extended season, limited hours, or by appointment; fee.

Through artifacts, paintings, and models, Kittery and neighboring seacoast towns' shipbuilding heritage comes alive; 300 years of maritime history.

2. PORTSMOUTH NAVAL SHIPYARD MUSEUM. Off Rte. 103. Entrance at Gate 2 of Naval Yard. Open by appointment.

Established June 12, 1800, nation's oldest federally owned shipyard; over 44 surface ships and 137 submarines built here. Today yard overhauls and repairs nuclear submarines; museum interprets yard's shipbuilding heritage with models, photographs, paintings, and artifacts.[37]

3. FIRST CONGREGATIONAL CHURCH AND VILLAGE GREEN, *c. 1730*; Pepperrell Rd. Old Graveyard.

Church oldest remaining one in Maine; congregation began 1694 under Reverend John Newmarch, who served over half a century during era of Indian attacks. When threats decreased, parishioners built first church building in 1727, destroyed by lightning 1729, present building erected 1730; basic structure and altar remain. Tradition suggests this church as setting for Nathaniel Hawthorne's *The Scarlet Letter;* characters and roles were changed. George Washington visited church minister Dr. Benjamin Stevens in **Old Parsonage** on Village Green built 1729. Across Pepperrell Road in **Old Graveyard** poet Celia Thaxter's husband is buried, epitaph written by Robert Browning. On Lawrence Lane beyond cemetery, Vice President Hannibal Hamlin lived in small red house on right; he served during Civil War; probably only man to go from vice president to private. Large white house on corner is summer home of New Hampshire governor John G. Winant.

4. LADY PEPPERRELL HOUSE, *1760*, NRHP, NHL, SPNEA. Pepperrell Rd. Private.

Georgian home built for Lady Pepperrell after death of husband, Sir William Pepperrell. Front entrance, with carved dolphins, depicts sea as source of Pepperrell wealth. Lady Pepperrell, born Mary Hirst, granddaughter of Chief Justice Samuel Sewall of Salem witch trials, moved to the mansion in 1760; died here in her eighties. Much of property confiscated during Revolution as family remained loyalists; Lady Pepperrell still respected as one of town's prominent citizens.

Lady Pepperrell House and First Congregational Church, Kittery   (Douglas Armsden)

5. FORT MCCLARY STATE PARK, NRHP. Pepperrell Rd. Open extended season, grounds all year. Fee. Views.

In 1715 Massachusetts ordered fort built to protect Maine settlers under Massachusetts' control from taxes levied by New Hampshire for use of river. Fort named for Pepperrells; when they remained loyal to England during the Revolution, renamed Fort McClary, honoring Andrew McClary, killed at Bunker Hill. Fort's view of harbor helped save Portsmouth and Kittery from British invasion during Revolution and War of 1812. Extensive changes during the Civil War never completed; granite slabs remain as they were when work was abandoned.

6. PEPPERRELL HOUSE, *c. 1682*, NRHP. Pepperrell Rd. opposite Post Office. Private.

William Pepperrell born in 1646 in England; arrived in New World as an apprentice on fishing schooner; settled on Isles of Shoals, then Kittery Point. Soon his ships found on all seven seas, warehouses full; wharves teemed with activity; married Margery Bray 1682.

With youngest son, William, enlarged shipping business and land holdings; Pepperrells powerful and popular.

During French and Indian Wars, French built a supposedly invincible fortress at Louisbourg, Nova Scotia; they harassed colonial shipping and supplied troops to assault Maine towns. Fortress had to be taken. Young William commanded attack; limited in military experience, he used influence, wealth, ingenuity, frontier type of fighting, courageous untrained troops, Lady Luck; took fortress June 1745. Pepperrell first native-born American created baronet by Great Britain; later lieutenant general in British Army; died 1759; buried in tomb across from home. In 1774 Pepperrell's grandson, William, loyal to both Colonies and England met Lord North in England, tried for reconciliation; efforts failed; remained in England working for legal claims of American loyalists. Pepperrell property confiscated, used to quarter troops.

Small red building was Pepperrell counting house in 1700s. Next door is **Bray House,** home of senior William Peppernell's father-in-law, John Bray, master shipwright; center section built 1662, making it oldest remaining dwelling in Maine.

7. TOWN DOCK. Behind general store, Pepperrell Rd. Open all year.

Magnificent views: To left picturesque Chauncey Creek runs between Gerrish Island and mainland; next Fort Foster with pier reaching toward old Coast Guard station on Wood Island; Whaleback Light at harbor entrance; to right New Castle with Fort Point Light and Fort Constitution; at extreme right Fort McClary.

8. FORT FOSTER, *1872.* Gerrish Island, Chauncey Creek Rd. Open summer, fee. Ball fields; picnicking, fishing, swimming, scuba diving; off-season park at gate and walk in.

Rocky coast, old fortifications, fort active 1872–1949; built as part of outer defense system of Portsmouth Harbor, typical fortification of that time; part of World War I coastal defense system; now owned by Kittery, used for recreation.

BEACHES, PARKS, OTHER POINTS OF INTEREST

A. **Seapoint Beach.** Chauncey Creek Rd., right on Cutts Island Ln., right on Seapoint Rd. Open all year. No fee. Swimming.

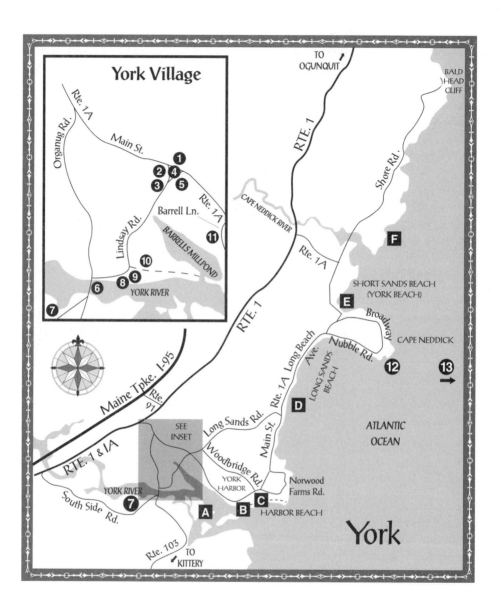

York Village

Rte. 1A

Organug Rd.

Main St.

① ② ④ ③ ⑤

Rte. 1A

Barrell Ln.

⑪

Lindsay Rd.

BARRELLS MILLPOND

⑩

⑧ ⑨

⑥

YORK RIVER

⑦

TO OGUNQUIT

BALD HEAD CLIFF

RTE. 1

Shore Rd.

CAPE NEDDICK RIVER

Rte. 1A

F

SHORT SANDS BEACH (YORK BEACH)

E

Broadway

CAPE NEDDICK

Rte. 1A Long Beach

Nubble Rd.

⑫

⑬ →

Maine Tpke. I-95

Rte. 91

RTE. 1

LONG SANDS AVE.

LONG SANDS BEACH

D

Main St.

SEE INSET

Long Sands Rd.

Woodbridge Rd.

YORK HARBOR

ATLANTIC OCEAN

RTE. 1 & 1A

YORK RIVER

⑦

Norwood Farms Rd.

A **B** **C**

South Side Rd.

HARBOR BEACH

York

Rte. 103

TO KITTERY

YORK

1. FIRST PARISH CHURCH, *c. 1747.* Rte. 1A and Lindsay Rd.

Church typical of early American architecture; building turned to face the road in 1872. Church of Reverend Samuel Moody; at age seventy he marched with William Pepperrell's expedition to Louisbourg, Nova Scotia; returned a hero; laid church cornerstone 1747, oldest remaining house of worship in York. It is said that in middle of sermon, Moody would shout, "Fire!" When hastily awakened one asked "Where?" reply was, "In hell for sleeping sinners!"[39] Son Joseph, next minister of the church, immortalized by Nathaniel Hawthorne in "The Minister's Black Veil." Joseph Moody accidentally shot and killed a friend while hunting; guilt caused him to wear handkerchief over face for rest of life, even in his casket. Earlier minister Shubael Drummer,1669–92, praised by Cotton Mather and victim of 1692 Indian massacre. Town Hall built on church-owned land, unusual circumstance technically united church and state.

2. JEFFERDS TAVERN, *c. 1750.* Lindsay Rd. and Rte. 1A. Old York Historical Society has combined tickets for attractions 2–5, 7, and 9; guided tours. Open summer, fees.

Fine example of early tavern required in every village to serve travelers; Colonial tavern keeper one of village's most respected citizens. Built by Captain Samuel Jefferds on King's Highway in Wells; served as a "Publick House" for stagecoach travelers; moved here 1942; replica taproom. Upstairs rooms feature wall murals by Mrs. Adela Ells depicting York scenes prior to 1820, in manner of Rufus Porter, plus exhibit on York County landscape and architecture.

3. THE OLD SCHOOLHOUSE, *c. 1745,* NRHP, HS. West branch Lindsay Rd. Open summer through attraction 2. Fee.

Old Schoolhouse features history of education in York; windows, originally covered with oiled brown paper, provided dull yellow glow. Horn book and New England primer main teaching materials; reading, writing, ciphering taught; benches only furniture in earliest schoolhouse; chairs and desks later additions. Building, rescued from use as workshop, moved to this location.

4. EMERSON WILCOX HOUSE, *c. 1740,* HS. Rte. 1A and Lindsay Rd. Open summer through attraction 2, fee. Museum shop, library.

Original two-story house built on parish land leased for 999 years; small rent still paid

First Parish Church; has been general store, tailor shop, tavern, post office, private home. Inside, mantels and paneling from Colonial through early Federal period; has unusual hallway cut through chimneys, creating medieval atmosphere; special display features bed hangings of beautiful crewel created more than 200 years ago by Mary Bulman while physician husband served at battle of Louisbourg. Home furnished with treasures, showcase of Old York's collections.

5. OLD GAOL, *c. 1653*, NRHP, HS. Rte. 1A and Lindsay Rd. Open summer through attraction 2, fee.

Oldest public building in use to survive from the English colonial period; feeling of penal institution remains in cavelike dungeon and thick walls; jailers' quarters adjacent to prison area; furnishings follow 1790s jailer William Emerson's inventory. Dungeon entered through old kitchen; museum features changing exhibits on York's past. On stairs, watch for "trip-stair," built a few inches higher than others, perhaps to trip anyone trying to escape. Old Gaol was jail until 1860, then warehouse, home, school, and museum since 1900.

6. SEWALL'S BRIDGE, *c. 1761*. Organug Rd. Spans tidal York River.

Created by Major Samuel Sewall, first pile drawbridge in New England, restored; rests on piles banded together at different heights, depending on depth needed; Sewall said to have invented a simple pile driver. Over this bridge, Maine's Minutemen marched to Lexington. York River scene of first "undershot" mill in United States; wheels turned, not by flow of water over top, but by pressure of changing tide against bottom of wheel.

7. ELIZABETH PERKINS HOUSE, *1732*, HS. South Side Rd., near bridge. Open summer through attraction 2, fee.

Summer home of York's leading preservationist; furnished as when Elizabeth died 1952; eighteenth-century building reflects life of wealthy New Yorker who wintered in Europe and summered in York. Furnishings from around the world combine with favorite Colonial pieces.

8. MARSHALL'S COUNTRY STORE AND WHARF, *c. 1867*, 140 Lindsay Rd. Open all year, no fee. Old York Historical Society office and research library.

Store once economic and social center of community; in late 1800s freight arrived by water, stored in big cellar open to wharf; common to see a three-masted schooner carrying 800 tons unload at wharf.

9. JOHN HANCOCK WAREHOUSE, *pre-Revolutionary*, NRHP, HS. Lindsay Rd. Open summer through attraction 2, fee. Self-guided tour.

Warehouse oldest standing commercial building in York; once owned in part by John

Hancock; served as customhouse, goods such as molasses, spices, rum from West Indies weighed and taxed; building features exhibit of York's maritime and farming past.

10. STEEDMAN WOODS NATURE PRESERVE AND RIVER PATH TO WIGGLEY BRIDGE, HS. Lindsay Rd.; from attraction 9, .1 mile after first house on right, path leads to Rte. 103, no fee.

Follow path through Nature Preserve north side York River; interesting birds in salt marshes, occasionally a moose ambles through; cross entrance to Barrell Mill Pond via Wiggley Bridge, walk over what was a dam, probably with sluice gate controlling water for waterwheel supplying power to mills. Barrell Mill Pond where Edward Godfrey, first settler of York, built home 1630.

11. SAYWARD–WHEELER HOUSE, *1718*, SPNEA. 79 Barrell Ln., York Harbor. Open extended season, fee.

Beautifully preserved Colonial home in Sayward family since 1718; bought by Joseph Sayward when original four-room section a year old. In 1740s Joseph sold to son Jonathan, who made fortune in West Indies trade; commissioned by Massachusetts Governor Shirley in 1745, Jonathan commanded sloop *Seaflower* in Battle of Louisbourg; returned victorious with bounty from battle, including rare floral gilt plates, on display. Jonathan remodeled house filling it with museum-quality pieces; family preserved Jonathan's furnishings, added own. Note sets of Queen Anne chairs and American Chippendale chairs, c. 1740–50, original moreen upholstery. In 1900 house bought by Sayward descendant Elizabeth Cheever Wheeler; heirs gave house to SPNEA in 1977.

12. NUBBLE POINT AND CAPE NEDDICK LIGHT. Nubble Rd.

Cape Neddick Light on island off Nubble Point; six-bedroom Victorian light keeper's house; one of most photographed spots on Maine coast. Site first recorded by Captain Bartholomew Gosnold, landed 1602, encountered Abenaki Indians, named it Savage Rock. Look up coast to Kennebunkport or out to Isles of Shoals and Boon Island Light. On maiden voyage, *Isadore,* out of Kennebunkport, dashed to pieces on Nubble Cliffs Thanksgiving night 1842 in blinding snowstorm; no survivors. As a result of such tragedies, in 1879 U.S. Department of Commerce erected light; now seen 15 nautical miles offshore.

13. BOON ISLAND LIGHTHOUSE. Off New Hampshire/Maine coast.

Boon Island Light stands tall against horizon; one of loneliest on Maine coast, 6.5 miles southeast of Cape Neddick; for years it was home to light keeper and family; during storms keepers went days without outside contact. Believed named for shipwrecked sailors who reached its safety 1682; lived off the island until signal fire attracted Indians atop Mount Agamenticus, rescued sailors; thankful for survival, sailors named island "Boon Island." Life of keepers immortalized by Celia Thaxter in poem "The Watch of Boon Island" and in Kenneth Roberts's book, *Boon Island*.

BEACHES, PARKS, OTHER POINTS OF INTEREST

A. **Town Wharf.** Harris Island Rd., off Rte. 103. Open all year. No fee. Commercial fishing boats moored alongside pleasure boats, wharf facilities, fishing, parking; boat rides.

B. **York Harbor Beach.** Open all year. No fee. Lifeguards; swimming.

C. **Cliff Walk.** York Harbor. Open all year. No fee. Walk north side of bath club end of Harbor Beach Rd.; walk hugs coast providing views of ocean and coastal homes; seacoast flora and fauna, interesting rock formations; after 45-minute walk arrive at rocky beach near Cow Beach Point; retrace steps.

D. **Long Sands Beach.** Rte. 1A. Open all year. Metered parking in summer. Lifeguards, refreshments, rest rooms; swimming.

E. **York Beach or Short Sands Beach.** York Beach, Rte. 1A. Open all year. Metered parking in summer. Amusement area, Animal Forest Park where guests hand feed animals; lifeguards, swimming.

F. **Passaconaway Beaches.** Off Shore Rd. Open all year. No fee. Swimming.

OGUNQUIT

1. MUSEUM OF ART. **Shore Rd. Open all year, no fee.**

Museum dedicated to art, beautifully situated above ocean, displays work of talented painters and sculptors; features permanent collection of North American art.

2. PERKINS COVE. **Oarweed Rd. Open extended season, no fee. Gift shops, art galleries, restaurants, boat rentals, boat rides; fishing, sailing; access by trolley, limited parking.**

Blend of Cape Cod and Rockport on smaller scale; artists' haven with room for lobstermen; narrow neck of land between Atlantic Ocean and Josiah River. Double-leaf draw footbridge opens for nearly every boat; unique in Maine. Boat horn sounds; someone—anyone—runs to the bridge controls; the bridge rises rapidly; the boat passes on way to ocean or upriver to harbor.

3. MARGINAL WAY. **Accesses: Perkins Cove parking lot, Israel's Head, and Shore Rd. opposite O'Bed's Ln. Open all year, no fee.**

Marginal Way offers fascinating 1-mile walk, Perkins Cove to Shore Road; enjoy nature's landscaping, listen to birds singing; observe unusual rock formations, some going back to Precambrian Age, markings from Glacial Age; watch lobstermen hauling traps, fishing boats followed by eager gulls, merchant ships, colorful saiboats, bobbing lobster markers. Foot of Ontio Hill, sewage treatment plant camouflaged as lighthouse.

4. OGUNQUIT LIBRARY, *c. 1897*, NRHP. **Shore Rd.**

Fieldstone building donated as village library by Mrs. George Connarroe in memory of lawyer husband; interior old English architecture; grandfather's clock made from a piano.

BEACHES, PARKS, OTHER POINTS OF INTEREST

*Parking available on Main Street for trolley, which makes frequent stops,
including beaches and Perkins Cove.*

A. Ogunquit Beach. Accesses: Beach St. and footbridge from end of Ocean St. Open all year. Metered parking in summer.

B. Moody Beach. End Bourne Ave., off Rte. 1. Open all year. Parking fee in summer.

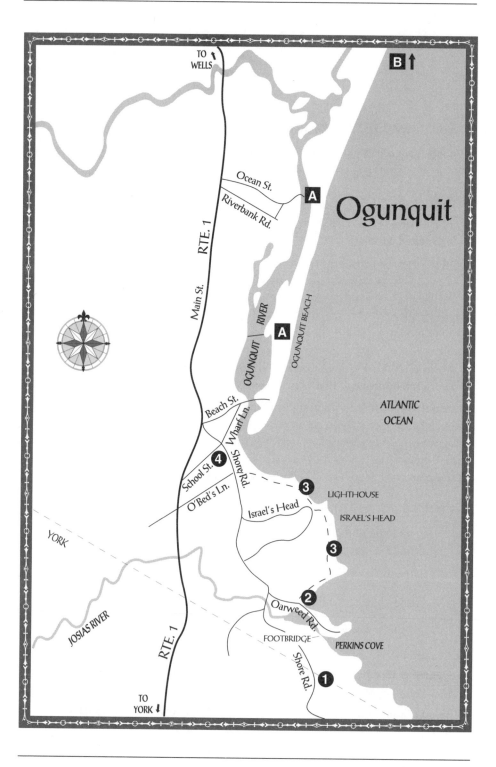

WELLS[40]

1. HISTORIC MEETINGHOUSE MUSEUM, *c. 1862*, NRHP, HS. Rte. 1 and Buzzell Rd. Open summer, limited hours. No fee.

New England church building with lofty steeples; built by first Congregational Church established 1642 under Reverend John Wheelwright. First building burned in 1692 Indians attack. Strength and courage of Reverend George Burroughs from Salem, Massachusetts, supported settlers during Indian attacks; sadly, later he was accused of witchcraft; ordered to Salem; convicted and hanged on testimony that, too late, was proved false. Present building, fourth on site, museum of local history containing memorabilia, artifacts, genealogies, research library.

2. WELLS NATIONAL ESTUARINE RESEARCH RESERVE AT LAUDHOLM FARM. Laudholm Farm Rd. Open all year, parking fee in summer. Visitor center, library, trails, exhibits, educational programs, teacher training, graduate courses, tours.

Unique estuarine sanctuary; view, study, understand, enjoy 1,600 acres of barrier beach, coastal salt marshes, upland fields and forests, estuaries where Little and Webhannet rivers join Atlantic Ocean. Estuarine areas among most productive natural resources in world. Reserve combines Rachel Carson Wildlife Refuge (D) and historic Laudholm Farm. Saltwater farm, started by Henry Boade 1643; home to Boade, Symonds, Clark, Lord families for more than 300 years; earliest section of farmhouse built 1717; main section, Federal style, built 1820, then altered to present Greek Revival style 1882. House and outbuildings restored as educational, environmental, research center. Research projects include: ecology of coastal and migratory fish; salt marsh restoration; sea level rise; long-term monitoring of songbirds and endangered shorebirds.

BEACHES, PARKS, OTHER POINTS OF INTEREST

A. Wells Beach. Along Webhannet Dr. and Atlantic Ave. to harbor; Mile Rd. and Atlantic Ave. Open all year. Summer parking fee. Lifeguards, rest rooms, boardwalk, arcade; swimming.

B. Wells Harbor. Atlantic Ave. Open all year. No fee. Safe inner harbor, passage to outer harbor may be rough, depending on tides; rest rooms; fishing, boating, swimming.

C. Drakes Island and Beach. Drakes Island Rd. Open all year. Summer parking fee. Swimming.

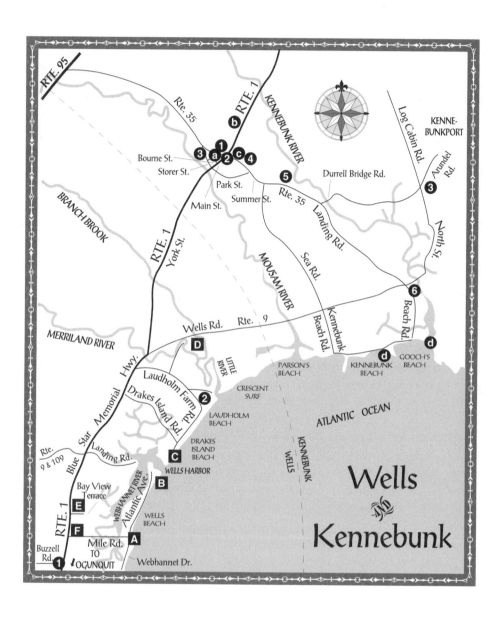

D. Rachel Carson National Wildlife Refuge. Rte. 9. Open all year. No fee. (See Wells 2). Key location along waterfowl migration; salt marsh, interpretative nature paths.

E. Wells Auto Museum. Rte. 1 and Bay View Terr. Open summer. Fee.

F. Storer Garrison Historic Marker. Rte. 1 near Ye Olde Garrison House Motel. In 1692 Storer Garrison, 4 watchtowers, commanded view of fields, sea, marsh; few soldiers and handful of gallant Wells settlers defended against several hundred French and Indians, 3-day siege; rare success in days of Indian massacres.

Wells Reserve at Laudholm Farm, Wells (Richard Magrath)

KENNEBUNK

(See locator map, page 444)

1. FIRST PARISH CHURCH UNITARIAN, *c. 1773*, and Hope Cemetery. Intersection Rtes. 1 and 35.

Considered by many most beautiful church in Maine; majestic Christopher Wren–style steeple; incorporated 1750 as Second Congregational Society of Wells. Though part of Wells, Kennebunk settlers wanted own church, erected building at Kennebunk Landing, called Daniel Little as minister. Little, teacher and preacher, led flock through French and Indian Wars, Revolutionary War; was dedicated missionary, known as "Apostle of the East," traveled hundreds of miles to backwoods people and Indians; helped translate language of Indians along Penobscot River; home, built c.1752, left of Wedding Cake House (5).

1773, Colonel Joseph Storer gave land for present church, built with wood from first church building; 1803 expanded, cutting church in half; moved rear half back 28 feet, added new midsection; year later added corn weather vane–topped steeple and belfry; bell cast in Paul Revere foundry. Behind church in **Hope Cemetery** grave of Sally S. Wood, Maine's first woman novelist; additional stone marker at Bourne grave was to be placed on Mount Washington, where Lizzie Bourne, twenty-two-year-old daughter of Judge Edward Bourne, died of exposure within 200 yards of the Summit House 1835; marker by Cog Railroad on mountain.

2. BRICK STORE MUSEUM, *1825*. 117 Main St. Open all year, fee.

Block of restored nineteenth-century buildings houses museum galleries, rotating exhibits of fine and decorative arts, maritime history. In 1825 William Lord erected building as general store; bricks from local Wonder Brook Kiln; goods sold first two floors, attic and cellar storage. By 1840 store leased; second floor used as meeting room; museum established in 1936, expanding to entire building; September 1940, Brick Store Museum incorporated.

3. STORER MANSION, *c. 1758*. 5 Storer St. Private.

Birthplace of Kenneth Roberts (1885–1957), novelist who made early New England come alive through books: *Arundel, Northwest Passage, Rabble in Arms*. House built by Colonel Joseph Storer, son of Wells's settler John Storer; first house in town painted; 1800s home to Colonel Storer's son, the Honorable Joseph Storer and wife Priscilla Cutts, descendant of first president of Royal Province of New Hampshire. President James Monroe entertained here 1817, General Lafayette 1825.

4. TAYLOR–BARRY HOUSE, *1803*. 24 Summer St. Open summer, fee. A Brick Store Museum property.

Federal-style house distinguished by hip roof, front and side formal facades, centered entrances surmounted with a fan-shaped light; interior hallway, black and white border stenciling against salmon-frescoed walls; Lord and Barry families' furnishings 1700–1905; fine collection of Oriental porcelain and American art.

5. WEDDING CAKE HOUSE, *1826*, NRHP. Landing Rd. Private.

Among old mansions is unique Wedding Cake House, basically plain, dignified brick house with Palladian window, plus facade of wooden gingerbread latticework dropped over its entirety; two brick chimneys surrounded by decorative balustrade with high ornamental pinnacles. House built for George W. Bourne, who owned shipyard by river; presumed Bourne, cabinetmaker and wood carver, added ornamentation. Local legend says decorations added by sea captain for his bride to make up for wedding cake she never had.

6. FRANCISCAN MONASTERY. Beach Rd. Open all year, no fee. Paths, shrines, chapel.

Magnificent estate, now retreat center and mother house for Lithuanian Franciscans in United States and Canada; monument of Triple Church is striking modern sculpture from Vatican Pavilion facade at 1964 New York World's Fair; open-air chapel depicting Stations of the Cross; unusual grotto illuminated at night; main building, Elizabethan design, houses monastery chapel. Early settler John Mitchell bought land c.1740 from Sir William Pepperrell; built garrison as protection against Indians; Kenneth Roberts refers to garrison in novel *Arundel;* in family for years; Franciscan Fathers purchased 1947.

BEACHES, PARKS, OTHER POINTS OF INTEREST

A. **Bourne Mansion.** c.1812 8 Bourne St. House built by John Usher Parsons; copy of wife's home in Newburyport, Massachusetts.

B. **Old Barnard Tavern.** c.1776 Rte. 1, north of Unitarian Church. Private. Built by post rider Joseph Barnard; in 1800s known as Frost Tavern, a busy stagecoach stop.

C. **William Lord Mansion.** c. 1760, NHRP 20 Summer St. Private. Low-ceiling ell built c.1760 by Jonathan Banks; 1801 Judge Jonas Clark added Federal wing; father Reverend Jonas Clark sheltered John Adams and John Hancock before battle of Lexington.

D. **Kennebunk Beach and Gooch's Beach.** Kennebunk Beach Rd. Open all year. Lifeguards; swimming; parking permits from Town Hall needed in summer.

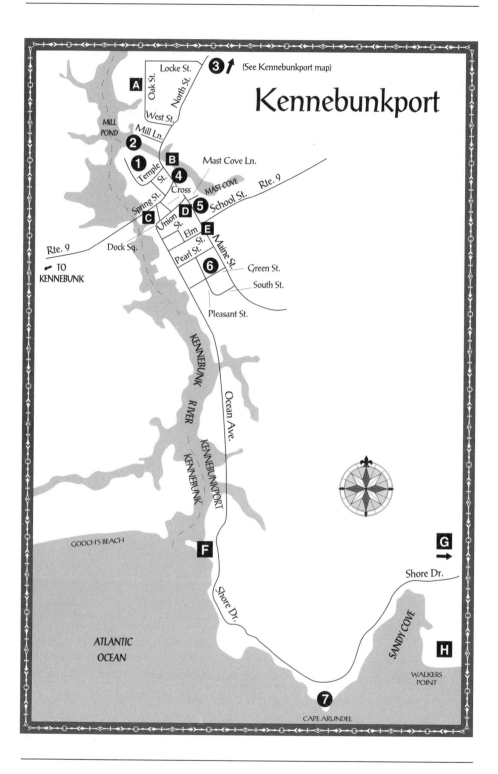

KENNEBUNKPORT

1. SOUTH CONGREGATIONAL CHURCH, *1824.* Temple St.

Often photographed church once overlooked busy David Clark's shipyard and nearby Tory Brass Foundry, where, in earlier times you might have heard the blow of hammers, ring of anvils, splash of hulls hitting water, or seen four-masted schooner *Savannah*, Kennebunkport's last famous ship. Church has 100-foot steeple with tower clock and a lantern-style cupola; Tuscan Doric portico entrance given by Henry Parsons 1912. Church sheds stabled horses during services.

2. OLDE GRIST MILL, *c. 1749*, NRHP. Mill Ln. Open summers as restaurant.

Older section of gristmill built by Thomas Perkins III, hand-hewn beams, ship's knees supports, inside wood shutters from the 1700s; see old scales, hoppers, grist elevator, old mill's equipment.

3. KENNEBUNKPORT HISTORICAL SOCIETY AND TOWN HOUSE SCHOOL, *1899*, HS. Intersection North St., Log Cabin and Arundel rds. (See 3, NE corner Wells/Kennebunk map.) Open summer and by appointment, no fee.

Old schoolhouse headquarters for historical society; museum features early life in sea-oriented town; sea captains' treasures mingle with exhibits of shipbuilding, wrecks, marine artifacts, town lock-up.

4. WHITE COLUMNS HOUSE/RICHARD A. NOTT MEMORIAL, HS. Maine St. Open summer, fee.

Home on site as early as 1802; Eliphalet Perkins bought original house for $600; turned it into impressive Greek Revival in 1851; sold three years later for $5,000. Today furnishings in high Victorian style, many from Nott family, who bequeathed home to historical society.

5. LOUIS T. GRAVES MEMORIAL PUBLIC LIBRARY, *c. 1813*, NRHP. Maine St.

Built as Kennebunk Bank of Arundel, upstairs soon became District of Kennebunk's customs offices; bank failed 1831, federal government purchased building; most popular cargoes registered were rum, molasses, sugar—port's contribution to triangular trade. Times changed, steam ships replaced sailing vessels, customs offices moved to Portland 1912; library opened on second floor; 1920 building puchased by Abbott

Graves, given to town as memorial to his son. Bank's granite vault, with iron-bound door requiring three men to close, is still intact as is customhouse sign. Gravestone of Ezra Thompson, beloved schoolmaster of the port, on outside wall.

6. NATHANIEL LORD MANSION, *c. 1812*, NRHP. Pleasant and Green sts. Open all year as guest house.

Nathaniel Lord was one of few people to own two homes back to back. In 1799 Daniel Walker gave land for his daughter and Nathaniel Lord to build white Federal house on Pleasant and Pearl streets; stands beside present Lord Mansion. During Jefferson's embargoes Nathaniel put unemployed shipbuilders to work building this mansion. It boasts twelve fireplaces, 36 rooms (one for each year of Nathaniel's age), three-story elliptical staircase, spiral staircase to large cupola. After Civil War, became home of Lord's grand nephew, Charles Peter Clark, president of New York, New Haven, and Hartford Railroad.

7. ST. ANN'S EPISCOPAL CHURCH, *c. 1887*. Shore Dr. at tip of Cape Arundel. Open summer for services.

Built by faithful parishoners who loved God and had deep appreciation for beauty and inspiration of ocean; raised stone church just above the waves, using ocean as back-drop for altar of outdoor chapel. Former President George Bush and his family worship here in summer.

BEACHES, PARKS, OTHER POINTS OF INTEREST

A. **Captain Thomas Perkins III House.** c.1724. Near end Oak St. Private. Believed oldest in town; 1787 smallpox innoculation hospital.

B. **Mast Cove.** North St. Early storage area for mast trees marked with king's "broad arrow"; best trees saved for use by the king.

C. **Bookport.** Center Dock Sq. Open as book shop. Oldest commercial building in town; was warehouse for Perkins's West India Goods, sailors' boardinghouse, post office, harness shop, fish market, artist's studio.

D. **Simon Nowell Tavern.** c.1802. Maine and Union sts. Private. Federal-style build-ing with murals of local scenes painted on dining room walls by Louis Norton.

E. **Alexander Gould House.** c.1803. Two houses south of library on Maine St. Pri-vate. Said to house Rustling Lady ghost.

F. **Henry Parsons Way and Colony Beach.** Shore Dr. Open all year. No fee. Views, benches, walk along river; swimming.

G. **Goose Rocks Beach.** Dyke Rd. off Rte. 9. Open summer. Swimming; town hall permit needed for beach parking.

H. **Summer Home of former president and first lady, George and Barbara Bush.** Walkers Point. Private.

SOURCES

1. *Greenwich Historic Collections,* Vol I, No. I, Jan 1970, Historical Society of the Town of Greenwich, Greenwich, CT, p. 10.

2. Resource: Susan Tritschler, Director, The Historical Society of the Town of Greenwich, quoted and paraphrased from letter 12/13/90.

3. Marcus, Ronald, "Elizabeth Clawson . . . Thou Deseruest to Dye," Stamford Historical Society, Inc., Ct., 1976.

4. Marcus, Ronald, "Fort Stamford", Stamford Historical Society, Inc. Ct., 1973.

5. Quotes from Elizabeth Tashjian, owner and curator of the Nut Museum, Old Lyme, CT., interview 6/7/91.

6. Field Enterprises Educational Corporation, *World Book Encyclopedia,* Nathan Hale, Vol. 9, 1968, p. 19.

7. Carpenter, Allan, *The New Enchantment of America,* Children's Press, Chicago, 1979. p. 28.

8. Lynch, Capt. Frank C., U.S.N. (Ret); *Battle of Stonington in Retrospect,* Its Strategy, Politics and Personalities, excerpted by author for "Historical Footnotes", Bulletin of the Stonington Historical Society, August, 1964.

9. Field Enterprises Educational Corporation, *World Book Encyclopedia,* Oliver Hazard Perry, Vol. 15, 1968, p. 259.

10. Field Enterprises Education Corporation, *World Book Encyclopedia,* Edward Everett Hale, Vol. 9, 1968, p. 18.

11. Resource: Walter Nebiker, President Warren Preservation Society, letter 1/16/91.

12. Resource: James Garman, author/photographer, letter 1/30/91.

13. Mark Twain's letters, Millicent Library, Fairhaven, MA.

14. Resource: Priscilla Hathaway, Historian, letter 2/16/91.

15. Rev. Robinson's words from plaque on wall of First Parish Church in Plymouth, Plymouth, MA.

16. Inscribed on facade of Church of the Pilgrimage, Plymouth, MA.

17. Inscribed on National Monument to the Forefathers, Plymouth, MA.

18. Longfellow, Henry Wadsworth, *Longfellow Leaflets,* "Priscilla's Answer," Houghton, Mifflin and Company, New York, 1881, p. 66.

19. Resource: Cynthia H. Krusell, author/historian, letters 2/91.

20. Hymn by Ralph Waldo Emerson sung at dedication of Battle monument in Concord, July 4, 1837.

21. Resource: Kathleen Laidlaw, Scituate Historical Society.

22. Deane, Samuel, *History of Scituate, Massachusetts,* Boston, James Loring, 132 Washington St., 1831, p. 246.

23. Scituate Historical Society pamphlet.

24. Trueblood, Rev. Roscoe E., *Historical Sketch of the First Parish and Its Meeting House,* Discourse delivered Dec. 14, 1947 on the 200th anniversary of the meetinghouse, p. 13.

25. Justine, Mildred L., Hingham Historical Society booklet, p. 2.

26. Resource: H. Hobart Holly, Historian Quincy Historical Society, letter 2/10/91.

27. Resource: Dorothy Anderson, Historian Swampscott Historical Society, letter 2/13/91.

28. Resource: Essex Institute, Salem, MA., letter, 3/1/91.

29. Beverly Historical Society booklet.

30. Inscribed on Gloucester statue *Man at the Wheel.*

31. "First Congregational Church of Essex", 1683–1983, 300th anniversary booklet, July, 1983, p. 24.

32. Waters, Thomas Franklin, *The Early Days of Ipswich in the Massachusetts Bay Colony* 1633–1917, abridged by Ipswich Public Library, Ipswich, 1962.

33. Dexter, Lord Timothy, "A Pickle for the Knowing Ones."

34. Currier, John J., *Ould Newbury: Historical and Biographical Sketches,* Damrell and Upham, Boston, 1896, p. 581.

35. *New Hampshire, A guide to the Granite State,* New Workers of the Federal Writer's Project of the WPA for state of NH, Houghton Mifflin Co., Boston, 1938, p. 226.

36. Resource: Frederick T. McGill, Jr., Isles of Shoals historian, letter 2/18/91.

37. Quote by James Dolph from letter by Joseph W. P. Frost, 2/20/91.

38. Resource: Sarah Giffen, Old York Historical Society, interview 2/28/91.

39. Banks, Charles Edward, *History of York, Maine,* Vol. II, Murray Printing Co., Cambridge, 1935, p. 134.

40. Resource: Hope M. Shelley, Museum Coordinator, Historical Society of Wells & Ogunquit, letter 2/11/91.

INDEX